MEDIEVAL ENGLISH PROSE
FOR WOMEN

MEDIEVAL ENGLISH PROSE FOR WOMEN

Selections from the
Katherine Group and
Ancrene Wisse

EDITED BY
BELLA MILLETT
AND
JOCELYN
WOGAN-BROWNE

CLARENDON PRESS · OXFORD

Oxford University Press, Great Clarendon Street, Oxford OX2 6DP

Oxford New York

Athens Auckland Bangkok Bogota Bombay Buenos Aires
Calcutta Cape Town Dar es Salaam Delhi Florence Hong Kong
Istanbul Karachi Kuala Lumpur Madras Madrid Melbourne
Mexico City Nairobi Paris Singapore Taipei Tokyo Toronto Warsaw

and associated companies in
Berlin Ibadan

Oxford is a trade mark of Oxford University Press

Published in the United States by
Oxford University Press Inc., New York

British Library Cataloguing in Publication Data

Medieval English prose for women: selections from the
"Katherine Group" and Ancrene Wisse.
I. Millett, Bella   II. Wogan-Browne, Jocelyn
828'.08

ISBN 0–19–811997–6

Library of Congress Cataloging-in-Publication Data
Medieval English prose for women.
Texts in English and Middle English.
1. English prose literature —Middle English,
1100–1500. 2. Christian literature, English (Middle).
3. Women—Conduct of life—Early works to 1800.
4. Monasticism and religious orders for women—Rules.
5. Christian saints, Women—Legends. 6. Sermons,
English (Middle). I. Milllett, Bella. II. Wogan-Browne,
Jocelyn.
PR1120.M374 1990 828'10808'09287 89–16014
ISBN 0–19–811997–6

5 7 9 10 8 6 4

Printed in Great Britain by
Biddles Ltd, Guildford and King's Lynn

PREFACE

AFTER some years of teaching specialist undergraduate courses on early Middle English literature at Liverpool and Southampton, we felt the need for an edition which would make the *Ancrene Wisse* and the works associated with it more accessible both to students and to a wider audience. This introductory selection includes three representative works from the 'Katherine Group' and the two final sections of *Ancrene Wisse*, and offers not only new critical texts, accompanied by a Glossary, for undergraduate use, but also translations for readers unfamiliar with Middle English. BM has taken the main responsibility for the texts and translations and JW-B for the Introduction, Textual Commentary, and Glossary, but each of us owes much to the other's collaboration.

We are grateful to Mr D. C. Lloyd of the University of Liverpool Computer Laboratory, Mrs G. Cooper, Oxford University Computing Service, and the secretarial staff of our own Departments, particularly Miss E. Birrell and Miss C. Rees at Liverpool and Mrs S. James and Mrs N. Martin at Southampton, for the help they have given us in preparing the edition; to Mr G. B. Jack of St Andrews University for advice on the text of *Ancrene Wisse* Part 8; to the British Academy for a grant to JW-B which has contributed to her work on these and other thirteenth-century texts; and to the Master and Fellows of Corpus Christi College, Cambridge, for allowing BM to consult their manuscript of the *Ancrene Wisse* and to use it as a basis for the text printed here. More generally, the edition would not have been a practical possibility without the substantial body of scholarly work on this group of texts which already exists, and we should like to acknowledge here, as well as in the detailed references given later, the extent of our debt to the work of earlier editors and commentators, and (in the case of *Ancrene Wisse*) an earlier translator, Mary Salu. For helpful points used in our revisions to the paperback edition we are grateful to our reviewers.

B.M.
J.W.-B.

Department of English, University of Southampton
Department of English Language and Literature, University of Liverpool

CONTENTS

LIST OF ABBREVIATIONS

Ackerman and Dahood	*Ancrene Riwle: Introduction and Part 1*, ed. Robert W. Ackerman and Roger Dahood (Binghamton, NY, 1984).
AW	*Ancrene Wisse* (references by part and line number to this edition).
Bennett and Smithers	*Early Middle English Verse and Prose*, ed. J. A. W. Bennett and G. V. Smithers, with a Glossary by Norman Davis, 2nd edn. (repr. with corrections, Oxford, 1974).
Colborn	*Hali Meiðhad: Edited from MS. Bodley 34 and MS. Cotton Titus D. xviii*, by A. F. Colborn (London, 1940).
Cooper	Josephine G. Cooper (Sister Ethelbert), 'Latin Elements of the *Ancrene Riwle*', Ph.D. diss. (Univ. of Birmingham, 1956).
Corpus MS	MS Corpus Christi College, Cambridge, 402. References by folio and line number. See the diplomatic edition by J. R. R. Tolkien, *The English Text of the Ancrene Riwle: Ancrene Wisse*, EETS, OS 249 (London, 1962).
d'Ardenne, *Iuliene*	*Þe Liflade ant te Passiun of Seinte Iuliene*, ed. S. R. T. O. d'Ardenne (Liège, 1936), repr. as EETS, OS 248 (London, 1961).
d'Ardenne, *KG*	*The Katherine Group*: see MS B below.
De custodia	*De custodia interioris hominis*, attrib. Anselm, ed. Southern and Schmitt (see below), 355–60.
Dobson, *Cotton Cleopatra*	*The English Text of the Ancrene Riwle, edited from B. M. Cotton MS. Cleopatra C. vi*, by E. J. Dobson, EETS, OS 267 (London, 1972).
Dobson, *Origins*	E. J. Dobson, *The Origins of 'Ancrene Wisse'* (Oxford, 1976).
EETS	Early English Text Society
OS	Original Series.
SS	Supplementary Series.
Furnivall	*Hali Meidenhad*, ed. F. J. Furnivall, EETS, OS 18 (London, 1922).
Hall	*Selections from Early Middle English 1130–1250*, ed. Joseph Hall (2 vols.; Oxford, 1920).
HM	*Hali Meiðhad* (references by line number to this edition).
Iuliene	See d'Ardenne, *Iuliene*, above.
JEGP	*Journal of English and Germanic Philology*.
Katerine	*Seinte Katerine*, ed. S. R. T. O. d'Ardenne and E. J. Dobson, EETS, SS 7 (Oxford, 1981).

Mack | *Seinte Marherete: Þe Meiden ant Martyr*, ed. Frances M. Mack, EETS, OS 193 (London, 1934; repr. with corrections 1958).

ME | Middle English.

MED | *Middle English Dictionary*, ed. H. Kurath and S. M. Kuhn (Michigan, 1956–).

Millett, *Hali Meiðhad* | *Hali Meiðhad*, ed. Bella Millett, EETS, OS 284 (London, 1982).

MS B | Bodleian Library, MS Bodley 34. See the *Facsimile of MS Bodley 34*, ed. N. R. Ker, EETS, OS 247 (London, 1960), and the diplomatic edition by S. R. T. O. d'Ardenne, *The Katherine Group edited from MS Bodley 34*, Bibliothèque de la Faculté de Philosophie et Lettres de l'Université de Liège, fasc. 215 (Paris, 1977).

MS R | British Library, MS Royal 17A xxvii.

MS T | British Library, Cotton MS Titus D. xviii.

NED | *A New English Dictionary on Historical Principles*, ed. J. A. H. Murray *et al.* (Oxford, 1888–1928).

Nero MS | British Library, Cotton MS Nero A. xiv. See the edition by Mabel Day, *The English Text of the Ancrene Riwle edited from Cotton Nero A xiv*, EETS, OS 225 (London, 1952).

OE | Old English.

PL | *Patrologiae Cursus Completus . . . Series Latina*, ed. J.-P. Migne (Paris, various years).

PMLA | *Publications of the Modern Language Association of America*.

RES | *Review of English Studies*.

Salu | *The Ancrene Riwle*, tr. M. B. Salu (London, 1955; repr. Exeter, 1990).

Shepherd | *Ancrene Wisse Parts 6 and 7*, ed. Geoffrey Shepherd (London, 1959; repr. Exeter, 1985).

SJ | *Seinte Iuliene*: see d'Ardenne, *Iuliene*, above.

SM | *Seinte Margarete* (references by line number to this edition).

Southern and Schmitt | *Memorials of St. Anselm*, ed. R. W. Southern and F. S. Schmitt, *Auctores britannici medii aevi*, 1 (London, 1969).

SW | *Sawles Warde* (references by line number to this edition).

Tolkien, 'Contributions' | J. R. R. Tolkien, 'Some Contributions to Middle-English Lexicography', *RES* 1 (1925), 210–15.

Warren | Ann K. Warren, *Anchorites and their Patrons in Medieval England* (Los Angeles and Berkeley, 1985).

Wilson | *Sawles Warde: An Early Middle English Homily*, ed. R. M. Wilson (Leeds School of English Language Texts and Monographs, 3; Leeds, 1938).

[handwritten annotations at top:] early 13th c. "Katherine Group" includes Hali M. & Ancrene R.

INTRODUCTION

THE texts edited in this anthology are all taken from a single group of religious prose works, written in the West Midlands in the early thirteenth century.

The longest of these works, and the best known both in the Middle Ages and today, is the *Ancrene Wisse*, a work of guidance for female recluses. The *ancre*—the anchorite or anchoress—was a man or woman who had chosen to be enclosed for life in an individual cell, usually built on to the wall of a church; the author explains, fancifully, that the anchoress is so called because she is 'anchored under a church like an anchor under the side of a ship'.[2] The first of the eight sections of his work prescribes the recluses' daily routine of prayers, and the last offers practical guidelines on their dress, diet, and general conduct. But he emphasizes that these recommendations on external behaviour, the 'Outer Rule', should be seen as no more than a handmaid to its lady, the 'Inner Rule'—the divine commands governing the heart and conscience—to which he devotes the main body of his work. Unlike some later medieval English writers, he has relatively little to say about the mystical union with God which was the ultimate aim of the contemplative life the recluses had chosen. He is more concerned with their practical problems and spiritual dangers, and although his account of the 'Inner Rule' culminates in a section on the love of God, it deals at much greater length with the custody of the senses and thoughts, and with temptation, confession, and penance.

Ancrene Wisse is anonymous, but it has close links with the tradition of monastic legislation running from the Augustinian canons to the Dominican friars, and recent research is pointing increasingly towards Dominican origin.[3] The author himself tells us something about his audience. The first version was written for three women in particular.

---

[1] For details of editions and translations see Further Reading. Explanations of brief references to particular texts are given in the List of Abbreviations. (*Ancrene Wisse* references are given both to the MSS (normally Corpus) and the Salu translation, but the translations given in the Introduction are not necessarily Salu's).

[2] Corpus MS 39^a/3–4; M. B. Salu (tr.), *The Ancrene Riwle* (London, 1955), 63. For a discussion of the actual etymology and medieval uses of the word, see the section on 'The Medieval Anchorite' in Ackerman and Dahood, pp. 7–16.

[3] See D. S. Brewer, 'Two Notes on the Augustinian and possibly West Midland Origin of the *Ancren Riwle*', *Notes and Queries*, 201 (1956), 232–5; E. J. Dobson, *The Origins of 'Ancrene Wisse'* (Oxford, 1976) (which follows Brewer in supporting

'There is a great deal of talk about you,' he says, 'what well-bred women you are, sought after by many for your goodness and kindness, and sisters of one father and mother, who in the flower of your youth renounced all the joys of the world and became recluses.'[4] From a revised version he made later, which has survived only in Corpus Christi College, Cambridge, MS 402, we learn that this little community of recluses eventually grew to twenty or more.[5]

Like many medieval religious works, however, *Ancrene Wisse* seems to have been intended from the first for more than its immediate audience. The author explains to them, for instance, that the section on Confession 'is equally relevant to everyone, so do not be surprised that I have not addressed you particularly in this section'.[6] Its later history confirms its effectiveness as a work of general spiritual guidance. It was adapted for nuns, for male religious communities, for laymen, and for a general audience; in a period when translation was normally from Latin or French into English, it was translated once into Latin and twice into French; and it continued to be read, copied, and borrowed from into the early sixteenth century.

A number of shorter works have come down to us which have close connections with *Ancrene Wisse* and with each other. They all seem to have been written originally in the same literary dialect, they are linked by verbal and thematic parallels, and sometimes several of them are found together in the manuscripts.[7] They are usually divided into two subgroups. Four lyrical meditations, dwelling particularly on the theme of Christ's love for the soul, make up the 'Wooing Group'. The remaining five works—lives of the virgin martyrs Katherine, Margaret, and Juliana, the letter on virginity called by its editors *Hali Meiðhad*, and an allegory on the custody of the soul, *Sawles Warde*—are collectively described as the 'Katherine Group'. It is uncertain whether the author of *Ancrene Wisse* also wrote any or all of these other works. It has been argued that there are significant variations in syntax, Augustinian authorship, and links *AW* specifically with Wigmore Abbey, Herefordshire, a house of Victorine canons); and Bella Millett, 'The Origins of *Ancrene Wisse*: New Answers, New Questions', *Medium Aevum*, 61 (1992) (which argues for Dominican origin).

---

[4] Nero MS 50^r/23–7; Salu, p. 84.   [5] Corpus MS 69^a/13–28; Salu, pp. 112–13.

[6] Corpus MS 93^a/2–5; Salu, p. 151.

[7] For their language, see J. R. R. Tolkien, '*Ancrene Wisse* and *Hali Meiðhad*', *Essays and Studies*, 14 (1929), 104–26; for their grouping in the MSS, see the useful diagram in G. Shepherd (ed.), *Ancrene Wisse Parts 6 and 7* (London, 1959; repr. Exeter, 1985), p. xiv; on verbal and thematic parallels, see n. 8 below.

vocabulary, and style, and perhaps also in authorial attitude, between
the different works of the group,[8] but these variations are not so wide
as to exclude the possibility of common authorship altogether. It is also
possible that they shared a common audience. All of the shorter works
would have been appropriate reading for recluses (the author of
Ancrene Wisse refers to 'your English book about St. Margaret'[9] which
may be the Life that we have), and in one of the meditations, 'The
Wooing of our Lord', the speaker is a recluse, her body fixed between
four walls as Christ's was fixed to the cross.[10] But these shorter works
are not addressed to individuals as *Ancrene Wisse* is, and most of them
assume, either implicitly or explicitly, a more general audience. There
is nothing in *Hali Meiðhad* which would not apply to any virgin
entering the religious life, and *Sawles Warde*, though it has more to say
on the reward of virgins in heaven than its source, deals with a theme
which is equally relevant to all Christians. The saints' lives, with their
melodramatic action and flamboyantly rhythmical and alliterative style,
were apparently intended in the first instance for public delivery to a
general audience: *Seinte Margarete* speaks of 'that holy maiden we
commemorate today', and addresses not only virgins but 'all those who
have ears to hear, widows with the married', while *Seinte Iuliene*, which
also calls on an audience of listeners, is for 'all lay-people who cannot
understand Latin'.[11]

Although this group of works can still be read for profit as well as
pleasure, there is little that is original about their content. They seem
to have been written mainly to make material already available in Latin
accessible to an audience whose first—and, in some cases, only—
language was English. Some of them, like *Sawles Warde* and the saints'
lives, are free translations from Latin sources, and even those works,
like *Ancrene Wisse* and *Hali Meiðhad*, which have no single Latin
source are heavily indebted for their material to earlier Latin writers.
What is distinctive about them is their treatment of this material. In a
period when few good writers chose to write in English, these works
show an unexpected literary skill and confidence. Even where they are
drawing directly on a Latin source they elaborate and develop it freely,
sometimes recreating its stylistic effects in English, more often adding
embellishments of their own. This remarkable flowering of English

[8] For fuller references and discussion, see Dobson, *Origins*, pp. 154–69, and *Hali Meiðhad*, ed. Bella Millett, EETS, os 284 (London, 1982), pp. xviii–xxii.

[9] Corpus MS 66ª/19; Salu, p. 108.

[10] *Þe Wohunge of Ure Lauerd*, ed. W. Meredith Thompson, EETS, os 241 (London, 1958), p. 36, ll. 590–5.   [11] *SM* 44/24–9; *SJ* (MS B) 5–6, d'Ardenne, *Iuliene*, p. 3.

prose in a largely barren age was probably the result of a combination of several factors. One major influence was certainly the native tradition of alliterative writing in prose and verse, which had survived the Norman Conquest more successfully in the West Midlands than elsewhere. English scholars between the wars tended to emphasize the 'Englishness' of the group and its link with Anglo-Saxon culture; J. R. R. Tolkien, for instance, described the literary dialect in which *Ancrene Wisse* and its group were written as 'an English . . . that has preserved some of its former cultivation . . . and has contrived in troublous times to maintain the air of a gentleman, if a country gentleman'.[12] This appealing image has some truth in it; the three saints' lives in particular draw mainly on this older native tradition for their language and style. But the stylistic origins of the group as a whole are more complex, and post-war scholarship has laid greater emphasis on the influence of contemporary French and Latin culture. M. T. Clanchy has pointed out that it is a mistake to assume that provincial culture in this period was necessarily backward, and for the West Midlands cites the example of Herefordshire, which acted as 'a meeting place of languages (Welsh, English, French, and Latin) and of cultures (Celtic, Anglo-Saxon, Anglo-Norman and cosmopolitan).'[13] In the twelfth century, this meeting of cultures had produced the 'Herefordshire school' of sculpture, which fused older native and newer Continental influences to produce what has been described as 'the most individual local school of stone carving that Romanesque art produced in England'.[14] A similar process of cultural fusion probably lies behind *Ancrene Wisse* and the works associated with it. Translated from Latin for an English- and French-speaking audience in the Welsh Marches, they draw stylistically on the resources of four languages; and their treatment of their sources shows the influence not only of the native literary tradition but of French courtly literature and the Latin prose of the twelfth-century Renaissance. But, like the sculpture of the 'Herefordshire School', these works add up to more than the sum of their parts; elements of diverse origin are transmuted into something with a fresh and distinctive character of its own.

Hali Meiðhad (A Letter on Virginity)

Although the modern editors of this work have called it *Hali Meiðhad* ('Holy Virginity'), the only medieval title that survives to us is the

---

[12] Tolkien, *'Ancrene Wisse and Hali Meiðhad'*, p. 106.
[13] *England and its Rulers, 1066–1272* (London, 1983), 177.
[14] T. S. R. Boase, *English Art 1100–1216* (Oxford, 1953), 77.

scribe's description of it in MS Bodley 34 as 'A letter on virginity for
the encouragement of a virgin' (or 'virgins'). In 1866, the Revd Oswald
Cockayne's horror at its many 'coarse and repulsive passages' led him
to 'Latinize' much of his translation,[15] and there are still critics
who find *Hali Meiðhad*'s arguments for a single life for women
unpalatable, but the idea that they are the product of individual
peculiarity cannot survive attention to its literary context. Almost
everything in it has a direct source or at least a precedent in earlier and
contemporary Latin writings. Among other works, the author draws on
Bishop Hildebert of Lavardin's early twelfth-century letter to the
recluse Athalisa and on model sermons.[16] *Hali Meiðhad* is essentially
a form of preaching by written instruction and, like some contemporary
model and actual sermons, is directed *ad status*—to the occupational or
'estates' category of its audience. For women this is usually wife,
widow, or virgin.

Virginity as a way of life for Christian women has a long history and
a highly developed literature.[17] When medieval clerics like Hildebert
or the author of *Hali Meiðhad* write on the subject, they draw heavily
on the works of the Church Fathers. In early Christian thought, a
virginal habit of mind is even more important than literal intactness
(which can be rendered meaningless by the wrong interior disposition).
Virginity is the superlative form of an ideal from which no one is
technically disbarred, that of chastity, and virgins are frequently
warned against pride and despising widows and wives (as in *HM* 36/
20–40/15). The purpose of virginity is to help the soul develop the
power of seeing God. It also expresses the pervasive human intuition
that a general early state of blessedness has been lost and that we live
'now' in a 'land of unlikeness', as *Hali Meiðhad* calls it (10/28).
Virginity signifies humanity's pre-lapsarian wholeness: 'the command
to increase and multiply is fulfilled *after* the expulsion from Paradise',
writes Jerome in the fourth century to the Roman consecrated virgin,
Eustochium; 'virginity is natural . . . marriage came after the Fall.'[18]
Had man been content to replace the angels in God's creation and not
imitate Lucifer's disobedience, our nature could and should have been
like that of the angels. As it is, we are offered a promise of angelic life

---

[15] *Hali Meidenhad*, EETS, os 18 (London, 1866), p. v.
[16] On *Hali Meiðhad*'s sources, see Millett, *Hali Meiðhad*, pp. xlv–lii and *Notes on the Text, passim*.
[17] For fuller discussion, see ibid. xxiv–xlv.
[18] F. A. Wright (tr.), *Select Letters of St. Jerome*, Loeb Classical Library (London, 1933), *Ep.* 22, pp. 91–3 (italics added).

only after the resurrection.[19] Virginity, however, offers an earthly approximation (see *HM* 4/15–16, 10/18–30, 22/31–2) to the angelic life and is our best image of redemption as well as of our first home in Paradise. Christ's incarnation in a virgin mother shows that 'purity is the only complete indication of the presence of God.'[20] Far from being a life of negation, virginity is the fullest expression of human free will, since, as Jerome, Ambrose, Augustine, and others insist, virginity is not commanded but *counselled* by St Paul (1 Cor. 7: 1–9). As the free choice of the better course, virginity is associated with reason (who, in *Hali Meiðhad* 14/7–8, is Virginity's sister).

Virginity's superiority did not depend on seeing sexuality itself as the cause of the Fall. In orthodox thought, the Fall was the outcome of human pride and disobedience; and human sexuality was undeniably part of God's created universe, even though, as a powerful appetite capable of blurring and distorting fallen humanity's attention to God, its exercise was to be avoided if possible and constructively channelled at all times. Christian orthodoxy thus does not argue that virginity is good and marriage bad, but that marital sexuality, properly understood, is legitimate and virginity better. All the major writers on virginity insist that marriage is not wrong, merely third-best to chastity and virginity, though in argument marriage can slip from being less than virginity to being virginity's opposite, seen as entirely negative.[21]

Hali Meiðhad's denunciations of human sexuality, though apparently close to heterodoxy (e.g. 30/19–27), are at most extensions of established positions, for which parallels could be cited in patristic and later writing. Though *Hali Meiðhad* condemns 'that stinking and wanton deed' (8/14), the reservation is made that it is 'nevertheless to be tolerated to some extent within marriage' (8/14–15) and *Hali Meiðhad*'s *faute de mieux* presentation of marriage as a God-given bed on which the spiritually infirm can break their fall as they plummet down from the tower of virginity (18/11–27) is itself derived from patristic sources.[22]

---

[19] On patristic discussion of the *vita angelica*, see Millett, *Hali Meiðhad*, pp. xxviii–xxx.

[20] Gregory of Nyssa, *On Virginity*, tr. W. Moore and H. A. Wilson, in *Select Writings and Letters of Gregory, Bishop of Nyssa*, A Select Library of Nicene and Post-Nicene Fathers of the Christian Church, 2nd ser. (New York, 1893; repr. Grand Rapids, Mich., 1954), v. 344, col. 2.

[21] See Millett, *Hali Meiðhad*, pp. xxx–xxxviii, for further discussion and references.

[22] Ibid. 10/14–15 n., 10/15 n.

Medieval works on virginity commend it as emotionally and socially desirable for women. In *Ancrene Wisse* Part 7 Christ is presented (in an allegory also found elsewhere)[23] as the knightly lover of an ungrateful lady, the soul; *Hali Meiðhad* emphasizes on the one hand his beauty and riches, and the high rank he offers to the virgin in heaven, on the other the suffering and degradation she will inevitably endure if she marries. Loss of virginity is presented as selling oneself too cheaply, doing something unworthy. So, for instance, the allegorical battle between Virginity and Lechery (14/11–33) is presented as a public spectacle involving the virgin in an unpleasant and degrading struggle.[24] The virgin's fall here happens before an audience: angels, in the heavenly equivalent of the upper circle, sorrow at their sister's disgrace (14/25–6), while a vulgar mob of groundling devils, 'capering and clapping their hands together' (14/26–7) enjoy the public embarrassment and social catastrophe that has befallen her. 'Guard yourself, innocent maiden,' says the author (14/28),—beware of letting this happen to *you. Hali Meiðhad* builds adroitly on the desires and fears of young women to persuade them of virginity's social and emotional advantages, not disdaining but using its audience's aspirations. (Perhaps, too, the author is mindful of Gregory the Great's injunction, in one of *Hali Meiðhad*'s sources, that weaker audiences are to be won over with easier arguments.)[25]

Hali Meiðhad's arguments are sometimes objected to for being directed towards the self-interest of the virgin, for presenting spiritual rewards as social enticements. The heavenly courtesy which the Gawain-poet's Pearl maiden so carefully distinguishes from its earthly analogue is here made a mere continuation of worldly rank. The traditionally differing rewards of the three states of sexual experience— thirtyfold for wedlock, sixty for widowhood, but one hundred for virginity (20/17–25)—become an unspiritually literal idea of social degree. In the heavenly court, the virgin will have the prettiest crown and the most beautiful robes (16/17–19) as well as the dazzling *aureola* reserved for virgins (20/10–14); the highest social pre-eminence will be hers, and a special song denied to lower ranks (16/11–17, 18/28– 20/4). But medieval preaching theory would argue that it is good

---

[23] Rosemary Woolf, 'The Theme of Christ the Lover-Knight in Medieval English Literature', *RES* NS 13 (1962), 1–16.
[24] This emphasis is *Hali Meiðhad*'s: for its source here, see Millett, *Hali Meiðhad*, 8/7–31 n.
[25] Gregory the Great, *Regula Pastoralis*, Part 3, ch. 39 (*PL* 77. 124).

technique for the argument to begin in the status and interests of its particular audience, and medieval virginity literature characteristically literalizes spiritual metaphors in order to appeal to young women.[26]

Hali Meiðhad follows the homiletic procedure of stating and expounding a theme rather than using the more elaborate divisions of the thirteenth-century scholastic or 'university' sermon. Its argument falls roughly into four parts: an introduction (2/1–4/35); two central sections, the first (6/1–20/29) largely concerned with virginity and its rewards, and the second (20/30–34/21) with marriage and its troubles; and a concluding section warning against pride and other vices, citing exemplary virgins, and offering defences against temptation (34/22–42/26). There are many connections between and across these blocks of material, however, and the progression of the argument as a whole is carefully planned so that each section presupposes and draws on responses developed in the preceding ones.

The theme *Hali Meiðhad* preaches is withdrawal from the world, a theme used in other writings on virginity, but not exclusive to such works, since virginity is seen as one specially dedicated form of a detachment from the world which any Christian should try to cultivate. Here, following Alan of Lille in his sermon *To Virgins*,[27] the words of Ps. 44: 11–12 are particularly applied to the virgin as bride of Christ (rather than to the Church or the Christian soul, as is more usual). As with its account of virginity's heavenly reward, *Hali Meiðhad*'s tactic is to render the arguments of the sources as literal and vivid as possible. Thus a specialized version of the theme's traditional Augustinian development is used. Instead of opposing Jerusalem as heavenly city to the Babylon of exile in the world, *Hali Meiðhad* makes Jerusalem not the city itself, but the tower of Zion (a fortification in Jerusalem). By traditional etymology (as explained at 2/26–7) this is a watch-tower (*specula*) and hence a place for contemplation (*speculatio*).[28] The image of virginity as a high state of life becomes a major structural metaphor of this first section, in which *Hali Meiðhad* concentrates less on the virgin's power of contemplating God from her exalted position than on establishing that the sole direction in which one can move away from

---

[26] So, for instance, Goscelin's 11th-cent. *Book of Comfort* for the English recluse, Eve of Wilton, presents heaven as a social reunion of Anglo-Saxon royal virgins and martyrs (ed. C. H. Talbot, 'The *Liber confortatorius* of Goscelin of Saint Bertin', (Studia Anselmiana, 37; *Analecta Monastica*, 3; 1955), 115).

[27] For this sermon, see Gillian R. Evans (tr.), *Alan of Lille: The Art of Preaching* (Cistercian Studies, 23; Kalamazoo, Mich., 1981), 166–8.

[28] See Millett, *Hali Meiðhad*, pp. xxvii–xxviii and 2/3 n., 2/5 n.

virginity is downwards. The virgin can only leave her tower to descend,
by way of physical desire, to marriage or worse. In *Hali Meiðhad* her
fall is not only a sad recapitulation of Adam's, but a loss of prestige, of
rank and privileges (see esp. 4/11–35, 12/13–26, 20/17–25), and a
descent from the level of angel (4/4) to that of beast (22/11–32).

Hali Meiðhad's longest amplification of what, for the virgin, it is to
fall is an extended treatment of marital and maternal miseries,
constituting the second half of the work. A dual focus on arguments *for*
virginity and *against* marriage is typical of patristic virginity literature,
and *Hali Meiðhad*'s account of marriage is a rhetorically forceful use
of commonplaces. Many of its observations on household drudgery
and marital bickering come ultimately from the arguments of Paul and
Jerome. Patristic (and classical) traditions of the *molestiae nuptiarum*—
the tribulation of the flesh referred to by Paul in 1 Cor. 7: 28—were
taken up with special vigour in the twelfth-century debate over
marriage, particularly within university and clerical circles.[29]

The vivid and detailed account of the miseries of motherhood also
uses an established tradition—that of contempt of the world. This
is given powerful expression in a probable source of *Hali Meiðhad*,
Pope Innocent III's treatise, *On the Misery of the Human Condition*
(completed in 1195). For Innocent, as for Augustine, the post-
lapsarian sexual act is inevitably tainted to a greater or lesser degree
with lust and the human child is 'conceived therefore with lascivious-
ness and filth, brought forth with sorrow and pain, nourished with
trouble and labour, watched over with anxiety and fear'.[30] *Hali
Meiðhad*'s reworkings of this theme are, if anything, less extreme than
some better-known vernacular applications, such as the lyric 'lullaby'
in which the mother condoles with the child for the mere fact of its
earthly existence.[31] In virginity literature, the expression of *contemptus
mundi*, contempt of the world, as applied to childbearing is coupled
with a more or less standard list of the symptoms of pregnancy,
warning the virgin of the pains and unpleasantness to be expected.
The theological source of this topic is commentary on Eve's expulsion
from Paradise to painful childbirth, but the list of signs occurs
in contemporary encyclopaedists and medical writers. As well as

[29] See ibid. xxx–xxxvii; R. A. Pratt, 'Jankyn's "Book of Wikked Wyves": Anti-Matrimonial Propaganda in the Universities', *Annuale Medievale*, 3 (1962), 5–27.
[30] M. Maccarrone (ed.), *De miseria humanae conditionis* (Verona, 1955), Bk. 1, ch. 6, §2, pp. 13–14; and see Millett, *Hali Meiðhad*, 17/3–6 n.
[31] See e.g. Carleton Brown (ed.), *Religious Lyrics of the Fourteenth Century*, 2nd edn. revised by G. V. Smithers (Oxford, 1952; corr. repr. 1957), no. 28, pp. 35–6.

shame

including the usual symptoms of pallor, darkness under the eyes, distension, vomiting, etc.[32], *Hali Meiðhad* adds embarrassment in front of the midwife (32/11–12), characteristically appealing to the virgin's sense of shame.

Critics who have found these arguments distasteful have sometimes assumed that they *must* be addressed to professed religious. *Hali Meiðhad* may well be directed towards sustaining those who have already chosen the virgin life, but is equally suitable for young girls facing the choice of marrying or of consecrating themselves to Christ. It is also of course true, whatever its original audience, that the piece's appeal need not be confined to them; in so far as it presents the meaning of virginity as an ideal, it can be received by a variety of audiences. Skilful rhetorical exploitation of source material and sermon techniques make *Hali Meiðhad* (as one Victorian scholar wrote) 'that most vivid sketch of an English girl's temptation to forsake marriage and maternity'[33] for the peace and freedom of a room of her own, but *Hali Meiðhad*'s framing assumptions are those of the long tradition of Christian thought on virginity and the spiritual life.

Seinte Margarete ('Saint Margaret')

Most writers on virginity cite models and examples, and virginity is a major theme of hagiographic literature.[34] Latin and vernacular lives of virgin saints were re-copied and rewritten in Britain in many forms and served a variety of occasions and purposes both in and outside church services, especially since opportunities for spectacle and narrative drama in these lives made them entertaining as well as edifying.[35] Like its Katherine Group sister-legends of St Katherine of Alexandria and St Juliana of Nicomedia, *Seinte Margarete* takes a virgin martyr for its

---

[32] M. C. Seymour *et al.* (eds.), *On the Properties of Things: John Trevisa's Translation of Bartholomaeus Anglicus' 'De Proprietatibus Rerum'* (Oxford, 1975), i. 265, 303.

[33] F. J. Furnivall (ed.), *The Stacions of Rome and the Pilgrims Sea-Voyage*, EETS, os 25 (London, 1867), p. vii.

[34] The hagiography of virgin saints in the British Isles extends from Aldhelm in the 7th cent. to Baring-Gould and beyond in the 19th: see e.g. D. H. Farmer, *The Oxford Dictionary of Saints* (Oxford, 1978); T. Wolpers, *Die Englische Heiligenlegende des Mittelalters* (Tübingen, 1964).

[35] On the mixed lay and religious audiences of saints' lives see J. Frankis, 'The Social Context of Vernacular Writing in Thirteenth Century England: The Evidence of the Manuscripts', in P. R. Coss and S. D. Lloyd (eds.), *Thirteenth Century England 1* (Woodbridge, 1986), 175–84.

heroine.[36] Unparalleled in contemporary and earlier sources, this group of saints, it has been suggested, may have been chosen to fit the names of the three sisters who formed *Ancrene Wisse*'s first audience.[37]

While such a principle of selection can only be speculated upon, internal evidence can tell us something of the way in which these Lives were designed to be read. Each is a reinforcement of the others, with exactly the same type of saint selected in each case and strong similarities of treatment in structure, themes, and style. The legends are all set in the Diocletian persecutions of the early fourth century in exotic locales in Asia Minor. All three saints are either entirely legendary martyrs or have only dubious traces of genuine early cults. They are presented as brides of Christ, interrogated and tortured by tyrant officials who want them to abandon both their virginity and their faith. Specific narrative motifs are shared, as well as setting and plot line: Juliana and Katherine both face torture on a wheel, Margaret and Juliana both interrogate demons. All three are high-born, but displaced from their natural, pagan families in some way, either by parental deaths, or by conflict with their fathers when they exercise their own choice of a spiritual father and bridegroom. All three die joyfully when, unable to think of further arguments or tortures, their persecutor has them beheaded in the formal execution of Roman law. Though there is some thematic variation between the Lives, this shared design and purpose make it possible for a single Life to give a good idea of all three.

Among these legendary or semi-legendary virgins, Margaret of Antioch (or Marina, as she was known to the Greek church) is an entirely unhistorical figure, and her cult was expunged from the Roman Calendar of Saints in 1969. Her popularity was, however, widespread and long-enduring, from her earliest Greek and Latin Lives before the ninth century throughout the Middle Ages, even though some medieval hagiographers reserved their position about the credibility of her encounter with a dragon.[38] Versions of her life survive in many vernaculars, partly because of the spectacular nature of her legend and partly because it included many promises of help and

---

[36] For editions of the Lives of St Juliana and St Katherine, see Further Reading.

[37] Dobson, *Origins*, pp. 138–9.

[38] Cf. e.g. *The South English Legendary 'Life of St. Margaret'* (ed. Charlotte d'Evelyn and Anna Mills, EETS, os 235 (London, 1956), i. 297, ll. 157–70), which follows the *Golden Legend* of James of Voragine (*Legenda Aurea*, ed. J. G. Th. Graesse (Vratislavia, 1890; repr. Osnabrück, 1969), 401).

intercession. Margaret's help in childbearing was especially important
in the success of her cult (see *Seinte Margarete* 78/25–8), and it was
widely believed that a reading of her passion would expedite safe
childbirth. Copies of her legend seem sometimes to have been given
to pregnant women in the form of amulets.[39] While childbirth is an
experience foreign to all virgin saints apart from the mother of God, a
popularly accepted logic founded Margaret's special powers in the
ease with which she is expelled from her dragon's jaws or stomach. In
England there are numerous early church dedications and vernacular
Lives of the saint. Interest was undiminished after the Conquest,
especially when the First Crusade's capture of Antioch in 1098
brought an influx of Margaret relics to Western Europe, and the
Katherine Group version is one of many insular medieval retellings.[40]

Seinte Margarete's author uses the more elaborate of the two
principal medieval Latin versions as his main source. He follows this
'Mombritius' version closely, but not slavishly.[41] His version is
addressed to 'widows with the married, and maidens above all' (44/
24–5); he explains or omits difficult theological points for his audience
and elaborates at will, emphasizing particular themes and adding fresh
material. The largest addition is an account of the Devil's attacks on
chastity and the defences against lechery. Spoken under duress by a
demon (66/5–70/13), it is a vivid account of everyday temptation,
homiletically relating the values represented in Margaret's heroic
virginity to the audience's lives. There is no source (though there is an
opportunity) for this miniature homily in the Latin *vita*, but it can be
readily paralleled in other Latin and vernacular writings.[42] Like all its

[39] E. A. Francis, 'A Hitherto Unprinted Version of the *Passio Sanctae Margaretae* with
some Observations on Vernacular Derivatives', *PMLA* 42 (1927), 94; L. Carolus-Barré,
'Un nouveau parchemin amulette et la légende de sainte Marguerite patronne des
femmes en couches', *Comptes rendus de l'Académie des Inscriptions et Belles Lettres* (1979),
256–75.

[40] For English Lives of Margaret, see C. d'Evelyn and F. A. Foster, 'Saints'
Legends', in Albert E. Hartung (ed.), *A Manual of the Writings in Middle English 1050–
1500*, rev. edn. by J. Burke Severs (Hamden, Conn., 1970), ii. 606–8; for Anglo-
Norman Lives, see P. Meyer, 'Légendes hagiographiques en Français', *Histoire de la
littérature française*, xxxiii (Paris, 1906), 362–3, and E. A. Francis (ed.), *Wace, la vie de
sainte Marguerite*, Les classiques français du moyen âge (Paris, 1932), p. xix, n. 4.

[41] On the Mombritius Latin version and *SM*, see Wolpers, pp. 170–7, 182–4.

[42] *Ancrene Wisse*, for instance, uses some of the same Latin material in its discussion of
remedies against temptation in Part 2 (Corpus MS 65ª/8–65ᵇ/9; Salu, pp. 106–7), and
Thomas of Froidmont has a similar treatment in his *De modo bene vivendi ad sororem*,
PL 184. 1299–1300, §159.

expansions to the Mombritius Latin text, *Seinte Margarete*'s homiletic
material is traditional rather than original, effectively adapted for its
audience. The demon's portrait of the godly man and woman at first
scrupulously talking together only of divine things while they gain
confidence and the demon prepares his attack (66/12–22) speaks
directly to the situation of the pious woman and her confessor or
spiritual director.

The Katherine Group legends function as exemplary rather than
historical biography. Their violence, though graphic and disturbing, is
highly stylized. An escalating sequence of tortures leaves the virgin
more untouched and the tyrant more unmanned. In no virgin-martyr
passio does the tyrant simply rape the saint; the official focus of these
narratives is upon the contest of wills between the tormentor and the
virgin.[43] A supporting cast of angelic and demonic manifestations
underlines this opposition. Margaret's dragon and his brother demon
belong to a tradition of demonology reaching far back through
apocryphal Christian traditions of the Babylonian idol Bel and the
dragon (Dan. 14: 2–21, 22–6) to Jewish and Eastern apocrypha.[44]
Seinte Margarete describes the dragon with a vividness beyond even that
of its graphic Latin source, emphasizing the horror of its appearance
and the saint's human fear and unshakeable faith (58/8–29).
Margaret's sancity is fully established within the dungeon: when the
dragon, like a grotesquely mobile hell-mouth, tries to swallow her,
he is split assunder as she makes the sign of the cross (60/16–25).
His demonic brother is then defeated by Margaret, and under
her interrogation reveals his provenance and professional tricks
(64/19–70/13). From now on, Margaret's passion becomes increasing
like that of Christ. When Olibrius resumes his fruitless tortures, the
spectators become Margaret's disciples and are themselves martyred at
the prefect's orders (76/27–31). In a scene which recalls the dialogue
with the good thief on Calvary (Luke 23: 43), Margaret assures her
reluctant executioner that he must continue his work in order to share
with her in the kingdom of heaven (80/34–82/4).

While Margaret's emotions are vividly realised, they are not used to
define her as an individual but to demonstrate exemplary responses.

---

[43] On the problematic nature of the Katherine Group saints' lives as exemplary
narratives of female torture, see J. Wogan-Browne, 'The Virgin's Tale', in *The Wife of
Bath and All Her Sect*, ed. R. Evans and L. Johnson (London, forthcoming).
[44] See further F. M. Mack (ed.), *Seinte Marherete*, EETS, os 193 (London, 1934;
corr. edn., 1958), pp. xxvi–xxix.

As in many medieval saints' lives, there is no attempt at realistic characterization; the saint is not a psychologically complex figure, vulnerable to doubts and inner conflicts, but is idealized to the point of impersonality. Margaret can feel fear (58/23–7), but not uncertainty, and her desire for God, stated firmly at the outset (46/9–17), can only be confirmed, not developed, in the course of the narrative. The consistency with which she looks through her experience to its ultimate source in God is, indeed, a hallmark of her sanctity. Similarly, the power and ornateness of Margaret's prayers does not express her sensibility but the majesty of God. Their psalm-based imagery is vivid, visual, and yet formulaic, drawing on long-established tradition to catalogue God's universe, from the sun and moon in their courses to the wild animals in the wood, from the angels to the demons and all that is created (58/29–60/9, 78/11–18). As in Daniel's encounter with Bel (Dan. 14: 4), this living and ordered creation is opposed to Olibrius' idolatrous statues, 'gods, who are deaf and dumb, and blind and helpless, made by human hands' (54/2–3, and cf. 74/12–13), and Margaret's triumph is important for illustrating such oppositions rather than simply as a personal victory.

Though heresies within Christianity and Islamic conquests from without were part of European experience at the time of *Seinte Margarete*'s composition, the legend is designed to reinforce faith rather than to combat paganism.[45] Olibrius is given a loosely defined historical context (there were more heathen people 'in those days' than 'now', 44/8), but more importantly he dramatizes, at the level of human agent, the Devil's side in humanity's continuing choice of allegiance. *Seinte Margarete* makes the contest with paganism a perennially relevant spiritual drama for its audience. Although a large proportion of the text consists of expository prayer and homiletic discourse, without the exclusive concentration on action and spectacle of some other vernacular retellings, spectacle and action are not lacking (most famously in the account of Margaret and the dragon, 58/6–60/25),[46] and stylistic lavishness and rhetorical skill make *Seinte*

[45] As *Ancrene Wisse* comments, 'heresy, thank God, is not prevalent in England' (Corpus MS 21ᵃ/12–13; Salu, p. 35). On contemporary Continental heresies, see R. I. Moore, *The Origins of European Dissent* (London, 1977; rev. ed., Oxford, 1985).

[46] For a discussion of this passage, see Cecily Clark, 'Early Middle English Prose: Three Essays in Stylistics', *Essays in Criticism*, 18 (1968), 366–8; for discussion of the *Seinte Margarete* author as stylist, see Bella Millett, 'The Saints' Lives of the Katherine Group and the Alliterative Tradition', *JEGP* 87 (1988), 33–4.

Margarete an entertaining as well as instructive legend, well-adapted for delivery to a general audience.

Nevertheless, it remains—as its author says (44/25–6)—a work with special relevance for virgins. In its presentation of heroic virginity *Seinte Margarete*, like its sister legends, exemplifies the strength of will required to resist parental and social pressures towards marriage and aligns this with spiritual strength against temptation.[47] In this way it makes a good companion-piece for *Hali Meiðhad*, the audience of which are adjured to think of Margaret and the other 'holy virgins in heaven', who have 'not only renounced the sons of kings and noblemen, with all worldly riches and earthly pleasures, but suffered cruel tortures rather than accept them', and now 'rejoice . . . in the arms of God, as queens of heaven' (*Hali Meiðhad* 40/20–4).

Sawles Warde ('The Custody of the Soul')

The source of *Sawles Warde* is a Latin treatise in dialogue form, *De custodia interioris hominis* ('On the Custody of the Soul'), one of many contemporary treatises giving instruction on the nature of the soul and its faculties.[48] *Sawles Warde* reworks this material into a homily (an important vehicle of instruction and persuasion in the vernacular), presenting in a different, more compact way concerns which figure extensively in *Ancrene Wisse*, where Part 2 gives instruction on 'how you shall, through your five senses, guard your heart, in which reside order, religion and the life of the soul'.[49]

Like its source, *Sawles Warde* treats the human being allegorically, in this case as a household under the overlordship of God and open to unrest within and attack from without (86/8–25, 86/26–88/4). Peculiarly appropriate to the enclosed anchoress, though not exclusive to her, the metaphor of the human being as building comes from a long

[47] See J. Wogan-Browne, 'Saints' Lives and the Female Reader', *Forum for Modern Language Studies*, 27 (1991), 314–32.
[48] The Latin source is edited in R. W. Southern and F. S. Schmitt (eds.), *Memorials of St. Anselm*, in *Auctores britannici medii aevi* (London, 1969), i. 354–60. See also Dobson, *Origins*, pp. 146–54, and Wolfgang Becker, 'The Source Text of *Sawles Warde*', *Manuscripta*, 24 (1980), 44–8. On contemporary Latin *De anima* treatises, see O. Lottin, 'L'Identité de l'âme et de ses facultés avant saint Thomas d'Aquin', in *Psychologie et morale aux XIIe et XIIIe siècles*, (Gembloux, 1957), i. 483–502.
[49] Corpus MS 4ª/24–6; Salu, p. 6.

tradition with many medieval examples (among them *Ancrene Wisse*'s 'hidden allegory', in Part 7 (112/33–114/21), of the anchoress's soul as a lady besieged in a castle).[50] *Sawles Warde*'s action begins with the arrival of two messengers, Fear, from hell, and Love of Life, from heaven (88/35 and 98/25). Once admitted to the household, they report on these two other habitations of the soul (90/26–94/14, 98/36–104/35). The household is chastened into quiet by Fear's account (94/15–98/11), cheered by Love of Life (98/18–19), and revived into hope and obedience after he speaks of heaven (106/1–32). Its reaction offers a model for the homily's audience, who are not asked to choose between hell and heaven but to keep their vividly evoked images in mind (106/33–108/12), recalling them whenever necessary. *Sawles Warde* is in this way the literary equivalent of a Judgement Day tympanum or wall-painting in a medieval church, the fates of sinners and saved, hell and heaven, displayed as in the two panels of a diptych. The final scene of its allegory stresses man's natural affiliation to God's house of heaven, rather than hell ('Death's house', 94/1), and Love of Life is retained in the household and Fear temporarily dismissed until further need (106/22–5).

Dramatic exposition presents the arrival of the messengers as events in the narrative, but they represent two constantly available possibilities— the fear of hell and the love of God—which can be stimulated at any time by the individual's remembrance of his or her human condition. *Sawles Warde*'s human being is not a static house, but a household, alive with action, interaction, and reaction. The master of the house is Reason ('Wit' in early Middle English, 86/9), who, in the customary hierarchical conception of marriage, must control his unruly wife Will and the household servants who all too readily enjoy her indiscipline (86/9–13). The household includes two kinds of servants: the outer, who are the five senses, and the inner servants who 'plot in all kinds of ways to please the housewife against God's will . . . Although we do not hear it, we can feel their din and unruly disturbance' (86/21–2). These inner servants, classified in *Sawles Warde* only as 'the other senses', are

---

[50] See Roberta Cornelius, *The Figurative Castle: A Study in the Medieval Allegory of the Edifice* (Bryn Mawr, 1930), and for *Ancrene Wisse*'s image of the five wits as thralls to the lady of the soul, see Corpus MS 46^b/15–17; Salu, pp. 75–6. Other notable 13th-cent. examples include Grosseteste's *Templum Dei* (*c*.1220–30), ed. J. Goering and F. A. C. Mantello (Toronto Medieval Latin Texts 14; Toronto, 1984), and his (Anglo-Norman) *Chasteau d'Amour*; see Kari Sajavaara (ed.), *The Middle English Translations of Robert Grosseteste's 'Château d'Amour'* (Mémoires de la Société Néophilologique de Helsinki; Helsinki, 1967).

more fully explained in *De custodia* as mental powers and fleshly desires.[51] When the outer wits have brought in sense impressions, their colleagues, the inner wits, process them, since they are the faculties through which decisions are taken on the exercise or denial of appetites. (As *Sawles Warde*'s allegory makes clear, in their undisciplined state the inner wits naturally incline to accepting temptations.)

In developing the dramatic possibilities inherent in a treatise in dialogue form, the author modifies and amplifies his source in several ways, most of them directed to bringing understanding by seeing ('Through this you may *see and understand*', 104/10, emphasis added). At a local level, *Sawles Warde* clarifies and heightens *De custodia*'s allegory by increased sensuous (especially visual) detail. Thus, where the Latin text dramatizes the opposition of virtues and vices as dialogue and discussion, *Sawles Warde* also shows each of the vices 'seeking entry around the walls to murder [the opposite virtue] inside' (88/3–4). Its messengers are not just bidden to speak: both make a minstrel's plea for attention (88/34–90/2, 98/20–21, 98/24), and their appearance is described (88/30–1, 98/13, 98/19–20). Where, in the source, Fear is given a second name, *memoria mortis* ('Remembrance of Death'), in *Sawles Warde* he is presented with the memory of hell stamped on his very features: 'he is tall and thin, and his face is deathlike and pale and livid, and every hair in his head seems to be standing on end' (88/30–1). In the Latin, Love of Eternal Life sees God in heaven as if '*per speculum et in enigmate*' (358/7–8). *Sawles Warde* turns this reminiscence of St Paul (1 Cor. 13: 12) into a visible mirror (100/4) which protects Love of Life's eyes from a brightness of countenance that makes the sunlight seem dark and 'like a shadow' (100/2).

Other changes involve the allegorical characters. *Sawles Warde* makes its household not *conscientia* ('conscience') as in the Latin, but the 'man himself' (86/8).[52] This enables some technicalities of the source's discussion to be avoided, and more importantly allows for a complete household in which each interior function can be assigned its

---

[51] '*cogitationes et motus sui*', Southern and Schmitt, p. 355/6 (henceforth cited by page and line number in the text). For an account of early medieval and scholastic theories concerning the inner wits, see E. Ruth Harvey, *The Inward Wits: Psychological Theory in the Middle Ages and the Renaissance* (Warburg Institute Surveys, VI; London, 1975).

[52] For discussion of this change, see Wolfgang Becker, 'The Literary Treatment of the Pseudo-Anselmian dialogue *De custodia interioris hominis* in England and France', *Classica et Medievalia*, 35 (1984), 217–18.

own personification. Wit has a wife, unlike his predecessor, Reason (*animus rationalis* in the source) and instead of the source's 'treasury of virtues' (356/3), the cardinal virtues become, in *Sawles Warde*'s selectively expanded treatment, the four daughters of God, lent to Wit as officers of the household, to help him guard God's treasure, the soul. Twelfth- and thirteenth-century theorists agree as to the qualities and usually as to the hierarchy of these virtues, but they are seldom seen as God's daughters, an allegory normally reserved for the Mercy, Truth, Righteousness, and Peace of Ps. 84: 11.[53] *Sawles Warde* highlights aspects of the virtues fitting the role of each in the household.[54] The relationship of the four daughters becomes a working interdependence, a model of female co-operation and mutual esteem used as an image of the desired individual response to the visionary messengers. After Fear's message, for instance, *Sawles Warde* alters the source's order of speeches (94/15–98/4) to conform with its own previous presentation of the virtues (88/10–24), expands their scriptural quotations into dialogue,[55] and gives Justice a summary of what each has said, in which the sisters' interdependence and humbly precise delimiting of their separate functions is stressed (96/14–98/4).

Sawles Warde also expands the messengers' accounts of heaven (105 lines to *De custodia*'s 79) and hell (57 lines to 14), and its treatment of hell, in particular, is deservedly well-known. Though they are more usually set within a dream than within a representative human memory and inner vision, tours of hell and heaven are a common feature of twelfth- and thirteenth-century Latin and vernacular literature.[56] They come from a long tradition of visits to the other-world and provide the source material of many important vernacular literary works, including Dante's *Divine Comedy*. Distinctive accounts of heaven and hell had also long been a feature of Anglo-Saxon homily, with its privileged access to Anglo-Irish tradition, and *Sawles Warde* shares some of its motifs with sermons in this tradition.[57] It does not add sensational extra

[53] On the four daughters of God, see Sajavaara, pp. 62–90, and, for a contemporary English example (*c.*1200), F. Holthausen (ed.), *Vices and Virtues*, EETS, os 89 (London, 1888), 113–17.

[54] On the cardinal virtues, see Rosamund Tuve, *Allegorical Imagery: Some Medieval Books and their Posterity* (Princeton, 1966), and for a 12th-cent. Latin treatment, O. Lottin (ed.), 'Le Traité d'Alain de Lille sur les vertus, les vices et les dons du saint Esprit', *Medieval Studies*, 12 (1950), 28–35.

[55] Cf. Southern and Schmitt, p. 357/15–26.

[56] See D. D. R. Owen, *The Vision of Hell: Infernal Journeys in Medieval French Literature* (Edinburgh, 1970), chs. 1–3, for a good survey of British examples.

[57] See e.g. Joyce Bazire and J. E. Cross (eds.), *Eleven Old English Rogationtide Homilies* (Toronto Old English Series, 7; Toronto, 1982), Introduction to Homily no. 4, p. 58.

torments (a favourite method of expansion in many vernacular other-worldly voyages), but again heightens its source material with detail. This greater sensory vividness is carefully used in the management of narrative perspective and audience response. In the Latin, hell is measurelessly broad and without order (357/1, 3). The audience of *Sawles Warde* are invited to use their memory and sense experience in trying to quantify hell's misery, and are invited to draw comparisons with their own experience of earthly fire and stench (90/26–8). The experience of hell in *Sawles Warde* is a mental progress, not just a sightseeing tour of hell's geography.[58] Similarly, in its account of heaven (notoriously more difficult to describe than hell and often evoked *only* by declarations of its indescribability), *Sawles Warde* again provides a full account and again adds its own emphases and elaborations to the source. It includes the traditional inhabitants of heaven (98/36–102/17), offers a detailed account of the bliss available to every soul there (102/21–104/33), and particularly honours virgins (102/8–17). Where hell's unimaginable misery has been made palpable in the appeal to the audience's experience, the infinite joy of heaven is poignantly conveyed through the messenger's own limitations: the Trinity's radiance can be seen only obliquely (98/36–100/13), and the light of the Virgin cannot long be borne by him (100/14–20).

'O beloved sister, nothing keeps us so free from all sin as the fear of hell and the love of God,' says a contemporary writer in his moral and psychological treatise for a nun.[59] *Sawles Warde*'s treatment of the fear that 'encourages us to flee all vices' (108/9–10) and the joy that 'kindles our hearts towards the bliss of heaven' (108/10) offers not just a theory of reward and punishment but a vivid account of the interior and exterior forces among which the restless and teeming human household attempts its custodianship of God's treasure.

Ancrene Wisse ('Guide for Anchoresses')

The enclosed life of the anchoress, like other forms of religious life, was undertaken by increased numbers of women in the twelfth and thirteenth centuries. The office of inclusion, with the singing of part of the mass for the dead and (in some versions) ceremonial episcopal

---

[58] Many versions detail the sins and the matching punishments of different classes of sinners (cf. e.g. *Visio Pauli*, *Visio Tnugdali*, *St. Patrick's Purgatory*, discussed by Owen, pp. 3–7, 27–33, 39–44): *SW* presents collective, undifferentiated suffering, appropriate for any individual in its audience.

[59] *De modo bene vivendi ad sororem*, ch. 4, §7, 'De timore Dei', *PL* 184: 1203–4.

locking and sealing of the cell door after the recluse had entered it, dramatically (some have thought horribly) marks the sharp boundary between the anchoress and the world. Yet the reclusive life, austere and extreme as it was, was not of its nature the refuge of the marginal or the desperate, but a carefully regulated institution, under strict episcopal supervision, not permitted without previous adequate financial arrangements, and a favourite object of both aristocratic patronage and charitable donation from other social classes. Thirteenth-century recluses were often high-born and influential ladies, like the sisters for whom *Ancrene Wisse* was originally written, but village recluses of more humble origin were also admired and supported by their communities.[60]

Though there is no previous work quite like *Ancrene Wisse*, it has generic affiliations to several kinds of writings for anchorites and to less specialized devotional and pastoral literature. Anchoritic rules occur in a variety of forms, ranging from the informal personal letter to full-scale treatises and from simple prescription to doctrinal and theological discussion.[61] Most, like *Ancrene Wisse*, bear some relation to monastic rules and include or assume a regular daily *horarium* of prayers and devotions, reading, and meditation.[62] Reference to previous monastic or other rules and carefully eclectic provision for particular needs is also characteristic.[63] For its Outer Rule, *Ancrene Wisse* draws on the tradition of legislation inherited by the Dominicans from the Premonstratensian canons,[64] while for both Outer and Inner Rule, other works on the religius life, from the fourth-century *Lives of the Desert Fathers* to St Aelred of Rievaulx's *On the Reclusive Life* (*c.*1162), provide some precedents, source material, and generic conventions, all freely rehandled by the author.[65] The fruits of late twelfth-century Anglo-

---

[60] See Ann K. Warren, *Anchorites and their Patrons in Medieval England* (Los Angeles and Berkeley, 1985).

[61] Medieval anchoritic rules written in England are conveniently listed in Warren, app. 2.

[62] On *Ancrene Wisse*'s devotional prescriptions, see Robert W. Ackerman and Roger Dahood (eds.), *Ancrene Riwle: Introduction and Part 1* (Binghamton, NY, 1984), and Roger Dahood, 'Design in Part I of *Ancrene Wisse*', *Medium Ævum*, 56 (1987), 1–11.

[63] So, for instance, the founder of the Sempringham order, according to his biographer, 'picked what he needed like so many beautiful flowers from the statutes and customs of many churches and monasteries' in drawing up his rule (*The Book of St. Gilbert*, ed. and tr. Raymonde Foreville and Gillian Keir (Oxford, 1987), ch. 18, p. 49).

[64] See Dobson, *Origins*, chs. 1–2, and Millett, 'Origins' (both cited in n. 3 above).

[65] On sources, see Shepherd, pp. xxv–xxix, and see further his notes to Parts 6 and 7, pp. 31–69; also Josephine G. Cooper, 'Latin Elements of the *Ancrene Riwle*', Ph.D. diss. (Univ. of Birmingham, 1956).

Parisian scholarship are drawn on in the use of handbooks of exegesis and preaching aids such as theological dictionaries and dictionaries of natural and scientific lore; penitential handbooks and confessor's manuals are also used.[66] Particularly important to Part 7 and the author's exposition of love are the major twelfth-century devotional and theological writings offering a more personal and human Christ, especially the works of St Anselm of Canterbury (d. 1109), St Bernard of Clairvaux (d. 1153), and St Aelred (d. 1167).[67]

In his introduction to *Ancrene Wisse*, the author distinguishes between two types of rule. The first 'is always within and directs the heart . . . this rule is charity, [which comes] from a pure heart and a clear conscience and true faith' (the definition is based on I Tim. 1:5).[68] The second rule, which is 'entirely outward', governs the body and 'instructs you fully on your external conduct, how you should eat, drink, dress, say your prayers, sleep, keep vigil . . . and this rule is only to serve the other'.[69] The physical hardships of the recluse's life as laid down in the 'Outer Rule', the rigorous custody of her senses and thoughts, and the penances by which she expiates her sins are all designed to purify the heart from the sinful love of earthly things for their own sake, and to open it instead to charity, the love of God and of those earthly things which help to bring us to God (110/30–112/1). Without charity, the ascetic life loses its point, and the aim of Part 7 is to kindle this higher kind of love. It is significant, however, that the word *chearite* is used only once in Part 7, towards the end (128/3); elsewhere, the author prefers the broader term *luue*, and his avoidance of sharper definition is essential to the kind of argument he is using. As Geoffrey Shepherd has shown, he takes over from his twelfth-century Latin sources the idea that the 'carnal' love of Christ in his humanity is a legitimate first step towards the love of Christ in his divinity: 'Throughout Part 7, God as the object and subject of love is presented . . . almost entirely as the incarnate Christ.'[70] It is only towards the end of this section that the emphasis shifts to the love of Christ as God rather than as man (126/13–29). The dominant image of Part 7 is of Christ in his humanity, the crucified figure 'who stretches out his arms

---

[66] For a discussion of contemporary confessional material, see Alexandra Barratt, 'The Five Wits and their Structural Significance in Part II of *Ancrene Wisse*', *Medium Ævum*, 56 (1987), 12–24.

[67] Shepherd, pp. xlviii–lvi. Shepherd's Introduction, which includes detailed discussions of the content and style of this section, is still essential reading.

[68] Corpus MS 1ᵃ/18–21; Salu, p. 1.

[69] Corpus MS 1ᵇ/3–9; Salu, p. 2. [70] Shepherd, p. li.

so lovingly towards you, and bends his head downwards as if to offer a kiss' (122/29–30), loving the recluse in a way which differs in degree rather than kind from ordinary human love and demanding a similar love in return.

Shepherd has commented that the aim of *Ancrene Wisse* is 'not to prove but to move',[71] and it is true that much of Part 7 is written to appeal directly to the senses and emotions of its audience. Its language is heightened, making extensive and skilful use of the techniques of Latin rhetoric,[72] and at one point it draws effectively (though perhaps unexpectedly) on the conventions of contemporary secular literature for the evocative image of Christ as knight, proving his love by chivalric deeds 'as was the custom of knights once upon a time' (114/25–6) in the imaginary past of courtly romance.[73] But its techniques of persuasion differ in some ways from those used in *Hali Meiðhad* and *Seinte Margarete*; the approach is more obviously expository and didactic, and, as Shepherd says, we have 'at least the semblance of rational arguments'.[74] The audience is not allowed to forget that the analogy between Christ and an earthly suitor is no more than an analogy; the 'story' of the lover-knight is also a 'hidden allegory' (112/32), saying one thing and meaning another, and it is only one of a sequence of diverse, sometimes bizarre, metaphors, borrowed from a variety of sources, through which the author explores and illustrates the nature of divine love. Both the ingenuity of some of the metaphors and the author's tendency to present his arguments as a series of methodically numbered points—the four chief loves, the three components of a shield, the three baths—suggest that the audience is being encouraged not only to feel but to reflect and remember. Part 7 of *Ancrene Wisse* cannot be read as 'literary' prose, if by that we mean a prose where the aesthetic effect is an end in itself; the various stylistic techniques it uses should be seen rather (to borrow a phrase from the author) as 'tools to cultivate the heart with' (110/14).

Part 8, which covers every aspect of the 'Outer Rule' except the recluses' daily routine of devotions (dealt with in Part 1), is presented by the author as little more than a postscript to his discussion of the 'Inner Rule', and much of it is an unadorned listing of recommendations and prohibitions. But the author sometimes develops the moral

---

[71] Ibid. lx. [72] See ibid. lix–lxxiii for a detailed analysis.
[73] See note to 114/24–6 in the Textual Commentary; and Woolf, 'The Theme of Christ the Lover-Knight' (cited in n. 23 above).
[74] Shepherd, p. lx.

implications of his practical instructions, and when he does this
he draws on a variety of stylistic resources—illustrative anecdote
(exemplum) (138/24–9), metaphor (132/35–7, 134/29, 140/9–10,
144/11–20, 146/16–18), simile (146/23–6), epigram (132/5–7, 140/
31–2, 146/5–6), proverb (134/10), imaginary dialogue (136/31–4),
and rhetorical question (132/11–12, 27–8, 32–4, 138/5–6). He tells
us that he has divided Part 8 into seven subsections, and the topics they
cover are listed at the end of his introduction to *Ancrene Wisse*: 'First,
on food and drink and related matters; then on the things you can
accept and what things you are allowed to look after or own; then on
your clothes and related matters; then on your occupations; on
haircutting and bloodletting; on your maidservants' rule; finally, how
you must lovingly instruct them.'[75]

This kind of neat structural subdivision is very common in *Ancrene
Wisse*; but the argument in Part 8 turns out on closer inspection to be
less orderly than one might expect from its well-defined framework.
So, for example, the warning against excessive scourging and self-
mutilation (136/15–19) may follow in natural sequence from a
discussion of hair shirts and other penitential clothing, but it still does
not fit easily into the third section; and although giving presents of
handiwork and receiving visits from friends and relations may both
require a confessor's permission (138/21–4), the latter hardly belongs
under the fourth section.

To some extent this tendency can be paralleled elsewhere in *Ancrene
Wisse*, as recent work on its structure has shown;[76] its formal patterns
of subdivision, often outlined in advance by the author, are repeatedly
disrupted by his naturally digressive way of thinking. But some of the
apparent discontinuities in the text given here have a further
explanation. The 'Outer Rule' in the Corpus version has been heavily
revised. The likely method of revision can be deduced from the
Cleopatra manuscript, which was written earlier than Corpus; it
contains a number of deletions, alterations, and marginal additions in
another hand, probably the author's own, which seem to be a
preliminary version of the more thorough revisions which underlie the
Corpus text.[77] This piecemeal method of revision naturally encourages

[75] Corpus MS 4ᵇ/9–15; Salu, p. 6.
[76] See Dahood, 'Design in Part I' (n. 62 above); and Barratt, 'The Five Wits' (n. 66
above).
[77] The 'Scribe B' additions in the Cleopatra MS are examined in detail in Dobson,
Cotton Cleopatra, pp. xciii–cxl; Dobson makes a convincing case for the identity of
'Scribe B' and the author of *Ancrene Wisse*.

digressions and afterthoughts (the awkwardly-placed passage on family visits in 138/22–9, for instance, is an addition to the original text), but it is easy to see—especially given his parting comments on the first version, which are retained in the revised text (148/9–13)—why the author should have preferred it to redrafting the section as a whole.

The content of his alterations tells us much about the development of the community of recluses from the time when *Ancrene Wisse* was first written. Instead of the original three sisters, we have a larger community (whom the author at one point addresses as 'dear daughters' (134/32) rather than 'sisters'); it is now supported by 'good men and women' in general (134/17) rather than the original 'good friends', and apparently thrown back more on its own resources as a result, since the author qualifies his earlier prohibitions on the keeping of animals (e.g. *bute . . . reade* 134/18–19) and the sale of handiwork (e.g. 134/29–31). Although he adds a lengthy denunciation of wimples (136/30–138/13), and of the more worldly types of needlework (138/29–34), advises against too much attachment to friends and family (138/22–9), and warns twice (140/25, 148/5–8) that no earthly comfort should be valued by a recluse, the general tendency of his alterations is to discourage excessive asceticism. His recluses must now supply their needs 'moderately' rather than 'sparingly' (132/26–9), and be less inhibited about asking benefactors for what they need (some restrictions on this are deleted in 134/13–17). They should fast only when in good health (130/28–9), pay more attention to personal hygiene (*ant . . . licwurðe* 140/30–2), and not see their necessary detachment from the world as a justification for inhospitality or rudeness to visitors (*ihwear . . . scandle* 134/11–12). The revised version of Part 8 reinforces more strongly the message of Part 7, that the hardships of the anchoritic life are only a means to an end; it is characteristic that where the original version suggests that the recluse might sleep in 'drawers of haircloth tightly fastened', the revised version adds, 'but a mild and gentle heart is always best. I would rather have you bear a harsh word well than a harsh hair shirt' (136/25–8).

Style

Ancrene Wisse and the works associated with it are written in a prose indebted to both English and Latin literary traditions, but the balance varies from text to text.

The saints' lives of the Katherine Group, which were probably the

earliest to be written, have closer links than the other works with the
native tradition of alliterative writing. The nearest equivalents to their
style can be found in late Old English religious prose, particularly the
rhythmical prose of Ælfric and Wulfstan, which itself owed something
to an older tradition of alliterative poetry. In this native tradition, the
basic rhythmical unit is the two-stress phrase, based on normal
speech-patterns and with a varying number and distribution of
unstressed syllables; alliteration on the stressed syllables is used to
emphasize the individual phrase ('meidenes menske'), link it with
other phrases ('þet eadie meiden / þe we munneð todei'), or do
both simultaneously ('þis meiden þet we munieð / wes Margarete
ihaten'). This generalization, however, covers a wide variety of
different styles in prose and verse, and the use of rhythm and
alliteration in the saints' lives of the Katherine Group cannot be
exactly paralleled elsewhere.[78] Their dominant rhythmical unit is the
two-stress phrase; occasional phrases with three main stresses seem to
be an acceptable variation on this pattern. The rhythm is more sharply
defined in some passages (usually where the emotional tone is
heightened) than in others, but in *Seinte Margarete* in particular it is
regular and strongly marked. The rhythmical phrases are not
consistently linked in pairs by alliteration, as they are in Old English
and later Middle English alliterative verse and in Ælfric's rhymical
prose; the use of alliteration in the saints' lives is more decorative than
structural, and its pattern varies throughout the text. Sometimes long
runs of the same letter link all the phrases of a sentence:

Drihtin deide for us, / þe deorwurðe Lauerd, / ant ne drede Ich na deð /
for to drehen for him (52/3–4);

sometimes shorter runs of alliteration remain internal to the rhythmical
phrase:

ah send me þi sonde, / Helent, of heouene, / þet cuðe me ant kenne / hu
Ich onswerie schule / þes schuckes schireue (48/7–9);

sometimes alliterative linking of phrases is double-stranded with two
letters interweaving:

Send me þi sonde / i culurene heowe, / þe cume me to helpe . . . (54/22).

The alliterative patterning is sometimes so close to that of Old

[78] See Millett, 'Saints' Lives . . . and the Alliterative Tradition', pp. 16–34 (cited in
n. 46 above).

English verse and the later Middle English alliterative long line that it encourages division into verse lines:

þe kingene king art,	echeliche icrunet,
sorhfule ant sari	ant sunfule toturn,
wondrinde ant wrecches	ant wonlese wisent,
castel of strengðe	aȝein þe stronge unwiht,
meidenes murhðe	ant martyrs crune,
mel-seotel softest	ant guldene ȝerde,
alre gold smeatest,	ant glistinde ȝimstan . . .
	(62/13–17)

Such passages, however, are not long sustained, tend to occur for special rhetorical effect, and do not always follow the conventions of alliteration observed in the verse (the first line of the passage quoted above, for instance, lacks the alliteration on the first stressed syllable of the second phrase which would be required in verse, and there is no linking alliteration between the two phrases of the penultimate line). Sometimes the style of *Seinte Margarete* is heightened not only by the techniques of the native alliterative tradition but by the newer device of end-rhyme, as in the dove's lyrical address to Margaret:

Cum nu, for Ich kepe þe,/ brud to þi brud*gume*. /
Cum, leof, to þi lif, / for Ich copni þi *cume*. /
Brihtest bur abit *te*; / leof, hihe þe to *me*. /
Cum nu to mi kinedom, / leaf þet leode se *lah*, /
ant tu schalt wealde wið me / al þet Ich i wald *ah*. / (80/13–16);

and in a couple of passages the author shifts briefly into fairly regular rhyming verse.[79]

Sawles Warde, *Hali Meiðhad*, and *Ancrene Wisse* also draw to some extent on the native alliterative tradition; the influence is strongest in *Sawles Warde*, least obvious in *Ancrene Wisse*, which was probably the latest written of the group. Their prose often falls naturally into a sequence of two-stress phrases, its rhythms reinforced by alliteration; but it also makes much more use than the saints' lives of the resources of Latin rhetoric.[80] There are occasional cases where the saints' lives borrow a stylistic device from their Latin source for special effect, as in *Seinte Margarete*'s use of anaphora (initial repetition):

---

[79] See *SM* 68/13–16, 84/6–13; possibly also 76/8–11.
[80] See Bella Millett, '*Hali Meiðhad*, *Sawles Warde* and the Continuity of English Prose', in E. G. Stanley and Douglas Gray (eds.), *Five Hundred Years of Words and Sounds: A Festschrift for Eric Dobson* (Cambridge, 1983), 100–8; Shepherd, pp. lxvi–lxxiii.

Vidi enim Rufonem . . .	*Ich habbe isehen* hu þe feond . . .
Uidi prostratum infernum . . .	*Ich habbe isehen* þe wulf of helle . . .
	Ich habbe isehen his ouergart . . .
Vidi crucem meam florentem . . .	*Ich habbe isehe* þe rode þe arudde me . . .
oleum sanctum uenire *uidi* . . .	*Ich habbe isehen* hali ant halwende eoli . . .
Uideo gaudium . . .[81]	*Ich habbe isehen* blisse . . .

(60/38–62/9)

This exploitation of the stylistic features of the source, however, is much more common in the later works of the group. So, for instance, the repetition, antithesis, and chiasmus (inversion of word order in successive clauses or phrases) of *Hali Meiðhad*'s Latin source are used in

Ant hwet is lufsumre þing . . . þen þe mihte of meiðhad . . .
þe makeð of eorðlich mon ant wummon heouene engel,

of heane	hine,
of fa	freont,
	help
of þet te hearmeð?	

(10/12–16)

(Quid castitate decorius, quae mundum de immundo conceptum semine, de hoste domesticum, angelum denique de homine facit?).[82]

There is nothing slavish about this imitation; all the works freely expand, alter, discard, or follow the effects of their source material. *Sawles Warde*, for instance, sometimes follows its source's rhythms:

Vae habent, et vae clamant[83]
'Wa' ha ʒeieð ant wa ha habbeð (94/7),

and sometimes substitutes for, or expands the Latin:

[apostolos] . . . tribus et linguas omnes iudicare paratos[84]
ʒarowe for te demen / i þe dei of dome / kinges ant keiseres / ant alle cunreadnes / of alles cunnes ledenes (100/33–4)

and the translation in *Hali Meiðhad* is similarly free.[85]

---

[81] Mack, pp. 134/25–135/2.
[82] For further discussion of this and other examples see Millett, 'Continuity', p. 103.
[83] Southern and Schmitt, p. 357/11.   [84] Ibid. 358/32–3.
[85] See Millett, *Hali Meiðhad*, pp. liii–lvi for detailed exemplification.

The diction of these works, like their style, is drawn from more than one source. It exploits the resources of English, French, Latin, and even, for a few words, Welsh,[86] to create a literary language which can be formal or colloquial, archaic and formulaic or fresh and inventive, courtly or blunt to the point of coarseness. To some extent there is a correlation between diction and style: the works which are closest to the native alliterative tradition have the lowest proportion of borrowings from Latin and French, and Cecily Clark comments, 'Although Romance loanwords could be and were used to make alliterative phrases . . . a writer using traditional alliterative style must often have been led by the semi-formulaic phraseology conventional with this style into traditional choice of words.'[87]

The style of this group of works cannot be fully appreciated unless we remember that they were written to be heard as well as read. Both of the major influences on their style, the native technique of alliterative writing and the devices of Latin rhetoric, were methods largely designed to produce verbal symmetries and echoes which would appeal directly to the ear. While the works were intended at least partly for an audience of recluses, and must sometimes have been used for solitary study, even this kind of reading in the Middle Ages was rarely silent; and both the scarcity and expense of manuscripts and the limitations of literacy meant that medieval works usually had a larger audience of hearers than readers. *Ancrene Wisse* has long been recognized as a 'stylisation of serious conversation',[88] and although its author describes *Hali Meiðhad* as a *writ*, a letter or written treatise (6/ 33, 34/23), the stylistic marks of an oral performance are deliberately built in, with exclamations, rhetorical questions, passages of impassioned argument or heightened denunciation, and imagined audience responses and objections. *Seinte Margarete* seems to have been intended primarily for public delivery in church, and *Sawles Warde* may have served the same function; the style of *Seinte Margarete* in particular is difficult for a modern reader to come to terms with, but its heavy use of tautology and its elaborately rhythmical and alliterative technique make sense as ways of communicating more clearly and attractively with a listening audience.

[86] On the Welsh element, see Dobson, *Origins*, p. 115–16.
[87] Cecily Clark, '*Ancrene Wisse* and *Katherine Group*: A Lexical Divergence', *Neophilologus*, 50 (1966), 119. The figures she gives (recalculated slightly more precisely by Dobson, *Origins*, p. 157) are: *SM* 2.5%, *SW* 4.2%, *HM* 6.3%, *AW* (Parts 6 and 7 only) 10.7%.
[88] Shepherd, p. lxv.

FURTHER READING

1. General: The Historical and Literary Context

Ann K. Warren's *Anchorites and their Patrons in Medieval England* (Los Angeles and Berkeley, 1985) is an important recent study, concentrating particularly on the economic and social position of recluses but also informative on their way of life in general. Sharon K. Elkins, *Holy Women of Twelfth-Century England* (Chapel Hill, 1988), and Sally Thompson, *Women Religious: The Founding of English Nunneries after the Norman Conquest* (Oxford, 1991), are helpful on the broader contemporary context of institutional religion. *Medieval Women*, ed. Derek Baker (Oxford, 1978), and the two anthologies edited by John A. Nichols and Lillian Thomas Shank, *Distant Echoes: Medieval Religious Women I* and *Peaceweavers: Medieval Religious Women II*, Cistercian Studies Series 71, 72 (Kalamazoo, Michigan, 1984, 1987), are excellent collections of articles on the religious life of medieval women. Elizabeth Salter, *English and International: Studies in the Literature, Art, and Patronage of Medieval England*, ed. Derek Pearsall and Nicolette Zeeman (Cambridge, 1988), Part 1, chs. 1 and 2, offers a valuable account of the literary context.

2. *Ancrene Wisse* and the Katherine Group: Editions, Translations, etc.

This list is intended only as an introductory guide; for a general survey of research on these texts and a full bibliography, see Roger Dahood, '*Ancrene Wisse*, the Katherine Group, and the *Wohunge* Group', in A. S. G. Edwards (ed.), *Middle English Prose: A Critical Guide to Major Authors and Genres* (New Brunswick, NJ, 1984). Further references on particular points are given in the footnotes to the Introduction.

On the authorship and origins of *Ancrene Wisse* and the works associated with it, see E. J. Dobson, *The Origins of 'Ancrene Wisse'* (Oxford, 1976). The standard study of the literary dialect in which they were written is still that in S. R. T. O. d'Ardenne's edition of the life of St Juliana, *Þe Liflade ant te Passiun of Seinte Iuliene* (Liège, 1936), repr. as EETS, OS 248 (London, 1961), but this should be supplemented by Arne Zettersten's *Studies in the Dialect and Vocabulary of the 'Ancrene Riwle'* (Lund Studies in English, 34; Lund, 1965), which is often useful on the origin and meaning of individual words. The most recent literary study, covering *Ancrene Wisse* and the Katherine Group, is Elizabeth Robertson's *Early English Devotional Prose and the Female Audience* (Knoxville, Tennessee, 1990). There is also now a complete translation of *Ancrene Wisse*, the Katherine Group, and the Wooing Group by Anne Savage and Nicholas Watson, with a Preface by Benedicta Ward, in *Anchoritic Spirituality: Ancrene Wisse and Associated Works*, The Classics of Western Spirituality (New York and Mahwah, N. J., 1991).

Ancrene Wisse: There is no critical edition of *Ancrene Wisse* as a whole at present, although the Early English Text Society has published diplomatic editions of all the English manuscripts except the Vernon MS (see p. xlii), and editions of the French and Latin translations. The full text of the revised version edited here can be found in *The English Text of the Ancrene Riwle: Ancrene Wisse, edited from MS Corpus Christi College, Cambridge, 402*, by J. R. R. Tolkien, EETS, OS 249 (London, 1962). There is a very readable modern English translation based on this version by M. B. Salu, *The Ancrene Riwle* (London, 1955; repr. Exeter, 1990).

Some sections of *Ancrene Wisse* are available in good student editions. *Ancrene Riwle: Introduction and Part 1*, ed. Robert W. Ackerman and Roger Dahood (Binghamton, NY, 1984), takes its text from the Cleopatra MS; it includes a useful short history of anchoritism, a summary of *Ancrene Wisse*, full notes, bibliography, and an interleaved translation. *Ancrene Wisse Parts 6 and 7*, ed. Geoffrey Shepherd (rev. edn, Exeter, 1985) is based on the Corpus MS; it has an excellent introduction (including both perceptive discussions of the individual texts and a study of their broader historical, theological, and literary context), full notes, and a glossary.

Hali Meiðhad: *Hali Meiðhad*, ed. Bella Millett, EETS, OS 284 (London, 1982), includes a critical text based on MS Bodley 34, notes, glossary, and a general introduction covering theological background, sources, and style.

Seinte Margarete: *Seinte Marherete: Pe Meiden ant Martyr*, ed. Frances M. Mack, EETS, OS 193 (London, 1934; repr. with corrections, 1958), includes corrected texts of both manuscripts on facing pages, a text of the Latin source, introduction, notes, and glossary.

The sister Lives of Juliana and Katherine are also available in EETS editions. *Pe Liflade ant te Passiun of Seinte Iuliene*, ed. S. R. T. O. d'Ardenne (Liège, 1936), repr. as EETS, OS 248 (London, 1961), includes diplomatic texts of both manuscripts, an emended text based on MS Bodley 34, a text of the Latin source, and a full glossary, as well as the fundamental study of the language mentioned above. *Seinte Katerine*, ed. S. R. T. O. d'Ardenne and E. J. Dobson, EETS, SS 7 (London, 1981), gives a critical text based on MS Bodley 34, diplomatic texts of the other two manuscripts, a critical text of the Latin source, full notes, and a glossary.

Sawles Warde: A useful edition for students of early Middle English is the critical text based on MS Bodley 34 in *Early Middle English Verse and Prose*, ed. J. A. W. Bennett and G. V. Smithers, with a Glossary by Norman Davis, 2nd edn. (repr. with corrections, Oxford, 1974), 246–61. R. M. Wilson's edition, *Sawles Warde: An Early Middle English Homily* (Leeds School of English Language Texts and Monographs, 3; Leeds, 1938), includes texts of all three manuscripts, and its long literary-historical introduction is still worth consulting. There is a critical text of the Latin source, the *De custodia interioris hominis* attributed to Anselm, in *Memorials of St. Anselm*, ed. R. W. Southern and F. S. Schmitt (London, 1969), 355–60.

A NOTE ON THE TEXTS
AND TRANSLATIONS

THE texts in this edition are critical texts, not reproducing a single manuscript but using the evidence of all the surviving manuscripts to produce a text corresponding as far as possible to the author's original intentions. Detailed accounts of the relationships between the manuscripts can be found in the earlier editions of the Katherine Group cited in Further Reading and in E. J. Dobson's *The Origins of 'Ancrene Wisse'* (Oxford, 1976) (see especially the diagram of the family tree of *Ancrene Wisse* manuscripts on p. 287). The manuscripts which best preserve the literary dialect in which these works were originally written are Bodleian MS Bodley 34 (*HM, SM, SW*) and Corpus Christi College, Cambridge, MS 402 (*AW*), and they have been used as the base manuscripts for linguistic forms.[1] Although Bodley 34 has been preferred on linguistic grounds, its readings otherwise have no particular authority, and all non-linguistic variants between Katherine Group manuscripts have been assessed on their merits.[2] The Corpus manuscript, however, has a special position among *Ancrene Wisse* manuscripts, not only because it offers a text exceptionally free from errors but because it is the only surviving manuscript of a revised version of the original text. This means that its differences from other manuscripts may be the result of revision rather than scribal departures from the original text, and they have been corrected only when there is good reason to believe that they are not authorial.

For those who prefer their texts unretouched, all departures in the edited text from the base manuscript are recorded in the list of variants at the foot of each page. Full information about the variant readings found in other manuscripts is available in the EETS editions of *Ancrene Wisse* and the Katherine Group mentioned below and in Further Reading; in this edition, variants from other manuscripts are recorded only when they have been used for emendation of the base manuscript, or as a basis for emendation. Where the variant reading has been

---

[1] There is one exception to this: the final part of *Sawles Warde* (from line 106/10 onwards) is missing in MS Bodley 34 because of damage to the manuscript, and MS Royal 17A xxvii has been used as the base manuscript for this section.

[2] For a detailed discussion of some individual textual difficulties, see Bella Millett, 'Some Editorial Problems in the Katherine Group', *English Studies*, 71 (1990), 386–94.

adopted in the edited text, the manuscript form has been silently altered where necessary to conform to the linguistic forms of the base manuscript. Otherwise, where two or more manuscripts have substantially the same reading, only the form found in the first manuscript cited is given. Where the French and Latin versions of *Ancrene Wisse* are clearly translating one particular English variant, their text has not been given separately in the list of variants. Major emendations first made by other scholars have been attributed to them by name in the list of variants; where no further reference is given, the emendation was privately suggested. The word-division, capitalization, punctuation, and paragraphing of the manuscripts have been modernized throughout. Folio references appear in square brackets in the margin.

The manuscripts cited in the list of variants are:

A   Corpus Christi College, Cambridge, MS 402.
B   Bodleian Library, MS Bodley 34.
B²   A corrector of the early part of *Seinte Margarete* in B. Called C in Mack's edition; rechristened here to avoid confusion with . . .
C   British Library, Cotton MS Cleopatra C. vi (*AW*).
C²   An early corrector of C, probably the *Ancrene Wisse* author himself (called 'Scribe B' by Dobson in his edition of the Cleopatra MS).
F   British Library, Cotton MS Vitellius F. vii (early French translation of *Ancrene Wisse*).
G   Gonville and Caius College, Cambridge, MS 234/120 (*AW*).
L   The Latin translation of *Ancrene Wisse*; cited in Part 7 from Merton College, Oxford, MS C.1.5; Coxe 44, and in Part 8 from British Library, Cotton MS Vitellius E. vii.
N   British Library, Cotton MS Nero A. xiv (*AW*).
P   Magdalene College, Cambridge, MS Pepys 2498 (*AW*).
R   British Library, MS Royal 17A xxvii (*SM, SW*).
S   Trinity College, Cambridge, MS R. 14. 7 (later French translation of *Ancrene Wisse*).
T   British Library, Cotton MS Titus D. xviii (*HM, SW, AW*).
V   Bodleian Library, Oxford, MS Eng. poet. a. 1 (*AW*): the 'Vernon manuscript'.

All the *Ancrene Wisse* manuscripts in this list except V have been published in diplomatic editions (that is, editions reproducing the features of the individual manuscripts as closely as possible) by the Early English Text Society, and B has been published both in a photographic facsimile by EETS and in a diplomatic edition by S. R. T. O. d'Ardenne, *The Katherine Group: Edited from MS Bodley 34* (Paris, 1977).

The translations given here, although they remain fairly close to the Middle English throughout, are not always literal. One reason for this is that the translation is sense-for-sense rather than word-for-word, and sometimes paraphrases slightly or adds a gloss where a literal translation would have been misleading or made little sense to the reader. Another is that it is intended to reproduce not only the sense but (as far as possible) the style of these works, including their use of rhythm, alliteration, and rhyming verse and their varying proportions of native and Romance diction, and the translation sometimes renders the text a little more freely in order to do this. Where the match between text and translation is not immediately obvious, the Glossary should be consulted for the literal sense of the Middle English words.

In translating from an earlier stage of one's own language, there is always a temptation to stay closer to the original text by using the surviving forms of the words it uses rather than other words which have taken over their functions in current English. This temptation has been resisted wherever possible, but an exception has been made for 'maiden', since there is no current English word which can mean both 'girl' and 'virgin' as Early Middle English '*meiden*' does, and it is often difficult in these texts to tell which sense is dominant.

TEXTS

Hali Meiðhad

Epistel of meidenhad meidene froure

| *Avdi, filia, et uide, et inclina aurem tuam; et obliuiscere populum tuum et* [52ᵛ]
domum patris tui. Dauið þe psalmwruhte spekeð i þe Sawter towart
Godes spuse—þet is, euch meiden þet haueð meið þeawes—ant seið:
'Iher me, dohter, bihald ant bei þin eare; ant forӡet ti folc ant tines
5 feader hus.'
   Nim ӡeme hwet euch word beo sunderliche to seggen. 'Iher me,
dohter,' he seið. 'Dohter' he cleopeð hire forþi þet ha understonde
þet he hire luueliche liues luue leareð, as feader ah his dohter; ant heo
him as hire feader þe bliþeluker lustni. 'Iher me, deore dohter': þet is,
10 'ӡeorne lustne me wið earen of þin heauet.' 'Ant bihald': þet is,
'opene to understonde me þe ehnen of þin heorte.' 'Ant bei þin eare':
þet is, 'beo buhsum to mi lare.' Ha mei ondswerien ant seggen, 'Ant
hwet is nu þis lare þet tu nimest se deopliche, ant learst me se
ӡeorne?' Low, þis: 'Forӡet ti folc ant tines feader hus.'
15   'Þi folc' he cleopeð, Dauið, þe gederunge inwið þe of fleschliche
þonkes, þe leaðieð þe ant dreaieð wið hare procunges to flesliche
fulðen, to licomliche lustes, ant eggið þe to brudlac ant to weres
cluppunge, ant makieð þe to þenchen hwuch delit were þrin, hwuch
eise i þe richedom þet þeos leafdis habbeð, hu muche god mahte of
20 inker streon | awakenin. A, fals folc of swikel read, as þi muð uleð, as [53ʳ]
þu schawest forð al þet god þuncheð, ant helest al þet bittre bale þet
ter lið under, ant al þet muchele lure þet terof ariseð! 'Forӡet al þis
folc, mi deorewurðe dohter,' seið Dauið þe witege: þet is, 'þes þonkes
warp ut of þin heorte.' Þis is Babilones folc, þe deofles here of helle,
25 þet is umbe for te leaden into þe worldes þeowdom Syones dohter.
   'Syon' wes sumhwile icleopet þe hehe tur of Ierusalem; ant 'Syon'
seið ase muchel on Englische ledene ase 'heh sihðe'. Ant bitacneð þis
tur þe hehnesse of meiðhad, þe bihald as of heh alle widewen under
hire ant weddede baðe. For þeos, ase flesches þrealles, beoð i worldes

3 meið] meiið B   6 word] worð B   9 lustni] lustin B   10 ӡeorne]
ӡeornne B   12 Ha ... seggen] T, *om.* B   14 ӡeorne] ӡeone B
15 gederunge] ӡederunge B   16 hare] har B   18 makieð] makied B
19 god] T, *om.* B   21 bittre] bittri B   22 ter lið under] T, is þerunder B
23 deorewurðe] deȝrewrðe B   26-7 'Syon' seið] Syon B, seið Syon T;
E. G. Stanley   29 worldes] worlddes B

A Letter on Virginity

A letter on virginity for the encouragement of virgins

Listen, daughter, and behold, and incline your ear; and forget your people and your father's house. David the psalmist is speaking in the Psalter to the bride of God—that is, every virgin who has the virtues of virginity—and he says: 'Hear me, daughter, behold and incline your ear; and forget your people and your father's house.'

Take note of what each word separately means. 'Hear me, daughter,' he says. He calls her 'daughter' so that she may understand that he is lovingly teaching her the love of eternal life, as a father ought his daughter; and that she may listen to him the more gladly as her father. 'Hear me, dear daughter': that is, 'listen to me carefully with your bodily ears.' 'And behold': that is, 'open the eyes of your heart to understand me.' 'And incline your ear': that is, 'be obedient to my teaching.' She may say in answer, 'And now what is this teaching that you take so seriously, and instruct me in so earnestly?' It is this: 'Forget your people and your father's house.'

'Your people' are what David calls the carnal thoughts which crowd into your mind, which incite you and draw you on with their goadings to carnal filthiness, to physical desires, and urge you towards marriage and a husband's embrace, and make you think what pleasure there would be in them, what comfort in the riches that these ladies have, how much that is good might come from your children. Oh, false people, treacherous advisers, how your mouths flatter, as you put forward all that seems good, and hide all that bitter misery which lurks underneath, and all the great loss which will be the result! 'Forget all this people, my beloved daughter,' says David the prophet: that is, 'cast these thoughts out of your heart.' This is the people of Babylon, the army of the Devil of hell, who are plotting to lead the daughter of Zion into the world's servitude.

'Zion' was once the name of the high tower of Jerusalem; and 'Zion' corresponds to 'high vision' in English. And this tower signifies the high state of virginity, which as if from a height sees all widows below it, and married women too. For these, as slaves of the flesh, are in the

þeowdom, ant wunieð lahe on eorðe; ant meiden stont þurh heh lif i
þe tur of Ierusalem. Nawt of lah on eorðe, ah of þe hehe in heouene þe
is bitacnet þurh þis, of þet Syon ha bihalt al þe worlt under hire; ant
þurh englene liflade ant heouenlich þet ha lead, þah ha licomliche
5 wunie upon eorðe, ha stiheð gasteliche, ant is as i Syon, þe hehe tur of
heouene, freo ouer alle from worldliche weanen.

Ah Babilones folc þet Ich ear nempnede, þe deofles here of helle,
þet beoð flesches lustes ant feondes eggunge, weorrið ant warpeð
eauer | towart tis tur for te keasten hit adun, ant drahen hire into [53ᵛ]
10 þeowdom þet stont se hehe þerin, ant is icleopet forþi Syones dohter.
Ant nis ha witerliche akeast ant into þeowdom idrahen, þe of se swiðe
heh stal, of se muche dignete, ant swuch wurðschipe as hit is to beo
Godes spuse, Iesu Cristes brude, þe Lauerdes leofmon þet alle þinges
buheð, of al þe worlt leafdi, as he is of al lauerd; ilich him in halschipe,
15 vnwemmet as he is, ant þet eadi meiden his deorrewurðe moder; ilich
his hali engles ant his heste halhen; se freo of hireseoluen þet ha
nawiht ne þearf of oðer þing þenchen bute ane of hire leofmon wið
treowe luue cwemen, for he wule carie for hire þet ha haueð itake to of
al þet hire bihoueð, hwil ha riht luueð him wið soðe bileaue—nis ha
20 þenne sariliche (as Ich seide ear) akeast ant into þeowdom idrahen, þe
of se muchel hehschipe ant se seli freodom schal lihte se lahe into a
monnes þeowdom, swa þet ha naueð nawt freo of hireseoluen; ant
trukien for a mon of lam þe heouenliche Lauerd; ant lutlin hire
leafdischipe ase muchel as hire leatere were is leasse wurð ant leasse
25 haueð þen hefde ear hire earre; ant of Godes brude ant his freo dohter
(for ba togederes ha is), biki|með þeow under mon ant his þrel, to don [54ʳ]
al ant drehen þet him likeð, ne sitte hit hire se uuele; ant of se seli
sikernesse as ha wes in ant mahte beon under Godes warde, deð hire
into drecchunge, to dihten hus ant hinen, ant to se monie earmðen, to
30 carien for se feole þing, teonen þolien ant gromen, ant scheomen
umbe stunde, drehen se moni wa for se wac hure as þe worlt forȝelt
eauer ed ten ende—nis þeos witerliche akeast? Nis þis þeowdom inoh,
aȝein þet ilke freolec þet ha hefde hwil ha wes Syones dohter? Ant
þah nis inempnet her nawt of heouenliche luren, þe passið alle oðre
35 wiðuten euenunge.

---

1 lahe] e *and part of* h *cropped from margin in* B   eorðe] eorððe B   5 ha . . .
gasteliche] *om.* BT; *Dobson*   9 hire] T, *om.* B   12 wurðschipe] wurðhchipe B
14 þe] T, *om.* B   al²] T, *om.* B   16 þet] T, *om.* B   17 nawiht] nawhit B
26 togederes] toȝederes B   28 in] T, *om.* B   29 drecchunge] drechunge B
earmðen] earmden B   34 oðre] T, *om.* B

servitude of the world, and live low on earth; and the virgin stands through her exalted life in the tower of Jerusalem. Not from low on earth, but from the height in heaven which is signified by this, from that Zion she sees all the world below her; and through the angelic and heavenly life that she leads, although she lives on earth in the body, she ascends in spirit, and is as if in Zion, the high tower of heaven, incomparably free from worldly troubles.

But the people of Babylon that I mentioned before, the army of the Devil of hell, who are carnal lusts and the fiend's temptation, constantly make war on this tower and attack it, so as to cast it down and bring into servitude the woman who stands so high inside it, and is called for that reason the daughter of Zion. And is she not truly cast down and brought into servitude, who from such a high position, of such great dignity, and such honour as it is to be God's spouse, the bride of Jesus Christ, the lover of the Lord to whom all things do homage, lady of all the world as he is lord of all; like him in integrity, spotless as he is, and that blessed virgin his beloved mother; like his holy angels and his highest saints; with such freedom for herself that she need not think about anything at all apart from pleasing her beloved with true love, because the lover she has chosen will care for her in all that she needs while she loves him well with constant faith— is she not then (as I said before) wretchedly cast down and brought into servitude, who from so great an eminence and such blessed freedom must descend so low into the service of a man, so that she has nothing that is freely her own; and desert the heavenly Lord for a man of clay; and lessen her rank as lady by as much as her latter husband is worth less and owns less than her former husband did; and from being God's bride and his free daughter (for she is both together) becomes a serf to a man and his slave, to do and suffer all that he pleases, however little she likes it; and from such blessed security as she was and might be in under God's protection, gives herself up to drudgery, to managing house and servants, and to so many troubles, caring for so many things, suffering trials and annoyances, and humiliations sometimes, bearing so many miseries for such poor wages as the world always pays in the end—is not this woman truly cast down? Is not this servitude enough, compared with that freedom which she had while she was the daughter of Zion? And even so, there is no mention here of the heavenly losses, which exceed all the others beyond comparison.

Sikerliche, swa hit feareð. Serue Godd ane, ant alle þing schule þe
turne to gode; ant tac þe to him treowliche, ant tu schalt beo freo from
alle worldliche weanen, ne mei nan uuel hearmi þe; for as Seinte
Pawel seið, alle þing turneð þen gode to gode. Ne mei na þing wonti
5 þe þe berest him þet al wealt inwið i þi breoste. Ant swuch swettnesse
þu schalt ifinden in his luue ant in his seruise, ant habbe se muche
murhðe þrof ant licunge i þin heorte, þet tu naldest changin þet stat
þet tu liuest in for te beo cwen icrunet. Se hende is ure Lauerd þet
nule he nawt þet his icorene beon her wiðute mede; | for se muchel [54ʳ]
10 confort is in his grace þet al ham sit þet ha seoð, ant þah hit þunche
oþre men þet ha drehen hearde, hit ne derueð ham nawt, ah þuncheð
ham softe, ant habbeð mare delit þrin þen ei oðer habbe i licunge of þe
worlt. Þis ure Lauerd ȝeueð ham her as on earnesse of þe eche mede
þet schal cume þrefter. Þus habbeð Godes freond al þe frut of þis
15 worlt þet ha forsaken habbeð, o wunderliche wise, ant heouene ed ten
ende.

Nu þenne on oðer half, nim þe to þe worlde; ant eauer se þu mare
hauest, se þe schal mare trukien. Ant serue, hwen þu naldest Godd,
þes fikele worlt ant frakele; ant schalt beo sare ideruet under hire
20 as hire þreal on a þusent wisen, aȝeines an licunge habben twa
ofþunchunges, ant se ofte beon imaket earm of an eðlich mon þet tu
list under, for nawt oðer for nohtunge, þet te schal laði þi lif, ant
bireowe þi sið, þet tu eauer dudest te into swuch þeowdom for
worldliche wunne þet tu wendest to biȝeotene, ant hauest ifunden
25 weane þrin ant wontreaðe riue. Al is þet tu wendest golt iwurðe to
meastling; al is nawt þet ti folc (of hwam I spec þruppe) biheten þe to
ifinden. Nu þu wast þet ha hab|beð itricchet te as treitres; for under [55ʳ]
weole, i wunnes stude þu hauest her ofte helle, ant bute ȝef þu
wiðbreide þe, þu bredest te þet oðer. Easke þes cwenes, þes riche
30 cuntasses, þeos modie leafdis of hare liflade; soðliche, ȝef ha
biþencheð ham riht ant icnawlecheð soð, Ich habbe ham to witnesse,
ha lickið honi of þornes. Ha buggeð al þet swete wið twa dale of
bittre—ant þet schal forðre i þis writ beon openliche ischawet. Nis hit
nower neh gold, al þet ter schineð; nat þah na mon bute hamseolfen
35 hwet ham sticheð ofte.

---

5 i] T, *om.* B   8 beo] T, *om.* B   13 earnesse] earnnesse B   þe] T, *om.* B
18 serue] seruin B   21 ofþunchunges] T, ofþunchunge B   25 wontreaðe]
wontreðe B   27 itricchet] T, bichearret B   29 Easke] T, as doð B

Certainly, this is the way it goes. Serve God alone, and everything will turn out well for you; and commit yourself faithfully to him, and you will be free of all wordly troubles, nor can any evil harm you; for as St Paul says, for the good all things turn out well. And you can lack nothing when you carry the ruler of everything in your heart. And you will find such sweetness in his love and his service, and feel so much joy and pleasure in it, that you would not change your way of life to be a crowned queen. Our Lord is so generous that he does not wish his chosen ones to be without reward here in this world; for there is so much comfort in his grace that all they see pleases them, and though it may seem to other people that they have much to bear, it does not trouble them but seems easy to them, and they have more delight in it than anyone else would in wordly pleasure. Our Lord gives them this here as a pledge, as it were, of the eternal reward which is to come afterwards. So God's friends, in a marvellous way, have all the benefit of this world which they have renounced, and heaven in the end.

Now then, on the other hand, turn to the world; and always the more you have, the more will fail you. And serve, when you would not serve God, this false and worthless world; and you shall be cruelly oppressed by it as its slave in a thousand ways, have two regrets for every pleasure, and be made wretched so often by the worthless man you are subject to, for nothing or for a trifle, that your life will be hateful to you, and make you regret your choice, that you ever entered into such slavery for the worldly joy that you expected to gain, since you have found misery in it and all kinds of hardship. Everything that you thought was gold has turned into brass; everything is worthless that your people (of whom I spoke above) promised that you would find. Now you know that they have treacherously betrayed you; for under the outward appearance of happiness, instead of delight you often have hell on earth, and unless you draw back, you are preparing the other hell for yourself. Ask these queens, these rich countesses, these proud ladies, about their way of life; certainly, if they give it careful thought and admit the truth, I have them as witnesses, they are licking honey off thorns. They pay for all that sweetness with twice as much bitterness—and that will be clearly shown later in this treatise. It is nowhere near gold, all that glitters there; but no one but themselves knows what they often suffer.

Hwen þus is of þe riche, hwet wenest tu of þe poure, þe beoð
wacliche iȝeuen ant biset vuele?—as gentile wummen meast alle nu
on worlde þe nabbeð hwerwið buggen ham brudgume onont ham, ant
ȝeoueð ham into þeowdom of an eðeluker mon wið al þet ha habbeð.
5 Weilawei, Iesu Godd, hwuch unwurðe chaffere! Wel were ham weren
ha on hare brudlakes dei iboren to biburien. Forþi, seli meiden,
forȝet ti folc as Dauið bit: þet is, do awei þe þonckes þe prokieð þin
heorte þurh licomliche lustes, ant leaðieð þe ant eggið towart þullich
þeowdom for fleschliche fulðen.

10 Forȝet ec þi feader hus, as Dauið read þrefter. 'Þi fea|der' he [55ᵛ]
cleopeð þet unþeaw þet streonede þe of þi moder—þet ilke unhende
flesches brune, þet bearninde ȝeohðe of þet licomliche lust biuore
þet wleatewile werc, þet bestelich gederunge, þet scheomelese
sompnunge, þet ful of fulðe, stinkinde ant untohe dede. (Hit is þah i
15 wedlac summes weies to þolien, as me schal efter iheren.) ȝef þu
easkest hwi Godd scheop swuch þing to beonne, Ich þe ondswerie:
Godd ne scheop hit neauer swuch, ah Adam ant Eue turnden hit to
beo swuch þurh hare sunne, ant merden ure cunde, þet is þis
unþeawes hus, þet haueð—mare hearm is—al to muche lauerdom ant
20 meistrie þrinne. Þis cunde imerred tus, þet Dauið cleopeð þi feadres
hus (þet is, þe lust of lecherie þet rixleð þerwiðinnen)—
forȝet ant ga ut þrof wið wil of þin heorte, ant Godd wule efter þe
wil ȝeoue þe strengðe sikerliche of his deore grace. Ne þearf þu bute
wilnin, ant leote Godd wurchen. Haue trust on his help; ne schalt tu na
25 þing godes bisechen ne iunnen þet he hit nule endin. Eauer bidde his
grace; ant ouerkim wið hire help þe ilke wake cunde þe draheð into
þeowdom, ant into fulðe fenniliche akeasteð se monie.

Et concupiscet rex decorem tuum. 'Ant þenne wule', seið Dauið, 'þe
king wilni þi wlite,' þe king of alle kinges desiri þe to leofmon. Ant tu | [56ʳ]
30 þenne, eadi mciden, þet art iloten to him wið meiðhades merke, ne
brec þu nawt þet seil þet seileð inc togederes. Halt þi nome þurh
hwam þu art to him iweddet; ne leos þu neauer for a lust, ant for an
eðelich delit of an hondhwile, þet ilke þing þe ne mei neauer beon
acoueret. Meiðhad is þet tresor þet, beo hit eanes forloren, ne bið hit
35 neauer ifunden. Meiðhad is þe blostme þet, beo ha fulliche eanes

---

1 þe'] T, *om.* B   2 biset] T, biset on B   wummen] T, wummon B   4 into]
T, to B   8 þe] T, *om.* B   9 fleschliche] flecsliche B   12 bearninde]
bearnninde B   18 þis] T, *om.* B   19 þet] ant BT   hearm] hearrm B
20 imerred tus] T, merreð us B   23 þe] T, *om.* B   25 iunnen] luuien B,
bigunnen T   30 meiðhades] meidhades B   31 Halt]T, Hwalt B
32 an] T, *om.* B

When it is like this for the rich, what do you expect of the poor, who are wretchedly married and ill provided for?—like almost all gentle-women living at present who do not have the wherewithal to buy themselves a bridegroom of their own rank, and give themselves up to the service of a man of lower rank with all that they own. Alas, Lord Jesus, what a dishonourable bargain! It would be better for them if they were brought to burial on their wedding-day. Therefore, innocent maiden, forget your people as David tells you to: that is, put away the thoughts which stir your heart through physical desires, and incite and urge you on towards such slavery for the sake of carnal filthiness.

And forget your father's house too, as David advises next. 'Your father' he calls that sinful act through which your mother conceived you—that indecent heat of the flesh, that burning itch of physical desire before that disgusting act, that animal union, that shameless coupling, that stinking and wanton deed, full of filthiness. (It is, nevertheless, to be tolerated to some extent within marriage, as you will hear later.) If you ask why God created such a thing, this is my answer: God never created it to be like this, but Adam and Eve perverted it through their sin and corrupted our nature, which is the house of this vice, which has—unfortunately—far too much dominance and mastery there. The nature corrupted in this way, which David calls your father's house (that is, the lecherous desire which rules in it)—forget it and go out of it with a resolute heart, and God will surely give you strength according to that resolve from his precious grace. You need only will it, and let God dispose. Put your trust in his help; you will not ask or wish for anything good that he will not accomplish. Constantly pray for his grace; and overcome with its help that weak nature which draws so many into servitude, and casts them foully into filth.

And the king will desire your beauty. 'And then', says David, 'the king will desire your beauty,' the king of all kings desire you as a lover. And you then, blessed maiden, who are assigned to him with the mark of virginity, do not break that seal which seals you both together. Keep that name through which you are wedded to him; never lose for an impulse, and for a worthless momentary pleasure, that one thing which can never be recovered. Virginity is the treasure which, if it is once lost, will never be found again. Virginity is the blossom which, if it is once

forcoruen, ne spruteð ha eft neauer (ah þah ha falewi sumchere mid
misliche þonkes, ha mei eft grenin neauer þe leatere). Meiðhad is þe
steorre þet, beo ha eanes of þe est igan adun i þe west, neauer eft ne
ariseð ha. Meiðhad is þet an ȝeoue iȝettet te of heouene; do þu hit eanes
5 awei, ne schalt tu neauer nan oðer al swuch acourin. For meiðhad is
heouene cwen, ant worldes alesendnesse þurh hwam we beoð iborhen,
mihte ouer alle mihtes ant cwemest Crist of alle. Forþi þu ahest,
meiden, se deorliche te witen hit, for hit is se heh þing ant se swiðe
leof Godd ant se licwurðe, ant þet an lure þet is wiðuten couerunge.
10 Ȝef hit is Godd leof þet is himseolf swa ilich, hit nis na wunder, for he
is leoflukest þing, ant buten eauereuch bruche, ant wes eauer ant is
cleane ouer alle þing, ant ouer alle þinge luueð cleannesse. Ant hwet is
lufsumre þing ant mare to herien bimong eorðliche þing þen þe mihte
of meiðhad | bute bruche ant cleane, ibrowden on himseoluen, þe [56ʳ]
15 makeð of eorðlich mon ant wummon heouene engel, of heane hine, of
fa freont, help of þet te hearmeð? Vre flesch is ure fa, ant heaneð us
ant hearmeð se ofte as ha us fuleð; ah ȝef ha wit hire wiðute bruche
cleane, ha is us swiðe god freond ant help of treowe hine. For in hire
ant þurh hire þu ofearnest, meiden, to beon englene euening i þe eche
20 blisse of heouene—ant wið god rihte, hwen þu hare liflade i þi
bruchele flesch bute bruche leadest. Engel ant meiden beoð euening i
uertu i meiðhades mihte, þah eadinesse ham twinni ȝetten ant
totweame; ant þah hare meiðhad beo eadiure nuðe, þin is þe mare
strengðe to halden, ant schal wið mare mede beo þe forȝolden. Þis
25 mihte is þet an þet i þis deadliche lif schaweð in hire an estat of þe
blisse undeadlich i þet eadi lond as brude ne nimeð gume ne
brudgume brude; ant teacheð her on eorðe in hire liflade þe liflade of
heouene; ant i þis worlt þet is icleopet 'lond of unlicnesse' edhalt hire
burde in licnesse of heouenlich cunde, þah ha beo utlahe þrof ant i
30 licome of lam; ant i bestes bodi neh liueð heouene engel. Nis | þis [57ʳ]
mihte of alle swiðe to herien? Þis is ȝet þe uertu þe halt ure bruchele
ueat, þet is, ure feble flesch, as Seinte Pawel leareð, in hal halinesse;
ant as þet swote smirles ant deorest of oþre þet is icleopet basme wit
þet deade licome þet is þerwið ismiret from rotunge, alswa deð
35 meidenhad meidenes cwike flesch wiðute wemmunge. Halt alse hire

---

4 ȝeoue] T, *om.* B   5 al] T, *om.* B   8 te] T, *om.* B   9 wiðuten] wituten B
10 leof] T, *om.* B   nis] T, *om.* B   12 cleannesse] cleainnesse B
13 eorðliche] eordlich B   15 makeð] maked B   eorðlich] eordlich B   heane]
T, heame B   16 hearmeð] hearmið B   17 hearmeð] hearmið B
18 god] godd B   19 meiden] meden B   20 god] goð B

completely cut off, will never grow again (but though it may wither
sometimes through indecent thoughts, it can grow green again
nevertheless). Virginity is the star which, if it has once travelled from
the East to sink in the West, will never rise again. Virginity is the one
gift granted to you from heaven; if you once dispose of it, you will
never regain another quite like it. For virginity is the queen of heaven,
and the world's redemption through which we are saved, a virtue above
all virtues, and most pleasing of all to Christ. For this reason, maiden,
you should guard it carefully, because it is such a noble thing and so
very dear to God and so acceptable, and the one loss which cannot be
recovered. If what is so like God is dear to him, it is no wonder, for he
is more beautiful than anything, and without any sin, and always was
and is pure above all things, and above all things loves purity. And what
is more beautiful and more praiseworthy among earthly things than the
virtue of inviolate and pure virginity, modelled on his own, which
makes from an earthly man or woman an angel of heaven, from a tyrant
a servant, from a foe a friend, help from what harms you? Our flesh is
our foe, and oppresses and harms us as often as it defiles us; but if it
keeps itself pure and intact, it is a very good friend to us and gives us
help as a faithful servant. For in it and through it, maiden, you earn the
right to be the equal of angels in the eternal bliss of heaven—and with
good reason, when you lead their life in your frail flesh without
unchastity. Angel and maiden are equal in virtue through the power of
virginity, though as yet their degrees of blessedness divide them; and
though their virginity is more blessed now, yours is more difficult to
keep intact, and will be recompensed by a greater reward. This virtue
is the only one that in this mortal life foreshadows in itself a state of the
immortal bliss in that blessed land where bride does not take groom
nor bridegroom bride; and teaches here on earth by its way of life the
way of life in heaven; and in this world which is called 'land of
unlikeness' keeps its nature in the likeness of heavenly nature,
although it is an outlaw from there and in a body of clay; and in a
beast's body lives almost like an angel of heaven. Is not this virtue
above all to be greatly honoured? This is, furthermore, the virtue
which keeps our frail vessel, that is, our feeble flesh, as St Paul teaches,
in complete holiness; and as that sweet ointment, more costly than any
other, which is called balm protects the dead body which is anointed
with it against corruption, so virginity preserves a maiden's living flesh
without defilement. Likewise it keeps her body and her five senses—

limen ant hire fif wittes—sihðe ant herunge, smechunge ant smellunge
ant euch limes felunge—þet ha ne merren ne ne mealten þurh
licomes lustes i fleschliche fulðen þe Godd haueð þurh his grace se
muche luue ivnnen; þet ha ne beoð of þeo iliche, bi hwam hit is iwriten
5 þus þurh þe prophete, þet ha in hare wurðinge as eaueres
forroteden—þet is, eauereuch wif þet is hire were þreal ant liueð i
wurðinge, he ant heo baðe. Ah nis nawt bi þeos iseid þet ha forrotieð
þrin, ȝef ha hare wedlac laheliche haldeð; ah þe ilke sari wrecches þe
i þe fule wurðinge vnwedde walewið beoð þe deofles eaueres, þet rit
10 ham ant spureð ham to don al þet he wule. Þeos walewið i wurðinge
ant forrotieð þrin aþet ha arisen þurh bireowsunge, ant healen ham
wið soð schrift ant wið deadbote.

    Eadi meiden, understont te in hu heh dignete þe mihte of meiðhad
halt te. Ah se þu herre stondest, beo sarre offea|ret to fallen; for se herre [57ᵛ]
15 degre, se þe fal is wurse. Þe ontfule deouel bihalt te se hehe istihe
towart heouene þurh meiðhades mihte, þet him is mihte laðest; for
þurh ure Leafdi meiðhad þe hit bigon earst, þe meiden Marie, he
forleas þe lauerdom on moncun on eorðe, ant wes helle irobbet ant
heouene bið ifullet. Sið þe folhin hire troden, meiden, gan as heo dude
20 þe offrede hire meiðhad earst to ure Lauerd, for hwon þet he cheas
hire bimong alle wummen for te beon his moder ant þurh hire
meiðhad moncun alesen. Nu bihalt te alde feond, ant sið þe i þis mihte
stonde se hehe, ilich hire ant hire sune, as engel in heouene, i
meiðhades menske, ant toswelleð of grome; ant scheoteð niht ant dei
25 his earewen, idrencte of an attri healewi, towart tin heorte to wundi þe
wið wac wil, ant makien to fallen, as Crist te forbeode! Ant eauer se þu
strengeluker stondest aȝein him, se he o teone ant o grome wodeluker
weorreð; for swa muche þe hokerluker him þuncheð to beon
ouercumen, þet þing se feble as flesch is, ant nomeliche of wummon,
30 schal him ouerstihen.

    Euch fleschlich wil ant lust of leccherie þe ariseð i þe heorte is þes
feondes fla; ah hit ne wundeð þe nawt bute hit festni in þe, ant leaue se
longe þet tu waldest þet ti wil were ibroht to werke. Hwil | þi wit [58ʳ]
edstont, ant chastieð þi wil, þah þi lust beore to þet te leof were, ne
35 hearmeð hit te nawiht, ne suleð þi sawle; for wit is hire scheld under

3 licomes] licome B   lustes] lustest B   4 þeo iliche] þe ilich B, þa iliche T
7 wurðinge] wurdinge B   9 walewið] waleweð B   10 wurðinge] wurdinge B
12 wið¹] wid B   13 meiðhad] meidhad B   14 offearet] offeaaret B
17 ure] T, hire B   21 wummen] wummem B   22 þe] T, *om.* B
24 scheoteð] scheoted B

sight and hearing, taste and smell, and sensation in every limb—so that those to whom God has granted so much love through his grace do not perish or grow corrupt in carnal filthiness through physical desires; so that they are not like those about whom it is written by the prophet that they rotted in their filth like beasts of burden—that is, every woman who is subject to her man and lives in filth, he and she both. But it is not said of these that they rot there, if they keep their marriage lawfully; but those miserable wretches who wallow unmarried in that unclean filth are the Devil's cart-horses, and he rides them and spurs them on to do all that he wants. These wallow in filth and rot in it until they rise up through repentance, and heal themselves with true confession and penance.

Blessed maiden, understand in what high dignity the virtue of virginity holds you. But as you stand higher, be more greatly afraid of falling; for the higher the degree, the worse the fall. The envious Devil sees you have climbed so high towards heaven through the virtue of virginity, which is the most hateful of virtues to him; for through the virginity of our Lady who began it first, the maiden Mary, he lost dominion over mankind on earth, and hell was plundered and heaven will be filled. He sees you follow in her footsteps, maiden, and go as she did, who offered her virginity first to our Lord, for which reason he chose her among all women to be his mother and through her virginity to redeem mankind. Now the ancient enemy looks on, and sees you stand so high in this virtue, like her and her son, like an angel in heaven, in the glory of virginity, and swells with fury; and night and day he shoots his arrows, dipped in a venomous potion, towards your heart, to wound you with weakness of will and cause you to fall, which Christ forbid! And always the more strongly you stand against him, the more furiously he attacks out of chagrin and rage; because it seems to him so much the more shameful to be overcome, that something as weak as flesh is—and especially a woman's—should be able to surpass him.

Every carnal impulse and lecherous desire which arises in your heart is the Devil's arrow; but it does not wound you unless it is lodged in you, and remains so long that you wish your desire could be acted out. While your reason stands firm and controls your will, although your desire may incline towards pleasure, it does not harm you at all or defile your soul; for reason is its shield, under God's grace. While that

Godes grace. Hwil þe scheld is ihal—þet is, þe wisdom of þi wit—þet
hit ne breoke ne beie, þah þi fleschliche wil fals beo þerunder ant
walde as hire luste, þes feondes flan fleoð aȝein alle on himseoluen.
Ant loke wel hweruore: vre licomes lust is þes feondes foster; vre wit
5 is Godes dohter; ant ba beoð us inwið. Forþi her is aa feht, ant mot
beon aa nede; for ne trukeð neauer mare, hwil we her wunieð, weorre
ham bitweonen. Ah wel is him þet folheð Wit, Godes dohter, for ha
halt wið Meiðhad, þet is hire suster; ah þi wil, on oðer half, of þet
licomliche lust halt wið Leccherie, þet is þe deofles streon as heo is,
10 ant Sunne hire moder.
Leccherie o meiðhad, wið help of fleschlich wil, weorreð o þis wise.
Hire forme fulst is sihðe: ȝef þu bihaldest ofte ant stikelunge on ei
mon, Leccherie ananriht greiðeð hire wið þet to weorrin o þi meiðhad,
ant secheð earst upon hire nebbe to nebbe. Speche is hire oþer help:
15 ȝef ȝe þrefter þenne speokeð togedere folliche, ant talkið of unnet,
Leccherie seið scheome þe menske of þi meiðhad ant tukeð hire al to
wundre, ant | þreat to don hire scheome ant hearmin þrefter—ant halt [58]
hire forewart. For sone se cos kimeð forð, þet is hire þridde fulst,
þenne spit Leccherie, to scheome ant to schendlac, Meiðhad o þe
20 nebbe. Þe feorðe fulst to bismere ant to merren Meiðhad, þet is
unhende felunge. Wite hire þenne; for ȝef ȝe þenne hondlið ow in ei
stude untuliche, þenne smit Leccherie o þe mihte of Meiðhad ant
wundeð hire sare. Þet dreori dede on ende ȝeueð þet deaðes dunt.
Weila, þet reowðe! Ne acwikeð neauer Meiðhad efter þet wunde.
25 Wei! Þe sehe þenne hu þe engles beoð isweamet þe seoð hare suster
se seorhfulliche aueallet, ant te deoflen hoppin ant kenchinde beaten
honden togederes, stani were his heorte ȝef ha ne mealte i teares!
Wite þe, seli meiden. Me seið þet eise makeð þeof; flih alle þe þing,
ant forbuh ȝeorne, þet tus unbotelich lure mahe of arisen. Þet is, on
30 alre earst, þe stude ant te time þe mahten bringe þe on mis for te
donne. Wið oþre unþeawes me mei stondinde fehten; ah aȝein
lecherie þu most turne þe rug ȝef þu wult ouercumen, ant wið fluht
fehten. Ant soðes, ȝef þu þenchest ant bihaldest on heh towart te
muchele mede þet meiðhad abideð, þu wult leote lihtliche, ant
35 abeoren bliðeliche, þe derf þet tu drehest onont ti fleschliche wil ant ti

3 fleoð] T, beoð B   8 hire] T, ure B   oðer] oder B   13 greiðeð] greideð B
14 earst] erst B   15 speokeð] T, sweoked B   18 fulst] fulht B
22 Meiðhad] Meiðhað B   26 seorhfulliche] seorhfuliche B   27 togederes]
toȝederes B

shield is intact—that is, the wisdom of your reason—so that it does not break or bend, even though your carnal will may be false beneath it and would like to turn its desire into action, the Devil's arrows all rebound again on himself.

And observe carefully why: our physical desire is the Devil's offspring; our reason is God's daughter; and both are within us. So here there is always conflict, and must always be of necessity, because fighting between them will never cease while we live in this world. But it is well for whoever follows Reason, God's daughter, because she sides with Virginity, who is her sister; but, on the other hand, your desire for that physical pleasure sides with Lechery, who is the Devil's offspring as she is, and Sin her mother.

Lechery, with the help of physical desire, makes war on Virginity in this way. Her first help is sight: if you look often and intently at any man, Lechery at once prepares herself with that to make war on your virginity, and first advances on her face to face. Speech is her second help: if you then go on to talk together in a light way and speak of frivolous matters, Lechery slanders the honour of your virginity and abuses her outrageously, and threatens to do her shame and harm her later—and keeps her promise. For as soon as it comes to a kiss, which is her third help, then Lechery spits, as a sign of dishonour, in Virginity's face. The fourth help towards shame and the ruin of Virginity is indecent touching. Keep guard over her then; because if you then touch one another improperly in any place, then Lechery strikes at the virtue of Virginity and wounds her severely. The shameful act itself finally gives the death-blow. On, the pity of it! Virginity never revives after that wound. Oh, whoever saw then how the angels are distressed to see their sister so dreadfully overthrown, and the devils capering and clapping their hands together, laughing raucously, his heart would be stony if it did not melt in tears!

Guard yourself, innocent maiden. They say that opportunity makes a thief; flee all those things, and avoid them earnestly, from which such irremediable loss may arise. That is, first of all, the place and the time which might lead you on into doing wrong. Against other vices one can stand and fight; but if you want to overcome lechery you must turn your back, and fight by retreating. And certainly, if you reflect and look upwards towards the great reward which waits for virginity, you will easily accept, and joyfully endure, the restraints imposed on your

licomes lust, þet tu forberest her | ant ane hwile leauest for blisse þet [59ʳ
kimeð þrof wiðuten eani ende.

    Ant hwuch is þe blisse? Low, Godd himseolf seið þurh þe prophete,
'Þeo þe habbeð from ham forcoruen flesches lustes, ant haldeð mine
5 sabaz'—þet is, haldeð ham i reste from þet fleschliche werc ant haldeð
me forewart—'Ich bihate ham', he seið, 'i mi kineriche to ʒeouen
ham stude ant betere nome þen sunen ant dehtren.' Hwa mahte wilni
mare? *Eunuchus qui seruauerit sabata mea, et cetera.* Hwa mei þenche þe
weole, þe wunne ant te blisse, þe hehschipe of þis mede þet tes ilke lut
10 word bicluppeð abuten? 'Ich chulle', he seið, 'ʒeouen ham stude ant
nome betere þen sunen ant dehtren.' Sulli biheaste! Ah hit is ilich þet
þet ham is bihaten, to singen wið engles—hwas feolahes ha beoð þurh
liflade of heouene, þe-ʒet þe ha wunieð fleschliche on eorðe—to
singe þet swete song, ant þet englene drem vtnume murie, þet nan
15 halhe ne mei, bute meiden ane, singen in heouene; ant folhin Godd
almihti, euch godes ful, hwider se he eauer wendeð, as þe oþre ne
mahe nawt, þah ha alle beon his sunen ant alle hise dehtren. Ne nan of
þes oþres crunen, ne hare wlite, ne hare weden ne mahen euenin to
hare, se vnimete brihte ha beoð ant schene to biseon on.

20   Ant hwet bið hare anes song, ant efter Godd hare anes ʒong
hwider se he eauer | turneð, ant hare fare se feier biuoren alle þe [59ᵛ
oþre? Vnderstond ant nim ʒeme. Al hare song in heouene is for te
þonki Godd ant herien of his grace ant of his goddede. Þe iweddede
þonkið him þet ha lanhure, hwen ha alles walden fallen dunewart, ne
25 feollen nawt wið alle adun, for wedlac ham ikepte, þe ilke lahe þe
Godd haueð istald for þe unstronge. For wel wiste ure Lauerd þet alle
ne mahten nawt halden ham i þe hehe of meiðhades mihte, ah seide þa
he spec þrof, *Non omnes capiunt uerbum istud.* 'Ne underneomeð nawt',
quoð he, 'þis ilke word alle.' *Qui potest capere, capiat.* 'Hwa se hit mei
30 underneomen, underneome, Ich reade,' quoð he. Oþer is þet Godd
hat, ant oþer is þet he reat. Þe ilke þinges þet he hat, þeo mot mon
nede halden þe wule beon iborhen, ant þeo beoð to alle men o liue
iliche imeane. His reades beoð of heh þing, ant to his leoueste freond,
þe lut i þisse worlde, ant derue beoð to fullen; ant lihte þah, hwa se
35 haueð riht luue to him ant treowe bileaue. Ah hwa se halt ham earneð

2 þrof] þreof B   8 *seruauerit*] T, *seminauerunt* B   11 biheaste] biheste B
13 þe-ʒet þe] þe ʒet þer B   14–15 nan halhe ne mei] nan habbe ne mei B,
nane halhes ne mahen T   20 bið] bid B   23 þonki Godd ant herien] herien
Godd B, þonki Godd T   28 *istud*] *istu*ð B   underneomeð] T, underuoð B
29 *Qui*] T, *Quis* B   31 þet he²] T, Godd B   þeo] T, þet B   mot mon] mon mot
B, mot mon mot T

carnal will and your physical desire, which you renounce here and give up for a time in exchange for happiness which will last for ever.

And what is this happiness? Look! God himself says through the prophet, 'Those who have cut off from themselves the desires of the flesh, and keep my sabbaths'—that is, keep themselves at rest from that physical act, and keep faith with me—'I promise them', he says, 'to give them a place in my kingdom, and a better name than sons and daughters.' Who could wish for more? *The eunuch who keeps my sabbaths, etc.* Who can imagine the happiness, the joy and the bliss, the glory of the reward which this short sentence contains? 'I shall', he says, 'give them a place and a better name than sons and daughters.' A wonderful promise! But it is like the promise that they are given to sing with angels—whose equals they are through their heavenly way of life, while they are still living in the flesh on earth—to sing that sweet song and that angelic melody, surpassingly joyful, that no saint who is not a virgin may sing in heaven; and to follow God almighty, full of every good, wherever he goes, as the others may not, though they are all his sons and all his daughters. And none of these others' crowns, nor their beauty, nor their robes, can equal theirs, they are so incomparably bright and shining to look at.

And what is the song which is theirs alone, and the progress which is theirs alone, following God wherever he goes, and their array so splendid above all the rest? Understand, and take note. All those who are in heaven sing the praises of God, to thank him for his grace and for his kindness. The married thank him because at least, when they were in danger of falling headlong, they did not fall all the way, for marriage saved them, that law which God has established for the weak. For our Lord knew well that not all were able to remain on the heights of the virtue of virginity, but said when he spoke about it, *Not all take this advice.* 'Not all', he said, 'take this advice.' *Whoever can take it, should take it.* 'Whoever can take it,' he said, 'I advise to take it.' What God commands is one thing, what he advises is another. Those things that he commands must be observed by anyone who wishes to be saved, and they are common to everyone in this life. His recommendations are on exalted matters, and to his dearest friends, the few in this world, and are hard to carry out; and yet easy for anyone who has real love for him and constant faith. But whoever observes them

him ouerfullet ful ant ouereorninde met of heouenliche mede. Swuch is meiðhades read, þet Godd ne hat nawt, ah reat hwuch se wule beon of þe lut of his leoueste freond, ant, as his deorling deore, don his read ant earnin him crune upo crune. Alswa Seinte Pawel ʒeueð read to
5 meidnes to beon as he wes, ant seið þet wel is ham | þet swa ham [60ʳ mahen halden. Ne hat he hit nan oþer weis, for eauer se deorre þing, se is derure to biwitene; ant ʒef hit were ihaten ant nawt tenne ihalden, þe bruche were deadlich sunne. Forþi wes wedlac ilahet in Hali Chirche, as bed te seke, to ihente þe unstronge þe ne mahen nawt
10 stonden i þe hehe hul ant se neh heouene as meiðhades mihte.

    Þis is þenne hare song þe beoð i lahe of wedlac, þonki Godd ant herien þet he greiðede ham lanhure, þa ha walden of meidnes hehschipe, a swuch stude in to lihten þet ha neren nawt ihurt, þah ha weren ilahet; ant hwet se ha þrin hurten ham, wið ealmesdeden
15 healden. Þis singeð þenne iweddede, þet ha, þurh Godes milce ant merci of his grace, þa ha driuen dunewart, i wedlac etstutten ant i þe bed of his lahe softeliche lihten. For hwa se swa falleð of meiðhades menske þet wedlakes heuel bedd nawt ham ne iȝente, se ferliche ha driueð dun to þer eorðe þet al ham is tolimet, lið ba ant lire. Þeos ne
20 schulen neauer song singen in heouene, ah schulen weimeres leoð a mare in helle, bute ʒef bireowsunge areare ham to liue, ant heale ham wið soð schrift ant wið deadbote. For ʒef ha þus beoð acwiket ant imaket hale, ha beoð i widewene reng, ant schulen i widewene ring biuore þe iweddede singen in heouene. Þet is þenne hare song, to
25 herien hare Drihtin | ant þonkin him ʒeorne þet his mihte heolt ham i [60ᵛ cleanschipe chaste efter þet ha hefden ifondet flesches fulðe, ant ʒettede ham i þis worlt to beten hare sunnen.

    Swote beoð þeos songes; ah al is meidenes song unilich þeose, wið engles imeane, dream ouer alle þe dreames in heouene. In heore ring,
30 þer Godd seolf ant his deore moder, þe deorewurðe meiden, þe heouenliche cwen, leadeð i þet eadi trume of schimminde meidnes, ne moten nane buten heo hoppin ne singen. For þet is aa hare song, þonki Godd ant herien þet he on ham se muche grace ʒef of himseoluen þet ha forsoken for him euch eorðlich mon, ant heolden ham cleane aa

---

3 as] T, al B   5 to beon] T, þe meidnes beoð B   9 nawt] T, *om.* B
17 softeliche] fofteliche B   20 leoð] leo B, leod T   28 is] T, *om.* B
31 leadeð] leat BT

earns for himself a cup running over and an overflowing measure of heavenly reward. Such is the recommendation of virginity, which God does not command, but recommends to whoever wants to be among the small number of his best-loved friends, and, as his dear beloved, to follow his advice and earn for himself crown upon crown. Likewise St Paul gives advice to maidens to be as he was, and says that it is well for those who can keep themselves so. He does not command it in any other way, because always the more precious something is, the harder it is to protect; and if it were commanded and then not kept, the breach would be mortal sin. It was for this reason that marriage was made lawful within Holy Church, as a bed for the sick, to catch the weak who cannot stand on the high hill and so near heaven as the virtue of virginity.

This, then, is the song of those who are lawfully married, thanking and honouring God because, when they were about to fall from the virgin's high estate, he at least prepared such a place for them to land in that they were not hurt, although they were brought low; and whatever harm they did to themselves there, they healed with good works. This, then, is what the married sing, that through God's kindness and the mercy of his grace, when they were rushing downwards they stopped short at marriage and made a soft landing in the bed of his law. For if anyone falls from the honour of virginity so that the mattress of wedlock does not catch them, they rush down so fast towards the ground that they are torn all to pieces, limb from limb. These will never sing a song in heaven, but must sing a song of lamentation for evermore in hell, unless repentance should bring them back to life and heal them with true confession and penance. For if they are revived and made whole in this way, they are in the rank of widows, and will sing in the circle of widows before the married in heaven. This, then, is their song, to praise their Lord and thank him earnestly that his power kept them in chaste purity after they had experienced carnal filthiness, and allowed them to atone in this world for their sins.

These songs are sweet; but a virgin's song is quite different from these, shared with angels, a melody above all the melodies in heaven. In their circle, where God himself and his beloved mother, the precious Virgin, the queen of heaven, lead in that blessed company of shining virgins, only they may dance and sing. For that is always their song, thanking God and honouring him because he granted them so much of his grace that they gave up every earthly man for him, and

from fleschliche fulðen i bodi ant i breoste, ant i stude of mon of lam
token liues Lauerd, þe king of hehe blisse, forhwi he menskeð ham se
muchel biuoren alle þe oðre, as þe brudgume deð his weddede spuse.
Þis song ne muhen nane buten heo singen.

5   Al, as Ich seide ear, folhið ure Lauerd, ant tah nawt oueral; for i þe
menske of meiðhad ant in hire mihte ne muhe nane folhin him, ne þet
eadi meiden, englene leafdi ant meidenes menske, bute meidnes ane.
Ant forþi is hare aturn se briht ant se schene biuoren alle oþre, þet ha
gað eauer nest Godd hwider se | he turneð. Ant alle ha beoð icrunet [61ᵃ
10 þe blissið in heouene wið kempene crune; ah þe meidnes habbeð upo
þeo þe is to alle iliche imeane a gerlondesche schininde schenre þen
þe sunne, *aureola* ihaten o Latines ledene. Þe flurs þe beoð idrahe
þron, ne þe ʒimmes þrin, te tellen of hare euene nis na monnes
speche. Þus feole priuileges schawið ful sutelliche hwucche beoð þer
15 meidnes, ant sundrið ham from þe oðre wið þus feole mensken world
buten ende.

ʒet of þes þreo hat—meiðhad ant widewehad, ant wedlac is þe
þridde—þu maht bi þe degrez of hare blisse icnawen hwuch ant bi hu
muchel þe an passeð þe oþre. For wedlac haueð hire frut þrittifald in
20 heouene; widewehad, sixtifald; meiðhad wið hundretfald ouergeað
baþe. Loke þenne herbi, hwa se of hire meiðhad lihteð into wedlac, bi
hu monie degrez ha falleð dunewardes. Ha is an hundret degrez ihehet
towart heouene hwil ha meiðhad halt, as þe frut preoueð; ant leapeð
into wedlac—þet is, dun neoðer to þe þrittuðe—ouer þrie twenti ant
25 ʒet ma bi tene. Nis þis ed en cherre a muche lupe dunewart? Ant tah
hit is to þolien, ant Godd haueð ilahet hit, as Ich ear seide, leste hwa se
leope ant þer ne edstode lanhure, nawt nere þet kepte him, ant driue
adun swireuorð wiðuten ike|punge deope into helle. Of þeos nis nawt [61ᵛ
to speokene, for ha beoð iscrippet ut of liues writ in heouene.

30   Ah schawi we ʒet witerluker, as we ear biheten, hwet drehen þe
iweddede, þet tu icnawe þerbi hu murie þu maht libben, meiden, i þi
meiðhad ouer þet heo libbeð, teke þe murhðe ant te menske in
heouene þet muð ne mei munnen. Nu þu art iweddet, ant of se heh se
lahe iliht—of englene ilicnesse, of Iesu Cristes leofmon, of leafdi in
35 heouene, into flesches fulðe, into beastes liflade, into monnes

6 muhe] T, muhten B   9 gað] gad B   11 schininde] T, *om.* B
12 *aureola*] an urle B, auriole T   13 ʒimmes] *extra minim after* mm *in* B
te] T, ne B   15 meidnes] meiðnes B   17 ʒet] ʒef B, *om.* T
19 hire] T, *om.* B   23 preoueð] preoued B   leapeð] leaped B
26 haueð] haued B   29 beoð] beod B   32 teke] T, to eche B

always kept themselves pure from carnal defilements in body and mind; and instead of a man of clay took the Lord of life, the king of exalted bliss, which is the reason he honours them so much above all the others, as the bridegroom does his wedded wife. This song only they may sing.

All, as I said before, follow our Lord, but nevertheless, not entirely; for in the honour of virginity and in its virtue nobody may follow him, or that blessed virgin, lady of angels and glory of maidens, except virgins alone. And that is why their robes are so bright and shining above all others, because they always walk next to God wherever he goes. And all who rejoice in heaven are crowned with a victor's crown; but the virgins have, over and above what is common to all alike, a circlet shining brighter than the sun, called *aureola* in Latin. As for the flowers which are engraved on it, and the inset jewels, no one could find the words to describe what they are like. So many privileges show very clearly which are virgins there, and distinguish them from the rest with so many honours to all eternity.

Yet of these three states—virginity and widowhood, and marriage is the third—you can tell by the degrees of their bliss which one is superior to the others, and by how much. For marriage has its reward thirtyfold in heaven; widowhood, sixtyfold; virginity, with a hundred-fold, surpasses both. See then from this, whoever descends from her virginity into marriage, by how many degrees she falls downwards. She is raised a hundred degrees towards heaven while she keeps her virginity, as the reward proves; and leaps into marriage—that is, right down to the thirtieth—over three score and yet more by ten. Is this not a great leap downwards at one time? But nevertheless it is to be tolerated, and God has made it lawful, as I said earlier, lest if anyone leapt and did not stop there at least, there would be nothing that held him back and he would rush down headlong without restraint deep into hell. These people are not to be spoken of, because they are scratched out of the book of life in heaven.

But let us show still more plainly, as we promised earlier, what the married suffer, so that by this you may understand, maiden, how happily you might live in your virginity, compared with how they live, quite apart from the joy and honour in heaven which no tongue can tell. Now you are married, and have descended so low from so high— from the likeness of angels, from the beloved of Jesus Christ, from a lady in heaven, into carnal filth, into the life of an animal, into servitude to a man, and into the world's misery; say now what its benefit is, and

þeowdom, ant into worldes weane—sei nu hwet frut, ant for hwuch þing meast. Is hit al forþi, oðer ane dale þeruore—beo nu soð-cnawes—for te keli þi lust wið fulðe of þi licome, for te habbe delit of þi fleschliche wil of monnes imeane? For Gode, hit is speatewile for te

5 þenche þron, ant for te speoken þrof 3et speatewilre; loke, þenne, hwuch beo þet seolue þing ant þet dede to donne. Al þet fule delit is wið fulðe aleid as þu turnest þin hond; ah þet ladliche least leafeð ant lest forð, ant te ofþunchunge þrof, longe þrefter. Ant te vnseli horlinges þe vnlaheliche hit hantið habbeð in inwarde helle for þet

10 hwilinde lust endelese pine, bute 3ef heo hit leauen ant hit on eorðe under schrift bitterliche beten. Forhohe for te don hit, þet te þuncheð uuel of ant eil for te heren; for hwen hit is þullich, ant muche deale ladluker þen ei wel-itohe muð for scheome | mahe seggen, hwet [62 makeð hit iluuet bituhhe beasteliche men bute hare muchele vnþeaw,

15 þet bereð ham ase beastes to al þet ham lusteð, as þah ha nefden wit in ham ne tweire schad as mon haueð, ba of god ant of vuel, of kumelich ant vnkumelich, na mare þen beastes þet dumbe neb habbeð? Ah leasse þen beastes 3et; for þeos doð hare cunde, bute wit þah ha beon, in a time of þe 3er. Moni halt him to a make, ne nule efter þet lure

20 neauer neomen oþer. Ant mon, þet schulde habbe wit, ant don al þet he dude efter hire wilnunge, folheð þet fulðe in eauereuch time, ant nimeð an efter an; ant moni þet is wurse, monie togederes. Lo nu, hu þis vnþeaw ne eueneð þe nawt ane to witlese beastes, dumbe ant broke-rugget, ibuhe towart eorðe—þu þet art i wit iwraht to Godes

25 ilicnesse, ant iriht ba bodi up ant heaued towart heouene, forþi þet tu schuldest þin heorte heouen þiderwart as þin eritage is, ant eorðe forhohien—nim 3eme hu þis vnþeaw ne makeð þe nawt ane euening ne ilich ham, ah deð muchel eateluker, ant mare to witen, þe forschuptest te seolf willes ant waldes into hare cunde.

30 Þe leoseð þenne se heh þing, þe mihte ant te biheue of meiðhades menske, for se ful fulðe as is ischawet þruppe, hwa se of engel lihteð to iwurðen lahre | þen a beast for se ladli cheaffere, loki hu ha spede. [62ᵛ 'Nai,' þu wult seggen, 'for þet fulðe nis hit nawt; ah monnes elne is muche wurð, ant me bihoueð his help to fluttunge ant te fode. Of wif

35 ant weres gederunge worldes weole awakeneð, ant streon of feire

2–3 soð-cnawes] soð-cwawes B   3–4 for te² . . . imeane] T, *om.* B   7 least] beast BT; *Dobson*   9 habbeð] *om.* BT   12 muche deale] T, muchele B
17 þet] T, ant B   21 folheð] foheð B   22 togederes] to3ederes B
23 witlese] wittlese B   24 iwraht] T, wraht B   25 ba] T, *om.* B
30 meiðhades] meidhades B

its main purpose. Is it entirely for this reason, or partly for it—now admit the truth—to cool your lust by the defilement of your body, to satisfy your carnal desire through intercourse with a man? By God, it is disgusting to think about it, and even more disgusting to talk about it; see, then, what it is to commit the act itself. All that foul pleasure is sated with filthiness in the space of a moment; but that loathsome sin remains and lingers on, and the remorse for it, a long time afterwards. And those wretched fornicators who practise it unlawfully have endless torment in the depths of hell for that momentary desire, unless they give it up and atone for it painfully in a state of penitence here on earth. Scorn to act out what seems to you vile and harmful to hear about; for when it is like this, and a great deal more loathsome than anyone well-bred can decently describe, what makes it popular among brutish men but their great viciousness, which draws them on like animals to all that gives them pleasure, as though they had no reason in them or power of discrimination between one thing and another as a human being has, both of good and of evil, of what is decent and what is indecent, any more than animals which lack the power of speech? But less than animals, even; because animals mate naturally, although they lack reason, at one time of the year. Many confine themselves to a single mate, and after losing that one will never take another. And man, who should have reason and do all that he did with its consent, pursues that filthiness at all times, and takes one after another; and many, which is worse, take many together. See now how this vice not only brings you down to the level of animals which have no reason, dumb and hunchbacked, bowed down towards the earth—you who are created as a rational being in God's image, and made erect, both body and head raised towards heaven, so you should lift your heart to where your heritage is, and despise the earth—take note of how this vice does not simply make you their equal or like them, but makes you much more contemptible and more to blame for transforming yourself of your own accord into their nature.

Whoever, then, loses something so exalted, the virtue and the merit of the honour of virginity, for such foul indecency as is described above, whoever descends from the state of an angel to become lower than a beast for such a poor exchange, see what she gains. 'No,' you will say, 'for that indecency it is not worth while; but a man's strength is worth a great deal, and I need his help for support and food. Worldly wealth springs from the union of man and wife, and a brood of fine

children þe gleadieð muchel þe ealdren.' Nu þu hauest iseid tus, ant
þuncheð þet tu seist soð; ah Ich chulle schawin hit al wið falsschipe
ismeðet. Ah on alre earst, nu, hwet weole oðer wunne se þer eauer of
cume, to deore hit bið aboht þet tu þe seolf sulest fore, ant ʒeuest þin
5 beare bodi to tukin swa to wundre, ant feare wið se scheomeliche, wið
swuch uncouerlich lure as meiðhades menske is, ant te mede baðe, for
worldlich biʒete. Wa wurðe þet cheaffeare, for ei hwilinde weole
sullen meiðhad awei, þe cwen is of heouene! For alswa as of þis lure
nis nan acouerunge, alswa is euch wurð unwurð hertowart.
10 Þu seist þet muche confort haueð wif of hire were þe beoð wel
igederet, ant eiðer is alles weis ipaiet of oðer. Ʒe—ah hit is seltscene
on eorðe. Beo nu þah swuch hare confort ant hare delit, hwerin is hit al
meast buten i flesches fulðe, oðer in worldes vanite, þe wurðeð al to
sorhe ant to sar on ende? Ant nawt ane on | ende, ah eauer umbe hwile; [63
15 for moni þing schal ham wreaðen ant gremien, ant makie to carien, ant
for hare oþres uuel sorhin ant siken. Moni þing ham schal twinnin ant
tweamen, þet lað is leouie men, ant deaðes dunt on ende, eiðer from
oðer; swa þet ne bið hit nanes weis þet tet elne ne schal endin in
earmðe. Ant eauer, se hare murhðe wes mare togederes, se þe sorhe is
20 sarre ed te twinnunge. Wa is him forþi (as Seint Austin seið) þet is wið
to muche luue to ei eorðlich þing iteiet; for eauer bið þet swete aboht
wið twa dale of bittre, ant a fals wunne wið moni soð teone. Ah wel is
hire þet luueð Godd; for him ne mei ha nanes weis, bute ʒef ha lihe
him ant his luue leaue, neauer mare leosen, ah schal ifinden him aa
25 swetture ant sauurure from worlde into worlde, aa on ecnesse.
Þu speke þruppe of monnes help to flutunge ant to fode. Wala!
Lutel þerf þu carien for þin anes liueneð, a meoke meiden as þu art,
ant his deore leofmon þe is alre þinge Lauerd, þet he ne mahe
lihtliche—ant þet he nule gleadliche—ifinde þe largeliche al þet te
30 bihoueð. Ant tah þu wone hefdest oðer drehdest eani derf for his
deorew|urðe luue, as þe oðre doð for monnes, to goder heale þin he [63
hit þoleð, to fondi þe hweðer þu beo treowe, ant greiðeð þi mede
monifald in heouene. Vnder monnes help, þu schalt sare beon ideruet
for his ant for þe worldes luue, þe beoð ba swikele; ant wakien i moni
35 care, nawt ane for þe seolf, ase þearf Godes spuse, ah schalt for monie

---

2 seist] T, hauest iseid B   3 nu] T, *om.* B   6 baðe] T, *om.* B
11 ah] ahi B   17 leouie] T, luuie B   19 earmðe] earmde B   togederes]
toʒederes B   20 twinnunge] twinnnunge B   28 he] T, ʒe B
29 ant] T, *om.* B   31 þin] T, him B   he] T, þe B

children who give much happiness to their parents.' Now you have made this claim, and it looks as if what you say is true; but I shall show that it is all glossed over with falsehood. But now, first of all, whatever advantage or happiness comes of it, it is too dearly bought when you sell yourself for it, and give up your naked body to be so scandalously abused and treated so shamefully, with such an irrecoverable loss as the honour of virginity, and its reward too, for worldly gain. A bad bargain indeed, to sell off virginity, which is queen of heaven, for any transitory wealth! For just as there is no recovery from its loss, so everything valuable is worthless compared with it.

You say that a wife has much happiness from her husband when they are well matched, and each is pleased with the other in every way. Yes—but it is seldom seen in this world. And even supposing they do have such happiness and such delight, what does the greatest part consist in but carnal filthiness or worldly vanity, which all turns to sorrow and pain in the end? And not only in the end, but all the time; for many things will anger and offend them, and cause them to worry, and grieve and lament for each other's misfortune. Many things will separate and divide them one from the other, which is hateful to loving couples, and the stroke of death at last; so that there is no way that their happiness will not end in misery. And always, the greater their happiness was together, the more intense is the grief at parting. Woe to him, therefore (as St Augustine says), who is attached with too much love to any earthly thing; for that sweetness will always be paid for with twice as much bitterness, and one false joy with many real sorrows. But it is well for the woman who loves God; because unless she is false to him and abandons his love, she can never lose him again in any way, but will constantly find him sweeter and more delightful for ever and ever into eternity.

You spoke above of a man's help towards maintenance and food. Come now! You have little need to worry about your own support, a modest maiden as you are, and the dear beloved of him who is Lord of all things, that he cannot easily—and that he will not gladly—provide you generously with all that you need. And even supposing you did suffer want or endured any hardship for his precious love, as the others do for man's, he allows it for your own good, to test whether you are faithful, and prepares your reward in heaven many times over. Supported by a man, you will suffer cruelly for his sake and the world's, since neither can be relied on; and lie awake with many cares, not only for yourself, as God's bride should, but for many others, often

oþre, ase wel for þe laðe ofte as for þe leoue; ant mare beon idrechet
þen ei driuel i þe hus oðer ei ihuret hine; ant tin anes dale bruken ofte
wið bale ant bitterliche abuggen. Lutel witen herof þe selie Godes
spuses, þe i se swote eise wiðute swuch trubuil, i gastelich este ant i
5 breoste reste, luuieð þe soðe Luue, ant in his anes seruise hare lif
leadeð. Inoh wel ham is her (ah unlich elleshwer); alle worldes weole
ham is inoh riue. Al ha habbeð þerof þet ha wel wilnið; al þet eauer
Godd isið þet ham wule freamien. Ne mei na worldlich unhap bireauin
ham hare weole, for ha beoð riche ant weolefule inwið i þe heorte. Al
10 þe este ant al þe eise is þer, as þe oþre beoð godlese ant ignahene,
nabben ha neauer se muchel wiðuten i þe worlde, for þet ha beoð
offearet eauer for te leosen, ant ȝiscið þah, efter muchel, muche deale
mare. Wið earmðe biwinneð hit, wið fearlac biwiteð hit, forleoseð hit
wið sorhe; swinkeð | to biȝeotene, biȝeoteð for te leosen, leoseð for   [64
15 te sorhin. Þus þis worldes hweol warpeð ham abuten. Þeoues hit
steoleð ham, reauers hit robbið; hare ouerherren witið ham ant
wreaðeð; mohðe fret te claðes ant cwalm sleað þet ahte; ant tah nane
of þeos ne makie to forwurðen weole þer ase muchel is, eauer se þer
mare is, se ma beoð þet hit wastið. Ant nat Ich neauer hwi me seið þet
20 heo hit al weldeð, þet, wullen ha, nullen ha, biwinneð ant biwiteð hit to
se monie oþre, nawt ane to hare freond ah to hare fan fulle; ne habben
ne mahen þrof, þah ha hit hefden isworen, bute hare anes dale. Þis is
nu forþi iseid þet tu seidest þruppe þet ter walde wakenin of wif ant
weres somnunge richesce ant worldes weole, þet tu understonde hu
25 lutel hit freameð ham ȝet her i þis worlt, teke þet hit reaueð ham þe
hehe riche of heouene, bute ha poure beon þerin wið halinesse of
heorte.

Þus, wummon, ȝef þu hauest were efter þi wil ant wunne ba of
worldes weole, þe schal nede itiden. Ant hwet ȝef ha beoð þe wone,
30 þet tu nabbe þi wil wið him ne weole nowðer, ant schalt grenin godles
inwið westi wahes, ant te breades wone brede þi bearn-team; ant teke
þis, liggen under la|ðest mon, þet þah þu hefdest alle weole, he went   [64ᵛ
hit te to weane? For beo hit nu þet te beo richedom riue, ant tine wide
wahes wlonke ant weolefule, ant habbe monie vnder þe hirdmen in
35 halle, ant ti were beo þe wrað, oðer iwurðe þe lað, swa þet inker eiþer
heasci wið oþer, hwet worltlich weole mei beo þe wunne? Hwen he bið

4 se] T, þe B   6 leadeð] leaðeð B   9 Al] T, as B   16 steoleð] steoled B
hit] hit hit B   17 claðes] clades B   18 forwurðen] forwurden B
29 schal nede] T, ne schal B

for those you hate as well as those you love; and be more oppressed than any drudge in the house or any hired servant; and often acquire your own share with suffering and pay dearly for it. The blessed brides of God know little of this, who in such pleasant ease, without this kind of trouble, in spiritual joy and peace of mind love the true Love and lead their lives in his service alone. They are happy enough here (though not as they will be in heaven); all the wealth of the world is at their disposal. They have everything of it that they really want; God always sees to everything that will be for their good. And no earthly misfortune can deprive them of their wealth, because they are rich and fortunate within, in the heart. All their joy and all their comfort is there, where the others are poor and consumed with anxiety, however much they have outside in the world, because they are constantly afraid of losing it, and nevertheless they are greedy, after much, for a great deal more. They gain it with misery, they guard it with fear, they lose it with grief; they labour to gain it, gain it to lose it, lose it to grieve for it. So this world's wheel whirls them about. Thieves steal it from them, robbers plunder it; their overlords fine them unjustly and harass them; moths eat away the clothes and plague kills the livestock; and even though none of these things causes wealth to be destroyed where there is much of it, always the more there is, the more there are who consume it. And I never know why it is said that those people own it outright who, whether they want to or not, acquire it and preserve it for so many others, not only for their friends but for their mortal enemies; and can have nothing of it, though they had sworn the opposite, but their own share. Now this has been said because you said above that from the union of man and wife there would come riches and worldly wealth, so that you may understand how little good it does them even here in this world, quite apart from robbing them of the high kingdom of heaven, unless they remain poor with it in holiness of heart.

And this, woman, is what must happen to you if you have a husband after your own heart, and pleasure too in worldly riches. And what if they are missing, so that you do not have your heart's desire with him, or riches either, and must pine away in poverty between bare walls, and bring forth your children to lack of bread; and besides this, be subject to a husband you hate, so that even if you had every kind of wealth he would turn it into misery for you? For suppose now that you have

ute, hauest aȝein his hamcume sar care ant eie. Hwil he bið et hame,
alle þine wide wanes þuncheð þe to nearewe. His lokunge on ageasteð
þe; his ladliche nurð ant his untohe bere makeð þe to agrisen. Chit te
ant cheoweð þe ant scheomeliche schent te, tukeð þe to bismere as
5 huler his hore, beateð þe ant busteð þe as his ibohte þrel ant his eðele
þeowe. Þine banes akeð þe ant ti flesch smeorteð þe, þin heorte
wiðinne þe swelleð of sar grome, ant ti neb utewið tendreð ut of teone.
Hwuch schal beo þe sompnunge bituhen ow i bedde? Me, þeo þe best
luuieð ham tobeoreð ofte þrin, þah ha þrof na semblant ne makien ine
10 marhen; ant ofte of moni nohtunge, ne luuien ha ham neauer swa,
bitterliche bi hamseolf teonið eiðer oþer. Heo schal his wil muchel
hire unwil drehen, ne luuie ha him neauer swa wel, wið muche weane
ofte; alle his fulitoheschipes ant his unhende gomenes, ne beon ha
neauer swa wið fulðe bifunden, nomeliche i bedde ha schal, wulle ha,
15 nulle ha, þo|lien ham alle. Crist schilde euch meiden to freinin oþer to [65
wilnin for te witen hwucche ha beon; for þeo þe fondið ham meast
ifindeð ham forcuðest, ant cleopieð ham selie iwiss þe nuten neauer
hwet hit is, ant heatieð þet ha hantið. Ah hwa se lið i leifen deope
bisuncken, þah him þunche uuel þrof he ne schal nawt up acouerin
20 hwen he walde. Bisih þe, seli wummon; beo þe cnotte icnut eanes of
wedlac, beo he cangun oðer crupel, beo he hwuch se he eauer beo, þu
most to him halden. ȝef þu art feier, ant wið gleade chere bicleopest
alle feire, ne schalt tu o nane wise wite þe wið unword ne wið uuel
blame. ȝef þu art unwurðlich ant wraðeliche ilatet, þu maht ba to
25 oþre ant to þi were iwurðen þe unwurðre. ȝef þu iwurðest him
unwurð ant he as unwurð þe, oðer ȝef þu him muche luuest ant he
let lutel to þe, hit greueð þe se swiðe þet tu wult inohreaðe—ase
monie aweariede doð—makien him poisun, ant ȝeouen bale i bote
stude; oðer hwa se swa nule don, medi wið mede wicchen, ant
30 forsaken, for te drahen his luue towart hire, Crist ant hire Cristendom
ant rihte bileaue. Nu hwet blisse mei þeos bruken þe luueð hire were
wel, ant ha habbe his laððe, oþer cunqueari his luue o þulliche wise?

Hwenne schulde Ich al habben | irikenet þet springeð bituhe þeo þe [65
þus beoð igederet? ȝef ha ne mei nawt temen, ha is icleopet gealde;

---

1 hamcume] T, cume B   7 tendreð] tendreið B   9 þrof] T, *om.* B
11 oþer] T, *om.* B   12 drehen . . . wel] T, *om.* B   13 fulitoheschipes]
fulitohchipes B   gomenes] gonienes B   17 ifindeð] ifinðeð B
21 he³] T, *om.* B   23 tu] T, *om.* B   24 unwurðlich ant wraðeliche] T,
unwurðliche B   28 aweariede] T, *om.* B   29 mede] *om.* BT; *Tolkien,*
'Contributions', p. 214.   34 igederet] iȝederet B

wealth in abundance, and your wide walls are proud and splendid, and
you have many servants under you in hall, and your husband is angry
with you or you have come to hate him, so that each of you is at odds
with the other, what worldly wealth can give you pleasure? When he is
out, you are filled with anxiety and fear of his homecoming. While he is
at home, all your wide halls seem to you too narrow. His attention
makes you nervous; his detestable clamour and his ill-bred shouting
frighten you. He rails at you and scolds you and abuses you shamefully,
treats you disgracefully as a lecher does his whore, beats you and
thrashes you like his bought slave and his born serf. Your bones ache
and your flesh smarts, your heart within you swells with violent rage, and
your outward countenance burns with anger. What will your relations in
bed be like? But those who love each other best often differ there,
although they may give no sign in the morning; and often, however
much they love one another, each gives bitter offence to the other in
many small matters when they are on their own. She must often submit
to his will much against her own will, in great distress; and especially in
bed she must put up with all his indecencies and his improper games,
however obscenely devised, whether she wants to or not. May Christ
protect every maiden from asking or wanting to know what they are; for
those who have most experience of them find them most loathsome,
and call those women happy indeed who have no idea what they might
be, and detest what they are doing. But if someone lies deeply sunk in
the mire, even though he finds it unpleasant there he cannot climb out
of it again when he feels like it. Consider, innocent woman: once the
knot of wedlock is tied, even if he is an idiot or a cripple, whatever he
may be like, you must be faithful to him. If you are beautiful, and speak
to everyone pleasantly in a friendly way, you will not be able to protect
yourself in any way against slander and harsh censure. If you are plain
and bad-tempered, you may come to be less valued both by others and
by your husband. If you lose his respect, and he loses yours as well, or
if you love him deeply and he cares little for you, it distresses you so
much that you will perhaps—as many wicked women do—brew
poison for him, and kill instead of cure; or the woman who does not
want to do this will pay money to witches and, to attract his love
towards her, abandon Christ and her Christianity and the true faith.
Now what happiness may that woman enjoy who truly loves her
husband if she is hated by him, or wins his love in this kind of way?

When should I have finished an account of everything that comes
between those who are joined in this way? If she cannot have children,

hire lauerd luueð hire ant wurðgeð þe leasse, ant heo, as þeo þet wurst
is þrof, biwepeð hire wurðes, ant cleopeð ham wunne ant weole fulle
þe temeð hare teames. Ah nu iwurðe hit al þet ha habbe hire wil of
streon þet ha wilneð, ant loki we hwuch wunne þrof hire iwurðe. I þe
5 streonunge þrof is anan hire flesch wið þet fulþe ituket, as hit is ear
ischawet; i þe burðerne þrof is heuinesse ant heard sar eauer umbe
stunde; in his iborenesse, alre stiche strengest, ant deað oðerhwiles; in
his fostrunge forð, moni earm-hwile. Sone se hit lihteð i þis lif, mare
hit bringeð wið him care þen blisse, nomeliche to þe moder. For ȝef
10 hit is misboren, as hit ilome ilimpeð, ant wonti ei of his limen, oðer
sum misfeare, hit is sorhe to hire ant to al his cun scheome, upbrud in
uuel muð, tale bimong alle. Ȝef hit wel iboren is ant þuncheð wel
forðlich, fearlac of his lure is anan wið him iboren, for nis ha neauer
bute care leste hit misfeare aþet owðer of ham twa ear leose oþer. Ant
15 ofte hit itimeð þet tet leoueste bearn, ant iboht bitterlukest, sorheð ant
sweameð meast his ealdren on ende. Nu hwet wunne haueð þe moder,
þe | haueð of þet forschuppet bearn sar ant scheome baðe, ant fearlac [66ᵛ]
of þet forðlich aþet ha hit leose?

   For Gode, þah hit nere neauer for Godes luue, ne for hope of
20 heouene, ne for dred of helle, þu ahtest, wummon, þis werc for þi
flesches halschipe, for þi licomes luue, ant ti bodies heale, ouer alle
þing to schunien. For ase Seinte Pawel seið, euch sunne þet me deð is
wiðute þe bodi bute þis ane. Alle þe oþre sunnen ne beoð bute
sunnen; ah þis is sunne, ant ec uncumelicheð þe ant unwurðgeð þi
25 bodi, suleð þi sawle ant makeð schuldi towart Godd, ant fuleð þi flesch
ec. Gultest o twa half: wreaðest þen Alwealdent wið þet suti sunne, ant
dest woh to þe seolf, þet tu al willes se scheomeliche tukest. Ga we nu
forðre, ant loki we hwuch wunne ariseð þrefter i burþerne of bearn,
hwen þet streon in þe awakeneð ant waxeð, ant hu monie earmðen
30 anan awakenið þerwið, þe wurcheð þe wa inoh, fehteð o þi seolue
flesch, ant weorrið wið feole weanen o þin ahne cunde. Þi rudie neb
schal leanin, ant ase gres grenin; þine ehnen schule doskin, ant
underneoðe wonnin, ant of þi breines turnunge þin heaued aken sare.
Inwið i þi wombe, swel in þi butte þe bereð þe forð as a weater-bulge,

2 weole fulle] T, weolefule B   6 ischawet] ishawet B   ant] T, *om*. B
8 fostrunge] fosttrunge B   11 upbrud] upbrťud B   12 bimong] T, bi mon B
13 forðlich] forlich B   23 sunnen] sunen B   24 uncumelicheð]
uncumelecheð B   unwurðgeð] unwurdgeð B   26 Gultest] Gulteð BT
27 þet] T, ant B   28 bearn] bearne B   30 awakenið] awakeneð BT
34 swel in] swelin BT

she is called barren; her lord loves her and honours her less, and she, as the one who has the worst of it, bewails her fate, and calls those women who do bear children full of happiness and good fortune. But now suppose that it turns out that she has all she wanted in the child that she longs for, and let us see what happiness she gets from it. In conceiving it, her flesh is at once defiled with that filth, as has been shown before; in carrying it there is heaviness and constant discomfort; in giving birth to it, the cruellest of all pains, and sometimes death; in bringing it up, many weary hours. As soon as it comes into this life, it brings more anxiety with it than joy, especially to the mother. For if it is born handicapped, as often happens, and one of its limbs is missing or has some kind of defect, it is a grief to her and shame to all its family, a reproach for malicious tongues, and the talk of everyone. If it is born healthy and seems to promise well, fear of its loss is born along with it, for she is never without anxiety lest it should come to harm until one of the two of them first loses the other. And often it happens that the child which is most loved, and paid for with most suffering, grieves and distresses its parents most in the end. Now what joy does the mother have, who feels great sorrow and shame as well for the handicapped child, and fear for the healthy one until she loses it?

By God, woman, even if it were not at all for the love of God, or for the hope of heaven, or for the fear of hell, you should avoid this act above all things, for the integrity of your flesh, for the sake of your body, and for your physical health. For as St Paul says, every sin that is committed is outside the body except this one alone. All the other sins are only sins; but this is a sin, and also disfigures you and dishonours your body, defiles your soul and makes you guilty in God's sight, and pollutes your flesh too. You offend on both sides: you anger the Almighty with that filthy sin, and do harm to yourself, mistreating yourself quite voluntarily in such a shameful way. Let us now go further, and see what happiness comes to you afterwards during pregnancy, when the child inside you quickens and grows, and how many miseries come into being at the same time, which cause you much unhappiness, assail your own flesh, and attack your own nature with many afflictions. Your rosy face will grow thin, and turn green as grass; your eyes will grow dull, and shadowed underneath, and because of your dizziness your head will ache cruelly. Inside, in your belly, a swelling in your womb which bulges you out like a water-skin,

þine þearmes þralunge ant stiches i þi lonke, ant i þi lendene sar eche
riue; | heuinesse in euch lim; þine breostes burþerne o þine twa [66ᵛ]
pappes, ant te milc-strunden þe þerof strikeð. Al is wið a weolewunge
þi wlite ouerwarpen; þi muð is bitter, ant walh al þet tu cheowest; ant
5   hwet mete se þi mahe hokerliche underueð—þet is, wið unlust—
warpeð hit eft ut. Inwið al þi weole ant ti weres wunne, forwurðest a
wrecche. Þe cares aȝein þi pinunge þrahen bineomeð þe nahtes
slepes. Hwen hit þenne þerto kimeð, þet sore sorhfule angoise, þet
stronge ant stikinde stiche, þet unroles uuel, þet pine ouer pine, þet
10   wondrinde ȝeomerunge; hwil þu swenchest terwið, ant þine deaðes
dute, scheome teke þet sar wið þe alde wifes scheome creft þe cunnen
of þet wa-sið, hwas help þe bihoueð, ne beo hit neauer se uncumelich;
ant nede most hit þolien þet te þerin itimeð. Ne þunche þe nan uuel
of, for we ne edwiteð nawt wifes hare weanen, þet ure alre modres
15   drehden on us seoluen; ah we schawið ham forð for te warni meidnes,
þet ha beon þe leasse efterwart swuch þing, ant witen herþurh þe
betere hwet ham beo to donne.

Efter al þis, kimeð of þet bearn ibore þus wanunge ant wepunge, þe
schal abute midniht makie þe to wakien, oðer þeo þet ti stude halt, þe
20   þu most for carien. Ant hwet, þe cader fulðen, ant bearmes | umbe [67ʳ]
stunde, to ferkin ant to fostrin hit se moni earm-hwile, ant his waxunge
se let, ant se slaw his þrifte; ant eauer habbe sar care, ant lokin efter al
þis hwenne hit forwurðe, ant bringe on his moder sorhe upo sorhe.
Þah þu riche beo ant nurrice habbe, þu most as moder carien for al þet
25   hire limpeð to donne.

Þeose ant oðre earmðen þe of wedlac awakenið, Seinte Pawel
bilukeð in ane lut wordes: *Tribulaciones carnis, et cetera*: þet is on
Englisch, 'Þeo þet þulliche beoð schulen derf drehen.' Hwa se
þencheð on al þis, ant o mare þet ter is, ante nule wiðbuhe þet þing
30   þet hit al of awakeneð, ha is heardre-iheortet þen adamantines stan ant
mare amead, ȝef ha mei, þen is meadschipe seolf; hire ahne fa ant
hire feont, heateð hireseolfen. Lutel wat meiden of al þis ilke weane, of
wifes wa wið hire were, ne of hare werc se wleateful þe ha wurcheð
imeane, ne of þet sar ne of þet sut i þe burþerne of bearn ant his
35   iborenesse, of nurrices wecches, ne of hire wa-siðes of þet fode

3 þerof] þe of BT   5 mete] T, *om.* B   7 cares] carest B, care T   þrahen]
T, þraen B   9 stikinde] T, stinkinde B   15 meidnes] meiðnes B
19 þet ti] T, þe hire B   21 ferkin] feskin BT; *Colborn, p. 119*
22 þrifte] þriftre B   23 upo sorhe] T, *om.* B   33 werc] T, were B
34 sut] suti BT

discomfort in your bowels and stitches in your side, and often painful backache; heaviness in every limb; the dragging weight of your two breasts, and the streams of milk that run from them. Your beauty is all destroyed by pallor; there is a bitter taste in your mouth, and everything that you eat makes you feel sick; and whatever food your stomach disdainfully receives—that is, with distaste—it throws it up again. In the midst of all your happiness and your husband's delight, you are reduced to a wretch. Worry about your labour pains keeps you awake at night. Then when it comes to it, that cruel distressing anguish, that fierce and stabbing pain, that incessant misery, that torment upon torment, that wailing outcry; while you are suffering from this, and from your fear of death, shame added to that suffering with the shameful craft of the old wives who know about that painful ordeal, whose help is necessary to you, however indecent it may be; and there you must put up with whatever happens to you. You should not see this as morally wrong, for we do not blame women for their labour pains, which all our mothers suffered for ourselves; but we describe them as a warning to virgins, so that they should be the less inclined towards such things, and understand the better through this what they ought to do.

After all this, there comes from the child born in this way wailing and crying, which will keep you up in the middle of the night, or the woman who takes your place, who is your responsibility. And all the filth in the cradle, and in your lap sometimes, so many weary hours in feeding and rearing it, and its development so late, and its growth so slow; and always being anxious, and anticipating after all this the time when it will go astray and bring all kinds of unhappiness to its mother. Though you may be rich and have a nurse, you must as a mother concern yourself with everything that she has to do.

These and other miseries which arise from marriage St Paul summarizes in a few words: *Tribulations of the flesh, etc.*: that is in English, 'Those who are in this state will suffer hardship.' Whoever considers all this, and more that is involved, and will not avoid that act from which it all arises, is more hard-hearted than a stone of adamant, and madder, if she can be, than madness itself is; her own foe and her enemy, she hates herself. A virgin knows little of all this misery, of the unhappiness of a wife with her husband, or of the disgusting act they take part in together, or of the pain and misery in pregnancy and childbearing, of a nurse's vigils, or of her troubles in rearing the child,

fostrunge, hu muchel ha schule ed eanes in his muð famplin, nowðer
to bigan hit ne his cader-clutes; þah þis beon of to speokene
vnwurðliche þinges, þes þe mare ha schawið i hwuch þeowdom
wifes beoð, þe þullich mote drehen, | ant meidnes i hwuch freodom, [67ᵛ]
5 þe freo beoð from ham alle.

Ant hwet ȝef Ich easki ȝet, þah hit þunche egede, hu þet wif
stonde, þe ihereð hwen ha kimeð in hire bearn schreamen, sið þe cat
et te fliche ant ed te hude þe hund, hire cake bearnen o þe stan ant hire
kelf suken, þe crohe eornen i þe fur—*ant* te cheorl chideð? Þah hit beo
10 egede i sahe, hit ah, meiden, to eggi þe swiðre þerfrommart, for nawt
ne þuncheð hit hire egede þet hit fondeð.

Ne þerf þet seli meiden þet haueð al idon hire ut of þullich
þeowdom, as Godes freo dohter ant his sunes spuse, drehe nawiht
swucches. Forþi, seli meiden, forsac al þulli sorhe for utnume mede,
15 þet tu ahest to don wiðuten euch hure; for nu Ich habbe ihalden min
biheaste þruppe, þet Ich walde schawin wið falschipe ismeðet þet te
moni an seið—ant þuncheð þet hit soð beo—of þe selhðe ant te sy þet
te iweddede habbeð; þet hit ne feareð nawt swa as weneð þet sið
utewið, ah feareð al oðerweis, of poure ba ant riche, of laðe ant ec of
20 leouie, þet te weane ihwer passeð þe wunne, ant te lure oueral al þe
biȝete.

Nu þenne, seli meiden, þet Dauið cleopeð 'dohter', iher þi feader
ant hercne his read þet he þe i þe frumðe of þis writ readde. 'Forȝet
ti folc' þet liheð þe of weres ant worldes wunne, þet beoð þine þohtes
25 þe swikelliche lea|ðieð þe towart alle weane; ant forsac þi feader hus, [68ʳ]
as hit is þruppe iopenet; ant tac þe to him treowliche wið hwam þu
schalt wealden, as wið þi were iweddet, worlt buten ende, heouenliche
wunnen. Eadi is his spuse, hwas meiðhad is unwemmet hwen he on
hire streoneð, ant hwen ha temeð of him, ne swinkeð ne ne pineð.
30 Eadi is þe were, hwen nan ne mei beo meiden bute ȝef heo him luuie,
ne freo bute ȝef heo him serui, hwas streon is undeaðlich ant hwas
marheȝeue is þe kinedom of heouene.

Nu þenne, seli meiden, ȝef þe is weole leof, nim þe him to lauerd
þet wealdeð al þet is ant wes ant eauer schal iwurðen; for þah he beo
35 richest him ane ouer alle, þe alre measte poure þe him to were cheoseð
is him wel icweme. Ȝef þet tu wilnest were þe muche wlite habbe, nim

---

1 ha schule] T, hit is B   3 þeowdom] þeodom B   10 swiðre] T, swiðe B
15 ahest] ahtest B, ahes T   19 ant ec of] T, ba ant B   20 leouie] T, leoue B
26 hwam] him BT   33 lauerd] lauerð B

how much food she should put in its mouth at a single time, not to bespatter it or its baby-clothes; though these are trivial things to mention, all the more they show what slavery wives are in, who must endure such things, and what liberty virgins have, who are free from them all.

And what if I should ask further, though it may seem ridiculous, what kind of position the wife is in who, when she comes in, hears her child screaming, sees the cat at the flitch and the dog at the hide, her loaf burning on the hearth and her calf sucking, the pot boiling over into the fire—*and* her husband is complaining? Although it may sound ridiculous, it ought, maiden, to discourage you from it all the more, because it is no joke to the woman who tries it.

The horrors of motherhood

That innocent maiden who has escaped such slavery, as God's free daughter and his son's bride, need not suffer anything of the kind. Therefore, innocent maiden, renounce all such misery for supreme reward, which you ought to do without any reward at all; for now I have kept my promise above, that I would show that what many people tell you about the happiness and success that the married have—and which seems to be true—is glossed over with falsehood: that things do not go as the outside observer thinks that they do, but turn out quite otherwise, for both poor and rich, for those who hate each other and those who love each other too, so that everywhere the misery exceeds the happiness, and the loss universally exceeds the gain.

Now then, innocent maiden, whom David calls 'daughter', hear your father and listen to the advice which he gave you at the beginning of this treatise. 'Forget your people' who deceive you about the pleasure of a husband and the world, who are the thoughts which treacherously entice you towards every misery; and forsake your father's house, as it is explained above; and devote yourself faithfully to him with whom, as with your wedded husband, you will possess heavenly joys for ever and ever. Blessed is his spouse, whose virginity is unblemished when he begets offspring on her, and who, when she bears children by him, does not labour or suffer. Blessed is the husband, when no woman can be a virgin unless she loves him, or free unless she serves him, whose offspring is immortal and whose marriage gift is the kingdom of heaven.

Now then, innocent maiden, if you are fond of wealth, take him as your lord who possesses all that is and was and ever shall be; for although he is far richer than anyone else, the very poorest woman who chooses him as a husband is altogether pleasing to him. If you want a

him of hwas wlite beoð awundret of þe sunne ant te mone, upo hwas
nebscheft þe engles ne beoð neauer fulle to bihalden; for hwen he
ӡeueð feirlec to al þet is feier in heouene ant in eorðe, muchele mare
he haueð, wiðuten ei etlunge, ethalden to himseoluen. Ant þah,
hwen he þus is alre þinge feherest, he underueð bliðeliche ant
bicluppeð swoteliche þe alre ladlukeste, ant makeð ham seouesiðe
schenre þen þe sunne. Ӡef þe were leof streon, nim þe to him under
hwam þu schalt, i þi meiðhad, te|men dehtren ant sunen of gasteliche   [68ᵛ
teames, þe neauer deie ne mahen ah schulen aa biuore þe pleien in
10   heouene, þet beoð þe uertuz þet he streoneð in þe þurh his swete
grace; as rihtwisnesse ant warschipe aӡeines unþeawes, mesure ant
mete ant gastelich strengðe to wiðstonde þe feond ant aӡein sunne,
simplete of semblant, buhsumnesse ant stilðe, þolemodnesse ant
reowfulnesse of euch monnes sorhe, gleadschipe i þe Hali Gast ant þes
15   i þi breoste of onde ant of wreaððe, of ӡisceunge ant of euch
unþeawes weorre, meokelec ant miltschipe, ant swotnesse of heorte,
þe limpeð alre þinge best to meiðhades mihte. Þis is meidenes team,
Godes sune spuse, þet schal aa libben ant pleien buten ende biuoren
hire in heouene.
20   Ah þah þu, meiden, beo wið unbruche of þi bodi, ant tu habbe
prude, onde oðer wreaððe, ӡisceunge oðer wac wil inwið i þin
heorte, þu forhorest te wið þe unwiht of helle, ant he streoneð on þe
þe team þet tu temest. Hwen þi were alwealdent þet tu þe to weddest
sið ant understont tis, þet his fa forlið þe ant þet tu temest of him þet
25   him is teame laðest, he forheccheð þe anan—as hit nis na wunder—ant
cweðeð þe al cwite him þet tu of temest. Ne kepeð he wið na mon, ant
hure wið his famon, nan half dale. Þe luuieð eawiht | buten him, ant   [69
hwet se ha for him luuieð, ha wreaðeð him swiðe. Ouer alle þing, wite
þe þet tu ne temi prude bi þes deofles streonunge; for heo of alle
30   unþeawes is his ealdeste dohter. Earst ha wakenede of him þe-ӡet he
wes in heouene, forneh wið him euenald, ant swa ha keaste hire
feader, sone se ha ibore wes, from þe heste heouene into helle grunde
bute couerunge, ant makede of hehengel eatelukest deofel. Þe þus
adun duste hire heouenliche feader, hwet wule ha don bi hire
35   eorðliche modres þe temeð hire in horedom of þen laðe unwiht, þe
hellene schucke? Hwen Godd se wracfulliche fordemde his hehengel

11 rihtwisnesse] rihtwissnesse B   13 þolemodnesse] þolomodnesse B
16 meokelec] T, metelec B   17 meiðhades] meihades B   21 i þin] T, *om.* B
30 his] hiss B   31 ha keaste hire] T, hire keaste ure B   34 ha] T, he B

husband who is very handsome, take him whose beauty the sun and moon admire, whose face the angels are never weary of gazing at; for when he gives beauty to everything that is beautiful in heaven and on earth, he will have kept inestimably more for himself. And even though this means he is incomparably beautiful, he gladly receives and sweetly embraces the most hideous of all, and makes them seven times brighter than the sun. If you would like children, devote yourself to him with whom you shall, in your virginity, give birth to spiritual sons and daughters, who can never die but will play before you for ever in heaven, which are the virtues that he engenders in you through his sweet grace; such as justice and prudence against vices, moderation and temperance and fortitude of spirit to withstand the Devil and against sin, simplicity of manner, obedience and silence, patience and compassion for everyone's misery, joy in the Holy Ghost and peace in your heart from envy and anger, from avarice and from the attack of every vice, meekness and mildness, and sweetness of heart, which belongs best of all things to the virtue of virginity. These are the virgin's children when she is wife to God's son, and will always live and play eternally before her in heaven.

But, maiden, although you may have physical integrity, if you have pride, envy, or anger, avarice or weakness of will in your heart, you are prostituting yourself with the Devil of hell, and he fathers on you the children which you bear. When the almighty husband that you are married to sees and understands this, that his enemy is committing adultery with you and that you are pregnant by him with the offspring he hates most, he turns you out of doors at once—and no wonder— and surrenders you completely to the lover you are pregnant by. He does not go halves with anyone, least of all with his enemy. Those who love anything apart from him, whatever they love instead of him, make him very angry. Above all, take care that you do not give birth to pride engendered by this Devil; for she of all the vices is his eldest daughter. She sprang from him first while he was still in heaven, born almost as soon as he was, and as soon as she was born she cast her father irrecoverably from the highest heaven into the depths of hell, and made from an archangel the most loathsome devil. Since this is how she cast down her heavenly father, what will she do to her earthly mothers who bear her adulterously to the loathsome Devil, the infernal demon? When God so vengefully condemned his archangel who

þe streonede hire in heouene, hwet wule he don bi þet lam ant
wurmene mete þe of þe deofel temeð hire in eawbruche on eorðe?
ȝef þu hauest wið meiðhad meokelec ant mildschipe, Godd is i þin
heorte; ah ȝef þer is ouerhohe oðer ei prude in, he is utlahe þrof, for
5 ne muhen ha nanes weis beddin in a breoste, þe ne mahten nawt somet
eardin in heouene. Þeonne Godd weorp hire sone se ha iboren wes,
ant as þah ha nuste hwuch wei ha come þeonewart, ne con ha neauer
mare ifinden nan wei aȝeinwart; ah eardinde her on eorðe bihat eche
wununge alle hire modres, al beon ha meidnes, wið hire awea|riede [69ᵛ]
10 feader in inwarde helle. Wite þe, meiden, wið hire; ha cwikede of
cleane cunde, as is in engles euene, ant cleaneste breosten bredeð hire
ȝetten. Þe beste ha asaileð; ant wel ha der hopien to beo kempe ouer
mon þe ouercom engel. Nis ha nawt i claðes ne i feahunge utewið, þah
hit beo merke þrof ant makunge oðerhwiles; ah under hwit oðer blac,
15 ant ase wel under grei as under grene ant gra, ha luteð i þe heorte.
Sone se þu telest te betere þen anoðer, beo hit hweruore se hit eauer
beo, ant hauest of ei ouerhohe, ant þuncheð hofles ant hoker of eawt
þet me seið þe oðer deð ȝetten, þu merrest þin meiðhad, ant brekest
ti wedlac towart Godd, ant of his fa temest. Ne tele þu nawt eðelich, al
20 beo þu meiden, to widewen ne to iweddede. For alswa as a charbucle is
betere þen a iacinct i þe euene of hare cunde, ant þah is betere a briht
iacinct þen a charbucle won, alswa passeð meiden, onont te mihte of
meiðhad, widewen ant iweddede; ant tah is betere a milde wif oðer a
meoke widewe þen a prud meiden. For þeos, for hare sunnen þet ha i
25 flesches fulðe folhið oþer fulieð, leoteð ham lahe ant eðliche, ant beoð
sare ofdret of Godes luðere eie, ant as þe eadi sunegilt Marie
Magdaleine wið bittre wopes bireowsið hare gultes ant inwardluker
luuieð Godd, alswa as heo | dude, for hare forȝeuenesse; ant te oðre, [70ʳ]
þe haldeð ham unforgult ant cleane, beoð ase sikere unlusti ant
30 wlecche—unneaðe liuieð i Godes luue, wiðuten euch heate of þe Hali
Gast, þe bearneð se lihte wiðute wastinde brune in alle his icorene.
Ant te oþre in an heate of an honthwile beoð imelt mare ant iȝotten i
Godd þen þe oþre in a wlecheunge al hare lifsiðen.
     Forþi, eadi meiden, Godes sunes spuse, ne beo þu nawt to trusti ane
35 to þi meiðhad wiðuten oðer god ant þeawfule mihtes ant, ouer al,

5 þe] ne B, ha T   mahten] maken B, muhen T   8 eardinde] T, earmðe B
bihat] T, bihalt B   9 hire²] hare BT; *Furnivall, p. 60*   15 gra] T, aa B
16 Sone] Son B   20 charbucle] charbuche B   22 onont] onon B
26 as] T, al B   27 bireowsið] bireowseð BT   inwardluker] inwarðluker B
30 liuieð], T, *om.* B   34 to trusti] T, trust B   35 meiðhad] meidhad B

fathered her in heaven, what will he do to that clay and food for worms which adulterously conceives her by the Devil on earth? If together with virginity you have meekness and mildness, God is in your heart; but if there is arrogance or any pride there, he is an outlaw from it, for they cannot possibly cohabit in one heart, when they could not live together in heaven. God cast her out from there as soon as she was born, and as if she did not know which way she came from it, she can never find any way back again; but living here on earth promises an eternal home to all her mothers, virgins though they may be, with her accursed father in inmost hell. Guard yourself against her, maiden; she had her origin in a pure nature, of the kind that belongs to angels, and the purest hearts still breed her. She attacks the best; and she may well dare hope to triumph over man, since she overcame an angel. She is not found in clothes or in outward adornment, though it may be a sign of her, and sometimes the cause; but underneath either white or black, and as much under grey garments as under rich robes, she lurks in the heart. As soon as you think yourself better than someone else, for whatever reason, or despise anyone, and anything that is said or done to you seems to you stupid or a matter for contempt, you impair your virginity, and break your bond of marriage with God, and bear children to his enemy. Though you may be a virgin, do not undervalue widows and married women. For just as a ruby is better than a jacinth in its natural quality, and nevertheless a bright jacinth is better than a dull ruby, so a maiden by the virtue of virginity surpasses widows and married women; and nevertheless a modest wife or a meek widow is better than a proud virgin. For the former, because of the sins that they commit in the filth of the flesh, think themselves humble and worthless, and are greatly afraid of God's terrible anger, and like the blessed sinner Mary Magdalene repent their sins with bitter lamentations, and love God more deeply, just as she did, because of their forgiveness; and the latter, who think themselves guiltless and pure, are as certainly listless and lukewarm—they are barely alive in the love of God, without any heat from the Holy Ghost, who burns so brightly without consuming flame in all his elect. And the former are more melted and dissolved in God in a moment's ardour than the latter in lukewarmness all their lives.

Therefore, blessed maiden, wife to God's son, do not be too confident in your virginity alone without other good and virtuous

miltschipe ant meokeschipe of heorte, efter þe forbisne of þet eadi
meiden ouer alle oðre, Marie, Godes moder. For þa þe hehengel
Gabriel grette hire ant brohte hire to tidinge of Godes akennesse, loke
hu lah ha lette hire þa ha ontswerede þus bi hireseoluen: 'Efter þi
5 word', quoð ha, 'mote me iwurðen. Low, her mi Lauerdes þrel.' Ant
tah ha ful were of alle gode þeawes, ane of hire meokelec ha seide, ant
song to Elizabeth: 'For mi Lauerd biseh his þuftenes meokelec, me
schulen cleopien', quoð ha, 'eadi alle leoden.'

Nim ʒeme, meiden, ant understont herbi þet mare for hire
10 meokelec þen for hire meiðhad ha lette þet ha ifont swuch grace ed
ure Lauerd. For al meiðhad, meokelec is muche wurð; ant meiðhad
wiðuten hit is eðelich ant unwurð, for alswa is meiden i meiðhad bu|te [70ᵛ]
meokeschipe as is wiðute liht eolie in a lampe. Eadi Godes spuse, haue
þeos ilke mihte, þet tu ne þunche þeostri ah schine ase sunne i þi
15 weres sihðe. Feahe þi meiðhad wið alle gode þeawes þe þuncheð him
feire. Haue eauer i þin heorte þe eadieste of meidnes ant meiðhades
moder, ant bisech hire aa þet ha þe lihte, ant ʒeoue luue ant strengðe
for te folhin i meiðhad hire þeawes. Þench o Seinte Katerine, o Seinte
Margarete, Seinte Enneis, Seinte Iuliene, Seinte Lucie, ant Seinte
20 Cecille, ant o þe oþre hali meidnes in heouene, hu ha nawt ane ne
forsoken kinges sunes ant eorles, wið alle worldliche weolen ant
eorðliche wunnen, ah þoleden stronge pinen ear ha walden neomen
ham, ant derf deað on ende. Þench hu wel ham is nu, ant hu ha blissið
þeruore bituhe Godes earmes, cwenes of heouene.

25 Ant ʒef hit eauer timeð þet ti licomes lust, þurh þe false feont,
leaðie þe towart flesliche fulðen, ontswere i þi þoht þus: 'Ne geineð þe
nawt, sweoke! Þullich Ich chulle beon in meidenes liflade, ilich
heouene engel. Ich chulle halde me hal, þurh þe grace of Godd, as
Cunde me makede, þet Paraise selhðe underuo me al swuch as weren,
30 ear ha agulten, his eareste heamen. Allunge swuch Ich chulle beon as
is mi deore leofmon, mi deorewurðe La|uerd, ant as þet eadi meiden [71ʳ]
þe he him cheas to moder. Al swuch Ich chulle wite me treowliche
unwemmet, as Ich am him iweddet; ne nulle Ich nawt for a lust of ane
lutle hwile—þah hit þunche delit—awei warpe þet þing hwas lure Ich
35 schal biremen wiðvten couerunge, ant wið eche brune abuggen in

4 lah] T, þah B   7 his] T, þis B   13 wiðute] widute B
14 i þi] T, ant ti B   15 Feahe] Feahi B   18 Katerine] Katerrine B
19 Seinte Lucie] T, om. B   20 meidnes] meiðnes B   25 ti] T, tu B
26 þe] T, om. B   28 engel] e engel B   30 heamen] T, hinen B
31 deorewurðe] deorewurde B   32 me] T, om. B

qualities, and above all mildness and meekness of heart, after the example of that virgin blessed above all others, Mary, mother of God. For when the archangel Gabriel greeted her and brought to her news of God's conception, look how little she valued herself when she said of herself in answer: 'Let it happen to me according to your word. See, here is my Lord's handmaid.' And though she was full of all good qualities, she spoke only of her humility, and sang to Elizabeth: 'Because my Lord has considered the humility of his handmaid, all nations', she said, 'shall call me blessed.'

Take note, maiden, and understand by this that she thought that she found such favour with our Lord more for her humility than for her virginity. For all virginity, humility is precious; and virginity without it is a poor and worthless thing, for a maiden in virginity without humility is like oil in a lamp that has not been lit. Blessed spouse of God, have this virtue, that you may not seem dark but shine like a sun in your husband's sight. Adorn your virginity with all the good qualities which he finds attractive. Have always in your heart the most blessed of virgins and mother of virginity, and entreat her constantly to kindle you, and give you love and strength to follow her virtues in your virginity. Think of St Catherine, of St Margaret, St Agnes, St Juliana, St Lucy, and St Cecilia, and of the other holy virgins in heaven, how they not only renounced the sons of kings and noblemen, with all worldly riches and earthly pleasures, but suffered cruel tortures rather than accept them, and a painful death at last. Think how happy they are now, and how they rejoice accordingly in the arms of God, as queens of heaven.

And if it happens that your physical desire, through the false fiend, should ever incite you towards carnal filthiness, answer mentally in this way: 'It does you no good, traitor! In my way of life as a virgin, I shall be like an angel in heaven. I shall keep myself intact, through the grace of God, as Nature made me, so that the blessedness of Paradise may receive me in the same state as its first inhabitants before they sinned. I shall be in every way like my dear lover, my precious Lord, and like that blessed virgin he chose for his mother. I shall faithfully keep myself spotless, as I am now in my marriage to him; and I will not throw away for a momentary desire—though it may seem delightful— that thing whose loss I shall lament as irrecoverable, and expiate with

helle. Þu wrenchwile ful wiht, al for nawt þu prokest me to forgulten
ant forgan þe blisse upo blisse, þe crune upo crune of meidenes mede,
ant willes ant waldes warpe me as wrecche i þi leirwite, ant for þet
englene song of meiðhades menske, wið þe ant wið þine greden aa ant
5 granin i þe eche grure of helle.'
    3ef þu þus ontswerest to þi licomes lust ant to þe feondes
fondunge, he schal fleo þe wið scheome; ant 3ef he alles efter þis
inohreaðe etstonde, ant halt on to eili þi flesch ant prokie þin heorte, þi
Lauerd Godd hit þeaueð him to muchli þi mede. For as Seinte Pawel
10 seið, ne bið nan icrunet bute hwa se treoweliche i þulli feht fehte, ant
wið strong cokkunge ouercume hire seolf. For þenne is þe deofel wið
his ahne turn scheomeliche awarpen, hwen þu, as þe apostle seið, ne
schalt beon icrunet bute þu beo asailet. 3ef Godd wule cruni þe, he
wule leote ful wel þe | unwiht asaili þe, þet tu earni þerþurh kempene [71ᵛ
15 crune. Forþi hit is þe meast god hwen he greueð þe meast ant towart te
wið fondunge wodeluker weorreð, 3ef þu wel wrist te under Godes
wengen; for þurh his weorre he 3arkeð þe, unþonc in his teð, þe
blisse ant te crune of Cristes icorene.
    Ant Iesu Crist leue hire þe þurh his blescede nome, ant alle þeo þe
20 leaueð luue of lami mon for te beon his leofmon; ant leue ham swa
hare heorte halden to him þet hare flesches eggunge ne þe feondes
fondunge ne nan of his eorðliche limen ne wori hare heorte wit, ne
wrenche ham ut of þe wei þet ha beoð in i3ongen; ant helpe ham swa
in him to hihin towart heouene, aþet ha beon istihe þider as hare
25 brudlac schal, in al þet eauer sel is, wið þene seli brudgume þet siheð
alle selhðe of, sitten buten ende. AMEN.

1 wrenchwile] wrenchfule B, wrechwile T   4 meiðhades] meidhades B
8 þi²] T, ant ti B   13 schalt] T, schalt tu B   15 hwen] þet hwen BT
greueð] greued B   16 Godes] Goder B   19 hire þe] T, hire B   his] T, þi B
ant²] T, *om.* B   24 hihin] hihen T, hehin B; *Colborn, p. 122*

everlasting fire in hell. You crafty demon, all for nothing you incite me to commit sin, and forgo the bliss upon bliss, the crown upon crown of a virgin's reward, and cast myself wretchedly of my own accord into your punishment for fornication, and instead of that angelic song of the glory of virginity, cry out and groan with you and yours forever in the eternal horror of hell.'

If you reply in this way to your physical desire and to the fiend's temptation, he will fly from you with shame; and if he makes any stand at all after this, and still keeps trying to trouble your flesh and stir your heart, then your Lord God is allowing him to, to increase your reward. For as St Paul says, no one is crowned except for whoever fights truly in that fight, and with a hard struggle overcomes herself. For then the Devil is shamefully overthrown with his own strength, since, as the Apostle says, you will not be crowned unless you are attacked. If God wishes to crown you, he will certainly let the Devil attack you so that you may earn a victor's crown by it. Therefore it is best for you when he afflicts you most and assails you more fiercely with his temptations, if you shelter yourself well under God's wings; for through his attack he prepares for you, in spite of himself, the bliss and the crown of Christ's elect.

And may Jesus Christ grant this crown to you through his blessed name, and to all those who give up the love of a man of clay to be his beloved; and grant them to keep their hearts for him in such a way that neither their body's urges nor the fiend's temptation nor any of his earthly agents may trouble their minds, or force them out of the way that they have chosen; and help them in him to hasten towards heaven so that they may ascend to the place where their marriage, in everything that is blessed, with that blessed bridegroom who is the source of all happiness, will last forever. AMEN.

Seinte Margarete

I þe Feaderes ant i þes Sunes ant i þes Hali Gastes nome, her
biginneð þe Liflade ant te Passiun of Seinte Margarete.

Efter ure Lauerdes pine ant his passiun, ant his deað o rode ant his
ariste of deað, ant efter his upastihunge, as he steah to heouene, weren
monie martyrs, wepmen ba ant wummen, to deaðes misliche idon for
þe nome of Drihtin; ant, as icudde kempen, ouercomen ant akeasten
5 hare þreo cunne uan, þe ueont ant teos wake worlt ant hare licomes
lustes, ant wenden of þeos weanen to weole ant to eche wunne, icrunet
to Criste.

Þe-ȝet weren monie ma þene nu beon misbileuede | men, þe [18ᵛ]
heheden ant hereden heþene maumez, of stanes ant of stockes
10 wrecches iwrahte. Ah Ich, an Godes þeowe, Teochimus inemned,
ilered i Godes lei, habbe iredd ant araht moni mislich leaf, ant neauer i
nan stude ne mahte Ich understonden of nan þe were wurðe for to
beon iwurget as Drihtin deh to donne, bute þe hehe Healent an þet is
in heouene, þe wunede hwil his wille wes amonc worldliche men, ant
15 bottnede blinde, þe dumbe ant te deaue, ant te deade arerde to leome
ant to liue; ant cruneð his icorene, þe deð dreheð for him oðer eni
neowcin; ant alle Cristene men, þet beoð of Crist icleopet, swa ȝef ha
nutteð hare nome, hafeð ilened þet lif þet echeliche lesteð. Ich, fulhet
i font o þe almihti Fedres nome ant o þe witti Sunes nome ant o þes
20 Hali Gastes, wes i þe ilke time liuiende i londe þa þet eadie meiden,
Margarete bi nome, feht wið þe feond ant wið his eorðliche limen, ant
ouercom ant acaste ham; ant biȝet hit iwriten of þe writers þa, al hire
passiun ant hire pinfule deð þet ha dreh for Drihtin.

Hercneð, alle þe earen ant herunge habbeð, widewen wið þa
25 iweddede, ant te meidnes nomeliche lusten swiðe ȝeornliche hu ha
schulen luuien þe liuiende Lauerd ant libben i meiðhad, þet him his
mihte leouest, swa þet ha moten, þurh þet eadie meiden þe we
munneð todei wið meiðhades menske, þet seli meidnes song singen
wið þis meiden ant wið þet heouenliche hird echeliche in heouene. | [19ʳ]

Heading: biginneð] biginned B   3 wepmen] wepme B   10 inemned]
inemed B   11 habbe iredd ant araht] R, redde ant arahte B (B² *alters* redde *to*
iredd *and* arahte *to* araht)   mislich] mislihc B   14 ant]B²R, þe B   15 blinde]
B²R, *om.* B   16 cruneð] B², crunede BR   dreheð] B²R, drehen B
for him]B²R, *om.* B   17 þet . . . icleopet] B²R, *om.* B   18 fulhet] foˈuˈlhet B

Saint Margaret

In the name of the Father, and of the Son, and of the Holy Ghost, here begins the Life and Passion of St Margaret.

After the suffering and passion of our Lord, and his death on the cross and his resurrection from death, and after his ascension, when he rose to heaven, there were many martyrs, both men and women, cruelly put to death in the name of God; and, like seasoned fighters, they conquered and cast down their three kinds of foe, the Devil and this frail world and the lusts of the flesh, and departed from these pains with martyrs' crowns to Christ, to eternal joy and bliss.

There were still in those days many more infidels than there are now, who worshipped and honoured heathen idols, wretched things made out of stone and wood. But I, a servant of God, Teochimus by name, learned in God's law, have read and interpreted many kinds of writings, and could never find anywhere any who were worthy to be given the worship that we owe to God, except for one alone, the supreme Saviour who lives in heaven, who deigned to dwell for a time among earthly men, and who healed the blind, the dumb, and the deaf, and raised up the dead to life again; and gives crowns to his chosen ones, those who suffer death or any affliction for him; and has granted all Christians—who take their name from Christ—if they deserve the name, life everlasting. I, who was baptized in the almighty Father's name, and in the wise Son's name, and in the Holy Ghost's, was living at the time that that blessed maiden, Margaret by name, fought with the Devil and his agents on earth, and defeated and destroyed them; and obtained the documents written at the time describing all her passion and the painful death which she endured for God.

Listen, all those who have ears to hear, widows with the married, and maidens above all should attend most earnestly to how they should love the living Lord, and live in virginity, the virtue dearest to him, so that they may, through that holy maiden we commemorate today with the honour due to virgins, sing that blessed virgins' song together with this maiden and with the heavenly host eternally in heaven.

19 ant . . . nome] B²R, *om.* B   20 ilke] B²R, *om.* B   21 ant²] B²R, *om.* B
25 ȝeornliche] ȝeorliche B   28 singen] sinȝen B   29 þet] B², þe T, *om.* B

Þis meiden þet we munieð wes Margarete ihaten; ant hire flesliche
feder Theodosie hehte, of þet heþene folc patriarche ant prince. Ah
heo, as þe deorwurðe Drihtin hit dihte, into a burh wes ibroht to
ueden ant to uostrin, from þe muchele Antioche fiftene milen. Þa ha
5 hefde of helde ȝeres fiftene, ant hire moder wes iwend þe wei þet
worldliche men alle schulen wenden, ha warð þeo þe hefde iwist ant
iwenet hire swa lengre swa leuere; ant alle hire luueden þet hire on
lokeden, as þeo þet Godd luuede, þe heouenliche Lauerd, ant ȝef
hire þe grace of þe Hali Gast, swa þet ha ches him to luue ant to
10 lefmon, ant bitahte in his hond þe menske of hire meiðhad, hire wil ant
hire werc, ant al þet heo eauer i þe world i wald hahte, to witen ant to
welden wið al hireseoluen. Þus ha wes ant wiste, meokest alre milde,
wið oðre meidnes o þe feld hire fostermodres hahte; ant herde on
euich half hire hu me droh to deaðe Cristes icorene for rihte bileaue;
15 ant ȝirnde ant walde ȝeorne, ȝef Godes wil were, þet ha moste
beon an of þe moni moder-bern þet swa muchel drohen ant
drehheden for Drihtin.

Bitimde umbe stunde þet ter com ut of Asye towart Antioche þe
ueondes an foster, to herien i þe hehe burh hise heþene godes.
20 Olibrius hehte, schireue of þe lond, þet alle þe lefden o þe liuiende
Godd fordude ant fordemde. As he wende a dei his wei, seh þis seli | [19ᵛ
meiden Margarete as ha wes ant wiste upo þe feld hire fostermodres
schep, þe schimede ant schan al of wlite ant of westume. He het his
hird hetterliche, 'Nemeð hire swiðe! ȝef heo his freo wummon, Ich
25 hire wule habben ant halden to wiue; ant ȝef heo þeowe is, Ich cheose
hire to cheuese, ant hire wule freohin wið gersum ant wið golde; ant
wel schal hire iwurðen for hire lufsume leor wið al þet Ich welde.'

As þe knihtes wolden warpen honden on hire, ha bigon to clepien
ant callen to Criste þus: 'Haue, Lauerd, milce ant merci of þi
30 wummon; ne ne let tu neaure mi sawle forleosen wið þe forlorene, ne
wið þe luðere mi lif, þe beoð al blodi biblodeget of sunne. Iesu Crist,
Godes Sune, beo þu eauer mi gleo ant mi gledunge; þe mot Ich a mare
hehen ant herien. Hald, hehe Healent, min heorte, Ich biseche þe, in
treowe bileue; ant biwite þu mi bodi, þet is al bitaht to þe, from
35 flesliche fulþen; þet neauer mi sawle ne isuled beo in sunne þurh þet

6 þe] þe ha B, *corrected to* þe *by* B², þat R   7 hire¹] B²R, *om.* B   10 menske]
meske B   14 for . . . bileaue] B²R, *om.* B   16–17 ant drehheden] B², *om.* BR
21 a dei] B²R, *om.* B   22 fostermodres] fostmodres B   26 gersum]
ȝersum B   30 forleosen] forleosun B   33 Healent] R, Lauerd B
34 þu] B²R, *om.* B   35 flesliche] B²R, ulche B

This maiden we commemorate had the name of Margaret; and her natural father was called Theodosius, patriarch and prince of that infidel race. Now by the decree of our dearest Lord she was taken to a town to be raised and fostered, fifteen miles from Antioch the great. By the time she was fifteen years of age, her mother had gone the way that all people on earth must go, but she had become as time went by more and more dear to the nurse who had weaned her and brought her up; and all those who saw her loved her as one who was loved by God, the heavenly Lord, who had given her the grace of the Holy Ghost, so that she chose him as love and as suitor, and commended to him her virgin honour, her will and her deeds, and everything that she possessed in the world to keep and to use on her own account. So, meekest of the mild, she tended with other maidens out in the fields her foster-mother's sheep; and heard on every side how Christ's chosen ones were being put to death for the true faith; and eagerly longed, if it were God's will, that she might be one of the many people who bore and suffered so much for God.

It happened after a time that the Devil's own offspring arrived from Asia, travelling to Antioch to worship his idols in the capital city. He was called Olibrius, the governor of that land, and condemned to death all who believed in the living God. One day as he rode out he caught sight of Margaret, this innocent maiden, as she was tending her foster-mother's sheep out in the fields, and was dazzled by the beauty of her face and figure. He gave a rapid command to his retinue: 'Seize her at once! If she is a free woman, I will take her to wife, to have and to hold; and if she is a slave, I will make her my mistress, and give her her freedom with treasure and gold; and she will be well rewarded for her beauty with all that I own.'

But as the knights were about to seize her, she began to call upon Christ as follows: 'Take pity, Lord, and have mercy on your maiden; and never let my soul be lost among the damned, or my life among evil men bloodstained with sin. Jesus Christ, Son of God, may you always be my joy and my delight; let me praise you for ever. Heavenly Lord, hold my heart, I beseech you, in the true faith; and deliver my body, dedicated to you, from carnal defilement, so my soul may never be

licomes lust þet lutle hwile likeð. Lauerd, lustu to me. Ich habbe a
deore ʒimstan, ant Ich hit habbe iʒeue þe—mi meiðhad I mene,
blostme brihtest i bodi þe hit bereð ant biwit wel. Ne let tu neauer þe
unwiht warpen hit i wurðinc; for hit is þe leof, hit is him þinge loþest,
5 ant weorreð ant warpeð euer þertoward wið willes, wið wer|kes, wið   20a
alles cunnes wrenches. Lauerd, þu were me ant wite hit euer to þe. Ne
þole þu neuer þe unwiht þet he wori mi wit ne wonie mi wisdom; ah
send me þi sonde, Helent, of heouene, þet cuðe me ant kenne hu Ich
onswerie schule þes schuckes schireue. For Ich iseo me, Lauerd,
10 bisteaðed ant bistonden ase lomb wið wedde wulues, ant ase þe fuhel
þe is iuon in þes fuheleres grune, ase fisc ahon on hoke, ase ra inumen
i nette. Heh Helent, help me, ne leaf þu me neuer nu i luðere mennes
honde.'
     Þe knihtes, for ha spec þus, charden euchan aʒein, ant cweþen to
15 hare lauerd: 'Ne mei þi mihte habben na man wið þis meiden, for ha
ne heheð nan of ure heþene godes, ah leueð o þe Lauerd þe þe Gius
fordemden ant drohen to deaðe, ant heðene hongeden ant heuen on
rode.'
     Olibrius þe luðere, þa he þis iherde, changede his chere, ant het
20 biliue bringin hire biforen him. Sone se ha icume wes, he cleopede to
hire þus: 'Cuð me', quoð he, 'ʒif þu art foster of freomon oðer
þeowe-wummon.'
     Þe eadi meiden Margarete sone him ontswerede, ant softeliche
seide: 'Freo wummon Ich am, ant þah Godes þewe.'
25 'ʒe,' quoð he, 'ah hwet godd hehest ant herestu?'
     'Ich hehe', quoð ha, 'heh-feader, Healent in heouene, ant his
deorwurðe Sune, Iesu Crist hatte; ant him Ich habbe, meiden, mi
meiðhad iʒettet, ant lu|uie to leofmon ant leue on ase on Lauerd.'   [20a
     'Hu dele!' quoð he lude, 'Leuestu ant luuest te þe reufulliche deide
30 ant dreorliche on rode?'
     'Nai,' quoð ha, 'ah þeo þe wenden to fordon him, þine forðfedres,
beoð forfaren reuliche ant forloren luðerliche; ant he liueð, kine-
bern icrunet in his kinedom, keiser of kinges, echeliche in heouene.'
     Þe wari of þeos wordes wearð utnume wrað, ant het hire kasten in
35 cwarterne ant i cwalhus aþet he hefde betere biþoht him o hwucche

1 hwile] while B   2 ʒimstan] gimstan B   4 unwiht] unwhit B   hit is²]
B²R, ant B   9 Lauerd] Lauerð B   10 bisteaðed] R, bistepped B
12 luðere mennes] luðeres menne B   24 þah] B²R, om. B   25 ah] B², ant
R, om. B   28 on ase on] ase B, corrected by B², as on R   29 lude] B²R, om. B
30 dreorliche] R, reuliche B   34 þeos] þes B, corrected by B²   35 ant i] B²,
ant into R, om. B

soiled with sin through the fleeting pleasures of fleshly lust. Lord, listen to me. I have a precious jewel—my virginity, I mean—brightest of blossoms in the body that bears it and guards it well. Never let the Evil One cast it in the mire; because it is dear to you, he hates it most of all, and campaigns against it and attacks it constantly with wishes, with acts, with all sorts of wiles. Lord, defend me; keep it always for yourself. Never allow the Evil One to trouble my reason or impair my wisdom; but send me your messenger, Saviour, from heaven, to tell me how to answer the Devil's agent. For I see myself, Lord, harassed and beset like a lamb among rabid wolves, and like the bird that is held in the fowler's snare, like a fish caught on a hook, like a roe trapped in a net; help me, great Redeemer, and never abandon me in the hands of evil men.'

The knights, on hearing this, all turned back, and said to their lord: 'This maiden may not be raised to your rank, since she worships none of our heathen gods, but believes in the Lord whom the Jews judged and put to death, who was hanged by the heathen high on a cross.'

When the cruel Olibrius heard these words, his countenance darkened, and he ordered them to bring her quickly before him. As soon as she came, he questioned her as follows: 'Tell me', he said, 'whether you are a freeman's child or a bondwoman.'

The holy maiden Margaret answered him at once, and mildly said: 'I am a free woman, but God's servant too.'

'Indeed!' he said, 'and what god do you honour and worship?'

'I honour', she said, 'the Father on high, the Lord in Heaven, and his precious Son, who is called Jesus Christ; and have given my virginity inviolate to him, and love him as a lover and believe in him as Lord.'

'What!' he cried, 'do you love and believe in a man who suffered wretchedly and died on a cross?'

'No,' she said, 'but those who thought to destroy him, your predecessors, have perished miserably and been utterly destroyed; and he lives, a prince crowned in his kingdom, emperor of kings, eternally in heaven.'

The wicked man was goaded to fury by these words, and commanded that she should be cast into prison until he had had more

wise he walde merren hire meiðhad; ant ferde him þenne swa forð into
Antioche, ant hehede hise heþene godes, as hit lomp ant lei to his
luðere bileue.

    Het hire i þe oðer dei bringen biuoren him. Ha wes sone ibroht
5 forð, ant he bigon to seggen: 'Meiden, haue merci ant milce of þe
seoluen. Nim ȝeme of þi ȝuheþe ant of þi semliche schape, of þi
schene nebschaft. Wurch efter mi wil ant wurge mine maumez, ant þe
schal wel iwurðen biuoren þe heste of min hirt, wið al þet Ich i world
hah ant i wald habbe.'

10   Margarete, mildest ant meidene meokest, ontswerede him ant seide:
'Wite hit tu nu gif þu wult—for he hit wat ful wel þe haueð iseilet to
himseolf me ant mi meiðhad—þet tu ne maht nanes weis, wið weole
ne wið wune, wið wa ne wið wont|reþe, ne wið nan worldlich þing, [21ʳ
wenden me ne wrenchen ut of þe wei þet Ich am in bigunne to ganne.
15 Ant unwurð, þet wite þu, me beoð þine wordes; for him ane Ich luuie
ant habbe to bileue þe weld ant wisseð wið his wit windes ant wederes,
ant al þet biset is wið se ant wið sunne. Buuen ba ant bineoþen, al
buheð to him ant beieð. Ant to-eke þis, þet he is se mihti ant se
meinful, he is leoflukest lif for to lokin upon ant swotest to smellen; ne
20 his swote sauour ne his almihti mihte ne his makelese lufsumlec neuer
mare ne mei lutli ne aliggen, for he ne alið neuer, ah liueð a in are, ant
al þet in him lið lesteð a mare.'

    'Let,' quoð Olibrius, 'Ne beoð þes wordes noht wurð! Ah an-hwet
wite þu—bute ȝif þu swike ham, mi swerd schal forswelten ant
25 forswolhen þi flesc, ant þerefter þine ban schulen beon forbernde o
berninde gleden. Ah ȝif þu wult leue me, þu schalt beon mi leofmon
ant min iweddede wif, ant welden ase lefdi al þet Ich i wald hah ant am
of lauerd.' | [20ᵛ

    'Ich ileue þe', quoð ha, 'wel of þine biheaste; ah haue þu hit ant ti
30 luue, for Ich habbe a leouere þet Ich nulle for nan leosen ne leauen. Þu
swenchest þe to swiþe, ant warpest—me is wa fore—awei þine hwile,
for al me is an', quoð ha, 'þin olhnung ant þin eie. | Ich wulle bitechen [21ʳ

5 seggen] segen B   6 ȝuheþe] guheþe B   8 iwurðen] iwurden B
10 him] B²R, *om.* B   11 þe] R, he þe B *corrected to* þe *by* B²   iseilet] R, iseiset B
11–12 to himseolf me] me to himseolf B, *corrected by* B², to him me seolf R
12 meiðhad] meidhad B   nanes weis] nansweis B   14 ut] B²R, *om.* B
18 buheð] buhed B   ant beieð] B²R, *om.* B   19 he is] B²R, *om.* B   lif for]
B²R, *om.* B   20 swote ... makelese] B²R, *om.* B   22 al ... lið] R,

time to consider how he might best corrupt her virginity; and then he continued his journey to Antioch and worshipped his heathen gods according to the rites of his evil faith.

The next day he ordered her brought before him. She was brought out at once, and he began by saying, 'Maiden, relent and take pity on yourself. Think of your youth and your comely figure, of your beautiful face. Do what I want and worship my idols and you shall be well rewarded, more than the highest in rank in my court, with all the possessions that I have in the world.'

Margaret, the gentlest and humblest of maidens, gave him this answer: 'Understand this now if you will—for he knows it well who has placed his own seal on me and my virginity—that you cannot in any way, by riches or pleasure, by pain or by hardship, or by any worldly thing, turn me aside out of the way that I have begun to walk in. And I want you to know that I scorn your words; for the only man I love and put my faith in is the one who rules and guides with his wisdom winds and tempests, and all that is encircled by sea and by sun. Both above and below, everything obeys him and does him homage. And not only is he so mighty and powerful, but he is the fairest of creatures to look at, and sweetest to smell; and neither his fragrance nor his almighty power nor his matchless beauty can ever grow less or come to an end, for he will never die, but always lives in glory, and all that belongs to him will last for ever.'

'Stop!' said Olibrius, 'What you say is worthless! But understand one thing: unless you renounce it, my sword will bite into your flesh and destroy it, and afterwards your bones will be burnt to ashes on burning coals. But if you will accept me, you will be my beloved and my wedded wife, and possess as its lady everything I own and rule over as lord.'

'I am sure', she said, 'that you mean to keep your promise; but you can keep it for yourself, and your love too, for I have a dearer lover I would not lose or leave for any other man. You are taking too much trouble, and—I am afraid—wasting your time, for your flattery and

---

his muchele mihte B   23 wurð] wurhð B   25 flesc] flecs B
29–32 Ich . . . eie] *entered by* B² *on slip of parchment (fo. 20b) pasted into MS; also* R *(with minor variants)*, 'Me, leoue,' quoð ha, 'hwarto luste þe warpen al awei þine hwile?' B
29 Ich] Ihc B²   30 habbe] habe B²   leouere] leoueuere B²   31 þine] þine þine B²   olhnung] olhnig B²

mi bodi to eauereuich bitternesse þet tu const on biþenchen, ne beo hit
neauer so derf to dreien ne to drehen, wið þon þet Ich mote meidene
mede habben in heouene. Drihtin deide for us, þe deorwurðe Lauerd,
ant ne drede Ich na deð for to drehen for him. He haueð his merke on
5 me iseiled wið his in-seil; ne mei vnc lif ne deð noþer twemen otwa.'
   'Na,' quoð he, 'is hit swa? | Neomeð hire swiðe,' quoð he to his [21ᵛ
cwelleres, 'Strupeð hire steort-naket ant hongeð hire on heh up, ant
beteð hire bere bodi wið bittere besmen.' Þa awariede wiðerlahen
leiden se luðerliche on hire leofliche lich þet hit brec oueral ant
10 liðerede o blode.
   Þet eadie meiden ahef hire heorte, heaued uppward to þe heouene,
ant feng on þeos bone: 'Lauerd, in þe is al min hope. Hald me mi wit
wel swa, ant mi wil, to þe, þet hit ne forwurðe naut for wa þet me do
me ne for wele nowþer; ne lef þu neuer mine fan—þe feondes, I
15 mene—habben ne holden hare hoker of me, as ha walden ȝef ha me
mahten awarpen—ah swa ne schulen ha neuer me ne nan oðer þet
ariht luuieð þe. Heouenliche Lauerd, þin nome beo iblescet. Lauerd,
loke to me ant haue merci of me; softe me mi sar swa ant salue mine
wunden þet hit ne seme nohwer, ne suteli o mi samblant, þet Ich derf
20 drehe.'
   Þe cwelleres leiden se luðerliche on hire lich þet tet blod bearst ut
ant strac adun of hire bodi as streem deð of welle. Olibrius þe luðere,
reue bute rewðe, hwil me ȝerdede hire þus ȝeomerliche, ȝeide:
'Stute nu ant stew þine unwitti wordes, ant hercne, meiden, mi read,
25 ant wel þe schal iwurðen'.
   Alle þe þear weren, wepmen ba ant wum|men, remden of reowðe [22ʳ
ant meanden þes meiden, ant summe of ham seiden: 'Margarete,
Margarete, meide swa muche wurð ȝef þu wel waldest, wa is us þet
we seoð þi softe leofliche lich toluken se ladliche! Weila, wummon,
30 hwuch wlite þu leosest ant forletest for þi misbileaue! Þe reue is
reowliche wrað, ant wule iwis fordo þe; ah luue nu ant lef him ant tu
schalt, wummone meast, wunne ant weole wealden.'
   'O,' quoð ha, 'wrecches, unweoten bute wit, weila, hwet wene ȝe?
Ȝef mi lich is toluken, mi sawle schal resten wið þe rihtwise; sorhe
35 ant licomes sar is sawulene heale. Ah leue ȝe, Ich reade ow, o þe
liuiende Godd, mihti ant meinful ant euch godes ful, þe hereð þeo þe

1–2 ne . . . drehen] R, ne bite hit ne se sare B   8 wiðerlahen] R, werlahen B
11 heaued . . . þe] R, heh up towart B   12 feng . . . bone] R, cleopede to Criste B
17 Heouenliche] he heouenliche B   23 ȝerdede] ȝerddede B
26 ba] R, *om.* B   33 ȝe] ge B   34 ȝef] Gef B   35 ȝe] ge B
36 Godd] Ȝodd B

threats' (she said) 'are all one to me. I will submit my body to every kind of suffering that you can contrive, however hard it may be to bear or endure, as long as I may have the reward that virgins receive in heaven. God died for us, the beloved Lord, and I am not afraid to suffer any kind of death for his sake. He has set his mark on me, sealed with his seal; and neither life nor death can divide us again.'

'No?' he said, 'Is that so? Take her at once,' he told his executioners. 'Strip her stark naked and hang her up high, and flog her bare body with biting rods.' The accursed villains laid on so violently that her fair skin was broken all over and streamed with blood.

That blessed maiden summoned up her courage, looking towards heaven, and began this prayer: 'Lord, in you is all my hope. Guard my reason well, and my will too, so that it does not weaken through any harm done to me, or any good either; and never let my enemies—the devils, I mean—hold me in contempt, as they would if they were able to overthrow me—but that they will never do to me or to anyone who truly loves you. Heavenly Lord, blessed be your name. Lord, protect me and have mercy on me; lighten my suffering and heal my wounds so it may not appear, or show on my face, that I feel any pain.'

The executioners laid on so cruelly that the blood burst out and ran down her body like a stream from a spring. While she was being so brutally beaten, the cruel Olibrius, the merciless governor, called out to her, 'Now stop saying such foolish things, and listen to me, maiden, and you will be rewarded.'

All those who were there, both men and women, wept for compassion and pitied this maiden, and some of them said: 'Margaret, Margaret, maiden who might be worth so much if you wanted to be, we are sorry to see your soft, lovely body so cruelly torn to pieces! Alas, woman, what beauty you are throwing away because of your false faith! The prefect is dreadfully angry, and will surely have you killed; but if you give him your love now and accept his hand you will live in prosperity, the noblest of women.'

'Oh!' she said, 'wretches, you senseless fools, what do you expect? If my body is torn apart, my soul will be at peace among the righteous; through sorrow and bodily pain, souls are saved. But take my advice and put your trust in the living God, mighty and powerful and full of all

him cleopieð to, ant heouene-ӡetes openeð. For ow nulle Ich iheren,
ne heien nan of ower godes, þe dumbe beoð ant deaue, ant blinde ant
bute mihte, wið monnes hond imakede.

'Ah þu wurchest', quoð ha þa to Olibrium þe luðere, 'þine feader
5 werkes, þe feondes of helle. Me, þu heaðene hund, þe hehe Healent is
min help; ant ӡef he haueð iӡettet te mi licome to teluken, he wule,
þu heatele reue, arudde mi sawle ut of þine honden ant heouen hire
into heouene, þah þu hongi me her. Ant tu, grisliche gra, þu luðere
liun lað Godd, þi mihte schal unmutlin ant melten to riht noht, ant tu
10 schalt eauer i sar | ant i sorhe swelten, hwen Ich gomeni wið Godd ant [22
gleadie buten ende.'

He o wraððe warð forneh ut of his witte; ant het swiðe bitterliche
hongin hire ant heouen up herre þen ha ear wes, ant wið sweord
scharpe ant ewles of irne hire freoliche flesch toronden ant torenden.

15 Ant heo biseh on heh up, ant bigon to seggen: 'Helle-hundes,
Lauerd, habbet bitrummet me, ant hare read þet heaneð me haueð al
biset me; ah þu, hehe Healent, beo umbe me to helpen. Arude,
reowfule Godd, mi sawle of sweordes egge ant of hundes hond, for
nabbe Ich bute hire ane. Lowse me, Lauerd, ut of þe liunes muð, ant
20 mi meoke mildschipe of þe an-ihurnde hornes. Glede me, Godd, wið
þi gleo ant ӡef me hope of heale, þet mi bone mote þurh-þurli þe
heouene. Send me þi sonde i culurene heowe, þe cume me to helpe,
þet Ich mi meiðhad mote wite to þe unwemmet; ant lef me ӡet iseon,
Lauerd, ӡef þi wil is, þe awariede wiht þe weorreð aӡein me; ant cuð
25 þi mahte on me, almihti Godd, þet Ich him ouercume mahe, swa þet
alle meidnes eauer mare þurh me þe mare trusten on þe. Beo þi nome
iblescet, alre bleo brihtest, in alre worldene worlt, aa on ecnesse.
Amen.'

Hwil þet ha spec þus, me tolec hire swa þet te luðere | reue for þe [23
30 stronge rune of þe blodi stream, ne nan oðer þet ter wes, ne mahte
for muche grure lokin þiderwardes, ah hudden hare heafden þe
heardeste-iheortet under hare mantles for þet seorfule sar þet heo on
hire isehen.

ӡet spec ant seide Olibrius þe luðere: 'Hwet bihalt, meiden, þet tu
35 ne buhest to me, ne nult habbe milce ne merci of þe seoluen? ӡe, ne
felest tu þi flesch al tolimet ant toluken þurh þet Ich hit hate? Ah buh
nu ant bei to me ear þen þu deie o dreori deð ant derf; for ӡef þu ne

---

6 ant] R, *om.* B   9 liun] R, lim B   10 Godd] ӡodd B
18 hundes] hondes B   28 Amen] R, *om.* B   35 buhest] buest B

goodness, who listens to those who call on him, and opens heaven's gates. For I will not listen to you, or worship any of your gods, who are deaf and dumb, and blind and helpless, made by human hands.

'But you', she said then to the cruel Olibrius, 'are doing the work of your father, the Devil of hell. But, you heathen dog, the heavenly Saviour is my help; and if he has allowed you to destroy my body, he will rescue my soul, you cruel governor, out of your hands and raise it to heaven, though you may hang me here. And you, you loathsome fiend, you raging lion hateful to God, your power will diminish and dwindle to nothing, and you will suffer for ever in pain and misery while I rejoice with God in unending bliss.'

At this he was almost beside himself with fury; and angrily ordered that she should be suspended still higher than before, and that her fair flesh should be ripped and torn with a sharp sword and with hooks of iron.

And she looked upwards and began to speak: 'The hounds of hell, Lord, are all around me, and their malicious scheming has encompassed me completely; but may you, heavenly Saviour, make haste to help me. Merciful God, rescue my soul from the blade of the sword and the grip of the hounds, for it is all I have. Deliver me, Lord, from the lion's mouth, and my meek mildness from the unicorns' horns. Give me comfort, God, and hope of eternal life, so that my prayer may pierce the heavens. Send me your messenger in the shape of a dove to come to my help, so that I may preserve my virginity undefiled for you; and, Lord, if it is your will, let me see before I die the accursed creature who is attacking me; and show your power through me, almighty God, that I may overcome him, so that all virgins ever afterwards may put their trust in you more through me. Blessed be your name, whose beauty is brightest, world without end, for ever and ever. Amen.'

While she spoke, she was being so lacerated that neither the cruel governor nor anyone else there could bear to look at her, so great was their horror at the torrents of blood that streamed from her; but the hardest-hearted hid their faces under their cloaks because of the torments they saw her suffer.

The cruel Olibrius spoke to her again: 'Why is it, maiden, that you will not submit to me, or relent and take some pity on yourself? What, do you not feel your flesh all torn apart because of my orders? But submit now to me and do me homage before you die a cruel and painful death; because if you do not you will be put to the sword and

dest no, þu schalt swelten þurh sweord ant al beo limmel toloken; ant
þenne Ich wulle tellen, hwen þu al totoren art, in euchanes sihðe þe sit
nu ant sið þe, alle þine seonewen.'
'Me, heateliche hund,' quoð ha þa, 'þah þu al swa do, me ne
5 schendest tu nawt. Hwen mi sawle bið biuoren Godes sihðe in
heouene, lutel me is hwet me do mid mi bodi on eorðe. Ah þe schulde
scheomien, þu scheomelese schucke—ʒef þu scheome cuðest—þe
þulli mot haldest wið a ʒung meiden; ant spillest al þi hwile, ant ne
spedest nawiht. For ʒef Ich wrahte þe wil of þe flesch þet tu fearest al
10 as þu wult wið, mi sawle schulde sinken, alswa as þu schalt, to sorhen
in helle; ah for|þi Ich wulle wel þet mi flesch forfeare her, þet te softe [23]
Iesu cruni mi sawle i þe selhðen of heouene, ant efter Domesdei do
ham ba togederes, to weolen ant to eche wunnen þurhwuniende.'
He warð se wrað þet forneh wod he walde iwurðen. Bed bi liues
15 coste keasten hire i cwalmhus, ant swa me dude sone. Ant wes as þah
hit were þe seoueðe time of þe dei þet me droh hire þus into dorkest
wan ant wurst in to wunien; ant heo hef up hire hont ant blecede al
hire bodi wið þe taken of þe hali rode. As me reat hire inwart, ha bigon
to bidden þeos bone to ure Lauerd: 'Deorewurðe Drihtin, þah þine
20 domes dearne beon, alle ha beoð duhtie. Alle heouenliche þing, ant
heorðliche baþe, buheð þe ant beieð. Þu art hope ant help to alle þet te
herieð. Þu art foster ant feader to helplese children. Þu art iweddede
weole, ant widewene warant, ant meidenes mede. Þu art wunne of þe
world, Iesu Crist, kine-bern: Godd ikennet of Godd, as liht is of
25 leome. Loke, Lauerd, to me, mi lif, mi luue, mi leofmon, ant milce
me, þi meiden. Min ahne flesliche feader dude ant draf me awei, his
anlepi dohter, ant mine freond aren me for þi luue, Lauerd, famen ant
feondes; ah þe Ich halde, Healent, ba for feader ant for freont. Ne
forlet tu me nawt, | liuiende Lauerd. Bihald me ant help me, ant lef me [24]
30 þet Ich mote legge mine ehnen o þe luðre unwiht þe weorreð aʒein
me, ant lef me deme wið him, Drihtin of dome. He heaneð me ant
heateð—ant Ich neauer nuste þet he ewt of min hearm eauerʒete
hefde. Ah swuch is his cunde, ant swa is ful of atter his ontfule heorte,
þet he heateð euch god; ant euch hali þing ant halewinde is him lað.
35 Þu art, Drihtin, domesmon of cwike ant of deade; dem bituhen unc

2 þenne] R, *om.* B   3 seonewen] seonewwen B   4 ne] R, *om.* B
9 al] R, *om.* B   11 te] R, *om.* B   13 togederes] toʒederes B
14 warð] R, *om.* B   17 wunien] R, cumene B   20 Alle[2] Þah alle B
22 iweddede] weddede B, iweddedes R   30 unwiht] unwhit B
34 heateð] heated B

torn limb from limb; and when you are torn to pieces, in the sight of everyone sitting here now I will count all your sinews.'

'But, you vicious dog,' she said to him then, 'even if you do all this, you do me no harm. When my soul is in heaven, in the sight of God, it matters little to me what may be done with my body on earth. But you ought to be ashamed, you shameless devil—if you could feel shame— to speak in this way to a young maiden; and are wasting your time and achieving nothing. For if I gave in to the desires of that body which is at your mercy, my soul would descend, just as you will, to the pains of hell; but I am very willing that my body should perish here, so that gentle Jesus may crown my soul among the joys of heaven, and after the day of Judgement bring them both together, to joy and eternal bliss lasting for ever.'

He became so angry he was half out of his mind. He commanded them on pain of death to cast her into prison, and this they did at once. And so she was taken, about the seventh hour of the day, down to the darkest and worst of the dungeons; and she raised up her hand and blessed her whole body with the sign of the holy cross. As she was dragged in, she began to say this prayer to our Lord: 'Dear Lord, although your judgements may be mysterious, they are all for the best. Everything in heaven, and on earth too, is obedient to you and pays you homage. You are the hope and help of all who honour you. You are foster-parent and father to helpless children. You are the delight of the married, the protector of widows, and the virgins' reward. You are the joy of the world, Jesus Christ, royal son: God begotten of God, as light is of light. Lord, watch over me, my life, my love, my lover, and have mercy on me, your maiden. My own natural father rejected me and drove me away, his only daughter, and my friends are my enemies and hostile towards me because of your love, Lord; but I see you, Saviour, as both father and friend. Do not abandon me, living Lord. Watch over me and help me, and grant it to me that I may lay my eyes on the wicked devil who is waging war against me, and let me speak with him, Lord of judgement. He humiliates and hates me—and I am not aware that he ever received any harm from me. But his nature is such, and his malignant heart so full of poison, that he hates every good; and every holy or wholesome thing is hateful to him. You, Lord, are the judge of living and dead; decide between us, and do not be angry at what I say,

twa, ne wraðþe þu þe, mi wunne, for sahe þet Ich segge. For an þing I biseche þe eauer ant oueral, þet tu wite to þe mi meiðhad unmerret, mi sawle from sunne, mi wit ant mi wisdom from unwitlese wiht. In þe is, min Healent, al þet Ich wilni. Beo þu aa iblescet, Ordfrume ant
5 Ende, bute ende ant ord, aa on ecnesse.'

Hire uostermoder wes an þet frourede hire, ant com to þe cwalmhus ant brohte hire to fode bred ant burnes drunch, þet ha bi liuede. Heo þa ant monie ma biheolden þurh an eilþurl as ha bed hire beoden; ant com ut of an hurne hihendliche towart hire an unwiht of helle on ane
10 drakes liche, se grislich þet ham gras wið þet sehen þet unselhðe, glistinde as þah he al ouerguld were. His lockes ant his longe berd blikeden al of golde, ant his grisliche teð semden of swart irn. His twa ehnen | steareden steappre þen þe steoren ant ten ȝimstanes, brade [24ᵛ ase bascins in his ihurnde heaued on eiðer half on his heh hokede
15 nease. Of his speatewile muð sperclede fur ut, ant of his nease-þurles þreste smorðrinde smoke, smeche forcuðest; ant lahte ut his tunge, se long þet he swong hire abuten his swire; ant semde as þah a scharp sweord of his muð scheate, þe glistnede ase gleam deð ant leitede al o leie; ant al warð þet stude ful of strong ant of stearc stench, ant of þes
20 schucke schadewe schimmede ant schan al.

He strahte him ant sturede toward tis meoke meiden, ant geapede wið his genow upon hire ungeinliche, ant bigon to crahien ant crenge wið swire, as þe þe hire walde forswolhe mid alle. Ȝef ha agrisen wes of þet grisliche gra, nes na muche wunder! Hire bleo bigon to blakien
25 for þe grure þet grap hire, ant for þe fearlac offruht, forȝet hire bone þet ha ibeden hefde, þet ha iseon moste þen unsehene unwiht, ne nawt ne þohte þron þet hire nu were ituðet hire bone; ah smat smeortliche adun hire cneon to þer eorðe, ant hef hire honden up hehe toward heouene, ant wið þeos bone to Crist þus cleopede: 'Unseheliche
30 Godd, euch godes ful, hwas wreaðde is se gromful þet helle ware ant heouenes, | ant alle cwike þinges, cwakieð þeraȝeines: aȝein þis [25ʳ eisfule wiht, þet hit ne eili me nawt, help me, mi Lauerd. Þu wrahtest ant wealdest alle worldliche þing. Þeo þet te heieð ant herieð in heouene ant alle þe þinges þe eardið on eorðe, þe fisches þe i þe
35 flodes fleoteð wið finnes, þe flihinde fuheles þe fleoð bi þe lufte, ant al þet iwraht is, wurcheð þet ti wil is ant halt þine heastes, bute mon ane. Þe sunne reccheð hire rune wiðuten euch reste; þe mone ant te

7 bi liuede] bileuide B, bilede R; *Mack, p. 65*   9 ane] ana B   16 smeche] smecche BR; *d'Ardenne, KG, p. 68*   29 ant] R, *om.* B   30 wreaððe] wreaððe B
32 wiht] whit B   Lauerd] la Lauerd B

my joy. For one thing I beseech you, always and everywhere, that you guard my virginity inviolate for yourself, my soul against sin, my reason and wisdom against senseless idols. In you, my Saviour, is all I desire. May you be blessed for ever, Beginning and End, without end or beginning, for all eternity.'

One of the people who cared for her was her foster-mother, who came to the dungeon and brought her food, the bread and spring water that kept her alive. Now this woman and many others were watching through a window as she said her prayers; and suddenly out of a corner there came towards her a fiend from hell in the form of a dragon, so dreadful they were aghast at the sight of that horror, glittering all over as if he had been gilded. His hair and his long beard shone with gold, and his grisly teeth were like dark iron. His eyes gleamed brighter than stars or jewels, broad as basins in his horned head on either side of his great hooked nose. Flames were flickering from his hideous mouth, and from his nostrils there streamed dense smoke, the foulest of vapours; and he thrust out his tongue, so long he could swing it around his neck; and it looked as if a sharp sword was coming from his mouth, flashing like lightning and sparkling with fire; and the place was filled with an overpowering stench, and shimmered in the demon's reflected glare.

He began to close in on this gentle maiden, and threateningly opened his jaws above her, and started to stretch and arch over his neck as if he were about to swallow her whole. If she was afraid of that hideous monster, it was hardly surprising! Her face grew pale with the terror that seized her, and she was so frightened she forgot the plea she had made before, to be granted a sight of her unseen foe, and it did not occur to her that her prayer was answered; but at once she fell to her knees on the ground, and raised her hands high towards heaven, and with this prayer she prayed to Christ: 'Invisible God, full of all goodness, whose wrath is so terrible that all the inhabitants of hell and heaven, and all living things, tremble before it: help me, my Lord, against this dreadful creature, so that it may not harm me. You created and govern everything on earth. Those who glorify and praise you in heaven and all the creatures that inhabit the earth, the fish that flash with fins through the sea, the birds that fly through the air above, and all creation, do what your will is and keep your commandments, all but mankind. The sun travels its course without any rest; the moon and the

steorren þe walkeð bi þe weolcne ne stutteð ne ne studegið, ah sturieð
aa mare, ne nohwider of þe wei þet tu hauest iwraht ham ne wrencheð
ha neaure. Þu steorest þe sea-strem, þet hit flede ne mot fir þen þu
merkedest. Þe windes, þe wederes, þe wudes ant te weattres buheð þe
5 ant beið. Feondes habbeð fearlac, ant engles, of þin eie. Þe wurmes
ant te wilde deor þet o þis wald wunieð libbet efter þe lahe þet tu ham
hauest iloket, luuewende Lauerd; ant tu loke to me ant help me, þin
hondiwerc, for al min hope is o þe. Þu herhedest helle ant ouercome
ase kempe þe acursede gast þe fundeð to fordo me. Ah her me nu ant
10 help me, for nabbe Ich i min nowcin nanes cunnes elne bute þin ane. Wið
þis uuel wite me, for Ich truste al o þe, ant ti wil iwurðe hit, deorwurðe
Lauerd, þet Ich þurh þi strengðe mahe stonden wið him, ant his
muchele ouergart þet Ich hit mote afeallen. Low, he fundeð swiðe | me |25'
to forswolhen, ant weneð to beore me into his balefule hole þer he
15 wuneð inne. Ah o þin blisfule nome Ich blesci me nuðe.'
	Ant droh þa endelong hire, ant þwertouer þrefter, þe deorewurðe
taken of þe deore rode þet he on reste. Ant te drake reasde to hire mit
tet ilke, ant sette his sariliche muð, ant unmeaðlich muchel, on heh on
hire heaued, ant rahte ut his tunge to þe ile of hire helen ant swengde
20 hire in ant forswelh into his wide wombe—ah Criste to wurðmund ant
him to wraðer heale. For þe rode-taken redliche arudde hire þet ha wes
wið iwepnet, ant warð his bone sone, swa þet his bodi tobearst
omidhepes otwa; ant þet eadi meiden allunge unmerret, wiðuten
eauereuch wem, wende ut of his wombe, heriende on heh hire Healent
25 in heouene.
	As ha biheold, lokinde upon hire riht half, þa seh ha hwer set an
unsehen unwiht, muche deale blackre þen eauer eani blamon, se
grislich, se ladlich, þet ne mahte hit na mon redliche areachen, ant his
twa honden to his cnurnede cneon heteueste ibunden. Ant heo, þa ha
30 seh þis, feng to þonkin þus ant herien hire Healent: | 'Brihtest bleo of |26'
alle þet eauer weren iborene, blostme iblowen ant iboren of meidenes
bosum, Iesu Godd, Godes bearn, iblescet ibeo þu. Ich am gomeful ant
glead, Lauerd, for þi godlec, keiser of kinges, Drihtin undeadlich. Þu
haldest ant heuest up treowe bileaue. Þu art welle of wisdom, ant euch
35 wunne waxeð ant awakeneð of þe. Þu art englene weole, þet wealdest
ant witest ham wiðuten wonunge. Me gomeneð ant gleadeð al of
gasteliche murhðen; me, mihti Godd makeles, is þet eani wunder? Ʒe,
iseo Ich, Lauerd, blowinde mine bileaue. Ich habbe isehen hu þe

stars moving through the sky never cease or stop but are constantly in motion, and they never turn aside from the track you have marked out for them. You guide the sea's current so it cannot overflow the bounds that you gave it. The winds, the storms, the woods and the waters are obedient to you and pay you homage. Devils fear your anger, and angels too. The snakes and the wild beasts that live in the woods follow the law that you have ordained for them, beloved Lord; protect me too and help me, the work of your hands, for all my hope is in you. You harrowed hell and overcame as champion the accursed spirit who is trying to destroy me. But hear me now and help me, for I have no strength to resist this suffering except for yours. Guard me against this evil, for my trust is all in you, and may it be your will, dear Lord, that I through your strength may stand against him, and that I may cast down his arrogant pride. Look! he is doing his best to devour me, and hopes to drag me down to the dreadful pit where he has his lair. But I cross myself now in your blessed name.'

And then she traced on her body, downwards and then across, the precious sign of the beloved cross that he was raised on. And the dragon rushed at her as she did this, and poised his hideous mouth, cavernously huge, high above her head, and stretched out his tongue to the soles of her feet and tossed her in, swallowing her into his monstrous belly—but to Christ's honour and his own destruction. For the sign of the cross that she was armed with swiftly set her free, and brought him sudden death, as his body burst in two in the middle; and that blessed maiden, completely unharmed, without a mark on her, walked out of his belly, praising aloud her Saviour in heaven.

As she looked round, she saw sitting on her right a different demon, much blacker than any black man, so grisly, so loathsome, that no one could easily find words to describe it, with both his hands tightly bound to his gnarled knees. And she, when she saw this, began to thank and praise her Saviour as follows: 'Fairest of all who were ever born, blossom in full flower, born from a maiden's womb, Jesus, God son of God, may you be blessed. I am full of joy, Lord, because of your goodness, emperor of kings, immortal Ruler. You sustain true faith and raise it up. You are the fount of wisdom, and every joy arises and originates from you. You are the delight of angels, ruling over them and guarding them unceasingly. I rejoice and exult in spiritual joys; but, matchless, mighty God, is that any wonder? Yes, Lord, I see the flowering of my faith. I have seen how the devil who thought he would

feond þe wende to fordo me tofeol efne atwa, ant felde hu his fule
stench strac ant sturede aweiwart. Ich habbe isehen þe wulf of helle
her awarpen ant te monslahe islein, þe stronge þurs astoruen. Ich
habbe isehen his ouergart ant his egede orhel earheliche auellet. Ich
5 habbe isehe þe rode þe arudde me se redliche of his reowliche rake, hu
ha þet balefule wurm ant þet bittre beast makede to bersten. Ich habbe
isehen hali ant halwende eoli as hit lihte to me, ant Ich me seolf smelle
of þe, swote Iesu, swottre þen eauer eani þing þet is on eorðe. Ich
habbe isehen blisse ant Ich blissi me þrof; i weole ant i wunne is nu þet
10 Ich wunie, ne nes me neauer se wa as me is wel nu. Þe Ich hit þoncki,
þolemode Lauerd. Ich habbe adun | þe drake idust ant his kenschipe [26
akest, ant he swelteð þet me wende to forswolhen; Ich am kempe ant
he is crauant ant ouercumen. Ah þe Ich þonki þrof, þe kingene king
art, echeliche icrunet, sorhfule ant sari ant sunfule toturn, wondrinde
15 ant wrecches ant wonlese wisent, castel of strengðe aʒein þe stronge
unwiht, meidenes murhðe ant martyrs crune, mel-seotel softest ant
guldene ʒerde, alre gold smeatest, ant glistinde ʒimstan; of alle
seheliche ant unseheliche ba swotest ant swetest; alre schefte
schuppent; þrumnesse þreouald ant anuald þe-hweðere, þrile i þreo
20 hades ant an in an hehschipe; heh hali Godd, euch godes ful, beo þu
eauer ant aa iheret ant iheiet bute linnunge.'
    As ha hefde iheret þus longe ure Lauerd, com þet grisliche gra
creopinde hire towart, ant heold hire bi þe uet, ant ase sorhfulest þing
sariliche seide: 'Marherete, meiden, inoh þu hauest ido me. Ne pine
25 þu me na mare wið þe eadie beoden þet tu biddest se ofte; for ha
bindeð me swiðe sare mid alle, ant makieð me se unstrong þet Ich ne
fele wið me nanes cunnes strengðe. Þu hauest grimliche ibroht mi
broðer to grunde ant islein þen sleheste deouel of helle, þe Ich o drake
liche sende to forswolhe þe ant merren | wið his muchele mein þe [27
30 mihte of þi meiðhad, ant makien þet tu nere na mare imong moncun
imuneget on eorðe. Þu cwenctest ant acwaldest him wið þe hali rode,
ant me þu makest to steoruen wið þe strengðe of þine beoden, þe beoð
þe se munde. Ah leaf me ant let me gan, leafdi, Ich þe bidde.'
    Þet milde meiden Margarete grap þet grisliche þing, þet hire ne
35 agras nawiht, ant heteueste toc him bi þet eateliche top ant hef him up
ant duste him dunriht to þer eorðe, ant sette hire riht fot on his ruhe

2 þe wulf of helle] þe wurse of helle B, þene þurs of helle, helles wulf R
9 isehen] sehen B   16 murhðe] murhde B   20 Godd] Godð B
21 linnunge] *lacks one minim in* B   25 biddest] R, bidest B
30 meiðhad] meidhad B   33 leaf] R, lef B   34 Margarete] Margarte B

destroy me fell to the ground, torn quite in two, and felt how his foul stench rolled away. I have seen the wolf of hell overthrown here and the murderer slaughtered, the mighty demon destroyed. I have seen his arrogance and his foolish pride shamefully laid low. I have seen the cross which saved me so swiftly from his dreadful jaws, and how it made the dragon, that fierce and savage beast, burst asunder. I have seen holy and healing oil as it descended to me, and I myself share your fragrance, sweet Jesus, sweeter than anything that there is on earth. I have seen bliss, and so I am blissful; my dwelling-place now is in joy and delight, and I was never so unhappy as I am happy now. It is you that I thank for this, long-suffering Lord. I have cast down the dragon and dashed his courage, and he who thought to devour me is dying himself; I am the victor and he is defeated and vanquished. But it is you that I thank for this, you who are king of kings, crowned for eternity, refuge of the sorrowful, the afflicted and sinful, guide to those who wander, the wretched and hopeless, castle of strength against the powerful Devil, virgins' joy and martyrs' crown, softest seat at the feast and golden rod, the purest gold of all, and glittering jewel; at once the sweetest and most fragrant of all things visible and invisible; creator of all creatures; trinity, threefold and none the less one, triple in three persons and single in one glory; high, holy God, full of all goodness, may you be praised and honoured unceasingly for ever and ever.'

When she had praised our Lord for so long, that hideous monster came creeping towards her and grasped her by the feet, and, looking most abject, plaintively said: 'Margaret, maiden, you have done enough to me. Do not torture me any more with the blessed prayers that you say so often; for all in all they bind me most painfully, and make me so weak that I cannot summon up any kind of strength. You have overthrown my brother most terribly and killed the most cunning devil in hell, whom I sent to devour you in the form of a dragon and attack with his great power the virtue of your virginity, and make sure that your memory would not be kept alive among mankind on earth. You defeated and destroyed him with the holy cross, and are killing me too with the power of the prayers which are so often on your lips. But leave me and let me go, lady, I beg you.'

The gentle maiden Margaret seized that frightful creature, who frightened her not at all, and grasped him firmly by his hideous hair and swung him upwards and threw him down again straight to the ground, and set her right foot on his rough neck and addressed him as

swire ant feng on þus to speokene: 'Stute nu, earme steorue, ant swic
nuðe lanhure, swikele swarte deouel, þet tu ne derue me nawt mare for
mi meiðhad; ne helpeð þe nawiht, for Ich habbe to help min Healent
in heouene, ant te worldes wealdent is ihwer mi warant. Þah þu strong
5 were þa þu weorredest me, he wes muchele strengre þe hefde to biwite
me.' Wið þis, þa þudde ha o þe þurs feste wið hire fot wið euchan of
þeose word: 'Stute nu, uuele gast, to gremie me mare. Stute nu, alde
monslahe, þet tu ne slea heonneuorð Cristes icorene. Stute nu,
wleatewile wiht, to astenche me wið þe stench þe of þi muð stiheð. Ich
10 am mi Lauerdes lomb, ant he is min hirde. Ich am Godes þeowe ant
his þrel to don al þet his deore wil | is. Beo he aa iblescet þet bliðe [27ᵛ
haueð imaked me in endelese blissen.'

Hwil þet ha spec þus o þet speatewile wiht, se þer lihtinde com into
þe cwalmhus a leome from heouene; and semde as þah ha sehe i þe
15 glistende glem þe deorewurðe rode reache to þe heouene; ant set a
culure þron ant þus to hire cleopede: 'Meiden eadi an, Margarete, art
tu, for Paraise ȝeten aren ȝarowe iopenet te nu.' Ant heo leat lahe to
hire leoue Lauerd, ant þonkede him ȝeorne wið inwarde heorte.

Þet liht alei lutlen, ant heo biturde hire þa ant cweð to þet unwiht.
20 'Cuð me', quoð ha, 'swiðe, forcuðest alre þinge, of hweat cunde þu
beo.'

'Leafdi,' quoð he, 'leowse þi fot þenne of mi necke ant swa lanhure
leoþe me, meiden an eadiest, þet Ich eðie mahe; ant Ich mot nede—
noðeles min unwilles hit is—don þet ti wil is.'

25 Þe milde meiden dude swa: lowsede ant leoðede a lutel hire hele,
ant he bigon to breoken on speatewilliche þus to speokene: 'Wult tu
witen, lufsume leafdi, hu Ich hatte? Ah hwet se of mi nome beo, Ich
habbe efter Belzebub meast monnes bone ibeon, ant forswolhen hare
swinc, ant to aswinden imaket þe meden þet ha moni ȝer hefden ham
30 iȝarket wið sum of mi|ne wiheles, þet Ich wrencte ham adun hwen ha [28ʳ
lest wenden; ne neauer ȝet ne mahte me ouercume na mon bute þu
nuþe. Þu haldest me i bondes, ant hauest her iblend me; ant art mi
broðeres bone, Rufines þe rehest ant te readwisest of alle þeo in helle.
Crist wuneð in þe, forþi þu wurchest wið us al þet ti wil is. Ne nawt
35 nart tu, wummon, oþre wummen ilich. Me þuncheð þet tu schinest
schenre þen þe sunne; ah ouer alle þine limen þe leitið of leome, þe
fingres se freoliche me þuncheð, ant se feire, ant se briht blikinde, þet

6 wið³] wid B   8 monslahe] monslae B   heonneuorð] heonneuord B
19 unwiht] unwhit B   20 forcuðest] forcudest B   33 rehest] R, rehe B
34 wuneð] wuned B   37 feire] R, freoliche feire B

follows: 'Now stop it, you wretched and pestilent creature; it is high time you gave up tormenting me, you treacherous black devil, because of my virginity; it does you no good, for I have my Saviour in heaven to help me, and the ruler of the world will protect me everywhere. Although you were strong when you made your assault on me, he who had me in his charge was stronger by far.' With this, she stamped hard with her foot on the demon at every sentence: 'Now stop disturbing me, you evil spirit. Now stop attacking Christ's chosen ones, you age-old murderer. Now stop stifling me, you disgusting creature, with the stench of your breath. I am my Lord's lamb, and he is my shepherd. I am God's handmaid and his servant to do everything that is his dear will. May he always be blessed who has made me happy in endless bliss.'

While she spoke in this way to the horrible creature, a light from heaven descended into the dungeon; and she seemed to see in the dazzling brightness the precious cross reaching to heaven; and a dove perched on it and said these words to her: 'Margaret, you are a blessed maiden, for now the gates of Paradise are opened ready for you.' And she bowed low to her beloved Lord, and thanked him earnestly in her inmost heart.

The light dimmed a little, and then she turned round and spoke to the demon. 'Tell me at once,' she said, 'foulest of all things, what your nature is.'

'Lady,' he said, 'then lift your foot from my neck, and at least take the weight off me, most blessed maiden, so I can breathe; and I will be forced—though much against my will—to do what you want.'

The gentle maiden did this; she raised her heel and relaxed it a little, and he began to speak in his uncouth way: 'Do you want to know, lovely lady, what my name is? But no matter what it is, I have been the destruction of more men than anyone but Beelzebub himself, and eaten up their labours, and caused the rewards they had prepared for themselves over many years to vanish completely through some of my wiles, pulling them down when they least expected it; and no one was ever able to overcome me yet except for you now. You are holding me in bonds, and have blinded me here; and have killed my brother Ruffin, the fiercest and most crafty of all those in hell. Christ is present in you, and so you do everything that you want with us. And you, woman, are not at all like other women. It seems to me you are shining brighter than the sun; but although all your body is radiant with light, more than anything else the fingers you used to bless yourself, and to

tu þe wið blescedest ant makedest te merke of þe mihti rode þe reauede
me mi broðer, ant me wið bale bondes bitterliche bindest, þet Ich lokin
ne mei, swa þet liht leomeð ant leiteð, me þuncheð.'

'Þu fikest,' quoð ha, 'ful wiht; ah cuð me þet Ich easki.'

5   'Wumme, leafdi!' quoð he þa, 'wa me mine liues, bute Ich hit am
þet weorri a wið rihtwise. Of þe unseli sunfule me þuncheð Ich am al
siker; ah þe gode Ich ga aa bisiliche abuten, ant ham Ich folhi
neodelukest þe cunnið to beon cleane wiðuten monnes man ant fleoð
flesches fulðen, ʒef Ich mahte eanies weis makien ham to fallen ant
10 fulen hamseoluen.

'Monie Ich habbe awarpen þe wenden mine wi|heles ful witerliche [28ᵛ
etwrenchen, ant o þisse wise. Ich leote oðerhwiles a cleane mon
wunien neh a cleane wummon, þet Ich nawiht towart ham ne warpe ne
ne weorri, ah leote ham al iwurðen. Ich leote ham talkin of Godd ant
15 teuelin of godlec, ant trewliche luuien ham wiðuten uuel wilnunge ant
alle unwreste willes, þet eiðer of his ahne, ant of þe oðres ba,
treowliche beo trusti, ant te sikerure beon to sitten bi hamseoluen ant
gomenin togederes. Þenne þurh þis sikerlec seche Ich earst upon ham,
ant scheote swiðe dearnliche ant wundi, ear ha witen hit, wið swiðe attri
20 healewi hare unwarre heorte. Lihtliche on alre earest, wið luueliche
lates, wið steape bihaldunge eiðer on oðer; ant wið plohe-speche
sputte to mare, se longe þet ha toggið ant tollið togederes. Þenne
þudde Ich in ham luuefule þohtes—on earest hare unþonkes, ah swa
waxeð þet wa þurh þet ha hit þeauieð þet ham þuncheð god þrof. Ant
25 Ich þus, hwen ha leoteð me, ne ne letteð me nawt ne ne steorið
hamseolf ne ne stondeð strongliche aʒein, leade ham i þe leiuen ant i
þe ladliche lake of þet suti sunne.

'ʒef ha edstonden wulleð mine unwreste wrenches ant mine
swikele swenges, wreastlin ha moten ant wiðerin wið hamseoluen; ne
30 me akeasten ha ne mahen ear ha | hamseoluen ouercumen. Lað me is [29
ant noðeles nedlunge Ich do hit, cuðe þe hu ha mahen best ouercume
me. Lowse me þe hwile, leafdi, ant leoðe me, ant Ich þe wile seggen.
Þis beoð þe wepnen þet me wurst wundið, ant witeð ham
unwemmet ant strengeð ham sterclukest aʒein me ant aʒein ham ant
35 hare wake lustes—þet beoð:—Eoten meaðeliche ant meaðeluker
drinken. Do þet flesh i sum derf, ne neauer ne beon idel. Hali monne

3 leomeð] leomed B   5 leafdi] leasdi B   9 fulðen] fulden B
13 nawiht] nawˈhiˈt B   18 gomenin] gominen B   togederes] toʒederes B
32 ant Ich . . . seggen] R, *om.* B   34 ham ant] R, *om.* B
35 meaðeliche] meokeliche BR

make the sign of the mighty cross that stole my brother from me, and to bind me cruelly with vicious bonds, seem to me so beautiful, so fair, and so dazzling that I cannot bear to look at them, so much that light seems to me to blaze and flash.'

'You are flattering me, demon,' she said, 'but answer my question.'

'Alas, lady!' he said then, 'I wish I may die if I am not the devil who makes war at all times against the righteous. It seems to me I am sure of the miserable sinners; but I am always busily prowling around the good, and the ones that I have to follow most closely are those who are trying to keep themselves chaste and untouched by men and flee carnal filth, to see if I might somehow cause them to fall and defile themselves.

'I have cast down many who thought they could wholly escape my schemes, and in this way. Sometimes I let a chaste man stay in the neighbourhood of a chaste woman, and do not attack them in any way at all, but leave them entirely to their own devices. I let them talk about God and discuss the nature of goodness, and love each other virtuously without illicit desire or any improper thoughts, so that each one is confident of his own feelings and the other person's too, and they feel all the safer sitting by themselves talking pleasantly together. Then through this security I make my first attack on them, and shoot very secretly and wound their unwary hearts, before they realize it, with a most venomous drug. Lightly at first, with loving looks, with gazing intently at one another; and I incite them to more through playful speech, until they are romping and wrestling together. Then I strike home with amorous thoughts—at first against their will, but when they tolerate it that evil grows so greatly that to them it seems good. And so, when they allow me to, and do not prevent me or control themselves or make strong resistance, I lead them into the mire and the loathsome slough of that filthy sin.

'If they want to resist my evil wiles and my treacherous ruses, they must wrestle with themselves and struggle inwardly; and they cannot cast me down before they conquer themselves. I hate doing this, but must do it all the same—tell you how best they can overcome me. Loosen my bonds in the mean time, lady, and relax your hold, and I will tell you. These are the weapons which wound me most, and protect them unhurt and support them most strongly against me and themselves and their base desires—that is:—Eating in moderation, and drinking still more moderately. Mortifying the flesh in some way

bone for ham, wið hare ahne; ant beodefule þohtes þet ha schulen
þenchen bimong hare benen, aȝein unwreste þohtes þet Ich in ham
þudde; þenchen hit is þurh me þet hare lust leadeð ham to wurche to
wundre; þenchen ȝef ha beieð me, to hu bitter beast ha buheð, ant
5 hwas luue ha forleteð; hu lufsum þing ha leoseð, þet is, wið meiðhad
meidenes menske, ant te luue of þe luueliche Lauerd of heouene ant
of þe lufsume cwen, englene leafdi; ant henlunges makieð ham wið al
þet heouenliche hird, ant unmenskið hamseolf bimong worldliche
men, ant forleoseð þe luue nawt ane of heh in heouene ah of lah ec on
10 eorðe, ant makieð þe engles murne ant us of muche murhðe to lahhe
se lude, þe seoð ham lihte se lah of se swiðe hehe, from þe heste in
heouene to þe laheste in helle. Þis ha moten ofte munien bi hamseolfen, | [29ᵛ

Þenchen hu swart þing ant suti is þet sunne;
Þenchen of helle-wa ant of heoueriche wunne;
15 Hare ahne deað ant Drihtenes munegin ful ilome,
Ant te grisle ant te grure þet bið et te dome;

þenchen þet te licunge of þet fleschliche lust alið se swiðe sone, ant te
pine þeruore leasteð aa mare. Ant sone se ha gulteð eawiht, gan anan
uorðriht þet ha ne firstin hit nawt to schawen hit i schrifte, ne beo hit
20 ne se lutel ne se liht sunne. For þet is under sunne þinge me laðest,
þet me ofte eorne to schrift of his sunne. For þet lutle Ich mei makien
to mutlin unmeaðliche ȝef me hut ant heleð hit; ah sone se hit
ischawet bið birewsinde i schrifte, þenne scheomeð me þerwið, ant
fleo ham from schuderinde as Ich ischend were.
25 'Þah se feor ant se forð ha mahen beon istopen in sotliche to luuien
þet nanes weis ne schulen ha stewen hare heorten, ne etstutten ne
etstonden þe strengðe of mine swenges hwil þet ha somet beoð. Ne nis
þear na bote bute fleo þenne, þet nowðer ne beo nohwer ane wið oðer,
ne seon ham ne sompnin ne sitten togederes wiðuten wittnesse þet
30 mahe iseon hweat ha don ant heren hwet ha seggen. Ȝef ha þus ne
letteð me | nawt, ah þeauieð me ant þolieð, ant weneð þah to [30ʳ
edwrenchen, Ich leade ham wið leas luue lutlen ant lutlen into se deop
dunge þet ha druncnið þerin; ant sperki in ham sperken of lustes se
luðere þet ha forberneð inwið ant þurh þet brune ablindeð, þet ha
35 nabbeð sihðe nan hamseolue to biseonne. Þet mein of hare heorte
mealteð þurh þe heate, ant forwurðeð hare wit ant woreð hare

---

1 ant] R, *om.* B   2 unwreste] R, hare unwerste B   9 ec] R, hec *added by*
later hand in B   31 nawt] R, *om.* B   35 nan] R, *om.* B
36 forwurðeð] forwurdeð B

or other, and never being idle. The prayers of holy men for them, as well as their own; and pious thoughts, which they should reflect on during their prayers, to counteract the evil thoughts that I assail them with; thinking that it is through me that their desire leads them to shameful actions; thinking what a vicious creature they are paying homage to if they submit to me, and whose love they are forsaking; what a desirable thing they are losing, that is, virginity and the honour due to it, and the love of the gracious Lord of heaven and his beloved queen, the lady of angels; how they make themselves contemptible to all the heavenly host, and dishonour themselves among earthly men, and lose the love not only of those who are high in heaven but of those too who live low on earth, and make the angels weep, and us laugh so loud out of sheer pleasure at seeing them fall so low from such a great height, from the highest in heaven to the lowest in hell. This is what they should often recall when alone,

> Thinking of sin's blackness, and how filthily it stains;
> Thinking of heaven and its joys, of hell and its pains;
> Thinking often how Jesus died, how their own lives slip away,
> And the horror and the terror there will be on Judgement Day;

thinking that the pleasure of that physical desire ends almost at once, and the punishment for it lasts for evermore. And as soon as they commit any kind of sin, they should go at once without any delay to reveal it in confession, however small or venial the sin may be. For that is what I hate most under the sun, people hurrying often to confess their sins. For I can make that small sin increase immoderately if they cover it up; but as soon as it is admitted with remorse in confession, then I am ashamed of it, and flee them in fear and trembling as if I had been disgraced.

'But they may be so far advanced in foolish love that they cannot by any means subdue their hearts, or counter or resist the strength of my blows while they are together. And the only remedy for this is running away, so that neither is anywhere alone with the other, and they never see or meet each other or sit together without a witness who can see what they are doing and hear what they say. If they do not stop me like this but tolerate my presence, and still hope to escape, I lead them through false love little by little into such deep mire that they drown in it; and kindle in them sparks of such evil desires that they are inwardly consumed and blinded by that blaze, so they no longer have the power to see what they are doing. Their moral courage melts away in the heat,

wisdom, swa þet nulleð ha nawt wite þet ha ahten to witen wel. Loke
nu hwuch wunder: ha beoð se cleane ouercumen, ant swa Ich habbe
iblent ham, þet ha blindlunge gað forð ant forseoð Godd ant
hamseoluen forȝeoteð, swa þet ha luðerliche, hwen ha lest weneð,
5 ferliche falleð fule ant fenniliche i flescliche fulðen; ant for a lust þet
alið in an hondhwile, leoseð ba þe luue of Godd ant te worldes
wurðschipe.

'Ah þeo þe stealewurðe beoð ant sterke toȝein me, swa þet ha ham
wið me ant mine wrenches wecchinde werien, se uuel me þuncheð
10 þrof þet al Ich am dreori aþet ha beon þurh me sumdel ideruet, ant am
in hare beddes se bisi ham abuten þet summes weis ha schulen ham
slepinde sulen. Ah þe rode merke merreð me oueral, ant meast ed te
nuðe.'

Ant wið þis ilke bigon to ȝeien ant to ȝuren: 'Margarete, meiden,
15 to hwon schal Ich iwurðen? | Mine wepnen—wumme!—allunge aren [30
awarpen. Ȝet were hit þurh a mon—ah is þurh a meiden! Þis ȝet me
þuncheð wurst, þet al þet cun þet tu art icumen ant ikennet of beoð
alle in ure bondes, ant tu art edbroken ham—alre wundre meast, þet
tu þe ane hauest ouergan þi feader ant ti moder, meies ant mehes ba,
20 ant al þe ende þet tu ant heo habbeð in ieardet, ant Crist ane hauest
icoren to leofmon ant to lauerd. Beatest us ant bindest ant to deað
fordemest. Wei! wake beo we nu ant noht wurð mid alle, hwen a
meiden ure muchele ouergart þus auealleð.'

'Stew þe,' quoð ha, 'sari wiht, ant sei me hwer þu wunest meast; of
25 hwet cun þu art ikumen of, ant ti cunde, cuð me, ant þurh hwas heaste
heane ȝe hali men ant hearmið, ant weorrið hare werkes.'

'Ah sei me, seli meiden, hweonne is þe ilenet i þine leoðebeie limen
se stealewurðe strengðe? Of hwet cunde kimeð þe þi luue ant ti
bileaue, þet leið me se lahe? Cuð me nu ant ken me hwi þe worldes
30 wealdent wuneð, wummon, in þe, ant hu he com into þe, ant Ich
chulle makie þe war of alle mine wiheles.'

'Steu þe, steorue, still stille beo', quoð ha, 'of þin easkunge. Ȝe, nart
tu nawt wurðe, awariede ful wiht, to here mi steauene, ant hure to
understonden se dearne ant se derf þing of Godes dihel|nesse. Ah [31
35 hwet se Ich am ant hwuch se Ich am, þurh Godes grace Ich hit am—

---

1 ahten to] R, *om.* B   2 ha] R, ah B   7 wurðschipe] wurdschipe B
9 ant mine wrenches] R, *om.* B   12 slepinde] sclepinde B   12–13 ed te nuðe]
R, ed ten ende B   15 iwurðen] iwurden B   16 ȝet²] get B
22 ant] R, aſhl B   24 wiht] whit B   32 steorue] R, *om.* B

and their reason is weakened and their understanding troubled, so they refuse to recognize what they ought to know well. Now this is quite remarkable: they are so completely overcome, and I have so bemused them, that they press on blindly and pay no heed to God and forget themselves, so that in a shameful way, when they least expect it, they take a terrible fall into the foul and muddy mire of carnal filthiness; and, for a desire that is sated in a moment, lose both the love of God and honour in the world.

'But those who are valiant and strong against me, so that they are able to defend themselves vigilantly against me and my wiles—this seems to me so shameful that I am thoroughly unhappy until I have caused them some kind of harm, and I busy myself with them in their beds so that they may defile themselves in some way while sleeping. But the sign of the cross hinders me everywhere, and most of all now when it comes from you.'

And with this he began to cry out and howl: 'Margaret, maiden, what will become of me? My weapons—alas!—have all been overcome. Now if it had been a man—but it is by a maiden! And this seems worst to me, that all that race you came from and were born into are wholly in our bonds, and you have escaped from them—the greatest of all marvels, that you on your own have been able to surpass your father and your mother, both kinsmen and kinswomen, and the whole region that you and they were living in, and have chosen Christ alone as your lover and as lord. You beat us and bind us and condemn us to death. Alas! we are weak now and utterly helpless, when a maiden casts down our immense pride like this.'

'Be quiet,' she said, 'wretched creature, and tell me what places you frequent; let me know what race you come of, and your nature, and by whose command you are sent to persecute and harm holy men, and attack what they do.'

'But tell me, blessed maiden, where did you get the gift of such stalwart strength in your supple limbs? What is the source of your love and your faith, which lay me so low? Reveal to me now why the ruler of the world is present, woman, in you, and how he came into you, and I will explain to you all my wiles.'

'Be quiet,' she said, 'pestilent creature, and stop asking questions. Indeed you are not worthy, accursed devil, to hear my voice, let alone to understand such a secret and hidden part of the mysteries of God. But whoever I am and whatever I am, I am through the grace of God—

wilʒeoue unofseruet, þet he haueð me iʒettet, for to ʒelden hit
himseoluen. Ah swiðe cuð me ant ken þet Ich easki efter.'
'ʒe,' quoð he, 'Ich mot nede. Sathanas þe unseli, þe for his prude
of Parais lihte se lahe, he is keiser ant king, icrunet of us alle. Ant
5 hwerto schulde Ich telle þe ant wið talen tealen, lufsume leafdi, of ure
cunde ant ure cun, þet tu cost þe seolf iseon i Iames ant i Manbres
bokes ibreuet? Swuch fearlac Ich fele for sihðen þet Ich iseo Crist
seche to þe þet speoken I ne dear nawt, ah diueri ant dearie, drupest
alre þinge. Þah hwen þu wult witen, we liuieð bi þe lufte al þet measte
10 deal, eadi meiden, ant ure weies beoð abufen wið þe windes; ant beoð
aa wakere to wurchen al þet wa þet we eauer mahe moncun, ant mest
rihtwise men ant meidnes as þu art. For Iesu Crist, Godes bern, wes of
meiden iboren, ant þurh þe mihte of meiðhad wes moncun iborhen,
binumen ant bireauet us al þet we ahten. Nu þu wast, leafdi, þet tu
15 wite waldest: hwer we meast wunieð ant hwi we meast heaneð ant
heatieð þe meidnes. ʒet ʒef þu wite wult hwi we weorrið meast
rihtwise þeines, Ich þe onswerie: for onde þet et aa ant eauer ure
heorte. We witen | ha beoð iwrahte to stihen to þet stude þet we of [31ᵛ
feollen; ant us þuncheð hokerlich ant swiðe hofles þrof, swa þet teone
20 ontent us, ant we iwurðeð wode þurh þe grome þet us gromeð aa wið
þe gode—for þet is ure cunde, þet I þe schulde kennen: beon sorhful
ant sari for euch monnes selhðe, gomenin hwen he gulteð, ne neauer
mare ne beo gleade bute of uuel ane. Þis is ure cunde, makelese
meiden. Ah, deore Drihtines lomb, leoðe me a lutel, ant leowse, leafdi,
25 þi fot þe sit me se sare. Ich halsi þe o Godes half, heh heouenlich
Feader, ant o Iesues nome, his an sulliche Sune, þet mon ne wummon
ne mahe neauer mare heonneuorð warpe me heonne. Ah þu, brihte
burde, bind me on eorðe, ant ne warp þu me nawt neoðer into helle.
For Salomon þe wise, hwile he her wunede, bitunde us in a tunne; ant
30 comen Babilones men, ant wenden for te habben golthord ifunden, ant
tobreken þet feat; ant we forð ant fulden þa þe widnesse of þe worlde.'
'Stille beo þu, stille,' quoð ha, 'earmest alre steorue! Ne schalt tu,
alde schucke, motin wið me mare; ah flih, sorhfule feont, ut of min
ehsihðe, ant def þider as þu mon ne derue na mare.' Wið þet ilke þe
35 eorðe totweamde ant bitunde him, ant | he rarinde rad ruglunge into [32ʳ
helle.

1 unofseruet] unoseruet B   for to ʒelden] R, forʒelde B   6 Iames] Iamemes B
13 meiðhad] meidhad B   16 weorrið] weorið B   19 hofles] holes B
20 iwurðeð] iwurdeð B   32 steorue] R, þinge B   33 ut] R, *om.* B
34 ilke] illke B

a voluntary gift above my deserts, which he has granted to me so it should be restored to him. But tell me at once what I want to know.'

'Yes,' he said, 'I am forced to. The wicked Satan, who because of his pride fell so far down out of Paradise, is our emperor and king, crowned by us all. And what would be the point of describing to you, or speaking at length, beautiful lady, of our nature and our race, which you can see for yourself set down in the books of Jannes and Mambres? I feel such fear at the visions I see of Christ coming down to you that I dare not speak, but quake and tremble, completely overawed. But if you must know, we live in the air for the most part, blessed maiden, and the ways that we travel are up among the winds; and we are always on the watch to work all the harm we can to mankind, and especially the righteous and virgins like you. For Jesus Christ, son of God, was born of a virgin, and through the virtue of virginity mankind was saved, and all that we owned was taken away from us. Now you know, lady, what you wanted to know; what places we frequent, and why we persecute virgins and hate them most of all. But if you want to know why we wage war mainly against the righteous, this is my answer: through the envy that constantly gnaws at our hearts. We know they are created to ascend to that place that we ourselves fell from; and because that injury infuriates us so, this seems to us shameful and most unfair, and we are driven wild by the anger that we always feel against the good—for that is our nature, which I must reveal to you: to be full of regret when a man does well, rejoice when he sins, and never to be glad of anything but evil. This is our nature, matchless maiden. But, dear lamb of God, let go of me a little, and, lady, release your foot which is hurting me so much. I entreat you for the sake of God, the high heavenly Father, and in the name of Jesus, his wondrous only Son, that neither man nor woman at any time to come may cast me out of here. But, beautiful lady, bind me here on earth rather than casting me down into hell. For Solomon the wise, while he lived on earth, confined us in a jar; and the men of Babylon came, and thought they had discovered a hoard of gold, and broke the vessel to pieces; and we were let out, and then we overran all the wide world.'

'Be quiet!' she said, 'Quiet, you pestilent wretch! I will not allow you to argue with me any more, ancient demon; but flee, miserable fiend, out of my sight, and fall headlong to the place where you can do no more harm to anyone.' And as she spoke the earth split open and swallowed him, and he fell howling backwards into hell.

Ine marhen sende hise men Olibrius þe luðere to bringen hire
biuoren him; ant heo blescede hire ant com baldeliche forð. Striken
men þiderwart of eauereuch strete for to seo þet sorhe þet me walde
leggen on hire leofliche bodi ʒef ha to þe reues read ne buhe ne ne
5 beide.
'Meiden,' quoð he, 'Margarete, ʒet Ich bidde ant bodie þet tu
wurche mi wil ant wurðgi mine maumez, ant te tide ant te time schal
beon iblescet þet tu ibore were.'
'Nai,' quoð ha, 'ne kepe Ich nawt þet me blesci me swa. Ah hit were
10 þi gein ant ti god baðe þet tu þe geast unblescet efter blesceunge ga
ant heie Godd almihti, heh heouenliche Feader, ant his selcuðe Sune,
Iesu Crist, þet is soð mon ant Godd noðeletere. Ah þu witlese wiht
wurgest as þu art wurðe, blodles ant banles, dumbe ant deaue baðe;
ant ʒet tu wurchest wurse, for þe unsehene unwihtes wunieð ham
15 inwið, ant tu ase þine lauerdes luuest ham ant heiest.'
Him bigon to gremien, ant o grome gredde: 'Strupeð hire steort-
naket ant heoueð hire on heh up, swa þet ha hongi to mede of hire
hokeres, ant ontendeð hire bodi wið bearninde teaperes.'
Þe driueles unduhtie swa duden sone, þet te hude snawhwit
20 swartede as hit sner|cte, ant bearst on to bleinin as hit aras oueral; ant [32ᵛ]
hire leofliche lich reschte of þe leie, swa þet alle remden þet on hire
softe siden sehen þet rewðe. Ant heo bigon to bidden Dauiðes bone:
'Heh Healent Godd, wið þe halewende fur of þe Hali Gast, moncunne
froure, fure min heorte, ant let te lei of þi luue leiti i mine lenden.'
25 ʒet him cweð Olibrius, reuene luðerest, 'Lef, meiden, mi read;
wurch þet Ich wilni ear þen þu þet lif luðerliche lete.'
'Luðerliche Ich liuede', quoð ha, 'ʒef Ich þe ilefde. Ah ʒef Ich
þus deie, mi deað is deorewurðe, ant dure into eche liue. Þu
swenchest te swiðe ant ne spedest nawiht; ne mahtu ne þin unwiht
30 nawiht wurchen on me, meiden an þet Ich am, ah wergið ow seoluen.
Mi Lauerd haueð mine limen sunderliche iseilet, ant haueð to mi
ʒimstan þet Ich ʒettede him iʒarket ant iʒeue me kempene
crune.'
Þa warð he swiðe wod, ant bed o wreððe bringen forð a uetles ful of

10 gein] ʒein B   11 selcuðe] selcude B   12 Godd] Goð B
13 wurgest] R, wurchest B   23 moncunne] moncune B   24 fure] R, froure B
let] R, om. B   29 nawiht] nawhit B   29–30 ne mahtu . . . nawiht] R, for te B
30 wergið ow seoluen] R, wergest þe scoluen B   31 haueðⁱ] haued B

In the morning Olibrius the cruel dispatched his men to bring her before him; and she made the sign of the cross and came boldly out. People streamed in from every street to see the suffering that was to be inflicted on her lovely body if she did not submit to the prefect's wishes.

'Maiden,' he said, 'Margaret, once again I order and command you to do my will and worship my idols, and people will bless the day you were born.'

'No,' she said, 'I do not care for that kind of blessing. But it would profit you more, and be better for you too, if you who are unblessed should go in search of blessing and honour God almighty, the high heavenly Father, and his wondrous Son, Jesus Christ, who is true man and God nevertheless. But you are fit for nothing but to worship senseless idols, not made of flesh and blood, and dumb and deaf as well; and you do still worse, because they are haunted by invisible demons, and you give them adoration and praise them as your lords.'

He began to be angry, and furiously cried, 'Strip her stark naked and raise her up high, so she may hang as payment for her insults, and burn her body with lighted tapers.'

The wretched menials did so at once, so that the snow-white skin blackened as it was scorched, and broke into blisters as it swelled all over, and her beautiful body crackled in the flame, so that there was an outcry from all those who saw the pitiful injury to her soft sides. And she began to recite the prayer of David: 'High Saviour God, with the healing fire of the Holy Ghost, comfort of mankind, kindle my heart, and let the fire of your love burn in my loins.'

Olibrius, cruellest of governors, spoke once again: 'Listen to me, maiden; do what I wish rather than suffer a shameful death.'

'I would be living shamefully', she said, 'if I believed you. But if I die in this way, my death is worthwhile, and becomes the door to eternal life. You are taking much trouble and having no success; nor can you or your devils do anything to me, lone maiden as I am, but wear yourselves out. My Lord has put a seal on each of my limbs, and in return for the jewel that I gave to him has prepared and granted me a victor's crown.'

Then he became mad with fury, and angrily ordered that a vessel

weattre, ant binden hire baþe þe fet ant te honden, ant dusten to þe
grunde, þet ha deað drohe ant druncnede þerinne.

Me dude as he don het; ant heo biheold on heh up ant cleopede
towart heouene: 'Alre kingene king, brec mine bondes, þet Ich ant alle
5 þet soð hit heien þe ant herien. Þis weater mote iwurðe me wunsum
ant softe, ant lef me þet hit to me beo beað of blisse ant fulluht of
font-|stan, halhunge ant leome of echelich heale. Cume þe Hali Gast o [33
culures iliche, þe o þi blisfule nome blesci þeos weattres. Festne wið
fulluht mi sawle to þe seoluen, ant wið þes ilke weattres wesch me
10 wiðinnen, ant warp from me awei eauereuch sunne, ant bring me to þi
brihte bur, brudgume of wunne. Ich underuo her fulluht o deore
Drihtines nome, ant on his deorewurðe Sunes, ant o þes Hali Gastes;
on Godd i godlec ituinet ant untodealet.'

Nefde ha bute iseid swa, þet al þe eorðe ne bigon to cwakien ant to
15 cwauien. Ant com a culure beorinde, se briht as þah ha bearnde, a
guldene crune, ant sette hire o þet seli meidenes heaued. Wið þet ilke
breken ant bursten hire bendes; ant heo, ase schene ase schininde
sunne, wende up of þe weater, singinde a loft-song þet Dauið þe
witege wrahte feor þerbiuoren, Criste to wurðmunt. 'Mi lufsume
20 Lauerd,' quoð ha, 'he cuðeð ase king þet he rixleð ariht. Feierlec ant
strengðe beoð hise schrudes, ant igurd he is ham on, þet a cumeliche
fearen ant semliche sitten.'

'Cvm', quoð þe culure wið schilinde steuene, 'ant stih to þe wunne
ant to þe weole of heouene. Eadi were þu, meiden, þa þu chure
25 meiðhad, þe of alle mihtes is cwen; forþi þu schalt aa bruken in blisse
buten ende crunene brihtest.'

| O þet ilke time turden to ure Lauerd fif þusent men, ʒet wiðuten [33ᵛ
itald children ant wummen; ant alle weren ananriht, as þe reue het hit,
o Cristes kinewurðe nome hefdes bicoruen, in a burh of Armenie
30 Caplimet inempnet, alle heriende Godd wið up-aheue steuene, ant
stihen alle martyrs wið murhðe to heouene.

Þe reue rudnede al of grome se him gromede, ant warð swa wrað
ant swa awed þet he al o wodschipe demde hire to deaþe; ant het on
hot heorte þet me hire heued wið schimminde ant scharp sweord, wið
35 blikinde ant bitel brond, totweamde from þe bodie. Leiden honden on

2 deað] R, deah B   7 echelich] R, eche lif B   14 ha] R, om. B
eorðe] eorde B   15 beorinde] beornind B, beorninde R   19 wurðmunt]
wurdmunt B   20 cuðeð] cudeð B   31 murhðe] murhde B
32 warð] ward B   34 schimminde] lacks one minim in B   wið²] wid B

full of water should be brought out, and that she should be bound both hand and foot and thrown to the bottom, so she should suffer death and be drowned in its depths.

It was done as he ordered; and she looked up on high and cried to heaven:—'King of all kings, break my bonds, so that I and all who see it may praise and honour you. May this water become pleasant and mild to me, and grant that it may be for me a bath of bliss and baptism from the font, sanctification and light of eternal salvation. May the Holy Ghost come in the form of a dove to bless these waters in your blessed name. Secure my soul with baptism to yourself, and with the same waters wash me within, and cast out from me every kind of sin, so your bright bridal chamber may welcome me in. Here I receive baptism in the dear Lord's name, and in his precious Son's, and in the Holy Ghost's; one God in goodness, enclosed and undivided.'

She had only just said this when all the earth started to quake and tremble. And a dove came bearing a golden crown, as bright as if it burned, and settled on that blessed maiden's head. At this her bonds were broken and shattered; and she, as bright as the shining sun, came out of the water singing a song of praise that David the prophet composed long before, to the honour of Christ. 'My beloved Lord', she said, 'reveals as king that his rule is just. Beauty and strength are garments for him, and he is girded with them so that they may seem comely and sit well on him.'

'Come', said the dove in a ringing voice, 'and ascend to the joy and the bliss of heaven. You were blessed, maiden, when you chose virginity, which is queen of all virtues; therefore you shall enjoy for ever in endless bliss the brightest of crowns.'

At the time this happened five thousand men were converted to our Lord, and this not counting women and children; and all of them were, as the governor commanded, beheaded at once in Christ's royal name, in a city of Armenia called Caplimet, all honouring God with upraised voices, and all ascended as martyrs joyfully to heaven.

The governor reddened with the fury that he felt, and became so madly angry that, quite in a frenzy, he condemned her to death; and in the heat of passion ordered that her head should be severed from her body with a sharp and shining sword, with a bright and biting blade. Those who were ordered to laid hands on her, and bound

hire þeo þe ihaten weren, ant bunden hire þet tet blod bearst ut et te neiles, ant wiðute þe burh ledden to biheafdin.

'Meiden,' quoð Malcus, 'streche forð þet swire scharp sweord to underuon, for Ich mot þi bone beon, ant þet me is wa uore—ȝef Ich
5 mahte þerwið, for Ich iseo Godd seolf wið his eadie engles bitrumme þe abuten.'

'Abid me, þenne, broþer,' quoð ha, 'hwil þet Ich ibidde me, ant biteache him mi gast ant mi bodi baðe, to ro ant to reste.'

'Ibide þe,' quoð he, 'baldeliche hwil þe god likeð.'

10 Ant heo bigon on hire cneon for te cneolin adun, ant bliðe wið þeos bone ber on heh iheuen up honden towart heouene: | 'Drihtin, leodes [3ᵃ]
Lauerd, duhtie, þah ha dearne beon ant derue, þine domes. Me is nu deað idemet her, ant wið þe lif ilenet; þi milde milce Ich þonki hit. Þu folkes Feader of frumscheft, schuptest al þet ischepen is. Þu wisest
15 wurhte of alle, merkedest þe heouene ant mete wið þi strahte hond, ant wið þe icluhte þe eorðe; þu steoresmon of sea-stream, þu wissent ant wealdent of alle wiht þe iwrahte beoð, seheliche ant unsehene, buh þine earen, Healent Godd, ant bei to mine benen. Ich bidde ant biseche þe, þet art mi weole ant wunne, þet hwa se eauer boc writ of
20 mi liflade, oðer biȝet hit iwriten, oðer halt hit ant haueð oftest on honde, oðer hwa se hit eauer redeð oðer þene redere liðeliche lusteð, wealdent of heouene, wurðe ham alle sone hare sunnen forȝeuene. Hwa se on mi nome makeð chapele oðer chirche, oðer findeð in ham liht oðer lampe, þe leome ȝef him, Lauerd, ant ȝette him, of
25 heouene. I þet hus þer wummon pineð o childe, sone se ha munneð mi nome ant mi pine, Lauerd, hihendliche help hire ant her hire bene; ne i þe hus ne beo iboren na mislimet bearn, nowðer halt ne houeret, nowðer dumbe ne deaf ne ideruet of deofle. Ant hwa se eauer mi nome munegeð wið | muðe, luueliche Lauerd, et te leaste dom ales him from [3ᵇ]
30 deaðe.'

Wið þis þa þuhte hit as þah a þunre dunede; ant come a culure of heouene, se briht as þah ha bearnde, wið a rode leitinde of liht ant of leome, ant te meiden duuelunge feol dun to þer eorðe. Ant com þe culure ant ran hire ant rihte up wið þe rode, ant seide hire sweteliche
35 to, wið swotest a steauene: 'Eadi art tu, meiden, bimong alle wummen,

9 quoð he] R, *om.* B   12 þah] B *has* þet-*abbreviation instead of* þ
14 al] R, a B   21 liðeliche] R, bliðeliche B   24 him] ham BR
25 mi] R, þi B   26 Lauerd] Lauerd, Lauerd B   29 leaste] lelaste B
31–2 of heouene . . . bearnde] se briht as þah ha bearnde, of heouene B, briht as þah ha bernde, from heouene R

her so the blood burst out from her nails, and took her to be beheaded outside the city.

'Maiden,' said Malchus, 'stretch out your neck to receive the sharp sword, for I must be your murderer, and that distresses me—if I am allowed to strike the blow, for I see God himself with his blessed angels in a circle about you.'

'Wait for me, then, brother,' she said, 'while I say my prayers and commend my soul to him, and my body too, to rest and repose.'

'Pray freely', he said, 'for as long as it pleases you.'

And first of all she fell to her knees, then joyfully lifted her hands up to heaven as she said this prayer: 'God, Lord of men, mysterious though they may be, your judgements are just. Now a sentence of death has been passed on me here, and life with you granted; for this I give thanks to your gentle mercy. Father of men and the created world, you made all creation. You who are the wisest workman of all marked out and measured the heaven with your palm and the earth with your fist. You who direct the ocean, guide and ruler of all created things, visible and invisible, incline your ears, Saviour God, and accede to my prayers. I beg and beseech you, who are my bliss and joy, that whoever writes a book on my life, or acquires it when written, or whoever has it most often in hand, or whoever reads it aloud or with good will listens to the reader, may all have their sins forgiven at once, ruler of heaven. Whoever builds a chapel or church in my name, or provides for it any light or lamp, give him and grant him, Lord, the light of heaven. In the house where a woman is lying in labour, as soon as she recalls my name and my passion, Lord, make haste to help her and listen to her prayer; and may no deformed child be born in that house, neither lame nor hunchbacked, neither dumb nor deaf nor afflicted by the Devil. And whoever calls on my name aloud, gracious Lord, at the Last Judgement save him from death.'

At this there came what sounded like a clap of thunder; and a dove came down from heaven, as bright as if it burned, with a cross shining with light and radiance, and the maiden fell headlong down to the ground. And the dove came and touched her and raised her up with the cross, and said to her gently, with the sweetest of voices, 'You are blessed, maiden, among all women, you who have sought healing and

þet eoli halwende hauest, ant halsum, isoht efter, ant alle sunfule men imuneget i þine benen ant i þine eadie beoden. Bi me Seolf Ich swerie, ant bi min heouenlich hird, þet tine beoden beoð þe treoweliche ituðet, ant for alle þeo iherd þe þu uore ibeden hauest; ant muche
5 mare is iʒeuen to þeo þe munieð þi nome, ant iʒettet moni þing þet nu nis nawt imuneget. Ant hwer se eauer þi bodi oðer ei of þine ban beon, oðer boc of þi pine, cume þe sunfule mon ant legge his muð þerupon, Ich salui him his sunnen; ne ne schal nan unwiht wunien in þe wanes þer þi martyrdom is iwriten inne, ant alle of þe hus schulen
10 gleadien i Godes grið ant i gasteliche luue. Ant alle þe þe biddeð, to ʒarkin Ich ʒetti ham of hare bruchen bote. Ant tu art eadi ant te stude þet tu on restest, ant alle þeo þe þurh þe schulen turne to me. | [35
Cum nu, for Ich kepe þe, brud to þi brudgume. Cum, leof, to þi lif, for Ich copni þi cume. Brihtest bur abit te; leof, hihe þe to me. Cum nu to
15 mi kinedom, leaf þet leode se lah, ant tu schalt wealde wið me al þet Ich i wald ah.'

Þe steuene stutte ant heo stod up, alre burde bliðest, ant bigon to bidden þeo þe hire abuten weren ant hire deað biwopen þet ha schulde þolien. 'Leoteð nu ant leaueð', quoð ha, 'ower ladliche nurð,
20 ant gleadieð alle wið me þe me god unnen; for ʒe habbeð iherd, ʒef ʒe hercneden riht, hwet te hehe Healent haueð me bihaten. Ant as ʒe luuieð ow seolf, leofliche Ich ow leare þet ʒe habben mi nome muchel ine munde; for Ich chulle bidden for þeo bliðeliche in heouene þe ofte munneð mi nome ant munegeð on eorðe. Wið bliðe heorte
25 beoreð me genge for te herien þe king þet haueð icore me, worldes wurhte ant wealdent of alle iwrahte þinges. Þe Ich þonki þrof, þe Ich heie ant herie, heouenliche Healent. For þi deorewurðe nome Ich habbe idrohe nowcin, ant neome deað nuðe; ant tu nim me to þe, Godd, of al þet god is Ordfrume ant Ende. Beo þu aa iblescet, ant ti
30 blisfule Sune, Iesu Crist bi his nome, wið þe Hali Gast, þet glit of inc baðe: ʒe, þreo ant tah an, in hades totweamet, in | hehschipe [35ᵛ untodealet, iteit ant itunet, an Godd unagin. Wurðschipe ant wurðmunt wurðe to þe ane from worlde into worlde aa on ecnesse.'

Efter þeos bone þa beah ha þe swire, ant cweð to þe cwellere, 'Do
35 nu, broðer, hihendliche, þet te is ihaten.'

---

6 Ant] R, *om.* B   7 oðer] oder B   8 unwiht] unwhit B   9 hus] R, þus B
14 abit] abitd B   17 bliðest] blidest B   22 ʒe] ge B   24 mi] ni B
31 hehschipe] he hehschipe B   32 Wurðschipe] Wurdschipe B

wholesome oil, and remembered in your prayers and your blessed petitions all sinful men. I swear by my Self, and by my heavenly host, that your prayers have been faithfully granted to you, and heard on behalf of all those you have prayed for; and much more is given to those who commemorate your name, and many things granted which have not been mentioned here. And wherever your body may be, or any of your bones, or a book on your passion, if a sinful man comes and touches it with his lips, I will heal his sins for him; and no devil will remain within the walls where a written account of your martyrdom is kept, and everyone in the house will rejoice in the peace of God and in spiritual love. And as for all those who pray to you, I am ready to grant them remission of their sins. And you are blessed, and the spot you stand on, and all those who through you will turn to me. Come now, for I am waiting for you, bride to your bridegroom. Come, beloved, to your life; I long for you to come. The brightest chamber is ready; beloved, hasten to me. Come now to my kingdom, leave that lowly race, and you will rule with me all that I possess.'

The voice ceased, and she stood up, most joyful of maidens, and began to tell those who were standing around her and lamenting her death that they should be patient. 'Now leave off your dreadful outcry,' she said, 'and all those who wish me well rejoice with me; because you have heard, if you listened well, what the exalted Saviour has promised me. And as you love yourselves, I exhort you lovingly to have my name much in your thoughts; for I will pray gladly in heaven for those who often recall my name and remember it on earth. With joyful hearts accompany me to honour the king who has chosen me, maker of the world and ruler of all creation. It is you I thank for this, you that I praise and honour, heavenly Saviour. For your precious name I have suffered affliction, and now must endure death; and may you, God, take me to yourself, the Origin and End of all that is good. May you be always blessed, and your glorious Son, whose name is Jesus Christ, with the Holy Ghost, who proceeds from you both; yes, three and yet one, separate in persons, undivided in in glory, bound and enclosed together, one God without beginning. May there be honour and glory to you alone, world without end, always to eternity.'

After this prayer she bowed her neck and said to the executioner, 'Now, brother, quickly carry out your orders.'

'Nai,' quoð he, 'nulle Ich no, for Ich habbe iherd hu Drihtines deore muð haueð wið þe imotet.'

'Þu most', quoð þe meiden, 'nedunge don hit; for ȝef þu ne dest no, ne schalt tu habbe wið me dale in heoueriche.'

5 Ant he wið þet hef up hetelest alre wepne, ant smat smeortliche adun, þet te dunt defde in; ant þet scherpe sweord scher hire wið þe schuldren, ant sahede hire þurhut, ant te bodi beide ant beah to þer eorðe. Ant te gast ananriht steah up to þet istirrede bur, bliðe to heouene. He þe þene dunt ȝef ȝeide mit tet ilke, 'Drihtin, do me
10 merci ant milce of þis dede; of þis sunne, Lauerd, loke, me nu salue.' Ant feol of fearlac adun on hire riht halue.

Comen lihtinde þa þe engles of leome, ant seten ant sungen on hire bodi bilehwit, ant iblesceden hit. Þe feondes þe þer weren, deadliche idoruen, fengen to ȝeien: 'Margarete, meiden, leoðe nuðe lanhure
15 ant lowse ure bondes.' We beoð wel icnawen þet nis na lauerd bute Godd, þe þu on leuest. ' Turnden þa þurh þis to Crist swiðe monie; | [3●
ant comen dumbe ant deaue to hire bodi as hit lei, and botneden alle. Þe engles, as ha beren þe sawle in hare bearmes, sihen towart heouene, ant sungen ase ha stuhen up wið sweteste steuene: '*Sanctus,*
20 *sanctus, sanctus Dominus Deus Sabaot, et cetera.* Hali is, hali is þe Lauerd of heouenliche weordes; heouene is ful, ant eorðe, of þine wurðfule weolen. Alre wihte wealdent in hehnesse, heal us. Iblescet beo þe Bearnes cume þe com i Drihtines nome; heale in hehnesse!' Wið þet, þa bigunnen þe gastes of helle to þeoten ant to ȝellen. Ant tuhen alle
25 to hire bodi þe untrume weren, ant hefden hare heale.

Com Ich, Teochimus, ant toc hire leofliche lich, ant ber ant brohte hit aȝein into Antioches burh wið murðe unimete, ant dude hit i graue-stan in hire grandame hus, þe wes icleopet Clete. Ich ah wel to wite þis, for Ich, i pine of prisun þer ha wes iput in, font hire flutunge
30 ant fedde flesches fode; and Ich iseh hwer ha feaht wið þe ferliche feond, ant hire bonen þat ha bed wrat o boc-felle, ant hire liflade al lette don o leaue, ant sende hit soðliche iwriten wide ȝont te worlde.

Þus þe eadi meiden, Margarete bi nome, i þe moneð þet on ure ledene—þet is, ald Englis—is *Efterliðe* inempnet, ant *Iulius* o Latin, o

---

5 smeortliche] smeotliche B   6 ant] ant þet bodi beide ant B   7 schuldren] scluldren B   ant sahede . . . þurhut] R, *om.* B   ant te bodi . . . beah] R, ant ᵗte bodi¹ beah B   8 ananriht] R, *om.* B   10 nu] R, *om.* B   12 lihtinde] lihtinte B   33–4 on . . . is²] ure ledene, þet is ald Englis B, on ure ledene is—ald Englisch— R   34 *Iulius*] R, *Iulium* B

'No,' he said, 'I will not, because I have heard how God's beloved voice has spoken to you.'

'You have no choice', said the maiden, 'but to do it; because if you do not, you will not share with me in the kingdom of heaven.'

And then he lifted up the cruellest of all weapons, and struck sharply down, so that the blow sank in; and that sharp sword sheared into her flesh close to the shoulders, and cut right through her, and her body gave way and fell to the ground. And at once her soul joyfully ascended to that starry mansion, up towards heaven. Then the man who had struck the blow cried out: 'God, have mercy on me for this deed, and see to it, Lord, I am healed of this sin.' And he fell down out of fear at her right side.

Then the angels of light came down, and sat and sang over her innocent body, and gave it their blessing. The devils that were there, dreadfully distressed, began to cry out: 'Margaret, maiden, now at least let go and loosen our bonds. We have to confess that there is no Lord but the God you believe in.' Very many people were converted to Christ at the time through this; and the dumb and deaf came to her body as it lay, and all were healed. The angels, carrying her soul in their arms, ascended towards heaven, and sang as they rose up in most sweet voices: '*Holy, holy, holy Lord of Hosts, etc.* Holy, holy, is the Lord of heavenly hosts; heaven and earth are full of your glorious joys. Ruler of all creatures, in the height of heaven, heal us. Blessed be the coming of the Son who has come in the name of God; hosanna in the highest!' At this the hellish spirits began to howl and yell. And all those who were infirm made their way to her body, and received a cure.

I, Teochimus, came and took away her beautiful body, and brought it back again to the city of Antioch with great rejoicing, and laid it in a sarcophagus in the house of her grandmother, who was called Clete. Indeed I ought to know all this, for I, during the time of her sufferings in prison, supplied her with provisions and gave her the food for her bodily needs; and I saw where she fought with the dreadful demon, and wrote down on parchment the prayers that she said, and had her whole life set down in a book, and, when it was faithfully committed to writing, sent it out widely throughout the world.

So this blessed maiden, whose name was Margaret, on the twentieth day of the month that in our language—that is, old English—is called *Efterlithe*, and *Julius* in Latin, died a painful death, and departed from

þe twen|tuðe dei, deide wið tintrohe ant wende from þes weanen to lif [3❧
þet aa lesteð, to blisse bute balesið, to wunne buten euch wa.

Alle þeo þe þis iherd heorteliche habbeð, in ower beoden bliþeluker
munneð þis meiden, þet ha wið þe ilke bone þet ha bed on eorðe
5 bidde ȝet for ow i þe blisse of heouene,

Þear ha schineð seoueualt schenre þen þe sunne,
I sy ant i selhðe mare þen eani muð cuðen hit cunne,
Ant i þet englene hird singeð aa unsulet
Þet mon ne wummon ne mei þet his flesch-fulet;
10 Ant we bituhe þe engles, þurh hire erndunge,
Moten ȝet iseo hire ant heren hire singen.
Igret iwurðe Godd Feader, ant his Sune iseinet,
Þe Hali Gast iheiet, þeos þreo in an iþeinet

of engles ant of eorðmen wiðuten ende. Amen.

2 balesið] balesid B   4 ilke bone] R, bonen B   7 muð] mud B
8 Ant] An B, *om.* R

these sufferings to everlasting life, to bliss without misery, to joy untouched by grief.

All those who have gladly listened to this, remember this maiden more readily in your prayers, so that she, with the same prayer she prayed on earth, may still intercede for you in the bliss of heaven,

> Where seven times brighter than the sun she shines in blessedness,
> In joy and bliss much greater than any words might express,
> And in that host of angels sings always with the just,
> As no man or woman may whose flesh is fouled with lust,
> And through her intercession, among that heavenly throng
> We may yet stand to see her and listen to her song.
> May God the Father be magnified, and blessed be his Son,
> The Holy Ghost be glorified, and these three in one

served by angels and earthly men eternally. Amen.

Sawles Warde

I þe Feaderes ant i þe Sunes ant i þe Hali Gastes nome, | her
biginneð 'Sawles Warde'.

Si sciret paterfamilias qua hora fur uenturus esset, vigilaret utique et non sineret perfodi domum suam.

Ure Lauerd i þe Godspel leareð us ant teacheð þurh a forbisne hu
we ahen wearliche to biwiten us seoluen wið þe unwiht of helle, ant
5   wið his wernches. 'ʒef þe husebonde wiste', he seið, 'hwenne ant i
hwuch time þe þeof walde cume to his hus to breoken, he walde
wakien, ant nalde he nawt þolien þe þeof for te breoken hire.'
Þis hus þe ure Lauerd spekeð of is seolf þe mon. Inwið, þe monnes
wit i þis hus is þe huse-lauerd, ant te fulitohe wif mei beon Wil ihaten,
10 þet ga þet hus efter hire, ha diht hit al to wundre, bute Wit ase lauerd
chasti hire þe betere ant bineome hire ofte muchel of þet ha walde. Ant
tah walde al þet hird folhin hire oueral, ʒef Wit ne forbude ham, for
alle hit beoð untohene ant rechelese hinen, bute ʒef he ham rihte.
Ant hwucche beoð þeos hinen? Summe beoð wiðuten ant summe
15 wiðinnen. Þeo wiðuten beoð þe monnes fif wittes: sihðe ant herunge,
smechunge ant smeallunge ant euch limes felunge. Þeos beoð hinen
vnder Wit as under huse-lauerd, ant hwer se he is ʒemeles, nis hare
nan þe ne feareð ofte untoheliche ant gulteð ilome, oðer i fol semblant
oðer in vuel dede. Inwið beoð his hinen in se moni mislich þonc to
20 cwemen wel þe husewif aʒein Godes wille, ant swerieð sometreadliche
þet efter hire hit schal | gan. Þah we hit ne here nawt, we mahen felen
hare nurð ant hare untohe bere, aþet Wit cume forð ant ba wið eie ant
wið luue tuhte ham þe betere. Ne bið neauer his hus for þeos hinen
wel iwist, for hwon þet he slepe oðer ohwider fare from hame—þet is,
25 hwen mon forʒet his wit ant let ham iwurðen.
Ah ne bihoueð hit nawt þet tis hus beo irobbet, for þer is inne þe
tresor þet Godd ʒef himseolf fore, þet is, monnes sawle. For te
breoke þis hus efter þis tresor, þet Godd bohte mid his deað ant lette
lif o rode, is moni þeof abuten ba bi dei ant bi niht, vnseheliche gastes

Heading: biginneð] bigineð B   3 leareð ... teacheð] T, teacheð us B
3 forbisne] T, bisne B   5 þe husebonde] RT, þes lauerd B   i] RT, *om.* B
6 to breoken] T, *om.* B   7 ant] RT, ne B   10 þet²]RT, þe B
11 ofte muchel] T, muchel B, ofte R   12 þet] RT, hire B   ʒef] gef B
19 oðer] oder B   20 sometreadliche] sometreaðliche B   21 felen] RT,

The Custody of the Soul

In the name of the Father and of the Son and of the Holy Ghost, 'The Custody of the Soul' begins here.

If the head of the household knew at what time a thief would come, he would keep watch and not allow his house to be broken into.

Our Lord in the Gospel gives us instruction and teaching through a parable on how we should carefully guard ourselves against the Devil of hell and his wiles. 'If the head of the household knew', he says, 'when and at what time the thief would come to break into his house, he would keep watch, and would not allow the thief to break into it.'

The house which our Lord is talking about is man himself. Inside, man's reason is master in this house, and Will can be described as the unruly wife, who, if the household follows her lead, reduces it to chaos, unless Reason as master disciplines her better, and often deprives her of much she would like. And yet all that household would follow her in everything, if Reason did not forbid them, because they are all undisciplined and careless servants unless he corrects them.

And what are these servants? Some are outside and some are inside. The outer servants are man's five senses—sight and hearing, taste and smell, and sensation in every part of the body. These are subject to Reason, as the head of the household, and wherever he is negligent, there is not one of them who does not often behave in an unruly way and frequently offend, by an impudent manner or by criminal acts. His inner servants plot in all kinds of ways to please the housewife against God's will, and swear with one voice that things shall go as she wants them to. Although we do not hear it, we can feel their din and unruly disturbance, until Reason intervenes and, with both fear and love, disciplines them better. Because of these servants, his house will never be properly guarded if he falls asleep or travels anywhere away from home—that is, when man forgets his reason and lets them be.

But it is not right that this house should be robbed, for in it is the treasure for which God gave himself—that is, man's soul. There are many thieves—invisible spirits with all evil qualities—plotting day and night to break into this house after this treasure, which God bought with his death and for which he gave up his life on the cross; and

[?]iwelen B   22 Wit] RT, hit B   24 fare] R, fares T, *om.* B
27 tresor] RT, tre *at end of line* B   29 gastes] gasttes B

wið alle unwreaste þeawes; ant aȝein euch goa þeaw þe biwiteð i þis
hus Godes deore chatel vnder Wittes wissunge þet is huse-lauerd, is
eauer hire unþeaw for te sechen inȝong abute þe wahes to amurðrin
hire þrinne. Þet heaued þrof is þe feont, þe meistreð ham alle.
5 Aȝeines him ant his keis, þe husebonde—þet is, Wit—warneð his
hus þus. Vre Lauerd haueð ileanet him froure of his dehtren, þet beoð
to vnderstonden þe fowr heaued-þeawes. Þe earste is Warschipe
icleopet, ant te oþer is ihaten Gastelich Strengðe, ant te þridde is
Meað; Rihtwisnesse, þe feorðe.
10 Wit þe husbonde, Godes cunestable, cleopeð War|schipe forð ant [7.
makið hire durewart, þe warliche loki hwam ha leote in ant ut, ant of
feor bihalde alle þe cuminde, hwuch beo wurðe inȝong to habben
oðer beon bisteken þrute. Strengðe stont nest hire, þet ȝef ei wule in
Warschipes vnþonkes, warni Strengðe fore, þet is hire suster, ant heo
15 hit ut warpe. Þe þridde suster—þet is, Meað—hire he makeð meistre
ouer his willesfule hird þet we ear of speken, þet ha leare ham mete,
þet me meosure hat, þe middel of twa uueles (for þet is þeaw in euch
stude ant tuht for te halden) ant hateð ham alle þet nan of ham aȝein
hire nohwer wið vnmeað ne ga ouer mete. Þe feorðe suster,
20 Rihtwisnesse, sit on hest as deme, ant beateð þeo þe agulteð ant
cruneð þeo þe wel doð, ant demeð euchan his dom efter his rihte. For
dret of hire nimeð þis hird, euch efter þet he is, his warde to witene: þe
ehnen hare, þe muð his, þe earen hare, þe honden hare, ant euch
alswa of þe oþre wit, þet onont him ne schal nan unþeaw cumen in.
25 As þis is ido þus, ant is al stille þrinne, Warschipe, þet aa is waker, is
offearet lest sum fortruste him ant feole o slepe ant forȝeme his
warde, ant sent ham in a sonde þet ha wel cnaweð, of feorren icumen,
for te offearen þeo þe beoð | ouerhardi, ant þeo þe ȝemelese beoð [73
halden ham wakere. He is underuon in, ant swiðe bihalden of alle, for
30 lonc he is ant leane, ant his leor deaðlich ant blac ant elheowet, ant
euch her þuncheð þet stont in his heaued up. Warschipe hat him tellen
biuoren ham hwet he beo ant hweonene he come ant hwet he þer
seche.
'Ne mei Ich', he seið, 'nohwer speoken bute Ich habbe god lust.
35 Lustnið me þenne! Fearlac Ich hatte, ant am Deaðes sonde ant

---

2 chatel] R, castel B   16 hird] hirð B   20 agulteð] aȝulteð B
22 þis] RT, his B   hird] hirð B   his] RT, *om.* B   29 alle] RT, ham alle B
32 ham] RT, *om.* B   come] comme B

against every virtue keeping guard over God's precious property within this house under guidance from Reason, the head of the household, there is always the vice which is her opposite, seeking entry around the walls to murder her inside. The head of these vices is the fiend, who rules them all. Against him and his henchmen, the husband—that is, Reason—defends his house as follows. Our Lord has lent him the aid of his daughters, who are to be understood as the four cardinal virtues. The first is called Prudence, and the second has the name of Spiritual Fortitude, and the third is Temperance; Justice is the fourth.

Reason the husband, whom God has made the commander of this stronghold, calls out Prudence and makes her doorkeeper, so that she may keep a careful eye on those she allows to go in and out, and see from a distance all those approaching, and which of them deserves to be given admission, or to be locked out. Fortitude stands beside her, so that if anything attempts to get in against Prudence's will she can warn Fortitude (who is her sister), and she can throw it out. He makes the third sister—that is, Temperance—the director of his unruly household, which we mentioned before, to teach them moderation, which is called 'measure', the middle way between two evils (for that is a virtue in every case, and the right course to follow), and gives them all orders that none of them should ever defy her wishes and overstep the limit through lack of moderation. The fourth sister, Justice, sits as judge in the highest seat, and punishes those who offend and crowns those who do well, and gives everyone his judgement as he deserves. Out of fear of her every member of this household undertakes to keep watch according to his function: the eyes theirs, the mouth his, the ears theirs, the hands theirs, and also each one of the other senses, so that no vice should enter through his fault.

When this has been completed, and all is quiet inside, Prudence, who is always watchful, is afraid lest someone should grow over-confident and fall asleep and neglect his watch, and sends them in a messenger whom she knows well, who has come from far away, to frighten those who are too bold and encourage the careless to stay more alert. He is admitted, and much stared at by them all, as he is tall and thin, and his face is deathlike and pale and livid, and every hair in his head seems to be standing on end. Prudence instructs him to tell them publicly who he is and where he comes from, and what he is there for.

'I cannot speak anywhere', he says, 'unless I have full attention. So listen to me! I am called Fear, and am Death's messenger and the

Deaðes munegunge, ant am icumen biuore hire to warnin ow of hire
cume.'

Warschipe, þet best con bisetten hire wordes ant ec hire werkes,
spekeð for ham alle, ant freineð hweonene ant hwenne ha cume, ant
5 hwuch hird ha leade.

Fearlac hire ontswereð: 'Ich nat nawt þe time, for ha ne seide hit me
nawt; ah eauer lokið hwenne, for hire wune is to cumen bi stale,
ferliche ant unmundlunge, hwen me least weneð. Of hire hird þet tu
easkest, Ich þe ondswerie: ha lihteð hwer se ha eauer kimeð wið a
10 þusent deoflen, ant euchan bereð a gret boc al of sunnen iwriten wið
swarte smeale leattres, ant an unrude raketehe gledread of fure, for te
binden ant to drahen into inwarde helle hwuch se he mei preouin þurh
his boc, þet is on euch sunne enbre|uet, þet he wið wil oðer wið word [74
oðer wið werc wrahte in al his lifsiðe, bute þet he haueð ibet earþon
15 wið soð schrift ant wið deadbote.'

Ant Warschipe hire askeð: 'Hweonene cumest tu, Fearlac, Deaðes
munegunge?'

'Ich cume', he seið, 'of helle.'

'Of helle!' ha seið, Warschipe. 'Ant hauest tu isehen helle?'

20 'Ʒe,' seið Fearlac, 'witerliche, ofte ant ilome.'

'Nu,' seið þenne Warschipe, 'for þi trowðe treoweliche tele us
hwuch is helle, ant hwet tu hauest isehen þrin.'

'Ant Ich', he seið, Fearlac, 'o mi trowðe bluðeliche, nawt tah efter
þet hit is (for þet ne mei na tunge), ah efter þet Ich mei ant con,
25 þertowart Ich chulle reodien.

'Helle is wid wiðute met ant deop wiðute grunde; ful of brune
uneuenlich, for ne mei nan eorðlich fur euenin þertowart; ful of stench
unþolelich, for ne mahte in eorðe na cwic þing hit þolien; ful of sorhe
untalelich, for ne mei na muð for wrecchedom ne for wa rikenin hit ne
30 tellen. Se þicke is þrinne þe þosternesse þet me hire mei grapin. For
þet fur ne ʒeueð na liht, ah blent ham þe ehnen þe þer beoð wið a
smorðrinde smoke, smeche forcuðest. Ant tah i þet ilke swarte
þeosternesse swarte þinges ha iseoð: as deoflen þet ham meallið ant
derueð aa ant dreccheð wið alles cunnes pinen; ant iteilede draken,
35 grisliche ase deoflen, þe forswolheð ham ihal ant speoweð ham | eft ut [7.
biuoren ant bihinden, oðerhwile torendeð ham ant tocheoweð euch

4 hweonene ant hwenne] hweonene BR, hwenne T; *Dobson, Origins, p. 424*　　ha] T
(*corrected from* he), he B　　14 wrahte] wrahtte B　　24 tunge] tellen *interlined*
after tunge B　　26 wid] T, *om.* B　　36 tocheoweð] RT, tocheoweð ham B

remembrance of Death, and have come before her to warn you of her arrival.'

Prudence, who knows best how to order her words, and her actions too, speaks for them all, and asks where Death is coming from and when she is coming, and what kind of company it is that she leads.

Fear answers her: 'I do not know the time, as she did not tell me when it would be; but always watch out for it, because it is her habit to come by stealth, suddenly and unforeseen, when she is least expected. As for what you ask about her company, I will give you an answer: she descends wherever she comes with a thousand devils, and each one carries a great book written all over with sins in small black letters, and an enormous chain glowing red-hot, to bind and drag down into innermost hell whoever he is able to convict with his book, which contains a record of every sin which that man committed in thought, word, or deed throughout his life, unless he has atoned for it before that time with true confession and penance.'

And Prudence asks, 'Where do you come from, Fear, remembrance of Death?'

'I come', he says, 'from hell.'

'From hell!' says Prudence. 'And have you seen hell?'

'Yes, certainly,' says Fear, 'very often indeed.'

'Now,' says Prudence then, 'on your honour tell us truthfully what hell is like, and what you have seen there.'

And I will gladly,' says Fear, 'on my honour; not, however, as it is (because there is nobody who could describe that), but as far as I can I shall do my best.

'Hell is immeasurably wide and illimitably deep; full of incomparable burning, for no earthly fire can be compared with it; full of intolerable stench, for no living thing on earth could tolerate it; full of inexpressible suffering, for no one would be able, out of grief and distress, to describe or express it. The darkness there is so thick that it can be grasped. For that fire gives no light, but blinds the eyes of those who are there with a choking smoke, the foulest of fumes. And nevertheless in that black darkness they can see black things: such as devils who beat them and constantly afflict them with all kinds of torments; and dragons with tails, as dreadful as devils, which swallow them whole and vomit them out again before and behind, or at other

grot, ant heo eft iwurðeð hal to a swuch bale bute bote as ha ear weren. Ant ful wel ha iseoð, ham to grisle ant to grure ant to echen hare pine, þe laðe helle-wurmes, tadden ant froggen, þe freoteð ham ut te ehnen ant te nease-gristles; ant snikeð in ant ut neddren ant eauroskes, nawt
5 ilich þeose her ah hundret siðe grisluker, et muð ant et earen, ed ehnen ant ed neauele ant ed te breoste holke, as meaðen i forrotet flesch, eauerȝete þickest. Þer is remunge i þe brune ant toðes hechelunge i þe snawi weattres. Ferliche ha flutteð from þe heate into þe chele, ne neauer nuten ha of þeos twa hweðer ham þuncheð wurse,
10 for eiðer is unþolelich. Ant i þis ferliche mong, þe leatere þurh þe earre derueð þe mare. Þet fur ham forbearneð al to colen calde, þet pich ham forwalleð aðet ha beon formealte, ant eft acwikieð anan to drehen al þet ilke, ant muche deale wurse, a wiðuten ende. Ant tis ilke unhope is ham meast pine: þet nan naueð neauer mare hope of nan
15 acouerunge, ah aren sikere of euch uuel to þurhleasten i wa from world into worlde, aa on echnesse. Euch aþrusmeð oðer, ant euch is oðres pine, ant euchan heateð oðer, ant terteken himseoluen, as | þe [7. blake deouel; ant eauer se ha i þis world luueden ham mare, se ha þer heatieð ham swiðere, ant eiðer curseð oðer, ant fret of þe oðres earen
20 ant te nease alswa.

'Ich habbe bigunne to tellen of þing þet Ich ne mahte nawt bringe to ende, þah Ich hefde a þusent tungen of stele ant talde aðet ha weren alle forwerede. Ah þencheð nu herþurh hwuch þe measte pine beo: for þe alre leaste is se heard þet hefde a mon islein ba mi feader ant mi
25 moder ant al þe ende of mi cun, ant ido me seoluen al þe scheome ant te hearm þet cwic mon mahte þolien, ant Ich isehe þes mon i þe ilke leaste pine þet Ich iseh in helle, Ich walde, ȝef hit mahte beon, þolien her a þusent deaðes to arudden him ut þrof, swa is þe sihðe grislich ant reowðful to bihalden. For þah þer nere neauer nan oðer pine bute
30 to seon eauer þe unseli gastes ant hare grisliche schape, biseon on hare grimfule ant grurefule nebbes, ant heren hare rarunge, ant hu ha wið hokeres edwiteð ant upbreideð euchan his sunnen, þis schendlac ant te grure of ham were unimete pine, ant hure þolien ant abeoren hare unirude duntes wið mealles istelet, ant wið hare eawles gledreade hare
35 dustlunges as þah hit were a pilche-clut euchan towart oðer i misliche pinen.

1 grot] RT, greot B   17 terteken] T, *om*. B   22 ende] RT, eni ende B
24 alre leaste] T, leaste pine B   28 her] T, *om*. B   29 þer nere neauer] T,
neauer nere B   30 seon] RT, iseon B   32 schendlac] schenðlac B

times tear them to pieces and chew up every fragment; and then they are made whole again to face the same suffering, with no hope of remedy, that they went through before. And they see very clearly, to their horror and dismay, and to add to their pains, the hideous creeping things of hell, toads and frogs, which gnaw out their eyes and the gristle of their noses; and adders and water-frogs, not like those here but a hundred times loathsomer, crawl in and out through mouth and ears, through eyes and navel and the hollow of the chest, like maggots in rotten flesh, as thick as could be. There is wailing in the fire and gnashing of teeth in the icy waters. Suddenly they shift from the heat to the cold, and they never know which of the two seems worse to them, since either is unbearable. And in this dreadful exchange, each state gives more pain because of what went before. The fire consumes them down to cold ashes, they are boiled in the pitch till they melt away, and at once revived to suffer the same, and a great deal worse, for all eternity. And this very despair is their greatest torment: that none of them has hope of any recovery for evermore, but rather they are certain that all their suffering will still be as cruel, world without end, for ever and ever. Every one of them suffocates his neighbour, and each is the other's torment, and each detests his neighbour, and himself as well, like the black devil; and always the more they loved each other here in this world, the more they hate each other in the next, and each one curses the other, and gnaws off the other's ears, and the nose too.

'I have begun to tell of things I could not bring to any conclusion, even if I had a thousand tongues of steel and spoke until they were all worn out. But now imagine by this what the greatest torture must be: for the least of all is so cruel that, if a man had murdered both my father and my mother and every one of my family, and done to me myself all the shame and the harm that a living man might suffer, and I saw this man in the very least torture that I saw in hell, I would, if it were possible, suffer a thousand earthly deaths to free him from it, the sight is so terrible and pitiable to see. For even if there were never any other torment but constantly seeing the unholy spirits and their hideous shapes, looking at their savage and terrible faces, and hearing their roaring, and how they abuse and upbraid every man with insults for his sins, this shame and the horror of them would be infinite torture—let alone actually having to bear the heavy blows of their steel-bound clubs, and being tossed by them like a scrap of hide from one to another with red-hot flesh-hooks, into all kinds of torments.

'O helle, Deaðes hus, wununge of wanunge, of grure ant of granunge, heatel | ham ant heard, wan of alle wontreaðes, buri of bale [75] ant bold of eauereuch bitternesse, þu laðest lont of alle, þu dorc stude ifullet of alle dreorinesses, Ich cwakie of grisle ant of grure, ant euch
5 ban schekeð me ant euch her me rueð up of þi munegunge; for nis þer na steuene bituhhe þe fordemde bute "Wumme!" ant "Wa is *me*!" ant "Wa beo þe!" ant "Wa beo *þe*!" "Wa" ha ӡeieð ant wa ha habbeð, ne of al þet eauer wa is ne schal ham neauer wontin. Þe swuch wununge ofearneð for ei hwilinde blisse her o þisse worlde, wel were him ӡef
10 þet he neauer ibore nere.

'Bi þis ӡe mahen sumdel witen hwuch is helle; for þis Ich habbe þrin isehen ant þusent siðe wurse, ant from þeonne kimeð Deað wið a þusent deoflen hiderwart, as Ich seide, ant Ich com þus', quoð Fearlac, 'for te warnin ow fore ant tellen ow þeos tidinges.'
15 'Nu Lauerd Godd', quoð Warschipe, 'wardi us ant werie, ant rihte us ant reade hwet us beo to donne, ant we beon warre ant wakere to witen us on euch half under Godes wengen. Ӡef we wel werieð ant witeð ure hus, ant Godes deore tresor þet he haueð bitaht us, cume Deað hwen ha wule; ne þurue we nowðer beon ofdred for hire ne for
20 helle, for ure deað bið deore Godd, ant inӡong into heouene. Of þeos fikelinde world ne of hire fahe blisse ne neome we neauer ӡeme, for al þet is on eorðe nis bute as a schadewe, for al wurðeð | to noht bute [76] þet deore tresor, Godes deorewurðe feh, þet is us bitaht to witene. Ich habbe þeruore sar care, for Ich iseo', seið Warschipe, 'hu þe unwiht
25 wið his ferd ase liun iburst geað abuten ure hus, sechinde ӡeornliche hu he hit forswolhe. Ant tis Ich mei,' seið Warschipe, 'warnin ow of his lað, for his wrenches Ich con, ah Ich ne mei nawt aӡeines his strengðe.'

'Do nu,' quoð Strengðe, 'Warschipe suster, þet te limpet to þe, ant
30 warne us of his wiheles, for of al his strengðe ne drede we nawiht; for nis his strengðe noht wurð bute hwer se he ifindeð eðeliche ant wake, unwarnede ant unwepnede of treowe bileaue. Þe apostle seið, "Etstont þen feont, ant he flið ananriht." Schulde we þenne fleon him? Ӡe, nis Godd ure scheld? ant alle beoð ure wepnen of his deore grace,
35 ant Godd is on ure half ant stont bi us i fehte. Ӡef he schute towart me wið weole ant wunne of þe world, wið este of flesches lustes, of

---

11 þis²] T, iwis B   12 ant¹] T, a B   16 warre] RT, þe warre B
19 ha] RT, he B   21 fahe] RT, false B   24 unwiht] unwhiht B
25 geað] ӡeað B   27 for . . . con] T, ant for his wrenches B
32 ant unwepnede] T, *om.* B

'O hell, house of Death, habitation of lamentation, of horror and execration, harsh and hateful home and dwelling of all distresses, stronghold of sorrow and abode of every bitterness, most loathsome land of all, place of darkness and haunt of dreadful griefs, I tremble with terror and dread, and every bone shudders and every one of my hairs stands on end at your memory; for no words pass between the damned but "Woe is me!" and "Woe is *me!*" and "Woe to you!" and "Woe to *you!*" "Woe" they cry and woe they have, and shall never lack for anything that counts as woe. As for the man who earns such a home for any passing pleasure here in this world, it would be better for him if he had never been born.

'By this you may have some idea of what hell is like; because I have seen this there and a thousand times worse, and it is from there that Death is coming with a thousand devils in this direction, as I have said, and so I have come', says Fear, 'to warn you beforehand and tell you this news.'

'Now may the Lord God', says Prudence, 'guard and defend us, and guide and advise us on what we must do, and so may we be more alert and more watchful to protect ourselves on every side under God's wings. If we defend and protect our house well, and God's precious treasure which he has entrusted to us, let Death come when she will; we need not be afraid either of her or of hell, for our death will be precious to God, and our entrance into heaven. Let us not be concerned about this false world or its specious happiness, since everything on earth is only like a shadow, as all will come to nothing except that precious treasure, God's priceless property, which is entrusted to us to guard. I am very anxious about it,' says Prudence, 'because I see how the Devil with his army prowls around our house like a raging lion, seeking eagerly how he may devour it. And this I *can* do,' says Prudence, 'warn you against his hatred, since I know his wiles, but I can do nothing against his strength.'

'My sister Prudence,' Fortitude says, 'do now what you are meant to do, and warn us of his wiles, for we are not afraid of all his strength; for his strength is worth nothing except where he finds people frail and weak, without the defence or the weapons of true faith. The apostle says, "Withstand the fiend, and he will flee at once." Should we then flee from him? Why, is not God our shield? and all our weapons are from his precious grace, and God is on our side and stands by us in battle. If the Devil shoots at me with riches and worldly pleasure, with the gratification of physical desires, I might be troubled to some extent

þulliche nesche wepnen Ich mahte carien summes weis, ah ne mei me
na þing heardes offearen, ne nowcin ne na wone falsi min heorte ne
wursi mi bileaue towart him þet ʒeueð me alle mine strengðen.'
   'For ba me ah,' quoð Meað, 'ant for heart of nowcin ant for nesche
5 of wunne, dreden ant carien. For moni for to muchel heard of wa þet
he dreheð forʒet ure Lauerd; ant ma þah for nesche ant for flesches
licunge for|ʒemeð ham ofte. Bituhhen heard ant nesche, bituhhe wa [76ᵛ
of þis world ant to muche wunne, bituhhe muchel ant lutel, is in euch
worldlich þing þe middel wei guldene. ʒef we hire haldeð, þenne ga
10 we sikerliche, ne þerf us nowðer for Deað ne for deouel dreden. Hwet
se beo of heardes, ne drede Ich nawiht nesches, for ne mei me na
wunne ne na flesches licunge ne licomlich este bringe ouer þe middel
of mesure ant of mete.'
   Rihtwisnesse spekeð nu. 'Mi suster,' ha seið, 'Warschipe, þe haueð
15 wit ant schad bituhhe god ant uuel, ant wat hwet is in euch þing to
cheosen ant to schunien, readeð us ant leareð for te ʒeme lutel alle
fallinde þing, ant witen warliche þeo þe schulen a lesten. Ant seið, as
hwa soð seið, þet þurh unweotenesse ne mei ha nawt sunegin, ant tah
nis nawt siker of þe unwihtes strengðe, as þeo þe halt hire wac (þah ha
20 beo muche wurð at ure alre ehnen), ant demeð hire unmihti onont
hireseoluen to etstonden wið his turnes—ant deð ase þe wise. Mi
suster Strengðe is swiðe bald, ant seið þet nawiht heardes ne mei hire
offearen, ah þah ha ne trust nawt on hire ahne wepnen, ah deð o
Godes grace, ant þet Ich demi riht ant wisdom to donne. Mi þridde
25 suster, Meað, spekeð of þe middel sti bituhhe riht ant luft þet lut
cunnen halden, | ant seiþ i nesche ha is bald, ant heard mei hire [77ʳ
offearen, ant forþi ne ʒelpeð ha of na sikernesse; ant deð as þe wise.
Mi meoster is to do riht ant riht for te demen; ant Ich deme me seolf
þet Ich þurh me ne do hit nawt, for al þet god is of Godd þet we her
30 habbeð. Nu is riht, þenne, þet we demen us seolf eauer unmihtie to
werien ant to witen us oðer ei god to halden wiðute Godes helpe. Þe
rihtwise Godd wule þet we demen us seolf eðeliche ant lahe, ne beo
we neauer swucche, for þenne demeð he us muche wurð, ant gode, ant
halt for his dehtren. For þah mi forme suster war beo of euch uuel, ant
35 min oðer strong beo toʒeines euch nowcin, ant mi þridde meaðful in

---

4 nesche] T, wone B   11 me] T, *om.* B   12 bringe] T, bringe me B
middel] midel B   14 Rihtwisnesse] Rihtwissnesse B   18 hwa] ha BRT;
Dobson, Origins, p. 428   19 strengðe] strengde B   20 at] ant BT, to R:
Dobson, Origins, p. 428 ant] RT, *om.* B   28 ant riht for te] T, for te B, ant riht
fon ant R

by such soft weapons, but nothing hard can frighten me, and no suffering or want can make my heart false or lessen my faith in him who gives me all my powers.'

'People should be anxious and concerned about both,' Temperance says, 'the hardship of suffering and the softness of pleasure. For many forget our Lord because the misery they suffer is too hard to bear; and yet there are more who often go astray because of the softness of physical pleasure. Between hard and soft, between the misery of this world and too much pleasure, between too much and too little, in every worldly matter the middle way is golden. If we keep to it, then we can go in safety, and have no need to fear either Death or the Devil. Whatever there may be by way of hardship, I am not afraid of any kind of softness, for there is no joy or pleasure of the flesh or bodily delight which can lure me from the middle way of measure and moderation.'

Now Justice speaks. 'My sister Prudence,' she says, 'who discriminates by reason between good and evil, and knows in every case what is to be chosen and what is to be shunned, advises and teaches us to give little thought to all transitory things, and to guard carefully those which will last for ever. And she says—and truthfully—that she cannot sin through ignorance, but even so is unsure of herself when it comes to dealing with the Devil's strength, as she thinks herself weak (although we all see her as having great merit), and regards herself as not strong enough to stand firm on her own against his wiles—and in this she does wisely. My sister Fortitude is very courageous, and says that no hardship can make her afraid, but nevertheless she does not trust in her own weapons, but rather in God's grace, and that I judge right and wise to do. My third sister, Temperance, speaks of the middle way between right and left that few can keep to, and says that she is brave when it comes to softness, but hardship can frighten her, and therefore she does not boast of her security; and she does wisely. My occupation is to do what is right and to judge rightly; and in my judgement, I do not do this from my own resources, for all the virtue we have in this world comes from God. Now it is right, therefore, that we should always judge ourselves helpless to defend and protect ourselves or maintain any virtue without God's help. God, who is righteous, wishes that we should judge ourselves to be worthless and low, even if we are not, for then he judges us to be of great merit, and virtuous, and regards us as his daughters. For although my first sister may be wary of every evil, and my second may be strong against all adversity, and my

alles cunnes estes, ant Ich do riht ant deme, bute we wið al þis milde
beon ant meoke, ant halden us wake, Godd mei mid rihte fordemen us
of al þis þurh ure prude; ant forþi is riht dom þet we al ure god þonkin
him ane.'

5   Wit þe husebonde, Godes cunestable, hereð alle hare sahen ant
þonkeð God ʒeorne wið swiðe glead heorte of se riche lane as beoð
þeos sustren, his fowr dehtren, þet he haueð ileanet him on helpe for
te wite wel ant werien his castel, ant Godes deorewurðe feh þet is
biloke þrinne. Þe willesfule husewif halt hire al stille, ant al þet hird
10 þet ha wes iwunet to dreaien efter hire turneð | ham treowliche to Wit [77
hare lauerd ant to þeos fowr sustren.

    Vmben ane stunde spekeð eft Warschipe, ant seið: 'Ich iseo a sonde
cumen, swiðe glead-icheret, feier ant freolich ant leofliche aturnet.'

    'Let him in!' seið Wit. 'ʒef Godd wule, he bringeð us gleade
15 tidinges, ant þet us were muche neod, for Fearlac, Deaðes sonde,
haueð wið his offearet us swiðe mid alle.'

    Warschipe let him in, ant he gret Wit, þen lauerd, ant al þet hird
seoðen wið lahhinde chere, ant ha ʒeldeð him his gretunge ant beoð
alle ilihtet ant igleadet, ham þuncheð, of his onsihðe, for al þet hus
20 schineð ant schimmeð of his leome. He easkeð ʒef ham biluueð to
heren him ane hwile.

    'ʒe,' quoð ha, Rihtwisnesse, 'wel us biluueð hit, ant wel is riht þet
we þe liðeliche lustnin þet helden us swa stille hwil Fearlac us agrette.'

    'Hercnið nu þenne,' he seið, 'ant ʒeornliche understondeð. Ich am
25 Murðes sonde ant munegunge of eche lif, ant Liues Luue ihaten, ant
cume riht from heouene, þet Ich habbe isehen nu, ant ofte ear, þe
blisse þet na monnes tunge ne mei of tellen. Þe iblescede Godd iseh
ow offruhte ant sumdel drupnin of þet Fearlac talde of Deað ant of
helle, ant sende me to gleadien ow; nawt forþi þet hit ne beo al soð þet
30 he seide—ant þet schulen alle uuele fondin ant ifinden—ah ʒe, wið
þe fulst of Godd, ne þurue na þing dreden, for he sit on | heh þet is ow [78
on helpe, ant is Alwealdent þet haueð ow to witene.'

    'A!' seið Warschipe, 'welcume, Liues Luue, ant for þe luue of Godd
seolf, ʒef þu eauer sehe him tele us sumhwet of him ant of his eche
35 blisse.'

    'ʒe, i soð,' quoð Liues Luue, Murhðes sonde, 'Ich habbe isehen

10 treowliche] treowliliche B   20 easkeð] RT, easkeð ham B
23 þet helden . . . agrette] T, *om.* B   36 i soð] T, iseoð B   Murhðes] Murhdes B

third temperate in all kinds of pleasure, and I do right and judge, unless with all this we are mild and meek, and consider ourselves frail, God may rightly condemn us for all this because of our pride, and therefore it is just that we should give thanks to him alone for all our virtue.'

Reason the husband, whom God has made the commander of the stronghold, hears all their speeches and thanks God earnestly with a very glad heart for such a rich loan as these sisters are, the four daughters of God, whom he has lent him as a help to guard and defend his castle well, and God's precious treasure which is locked up inside. The wilful housewife remains quite silent, and all the household that she was used to attracting as followers transfer their loyalty to Reason their lord and to these four sisters.

After a while Prudence speaks again, and says: 'I see a messenger coming who looks very joyful, handsome and noble and finely dressed.'

'Let him in!' says Reason. 'If it is God's will, he brings us good news, and that we could do with, because Fear, Death's messenger, has frightened us terribly with the news he brought.'

Prudence lets him in, and he greets Reason, the lord, and then the whole household with a smiling countenance, and they return his greeting and are all cheered, and the very sight of him makes them feel happy, for all the house shines and shimmers with his radiance. He asks them if they would like to listen to him for a while.

'Yes,' says Justice, 'we would like it very much, and it is only right that we should listen to you courteously, since we kept so quiet while Fear was addressing us.'

'Now then, listen,' he says, 'and understand me well. I am the messenger of Joy and the remembrance of eternal life, and am called Love of Life, and come straight from heaven, where I have seen just now, and often before, the bliss that no man's tongue is able to tell. God, who is blessed, saw you afraid and rather downcast because of what Fear said about Death and hell, and sent me to cheer you; not because anything he said was not true—and that all the wicked will find out for themselves—but you, with the aid of God, need have no fear, for he who is your help sits on high, and it is the Almighty who has you in his keeping.'

'Ah!' says Prudence, 'welcome, Love of Life, and for the love of God himself, if ever you saw him tell us something about him and his eternal bliss.'

'Yes, certainly,' says Love of Life, the messenger of Joy, 'I have seen

him ofte, nawt tah alswa as he is—for aȝein þe brihtnesse ant te liht
of his leor þe sunne-gleam is dosc ant þuncheð a schadewe, ant forþi
ne mahte Ich nawt aȝein þe leome of his wlite lokin ne bihalden, bute
þurh a schene schawere bituhhe me ant him þet schilde mine ehnen.

5 Swa Ich habbe ofte isehen þe hali Þrumnesse, Feader ant Sune ant
Hali Gast, þreo an untodealt, ah lutle hwile Ich mahte þolie þe leome.
Ah summes weis Ich mahte bihalden ure Lauerd, Iesu Crist, Godes
Sune, þet bohte us o rode: hu he sit blisful on his Feader riht half þet
is alwealdent, rixleð i þet eche lif bute linnunge, se unimete feier þet te

10 engles ne beoð neauer ful on him to bihalden. Ant ȝet I seh etscene
þe studen of his wunden, ant hu he schaweð ham his Feader to cuðen
hu he luuede us ant hu he wes buhsum to him þe sende him swa to
alesen us, ant bisecheð him a for moncunnes heale.

'Efter him Ich iseh on heh ouer alle heouenliche wordes þe eadi

15 meiden, his moder, Marie inempnet, sitten in | a trone se swiðe brihte [78ᵛ]
wið ȝimmes istirret, ant hire wlite se weoleful, þet euch eorðlich liht
is þeoster þeraȝeines. Þear I seh as ha bit hire deorewurðe Sune se
ȝeornliche ant se inwardliche for þeo þet hire seruið, ant he hire
ȝetteð bliðeliche al þet ha bisecheð.

20 'Þet liht þa Ich ne mahte of hire na lengre þolien, Ich biseh to þe
engles ant to þe archangles ant to þe oðre þe beoð buuen ham,
iblescede gastes þe beoð a biuore Godd ant seruið him eauer, ant
singeð a unwerget. Nihe wordes þer beoð, ah hu ha beoð iordret ant
sunderliche isette, þe an buue þe oðre, ant euchanes meoster, were

25 long to tellen. Se muche murhðe Ich hefde on hare onsihðe þet ne
mahte Ich longe hwile elleshwider lokin.

'Efter ham Ich iseh towart te patriarches ant te prophetes, þe makieð
swuch murhðe þet ha aren nuðe i þet ilke lont of blisse þet ha hefden
of feor igret ear on eorðe, ant seoð nu al isoðet þet ha hefden longe ear

30 icwiddet of ure Lauerd, as he hefde ischawed ham i gastelich sihðe.

'Ich iseh þe apostles, of poure ant lah on eorðe, ifullet ant bigoten al
of unimete blisse, sitten i trones, ant al under hare uet þet heh is i þe
worlde, ȝarowe for te demen i þe dei of dome kinges ant keiseres ant
alle cunreadnes of alles cunnes ledenes.

10 I seh] T, Ich iseh B, is R   14 wordes] weoredes T, *om.* BR; *Bennett and
Smithers, p. 256*   15 brihte] T, briht B, brih R   16 wið] wid B
17 þeraȝeines] R, þe aȝeines B, þertoȝeines T   I seh] RT, Ich iseh B
19 bliðeliche] blideliche B   20 of hire . . . þolien] T, lengre þolien B, na mare of
hire iþolien R   23 ha] ha ha B   27 makieð] makied B   29 al] RT,
al þet B   31 of] T, *om.* B

him often, but not as he really is—for compared with the brightness and light of his countenance the sunlight is dark and seems like a shadow, and therefore I could not look towards the brilliance of his face or hold my gaze, except through a shining mirror between me and him which shielded my eyes. In this way I have often seen the Holy Trinity, Father and Son and Holy Ghost, three in one undivided, but I could bear the radiance only a little while. But to a certain extent I could see our Lord, Jesus Christ, Son of God, who redeemed us on the cross: how he sits in bliss on the right hand of his Father who is all-powerful, and rules perpetually in that eternal life, so immeasurably beautiful that the angels are never weary of gazing at him. And yet I saw plainly the places of his wounds, and how he shows them to his Father to reveal how he loved us and how he was obedient to him who sent him to save us in that way, and prays to him constantly for the salvation of mankind.

'After him I saw on high, above all heavenly hosts, the blessed maiden, his mother, called Mary, sitting on a throne so very brightly starred with gems, and her face so radiant, that every earthly light is darkness compared with it. There I saw how she prays to her beloved son so earnestly and so sincerely for those who serve her, and he grants her gladly all that she asks for.

'When I could no longer bear the light that came from her, I looked towards the angels and the archangels and the others which are above them, blessed spirits who are for ever before God and serve him always, and sing perpetually without ever tiring. There are nine hosts, but how they are ordered and separately arrayed, one above the other, and the function of each, would take long to describe. I took so much pleasure in gazing at them that I could not look elsewhere for a long time.

'After them, I looked towards the patriarchs and the prophets, who rejoice so much because they are now in the very land of bliss that they had once hailed from afar on earth, and now see proved all that they had long before prophesied of our Lord, as he had revealed it to them through visions.

'I saw the apostles, who were once poor and humble on earth, all filled and suffused with immeasurable bliss, sitting on thrones, with everything under their feet that is exalted on earth, ready to judge at Doomsday kings and emperors and all the tribes of every nation.

| 'Ich biheolt te martyrs, ant hare unimete murhðe þe þoleden her [7〈
pinen ant deað for ure Lauerd, ant lihtliche talden to alles cunnes
neowcins ant eorðliche tintreohen aʒeines þe blisse þet Godd in hare
heorte schawede ham to cumene.

5   'Efter ham Ich biheolt þe cunfessurs hird, þe liueden i god lif ant
haliliche deiden, þe schineð as doð steorren i þe eche blissen, ant seoð
Godd in his wlite þet haueð alle teares iwipet of hare ehnen.

'Ich iseh þet schene ant þet brihte ferreden of þe eadi meidnes,
ilikest towart engles, ant feolahlukest wið ham blissin ant gleadien—
10   þe, libbinde i flesche, ouergað flesches lahe ant ouercumeð cunde, þe
leadeð heouenlich lif in eorðe as ha wunieð. Hare murhðe ant hare
blisse, þe feierlec of hare wlite, þe swetnesse of hare song, ne mei na
tunge tellen. Alle ha singeð þe þer beoð, ah hare song ne mahe nane
buten heo singen. Se swote smeal ham folheð hwider se ha wendeð þet
15   me mahte libben aa bi þe swotnesse. Hwam se heo bisecheð fore is
sikerliche iborhen; for aʒein hare bisocnen Godd himseolf ariseð, þet
alle þe oðre halhen sittende ihereð.'

'Swiðe wel', quoð Warschipe, 'likeð us þet tu seist. Ah nu þu hauest
se wel iseid of euch a setnesse of þe seli sunderlepes, sumhwet sei us
20   nu hwuch blisse is to alle iliche meane.'

Ant Liues Luue hire ondswereð: | 'Þe imeane blisse is seouenfald: [7〈
lengðe of lif, wit, ant luue, ant of þe luue a gleadunge wiðute met
murie, loft-song, ant lihtschipe; ant sikernesse is þe seoueðe.'

'Þah Ich þis', seið Warschipe, 'sumdel understonde, þu most
25   unwreo þis witerluker ant openin to þeos oðre.'

'Ant hit schal beon,' seið Liues Luue, 'Warschipe, as þu wilnest.

'Ha liuieð a in a wlite þet is brihtre seoueualt ant schenre þen þe
sunne, ant eauer in a strengðe to don buten euch swinc al þet ha
wulleð, ant eauer mare in a steal in al þet eauer god is, wiðute
30   wonunge, wiðuten euch þing þet mahe hearmin oðer eilin, in al þet
eauer is softe oðer swote. Ant hare lif is Godes sihðe ant Godes
cnawlechunge, as ure Lauerd seide: þet is, quoð he, eche lif, to seon
ant cnawen soð Godd ant him þet he sende, Iesu Crist ure Lauerd, to
ure alesnesse. Ant beoð forþi ilich him, i þe ilke wlite þet he is, for ha
35   seoð him as he is, nebbe to nebbe.

'Ha beoð se wise þet ha witen alle Godes reades, his runes ant his
domes, þe derne beoð ant deopre þen eni sea-dingle. Ha seoð i Godd

---

6 haliliche] RT, haliche B   12 feierlec] feierlᵉlᵉlac B   33 soð] sod B

'I saw the martyrs, and the infinite joy of those who in this world suffered tortures and death for our Lord's sake, and held all kinds of hardship and earthly torment of little account, compared with the bliss to come which God had revealed to them in their hearts.

'After them I saw the company of confessors, who lived a virtuous life and died in holiness, who shine like stars in the eternal joys, and see in his splendour God who has wiped away all tears from their eyes.

'I saw that radiant and shining company of the blessed virgins, most like the angels, and best fitted as companions to rejoice and be glad with them—those who, living in the flesh, transcend its law and overcome nature, who lead a heavenly life while they live on earth. Their joy and their bliss, the beauty of their appearance, the sweetness of their song, no tongue can tell. All who are there sing, but none but they may sing their song. Such a sweet smell follows them wherever they go that one could live for ever on the sweetness. Whoever they intercede for is certainly saved; for, although he hears all other saints while seated, God himself rises in response to their prayers.'

'What you say', says Prudence, 'pleases us very much. But now you have spoken so well about every order of the blessed separately, tell us something now about what kind of bliss is common to all alike.'

And Love of Life answers her: 'The common bliss is sevenfold: length of life, understanding, and love, and from that love a delight which is infinitely joyful, a song of praise, and swift ease of movement; and security is the seventh.'

'Although I understand something of this,' says Prudence, 'you must reveal it more clearly and explain it to these others.'

'And it shall be as you wish, Prudence,' says Love of Life.

'They live always in a splendour that is seven times brighter and more radiant than the sun, and always with the strength to do all that they want to without any effort, and are given a place forever among everything that is good, without any decrease, without anything that can cause harm or injury, and in everything that may be soft or sweet. And their life is the vision of God and the knowledge of God, as our Lord said: that is eternal life, he said, to see and know the true God and him whom he sent for our salvation, Jesus Christ our Lord. And therefore they are like him, in the same glory as he is himself, because they see him as he is, face to face.

'They are so wise that they are aware of all God's designs, his secrets and his judgements, which are hidden in darkness and deeper than any abyss of the sea. They see all things through God, and know

alle þing, ant witen of al þet is ant wes ant eauer schal iwurðen, hwet hit beo, hwi ant hwerto, ant hwerof hit bigunne.

'Ha luuieð God wiðute met, for þet ha understondeð hu he haueð bi ham idon þurh his muchele godlec, ant hwet ha ahen his
5 deorewurðe milce to ȝelden; ant euchan luueð oðer ase muchel as himseoluen.

'Se gleade ha beoð of Godd þet al is hare blisse se muchel | þet ne [80ʳ mei hit munne na muð ne spealie na speche. Forþi þet euchan luueð oðer as himseoluen, euchan haueð of oðres god ase muche murhðe as
10 of his ahne. Bi þis ȝe mahen seon ant witen þet euchan haueð sunderlepes ase feole gleadschipes as ha beoð monie alle, ant euch of þe ilke gleadschipes is to eauereuch an ase muche gleadunge as his ahne sunderliche. Ȝet ouer al þis, hwen euchan luueð Godd mare þen himseoluen ant þen alle þe oðre, mare he gleadeð of Godd, wiðuten ei
15 etlunge, þen of his ahne gleadunge ant of alle þe oðres. Neomeð nu þenne ȝeme: ȝef neauer anes heorte ne mei in hire underuon hire ahne gleadunge sunderliche, se unimete muchel is þe anlepi blisse, hu is hit þet ha nimeð in hire þus monie ant þus muchele? Forþi seide ure Lauerd to þeo þe him hefden icwemet: *Intra in gaudium, et cetera.*
20 "Ga", quoð he, "into þi Lauerdes blisse." Þu most al gan þrin, ant al beon bigotten þrin, for in þe ne mei hit nanes weis neomen in.

'Herof ha herieð Godd ant singeð a unwerget, eauer iliche lusti in his loft-songes, as hit iwriten is: *Beati qui habitant, et cetera.* "Eadi beoð þeo, Lauerd, þe i þin hus wunieð; ha schulen herien þe from worlde
25 into worlde."

'Ha beoð alle as lihte ant as swifte as þe sunne-gleam, þe scheot from est into west ase þin | ehelid tuneð ant openeð; for hwer se eauer [80ᵛ þe gast wule, þe bodi is ananriht wiðute lettunge. For ne mei ham na þing aȝeines etstonden, for euchan is almihti to don al þet he wule,
30 ȝe, makie to cwakien heouene ba ant eorðe wið his an finger.

'Sikere ha beoð of al þis, of þulli lif, of þulli wit, of þulli luue ant gleadunge þrof, ant of þulli blisse þet hit ne mei neauer mare lutlin ne wursin ne neome nan ende.

'Þis lutle Ich habbe iseid of þet Ich iseh in heouene, ah nower neh
35 ne seh Ich al, ne þet ȝet þet Ich iseh ne con Ich half tellen.'

---

1 iwurðen] iwurden B   5 deorewurðe] deorewurde B   7 *Fos. 80ʳ, 80ᵛ are heavily stained and torn; some words or parts of words have been supplied from R and T*
9 oðres] odres B   14 oðre] odre B   16 underuon] RT, [. . .]ruon B
17 se unimete] RT, s[. . .]ete B   17–18 hu is hit þet] þet BRT
18 hire] RT, hi[. . .] B   24–5 worlde into worlde] RT, [. . .]lde B

about everything that is and was and ever shall be, what it is, why, and for what end, and where it began from.

'They love God beyond measure, because they understand what he has done for them through his great goodness, and what they ought to give in return for his precious mercy; and each one loves his neighbour as much as himself.

'They are so happy in God that their bliss is too great for any tongue to tell or speech to describe. Because each one loves his neighbour as he does himself, each has as much joy from his neighbour's good as he does from his own. Through this you may see and understand that every one has separately as many joys as they themselves are many, and each of those joys gives as much pleasure to every one as his own separately. Yet above all this, when each one loves God more than himself and than all the others, he rejoices inestimably more in God than in his own joy or that of all the others. Now then, consider this: if the heart of one of them can never take in its separate joy, so infinitely great is its individual bliss, how can it accommodate so many and such great joys? That is why our Lord said to those who had pleased him: *Enter into the bliss, etc.* "Enter", he said, "into your Lord's bliss." You must go into it completely, and be immersed in it completely, for it cannot in any way enter into you.

'For this they honour God and sing for ever unwearied, always rejoicing equally in songs of praise to him, as it is written: *Blessed are those who live, etc.* "Blessed are those, O Lord, who live in your house; they shall honour you world without end."

'They are all as light and swift as the sunbeam which darts from east to west in the blink of an eye; for wherever the spirit may wish to go, the body is at once without any delay. For nothing may stand against them, since each one is all-powerful to do all that he wants, yes, to make heaven tremble, and earth as well, with one touch of his finger.

'They are assured of all this, of such life, of such understanding, of such love and the delight from it, and of such bliss that it may never diminish or change for the worse or come to an end.

'This little I have said of what I saw in heaven, but nevertheless I saw nowhere near everything, nor can I even describe half of what I did see.'

---

26 lihte . . . sunne-gleam] R, lih[. . .]gleam B   26–7 scheot . . . þin] RT, sch[. . .] B
35 seh] T, neh B   iseh] *supplied from* R

'Witerliche,' quoð Warschipe, 'wel we understondeð þet tu hauest
ibeo þear ant soð hauest iseid trof efter þi sihðe. Ant wel is him þet is
war ant bisið him hu he mahe beast halden his hus, þet Godes tresor is
in, aʒeines Godes unwine, þe weorreð þertowart a wið unþeawes; for
5 þet schal bringen him þider as he schal al þis þet tu hauest ispeken of,
ant hundret siðe mare, of blisse buten euch bale fondin ant ifinden.'

Quoð Strengðe, 'Hwen hit swa is, hwet mei tweamen us from Godd
ant halden us þeonne? Ich am siker ine Godd þet ne schal lif ne deð,
ne wa ne wunne nowðer, todealen us ant his luue þet al þis us haueð
10 iʒarket, ʒef we as treowe tresurers witeð wel his tresor þet is bitaht
us to halden, as we schulen ful wel under his wengen.'

'Varpeð ut', quoð Rihtwisnesse, 'Farlac ure fa! Nis nawt riht þet an
hus halde þeos tweien; for þer as Murðes sonde is, ant soð Luue of
eche Lif, Farlac is fleme.'

15 'Nu ut,' quoð Strenðe, 'Farlac! Ne schaltu na lengere leuen in ure
ende.'

'Nu, nu!' quoð Farlac, 'Ich seide for god al þet Ich seide; ant þah hit
muri nere, nes na lessere mi tale þen wes Murhðes sondes, ne
unbihefre to ow, þah hit nawt ne beo so licwurðe ne icweme.'

20 'Eiðer of ow', quoð Meað, 'haueð his stunde to speokene, ne nis
incker noðres tale to schunien in his time. Þu warnest of wa, he telleð
of wunne. Muche neod is þet me ow ba ʒeornliche hercni. Flute nu,
Farlac, þah, hwil Liues Luue is herinne, ant þole wið efne heorte þe
dom of Rihtwisnesse; for þu schal ful blieðliche beon underfon in as
25 ofte as eauer Liues Luue stutteð for to spekene.'

Nv is Wil, þet husewif, al stille þet er wes so willesful, al ituht efter
Wittes wissunge, þet is husebonde; ant al þet hird halt him stille, þet
wes iwunet to beon fulitohen ant don efter Wil, hare lefdi, ant nawt
efter Wit; lustneð nu his lare ant fondeð eauereuch an efter þet him
30 limpeð to, þurh þeos twa sonden þet ha iherd habbeð ant þet teo fowr
sustren lerden þruppe, for euch unþeawes inʒong his warde te witene
ant te warden treowliche.

| Þus ah mon te þenchen ofte ant ilome, ant wið þulliche þohtes [Rı
awecchen his heorte, þe i þe slep of ʒemeles forʒet hire sawle heale,

---

1 Witerliche, quoð] RT, witerl[. . .] B   tu hauest] RT, t[. . .]auest B   6 ant]
RT, an B   fondin] T, folhin B   8 halden . . .Ich] RT, hald[. . .] B
8–9 þet . . . wa] RT, [. . .]a B   9 todealen . . . luue] *supplied from* RT
þet] *supplied from* T   al þis] *supplied from* RT   haueð *After this word the rest of the* B
text is lost through MS damage, and R *replaces it as base MS*   10 tresurers] T, tresures R
12 Rihtwisnesse] T, Warschipe R   17 Nu, nu] T, Nu R   Farlac] T, ᶦheᶦ R

'Certainly', says Prudence, 'we understand well that you have been there and have told the truth about it according to what you saw. And it is well for him who is prudent and considers how he may best hold his house, where God's treasure is, against God's enemy, who is attacking it constantly with vices; for that will bring him to a place where he will discover and experience all this, the bliss unmixed with sorrow that you have spoken of, and a hundred times more.'

Fortitude says, 'When this is the case, what may separate us from God and keep us from that place? I am sure in God that neither life nor death, sorrow nor joy, will separate us from the love of him who has prepared all this for us, if we as faithful treasurers guard well the treasure he has entrusted to our keeping, as we shall very well under his wings.'

'Cast out our enemy Fear!' says Prudence. 'It is not right that one house should hold these two; for where Joy's messenger is, and the true Love of eternal Life, Fear is put to flight.'

'Now out, Fear!' says Fortitude. 'You are not to stay with us any longer.'

'Now, now!' says Fear. 'I said for good all that I said; and though it was not cheering, my news was as important as that of Joy's messenger, and no less useful to you, although it may not be so delightful or pleasant.'

'Each of you,' says Temperance, 'has his time to speak, and neither of your accounts should be shunned in its time. You warn of sorrow, he tells of joy. It is very necessary that both of you should be heard with attention. But go away now, Fear, while Love of Life is here, and resign yourself to the judgement of Justice; for you will be very gladly received again whenever Love of Life ceases to speak.'

Now Will the housewife, who was formerly so wilful, is entirely subdued, completely directed by the guidance of Reason, who is master of the house; and all the household remain in peace, who were accustomed to be undisciplined and follow the lead of Will, their lady, instead of Reason; now they listen to his teaching, and because of those two messengers that they have heard and what the four sisters taught above, each does his best in the post assigned to him to maintain his watch and to keep guard faithfully against the entry of every vice.

We should all meditate often on this theme, and with such meditations awaken our hearts, which in the sleep of heedlessness

19 nawt] T, *om.* R   20 quoð Meað] T, *om.* R   25 eauer] T, *om.* R
30 þet teo] þet R, to T   34 þe²] T, *om.* R

efter þe tiðinges of þeos twa sonden; from helle sihðe biseon to þe
blisse of heouene; to habben farlac of þet an, luue toward þet oðer, ant
leaden him ant his hinen, þet beoð his limen alle, nawt efter þet his
Wil, þe untohe lefdi, ant his lust leareð, ah efter þet Wit wule, þe wise
5 husebonde; tuhten ant teachen þet Wit ga euer biuore ant drahe Wil
efter him to al þet he dihteð ant demeð to donne; ant wið þe fowr
sustren, þe fowr heued-þeawes—Warschipe ant Strencðe in Godd,
Með ant Rihtwisnesse—witen Godes treosor, þet is his ahne sawle, i
þe hus of þe bodi from þe þeof of helle. Þulli þoht makeð mon te fleon
10 alle unþeawes ant ontent his heorte toward þe blisse of heouene, þet
ure Lauerd ȝeue us þurh his hali milce, þet wið þe Feder ant e Hali
Gast rixleð in þreohad a buten ende. AMEN.

Par seinte charite biddeð a Pater Noster for Iohan þet þeos boc wrat.

Hwa se þis writ haueð ired
15 Ant Crist him haueð swa isped,
Ich bidde par seinte charite
Þet ȝe bidden ofte for me—
Aa Pater Noster ant Aue Marie—
Þet Ich mote þet lif her drehen,
20 Ant ure Lauerd wel icwemen
I mi ȝuheðe ant in min elde,
Þet Ich mote Iesu Crist mi sawle ȝelden. AMEN.

1 þe tiðinges of] T, *om.* R   3 his[1]] T, *om.* R   þet his] T, *om.* R
4 þe wise] T, þet is R   5 drahe] T, teache R   7 þe fowr] T, þerfore
þe fowr R   ant] T, *om.* R   8 Með] T, ant Með R   11 Feder] T, Feder
ant e Sune R   13–22 *in R only*

forget the soul's salvation, drawing on the news brought by these two messengers; we should look from the vision of hell to the joy of heaven, feel fear of the one, love towards the other, and conduct ourselves and our servants, which are all the parts of the body, not in accordance with the instructions of Will, the unruly lady, and our desire, but according to what is required by Reason, the wise head of the household; we should instruct them and teach them that Reason should always lead the way and guide Will after him in all that he plans and decides should be done; and with the four sisters, the four cardinal virtues—Prudence and Fortitude in God, Temperance and Justice—we should guard God's treasure, which is our own soul, in the house of the body from the thief of hell. This kind of meditation encourages us to flee all vices and kindles our hearts towards the bliss of heaven. May our Lord grant us that bliss through his holy grace, who with the Father and the Holy Ghost rules in trinity for ever without end. AMEN.

Out of holy charity pray an *Our Father* for John who copied this book.

> Whoever reads the text I write
> With Jesus Christ to give him light,
> I ask for holy charity
> That you will often pray for me—
> *Pater* and *Ave* constantly—
> To lead my life as best I may,
> And please God well in every way
> In youth and when my youth is past,
> And yield my soul to Christ at last. AMEN.

| Seinte Pawel witneð þet alle uttre heardschipes, alle flesches [10
pinsunges ant licomliche swinkes, al is ase nawt aʒeines luue, þe
schireð ant brihteð þe heorte. *Exercitio corporis ad modicum ualet, pietas
autem ualet ad omnia*: þet is, licomlich bisischipe is to lutel wurð, ah
swote ant schir heorte is god to alle þinges. *Si linguis hominum loquar et
angelorum, et cetera; si tradidero corpus meum ita ut ardeam, et cetera; si
distribuero omnes facultates meas in cibos pauperum, caritatem autem non
habeam, nichil michi prodest.* 'Þah Ich cuðe', he seið, 'monne ledene ant
englene, þah Ich dude o mi bodi alle pine ant passiun þet bodi mahte
þolien, þah Ich ʒeue poure al þet Ich hefde, ʒef Ich nefde luue
þerwið, to Godd ant to alle men in him ant for him, al were ispillet.'
For as þe hali abbat Moyses seide, al þet wa ant al þet heard þet we
þolieð o flesch, ant al þet god þet we eauer doð, alle swucche þinges
ne beoð nawt bute as lomen to tilie wið þe heorte. Ʒef þe axe ne
kurue, ne spitelsteaf ne dulue, ne þe sulh ne erede, hwa kepte ham to
halden? Alswa as na mon ne luueð lomen for hamseolf, ah deð for þe
þinges þet me wurcheð wið ham, alswa na flesches derf nis to luuien
bute forþi, þet Godd te reaðere þiderward loki mid his grace, ant makie
þe heorte schir ant of briht sihðe, þet nan ne mei habben wið
monglunge of unþeawes, ne wið eorðlich luue of worltliche þinges; for
þis mong woreð swa þe ehnen of þe heorte þet ha ne mei cnawen
Godd ne gleadien of his sihðe. Schir heorte, as Seint Bernard seið,
makieð twa þinges: þet tu al þet tu dest, do hit oðer for luue ane of
Godd, oðer for oþres god ant for his biheue. | Haue in al þet tu dest an [10
of þes twa ententes—oðer ba togederes, for þe leatere falleð into
þe earre. Haue eauer schir heorte þus, ant do al þet tu wult; haue wori
heorte, al þe sit uuele. *Omnia munda mundis, coinquinatis uero nichil est
mundum (Apostolus). Item. Augustinus: Habe caritatem, et fac quicquid
uis—uoluntate uidelicet rationis.* Forþi, mine leoue sustren, ouer alle
þing beoð bisie to habben schir heorte. Hwet is schir heorte? Ich hit
habbe iseid ear: þet is, þet ʒe na þing ne wilnin ne ne luuien bute
Godd ane, ant te ilke þinges for Godd þe helpeð ow toward him—for
Godd, Ich segge, luuien ham, ant nawt for hamseoluen—as is mete

5

10

15

20

25

30

18 makie] NTS, makeð ACFLP

Guide for Anchoresses, Part 7

St Paul testifies that all external hardships, all mortifications of the flesh and physical labours count as nothing compared with love, which purifies and enlightens the heart. *Physical exertion is of little use, but piety can achieve everything*: that is, physical exertion is of little use, but a gentle and pure heart can achieve everything. *If I speak with the tongues of men and angels, etc.; if I surrender my body to be burned, etc.; if I give away all my goods to feed the poor, but do not have charity, it is useless to me.* 'If I knew the languages of men and angels,' he says, 'if I inflicted on my body every torture and suffering that the body could bear, if I gave the poor all that I had, and I did not have love as well, for God and for all men in him and for his sake, it would all be wasted.' For as the holy abbot Moses said, however much misery and physical hardship we may endure, and however much good we may bring about, all such things are nothing unless they are used as tools to cultivate the heart with. If the axe did not cut, or the spade dig, or the plough turn up the soil, who would want to keep them? Just as tools are not valued for their own sake, but only for the things that are done with them, so no physical hardship is to be valued except for this reason: that God may look towards it sooner with his grace, and purify the heart and give it clear sight, which nobody can have who is polluted by vices, or by earthly love of worldly things; because this pollution clouds the eyes of the heart so much that it cannot know God or rejoice in seeing him. Two things, as St Bernard says, make a pure heart: that everything you do, you do either solely for the love of God, or for someone else's good and advantage. In everything that you do, have one of these two intentions—or both together, because the second is included in the first. If you always keep your heart pure in this way, you can do all you want; if you have a troubled heart, everything troubles you. *To the pure all things are pure, but nothing is pure to those who are defiled,* says the Apostle. Similarly, *Augustine says: Have charity and do what you wish—that is, with the consent of the reason.* Because of this, my dear sisters, try above all to have a pure heart. What is a pure heart? I have said what it is already: that is, that you should not desire or love anything except for God and those things which help you towards

oðer cla$\eth$, mon oðer wummon þe ʒe beoð of igodet. For ase seið
Seint Austin, ant spekeð þus to ure Lauerd, *Minus te amat qui preter te*
aliquid amat quod non propter te amat: þet is, 'Lauerd, leasse ha luuieð
þe þe luuieð eawt bute þe, bute ha luuien hit for þe.' Schirnesse of
5 heorte is Godes luue ane. I þis is al þe strengðe of alle religiuns, þe
ende of alle ordres. *Plenitudo legis est dilectio*: 'Luue fulleð þe lahe,' seið
Seinte Pawel. *Quicquid precipitur, in sola caritate solidatur*: alle Godes
heastes, as Sein Gregoire seið, beoð i luue irotet. Luue ane schal beon
ileid i Seinte Mihales weie. Þeo þe meast luuieð schulen beo meast
10 iblisset, nawt þeo þe leadeð heardest lif, for luue hit ouerweieð. Luue
is heouene stiward for hire muchele freolec, for heo ne edhalt na þing,
ah ʒeueð al þet ha haueð, ant ec hireseoluen—elles ne kepte Godd
nawt of þet hiren were.

Godd haueð ofgan ure luue on alle cunne wise. He haueð muchel
15 idon us, ant mare bihaten. Muchel ʒeoue ofdraheð luue. Me, al þe
world he ʒef us in Adàm, | ure alde feader; ant al þet is i þe world he [16
weorp under ure fet, beastes ant fuheles, ear we weren forgulte.
Omnia subiecisti sub pedibus eius: oues et boues uniuersas, insuper et pecora
campi, volucres celi, et pisces maris qui perambulant semitas maris. Ant ʒet
20 al þet is, as is þruppe iseid, serueð þe gode to sawle biheue. Ʒet te
uuele seruið eorðe, sea, ant sunne. He dude ʒet mare: ʒef us nawt
ane of his, ah dude al himseoluen. Se heh ʒeoue nes neauer iʒeuen
to se lahe wrecches. *Apostolus: Christus dilexit Ecclesiam et dedit*
semetipsum pro ea. Crist, seið Seinte Pawel, luuede swa his leofmon þet
25 he ʒef for hire þe pris of himseoluen. Neomeð nu gode ʒeme, mine
leoue sustren, forhwi me ah him to luuien. Earst, as a mon þe woheð,
as a king þet luuede a gentil poure leafdi of feorrene londe, he sende
his sonden biuoren, þet weren þe patriarches ant te prophetes of þe
Alde Testament, wið leattres isealet. On ende he come himseoluen,
30 ant brohte þe Godspel as leattres iopenet; ant wrat wið his ahne blod
saluz to his leofmon, luue-gretunge for te wohin hire wið ant hire luue
wealden. Herto falleð a tale, a wrihe forbisne.

A leafdi wes mid hire fan biset al abuten, hire lond al destruet, ant
heo al poure inwið an eorðene castel. A mihti kinges luue wes þah
35 biturnd upon hire swa unimete swiðe þet he for wohlech sende hire his
sonden, an efter oðer, ofte somet monie; sende hire beawbelez baðe
feole ant feire, sucurs of liueneð, help of his hehe hird to halden hire

23 wrecches] wrecchces A   28 prophetes] prophes A

God, for his sake—love them for his sake, I say, and not for themselves—such as food or clothing, or a man or woman who gives you help. For as St Augustine says, addressing our Lord, *He loves you less who loves anything other than you which he does not love for your sake*: that is, 'Lord, they love you less who love anything but you, unless they love it because of you.' Purity of heart is the love of God alone. In this lies all the strength of every kind of religious life, the purpose of all orders. *The fulfilment of the law is love*: 'Love fulfils the law,' says St Paul. *Whatever is commanded, it is confirmed by love alone*: all God's commandments, as St Gregory says, are rooted in love. Love alone will be laid in St Michael's scales. Those who love most will be most blessed, not those who lead the hardest life, for love outweighs it. Love is the steward of heaven for her great generosity, since she does not withhold anything, but gives all that she has, and herself too—else God would care nothing for anything that she did.

God has earned our love in every kind of way. He has done much for us, and promised more. A generous gift attracts love. Why, he gave us the whole world through Adam, our forefather; and everything that is in the world, animals and birds, he cast under our feet, before we fell through sin. *You have put all things under his feet: all sheep and cattle, and moreover the beasts of the field, the birds of the air, and the fish of the sea which travel the paths of the sea.* And everything that exists, as has been said above, still serves the virtuous for the good of their souls. Even the wicked are served by the earth, sea, and sun. He did still more: not only gave us things which were his, but gave himself completely. Such a noble gift was never given to such base wretches. *The Apostle says: Christ loved the Church and gave himself for it.* Christ, says St Paul, loved his beloved so much that he gave for her the price of himself. Now note carefully, my dear sisters, why he ought to be loved. First, like a suitor, like a king who was in love with a noble but poor lady in a distant land, he sent his messengers in advance—the patriarchs and the prophets of the Old Testament—with sealed letters. At last he came himself, and brought the Gospel as open letters; and with his own blood wrote greetings to his lady, a lover's homage to woo her with and gain her love. There is a story linked with this, a hidden allegory.

A lady was completely surrounded by her enemies, her land laid waste, and she herself quite destitute, in a castle of clay. But a powerful king had fallen in love with her so inordinately that to win her love he sent her his messengers, one after another, often many together; he sent her many splendid presents of jewellery, provisions to support

castel. Heo underfeng al as on unrecheles, ant swa wes heard-iheortet
þet hire luue ne mahte he neauer beo þe neorre. Hwet wult tu mare?
He com himseolf on ende; schawde hire his feire neb, as þe þe wes of
alle men feherest to bihalden; spec se swiðe swoteliche, ant wordes se
5   murie | þet ha mahten deade arearen to liue; wrahte feole wundres [10
ant dude muchele meistries biuoren hire ehsihðe; schawde hire his
mihte; talde hire of his kinedom; bead to makien hire cwen of al þet he
ahte. Al þis ne heold nawt. Nes þis hoker wunder?—for heo nes
neauer wurðe for te beon his þuften. Ah swa þurh his deboneirte luue
10 hefde ouercumen him þet he seide on ende: 'Dame, þu art iweorret,
ant þine van beoð se stronge þet tu ne maht nanes weis wiðute mi
sucurs edfleon hare honden, þet ha ne don þe to scheome deað efter al
þi weane. Ich chulle, for þe luue of þe, neome þet feht upo me, ant
arudde þe of ham þe þi dead secheð. Ich wat þah to soðe þet Ich schal
15 bituhen ham neomen deaðes wunde; ant Ich hit wulle heorteliche for
te ofgan þin heorte. Nu, þenne, biseche Ich þe, for þe luue þet Ich
cuðe þe, þet tu luuie me lanhure efter þe ilke dede dead, hwen þu
naldest liues.' Þes king dude al þus: arudde hire of alle hire van, ant
wes himseolf to wundre ituket ant islein on ende. Þurh miracle aras
20 þah from deaðe to liue. Nere þeos ilke leafdi of uueles cunnes cunde
ȝef ha ouer alle þing ne luuede him herefter?

Þes king is Iesu, Godes Sune, þet al o þisse wise wohede ure sawle,
þe deoflen hefden biset. Ant he, as noble wohere, efter monie
messagers ant feole goddeden com to pruuien his luue, ant schawde
25 þurh cnihtschipe þet he wes luuewurðe, as weren sumhwile cnihtes
iwunet to donne. Dude him i turneiment, ant hefde for his leoues luue
his scheld i feht, as kene cniht, on euche half iþurlet. His scheld, þe
wreah his goddhead, wes his leoue licome, þet | wes ispread o rode: [10
brad as scheld buuen in his istrahte earmes, nearow bineoðen, as þe an
30 fot (efter monies wene) set upo þe oðer. Þet þis scheld naueð siden is
for bitacnunge þet his deciples, þe schulden stonden bi him ant
habben ibeon his siden, fluhen alle from him ant leafden him as
fremede, as þe Godspel seið: *Relicto eo omnes fugerunt.* Þis scheld is
iȝeuen us aȝein alle temptatiuns, as Ieremie witneð: *Dabis scutum*
35 *cordis, laborem tuum.* Nawt ane þis scheld ne schilt us from alle uueles,
ah deð ȝet mare: cruneð us in heouene. *Scuto bone uoluntatis—*

her, help from his noble army to hold her castle. She accepted everything as if it meant nothing to her, and was so hard-hearted that he could never come closer to gaining her love. What more do you want? At last he came himself; showed her his handsome face, as the most supremely handsome of men; spoke so very tenderly, and with words so beguiling that they could raise the dead to life; worked many wonders and did great feats before her eyes; showed her his power; told her about his kingdom; offered to make her queen of all that he owned. All this had no effect. Was not this scorn surprising?—for she was never fit to be his maidservant. But because of his gentle nature love had so overcome him that at last he said: 'You are under attack, lady, and your enemies are so strong that without my help there is no way that you can escape falling into their hands, and being put to a shameful death after all your troubles. For your love I am willing to take on that fight, and rescue you from those who are seeking your death. But I know for certain that in fighting them I shall receive a mortal wound; and I will accept it gladly in order to win your heart. Now, therefore, I beg you, for the love I am showing towards you, to love me at least when this is done, after my death, although you refused to during my life.' This king did just as he had promised; he rescued her from all her enemies, and was himself shamefully ill-treated and at last put to death. But by a miracle he rose from death to life. Would not this lady have a base nature if she did not love him after this above all things?

This king is Jesus, Son of God, who in just this way wooed our soul, which devils had besieged. And he, like a noble suitor, after numerous messengers and many acts of kindness came to prove his love, and showed by feats of arms that he was worthy of love, as was the custom of knights once upon a time. He entered the tournament and, like a bold knight, had his shield pierced through and through in battle for love of his lady. His shield, which hid his divinity, was his dear body, which was stretched out on the cross: broad as a shield above in his extended arms, narrow below, where the one foot (as many people think) was fixed above the other. That this shield has no sides is to signify that his disciples, who should have stood by him and been his sides, all fled from him and abandoned him like strangers, as the Gospel says: *They all abandoned him and fled.* This shield is given to us against all temptations, as Jeremiah testifies: *You will give your labour as a shield for the heart.* This shield not only protects us against all evils, but does still more: it crowns us in heaven. *With the shield of good will—*

'Lauerd,' he seið, Dauið, 'wið þe scheld of þi gode wil þu hauest us icrunet.' 'Scheld', he seið, 'of god wil', for willes he þolede al þet he þolede. *Ysaias: Oblatus est quia uoluit.*

'Me, lauerd,' þu seist, 'hwerto? Ne mahte he wið leasse gref habben
5 arud us?' ʒeoi, iwiss, ful lihtliche; ah he nalde. Forhwi? For te bineomen us euch bitellunge aʒein him of ure luue þet he se deore bohte. Me buð lihtliche þing þet me luueð lutel. He bohte us wið his heorte blod—deorre pris nes neauer—for te ofdrahen of us ure luue toward him, þet costnede him se sare. I scheld beoð þreo þinges: þe
10 treo, ant te leðer, ant te litunge. Alswa wes i þis scheld: þe treo of þe rode, þet leðer of Godes licome, þe litunge of þe reade blod þet heowede hire se feire. Eft þe þridde reisun: efter kene cnihtes deað, me hongeð hehe i chirche his scheld on his mungunge. Alswa is þis scheld—þet is, þe crucifix—i chirche iset i swuch stude þer me hit
15 sonest seo, for te þenchen þerbi o Iesu Cristes cnihtschipe þet he dude o rode. His leofmon bihalde þron hu he bohte hire luue: lette þurlin his scheld, openin his side to schawin hire his heorte, to schawin hire | [1●] openliche hu inwardliche he luuede hire, ant to ofdrahen hire heorte.

Fowr heaued-luuen me ifind i þis world: bitweone gode iferen;
20 bitweone mon ant wummon; bitweone wif ant hire child; bitweone licome ant sawle. Þe luue þet Iesu Crist haueð to his deore leofmon ouergeað þeos fowre, passeð ham alle.

Ne teleð me him god fere þe leið his wed i Giwerie to acwitin ut his fere? Godd almihti leide himseolf for us i Giwerie, ant dude his
25 deorewurðe bodi to acwitin ut his leofmon of Giwene honden. Neauer fere ne dude swuch fordede for his fere.

Muche luue is ofte bitweone mon ant wummon. Ah þah ha were iweddet him, ha mahte iwurðen se unwreast, ant swa longe ha mahte forhorin hire wið oþre men, þet þah ha walde aʒein cumen, he ne
30 kepte hire nawt. Forþi Crist luueð mare: for þah þe sawle, his spuse, forhori hire wið þe feond under heaued-sunne feole ʒeres ant dahes, his mearci is hire eauer ʒarow hwen ha wule cumen ham ant leten þen deouel. Al þis he seið himseolf þurh Ieremie: *Si dimiserit uir uxorem suam, et cetera . . . Tu autem fornicata es cum multis amatoribus;*
35 *tamen reuertere ad me, dicit Dominus.* ʒet he ʒeiʒeð al dei, 'Þu þet hauest se unwreaste idon, biturn þe ant cum aʒein; welcume schalt tu beo me.' *Immo et occurrit prodigo uenienti.* ʒet he eorneð, hit seið,

---

20 bitweone²] CGNTP, bi (*at end of line*) A

'Lord,' says David, 'you have crowned us with the shield of your good will.' He says 'shield of good will' because he suffered willingly all that he suffered. *Isaiah says: He was offered because he wished to be.*

'But, master,' you say, 'what was the point? Could he not have saved us without so much suffering?' Yes, indeed, very easily; but he did not wish to. Why? To deprive us of any excuse for denying him our love, since he had paid so dearly for it. You buy cheaply what you do not value highly. He bought us with his heart's blood—a higher price was never paid—to attract our love, which cost him so much suffering. In a shield there are three things: the wood, and the leather, and the painted design. So it was in this shield: the wood of the cross, the leather of God's body, the painting of the red blood which coloured it so brightly. The third reason, then: after a brave knight's death, his shield is hung high in the church in his memory. Just so this shield— that is, the crucifix—is placed in church where it can be seen most easily, to be a reminder of the knightly prowess of Jesus Christ on the cross. His beloved should see in this how he bought her love: he let his shield be pierced, his side opened up, to show her his heart, to show her openly how deeply he loved her, and to attract her heart.

Four main kinds of love are found in this world: between good friends; between man and woman; between a woman and her child; between body and soul. The love which Jesus Christ has for his dear beloved transcends these four, surpasses them all.

Is not that man considered a good friend who leaves his security for payment with the Jews to release his friend? Almighty God gave himself to the Jews as security for us, and gave his precious body to release his beloved from the hands of the Jews. No friend ever did such a favour for his friend.

There is often great love between a man and a woman. But even if she were married to him, she might become so depraved, and might prostitute herself with other men for such a long time that, even she wanted to come back to him, he would have nothing to do with her. Christ, then, loves more than this: because even if the soul, his bride, fornicates with the Devil in mortal sin for many long years, his mercy is always waiting for her when she is willing to come home and leave the Devil. He says all this himself through Jeremiah: *If a man should put away his wife, etc. . . . But you have fornicated with many lovers; nevertheless, return to me, the Lord says.* He still cries constantly, 'You who have behaved so scandalously, turn and come back; you will be welcome to me.' *Indeed, he even ran to meet the returning prodigal.* Even

aʒein hire ʒeincume ant warpeð earmes anan abuten hire swire.
Hweat is mare milce? Ʒet her gleadfulre wunder: ne beo neauer his leof
forhoret mid se monie deadliche sunnen, sone se ha kimeð to him
aʒein, he makeð hire neowe meiden. For as Seint Austin seið, swa
5 muchel is bitweonen—bituhhen Godes neoleachunge ant monnes to
wummon—þet monnes neoleachunge makeð of meiden wif, ant Godd
makeð of wif meiden. *Restituit,* | *inquit Iob, in integrum.* Gode werkes [10
ant treowe bileaue—þeose twa þinges beoð meiðhad i sawle.

Nu of þe þridde luue. Child þet hefde swuch uuel þet him bihofde
10 beað of blod ear hit were ihealet, muchel þe moder luuede hit þe
walde þis beað him makien. Þis dude ure Lauerd us þe weren se seke
of sunne, ant swa isulet þerwið, þet na þing ne mahte healen us ne
cleansin us bute his blod ane, for swa he hit walde. His luue makeð us
beað þrof—iblescet beo he eaure! Þreo beaðes he greiðede to his
15 deore leofmon for te weschen hire in ham se hwit ant se feier þet ha
were wurðe to his cleane cluppunges. Þe earste beað is fulluht. Þe
oðer beoð teares, inre oðer uttre, efter þe forme beað ʒef ha
hire suleð. Þe þridde is Iesu Cristes blod, þet halheð ba þe oþre, as
Sein Iuhan seið i þe Apocalipse: *Qui dilexit nos et lauit nos in sanguine*
20 *suo.* Þet he luueð us mare þen eani moder hire child, he hit seið
himseoluen þurh Ysaie, *Nunquid potest mater obliuisci filii uteri sui? Et si*
illa obliuiscatur, ego non obliuiscar tui. 'Mei moder', he seið, 'forʒeoten
hire child? Ant þah heo do, Ich ne mei þe forʒeoten neauer.' Ant seið
þe resun efter: *In manibus meis descripsi te.* 'Ich habbe', he seið, 'depeint
25 te i mine honden.' Swa he dude mid read blod upo þe rode. Me cnut
his gurdel to habben þoht of a þing. Ah ure Lauerd, for he nalde
neauer forʒeoten us, dude mearke of þurlunge in ure munegunge i ba
twa his honden.

Nu þe feorðe luue. Þe sawle luueð þe licome swiðe mid alle, ant þet
30 is etscene i þe twinnunge; for leoue freond beoð sari hwen ha schulen
twinnin. Ah ure Lauerd willeliche totweamde his sawle from his bodi
for te veien ure baðe togederes world buten ende i þe blisse of
heo|uene. Þus, lo, Iesu Cristes luue toward his deore spuse—þet is, [1
Hali Chirche oðer cleane sawle—passeð alle ant ouerkimeð þe fowr
35 measte luuen þet me ifind on eorðe. Wið al þis luue ʒetten he woheð
hire o þis wise.

'Þi luue', he seið, 'oðer hit is for te ʒeouen allunge, oðer hit is to
sullen, oðer hit is to reauin ant to neomen wið strengðe.

so, it says, he runs to meet her and throws his arms around her neck. What is greater mercy than this? Here is a more joyful wonder still: no matter how many mortal sins his love has been dishonoured by, as soon as she comes back to him, he makes her a virgin again. For as St Augustine says, there is so much difference—that is, between God's advances to a woman and a man's—that a man's advances make a virgin into a woman, and God makes a woman into a virgin. *He has made me whole again, says Job.* Good works and true faith—these two things are virginity in the soul.

Now something about the third love. If a child had such an illness that it needed a bath of blood before it could be healed, the mother who was willing to provide this bath for it would love it very much. Our Lord did this for us—who were so infected with sin, and so polluted with it, that nothing could heal or cleanse us except for his blood—because that was what he wished. His love makes a bath of his blood for us—may he always be blessed! He prepared three baths for his dear beloved to wash herself in, and make herself white and fair enough for his pure embraces. The first bath is baptism. The second is tears, inward or outward, after the first bath if she makes herself unclean. The third is the blood of Jesus Christ, which sanctifies both the others, as St John says in the Apocalypse: *Who loved us and washed us in his own blood.* He says himself through Isaiah that he loves us more than any mother her child: *Isaiah: Can a mother forget the child of her womb? Even if she forgets, I shall not forget you.* 'Can a mother', he says, 'forget her child? And even if she does, I can never forget you.' And then he gives the reason: *I have painted you in my hands.* 'I have painted you in my hands,' he says. So he did, with red blood on the cross. You tie a knot in your girdle to remind you of something. But our Lord, because he wished never to forget us, put a pierced mark to remind him of us in both his hands.

Now the fourth love. The soul loves the body very much indeed, and that is clearly seen when they part company; for close friends are sorry when they have to part. But our Lord willingly parted his soul from his body to join ours together for all eternity in the bliss of heaven. In this way, as you can see, Jesus Christ's love for his dear wife—that is, Holy Church or the pure soul—surpasses and overcomes the four greatest loves to be found on earth. With all this love he still woos her in this way:

'Your love', he says, 'is either to be given outright, or it is for sale, or it is to be seized and taken by force.

'3ef hit is for te 3eouen, hwer maht tu biteon hit betere þen upo
me? Nam Ich þinge feherest? Nam Ich kinge richest? Nam Ich hest
icunnet? Nam Ich weolie wisest? Nam Ich monne hendest? Nam Ich
þinge freoest?—for swa me seið bi large mon þe ne con nawt edhalden,
5 þet he haueð þe honden, as mine beoð, iþurlet. Nam Ich alre þinge
swotest ant swetest? Þus alle þe reisuns hwi me ah to 3eoue luue þu
maht ifinden in me, nomeliche 3ef þu luuest chaste cleannesse; for
nan ne mei luuie me bute ha hire halde (ah ha is þreouald: i
widewehad; i spushad; i meidenhad, þe heste).
10   '3ef þi luue nis nawt to 3eouene, ah wult þet me bugge hire—
buggen hire? Hu? Oðer wið oðer luue oðer wið sumhweat elles. Me
suleð wel luue for luue; ant swa me ah to sulle luue, ant for na þing
elles. 3ef þin is swa to sullen, Ich habbe iboht hire wið luue ouer alle
oþre; for of þe fowr measte luuen Ich habbe icud toward te þe measte
15 of ham alle.
    '3ef þu seist þu nult nawt leote þron se liht chap, ah wult 3ette
mare, nempne hweat hit schule beon. Sete feor o þi luue; þu ne schalt
seggen se muchel þet Ich nule 3eoue mare. Wult tu castles,
kinedomes, wult tu wealden al þe world? Ich chulle do þe betere—
20 makie þe wið al þis cwen of heoueriche. Þu schalt te seolf beo
seoueuald brihtre þen þe sunne. Nan uuel ne schal | nahhi þe, na [1(
wunne ne schal wonti þe. Al þi wil schal beon iwraht in heouene ant ec
in eorðe—3e, ant 3et in helle. Ne schal neauer heorte þenchen
swuch selhðe þet Ich nule 3eouen for þi luue unmeteliche,
25 vneuenliche, unendeliche mare. Al Creasuse weole, þe wes kinge
richest; Absalones schene wlite, þe as ofte as me euesede him, salde
his euesunge—þe her þet he kearf of—for twa hundret sicles of
seoluer iweiet; Asaeles swiftschipe, þe straf wið heortes of urn;
Samsones strengðe, þe sloh a þusent of his fan al ed a time, ant ane
30 bute fere; Cesares freolec; Alixandres hereword; Moysese heale:—
nalde a mon for an of þeos 3eouen al þet he ahte? Ant alle somet
a3ein mi bodi ne beoð nawt wurð a nelde.
    '3ef þu art se swiðe anewil, ant swa ut of þi wit þet tu, þurh nawt to
leosen, forsakest swuch bi3ete, wið alles cunnes selhðe, lo! Ich halde
35 her heatel sweord upo þin heaued to dealen lif ant sawle, ant
bisenchen ham ba into þe fur of helle, to beon þer deofles hore

11 buggen hire? Hu?] CG, buggen hire? A, achatez-le. Coment? F, quomodo potest
emi? L, do seie hwu N, dites coment vus la uolez doner S, hu? T   12 for luue]
CFGNTSLP, *om.* A   24 swuch] CGNT, hwuch A   36 þer] CFGNTSL, *om.*
A, þe P

'If it is to be given, where can you bestow it better than on me? Am I not fairer than anything else? Am I not the richest of kings? Am I not of the noblest ancestry? Am I not the wisest of the wise? Am I not the most courteous of men? Am I not supremely generous?—because it is said of a generous man who can keep nothing back that he has holes in his hands, as I have. Am I not the sweetest and most fragrant of all things? So you can find in me all the reasons why love should be given, especially if you love chaste purity; because nobody can love me unless she preserves it (but there are three kinds: in widowhood, in marriage, and in virginity, the highest).

'If your love is not to be given, but you want it to be bought, how is it to be bought? Either with another love or with something else. Love for love is a fair exchange; and that is how love should be sold, and for nothing else. If your love is to be sold in this way, I have bought it with a love greater than all others; since, of the four greatest loves, I have shown towards you the greatest of them all.

'If you say that you do not want to value your love so cheaply, but want still more, say what it is to be. Set a price on your love; you cannot ask so much that I will not give more. Do you want castles, kingdoms, do you want to have power over the whole world? I will do better for you—make you, as well as all this, queen of the kingdom of heaven. You yourself shall be seven times brighter than the sun. No evil shall approach you, no joy shall fail you. All your will shall be done in heaven and on earth—yes, and even in hell. No heart can ever imagine such bliss that I will not give for your love immeasurably, incomparably, infinitely more. All the wealth of Croesus, who was the richest of kings; the radiant beauty of Absalom, who, as often as his hair was cut, sold the clippings—the hair that he cut off—for two hundred shekels of silver weighed out; the swiftness of Asahel, who could race with the deer; the strength of Samson, who killed a thousand of his enemies all at one time, and alone without a companion; Caesar's generosity; Alexander's fame; Moses' health:—surely a man would give all that he had for one of these? And all together, compared with me, are not worth a needle.

'If you are so very stubborn, and so out of your senses, that for fear of losing anything you reject such a gain, with every kind of happiness, look! I am holding a cruel sword here above your head to separate body and soul, and plunge them both into the fire of hell, to be the Devil's

schentfulliche ant sorhfulliche world abuten ende. Ondswere nu ant
were þe—ȝef þu const—aȝein me; oðer ȝette me þi luue þe Ich
ȝirne se swiðe, nawt for min, ah for þin ahne muchele biheue.'
Lo, þus ure Lauerd woheð. Nis ha to heard-iheortet þet a þulli
5 wohere ne mei to his luue turnen, ȝef ha wel þencheð þeose þreo
þinges, hwet he is ant hwet heo is, ant hu muchel is þe luue of se heh
as he is toward se lah as heo is? Forþi seið þe salmwruhte: *Non est qui se
abscondat a calore eius*—nis nan þet mahe edlutien þet ha ne mot him
luuien. Þe soðe sunne i þe undertid wes forþi istihen on heh o þe hehe
10 rode, for te spreaden oueral hate luue-gleames. Þus neodful he wes—
ant is aþet tes dei—to ontenden his luue in his leoues heorte; ant seið i
þe Godspel, *Ignem | ueni mittere in terram, et quid uolo nisi ut ardeat?* 'Ich   [1
com to bringen', he seið, 'fur into eorðe'—þet is, bearninde luue into
eorðlich heorte—'ant hwet ȝirne Ich elles bute þet hit bleasie?'
15 Wlech luue is him lað, as he seið þurh Sein Iuhan i þe Apocalipse:
*Vtinam frigidus esses aut calidus! Set quia tepidus es, incipiam te euomere de
ore meo.* 'Ich walde', he seið to his leofmon, 'þet tu were i mi luue oðer
allunge cald oðer hat mid alle. Ah forþi þet tu art ase wlech bitweone
twa, nowðer hat ne cald, þu makest me to wleatien, ant Ich wulle
20 speowe þe ut bute þu wurðe hattre.'
Nu ȝe habbeð iherd, mine leoue sustren, hu ant forhwi Godd is
swiðe to luuien. For te ontenden ow wel, gederið wude þerto wið þe
poure wummon of Sarepte, þe burh þe spealeð 'ontendunge'. *'En',
inquit, 'colligo duo ligna' (Regum iiiº).* 'Lauerd,' quoð ha to Helye þe hali
25 prophete, 'lo, Ich gederi twa treon.' Þeos twa treon bitacnið þet a treo
þet stod upriht, ant þet oþer þe eode þwertouer, o þe deore rode. Of
þeos twa treon ȝe schulen ontende fur of luue inwið ower heorte.
Biseoð ofte towart ham; þencheð ȝef ȝe ne ahen eaðe to luuien þe
king of blisse, þe tospreat swa his earmes toward ow, ant buheð as to
30 beoden cos duneward his heaued. Sikerliche Ich segge hit, ȝef þe
soðe Helye, þet is, Godd almihti, ifint ow þeose twa treon bisiliche
gederin, he wule gestnin wið ow, ant monifalden in ow his deorewurðe
grace, as Helie dude hire liueneð ant gestnede wið hire þet he ifond þe
twa treon gederin i Sarepte.
35 Grickisch fur is imaket of reades monnes blod, ant þet ne mei na

---

11 in] CFGNTL, ant A

whore there in shame and misery for all eternity. Now answer and defend yourself—if you can—against me; or grant me your love which I long for so much, not for my sake, but for your own great advantage.'

This, you see, is how our Lord woos. Surely that woman is too hard-hearted whose love cannot be won by such a suitor, if she seriously considers these three things: what he is, what she is, and how great is the love of such a noble man towards a woman as base as she is. That is why the Psalmist says: *there is no one who can hide himself from his heat*—there is no one who can hide herself so that she will not be forced to love him. It is for this reason that the true sun rose high on the lofty cross at the third hour of the day, so as to send out hot rays of love in all directions. This is how anxious he was—and is to this day—to kindle his love in his beloved's heart; and he says in the Gospel, *I have come to send fire into the earth, and what else do I want except that it should be kindled?* 'I came', he says, 'to bring fire into the earth'—that is, burning love into an earthly heart—'and what else do I want but that it should blaze?' Lukewarm love is hateful to him, as he says through St John in the Apocalypse: *If only you were hot or cold! But because you are lukewarm, I will vomit you out of my mouth.* 'I would wish you', he says to his beloved, 'to be either entirely hot or entirely cold in your love for me. But because you are (as it were) lukewarm between the two, neither hot nor cold, you sicken me, and I will vomit you out unless you become hotter.'

Now, my dear sisters, you have heard how and why God is greatly to be loved. To set yourselves well alight, gather wood for the purpose with the poor woman of Sarepta, the city whose name means 'kindling'. *'Look,' she said (in the third Book of Kings), 'I am gathering two sticks.'* 'Look, sir,' she said to Elijah the holy prophet, 'I am gathering two sticks.' These two sticks signify the one piece of wood which stood upright, and the other which went across it, which made up the precious cross. With these two pieces of wood you must kindle a fire of love in your heart. Often look towards them; think whether you ought not to give your love readily to the King of bliss, who stretches out his arms so lovingly towards you, and bends his head downwards as if to offer a kiss. You can be sure that if the true Elijah, that is, almighty God, finds you busily gathering these two pieces of wood, he will stay with you as your guest, and multiply his precious grace in you, as Elijah multiplied the woman's food, and lodged with her, after he found her gathering the two sticks in Sarepta.

Greek fire is made from the blood of a red man, and nothing can

þing bute migge ant sond ant eisil, as me seið, acwenchen. Þis
Grickisch fur is þe luue of Iesu ure Lauerd, ant ʒe hit schule makien
of reade | monnes blod, þet is, Iesu Crist ireadet wið his ahne blod o   [▪
þe deore rode—ant wes inread cundeliche alswa as me weneð. Þis
5 blod, for ow isched upo þe earre twa treon, schal makien ow
Sareptiens—þet is, ontende mid tis Grickisch fur, þet, as Salomon
seið, nane weattres (þet beoð worldliche tribulatiuns), nane temptatiuns,
nowðer inre ne uttre, ne mahen þis luue acwenchen. Nu nis þenne on
ende bute witen ow warliche wið al þet hit acwencheð: þet beoð migge
10 ant sond ant eisil, as Ich ear seide. Migge is stench of sunne. O sond
ne groweð na god, ant bitacneð idel. Idel akeldeð ant acwencheð þis
fur. Sturieð ow cwicliche aa i gode werkes, ant þet schal heaten ow ant
ontenden þis fur aʒein þe brune of sunne; for alswa as þe an neil
driueð ut þen oþer, alswa þe brune of Godes luue driueð brune of ful
15 luue ut of þe heorte. Þe þridde þing is eisil—þet is, sur heorte of nið
oðer of onde. Vnderstondeð þis word: þa þe niðfule Giws offreden ure
Lauerd þis sure present upo þe rode, þa seide he þet reowðfule word,
Consumatum est. 'Neauer', quoð he, 'ear nu nes Ich ful pinet'—nawt
þurh þet eisil, ah þurh hare ondfule nið, þet tet eisil bitacnede þet heo
20 him duden drinken. Ant is ilich as þah a mon þet hefde longe
iswunken, ant failede efter long swinc on ende of his hure. Alswa ure
Lauerd mare þen twa ant þritti ʒer tilede efter hare luue, ant for al his
sare swinc ne wilnede na þing bute luue to hure. Ah i þe ende of his lif,
þet wes as i þe euentid, hwen me ʒelt wercmen hare deies hure, loke
25 hu ha ʒulden him for piment of huni luue eisil of sur nið ant galle of
bitter onde. 'O!' quoð ure Lauerd þa, '*consumatum est.* Al mi swinc on
eorðe, al mi pine o rode | ne sweameð ne ne derueð me nawiht aʒein   [▪
þis, þet Ich þus biteo al þet Ich idon habbe. Þis eisil þet ʒe beodeð
me, þis sure hure, þurhfulleð mi pine.' Þis eisil of sur heorte ant of
30 bitter þonc ouer alle oðre þing acwencheð Grickisch fur, þet is, þe
luue of ure Lauerd; ant hwa se hit bereð i breoste toward wummon
oðer mon, ha is Giwes make. Ha offreð Godd þis eisil, ant þurhfulleð
onont hire Iesues pine o rode. Me warpeð Grickisch fur upon his
famen, ant swa me ouerkimeð ham. ʒe schule don alswa hwen Godd
35 areareð ow of ei va eani weorre. Hu ʒe hit schule warpen Salomon
teacheð: *Si esurierit inimicus tuus, ciba illum; si sitierit, potum da illi. Sic
enim carbones ardentes congeres super caput eius*—þet is, 'ʒef þi fa

extinguish it, so they say, but urine and sand and vinegar. This Greek fire is the love of Jesus our Lord, and you must make it from the blood of a red man, that is, Jesus Christ, who was reddened with his own blood on the precious cross—and was, it is thought, naturally red in complexion. This blood, shed for you on the two pieces of wood mentioned above, will make you Sareptans—that is, kindled with this Greek fire, this love which, as Solomon says, cannot be quenched by any waters (which are earthly tribulations) or any temptations, either inner or outer. Now all that remains is to guard yourself carefully against everything which quenches it: that is, urine and sand and vinegar, as I said before. Urine is the stench of sin. Nothing good grows on sand, and it stands for idleness. Idleness cools this fire and puts it out. Always be active in good works, and that will warm you and kindle this fire against the flames of sin; for just as one nail drives out the other, so the flames of God's love drive the flames of sinful love out of the heart. The third thing is vinegar—that is, a heart sour with envy or hatred. Undertand this saying: when the envious Jews offered our Lord this sour present on the cross, he said those heart-breaking words, *It is finished*. 'My sufferings', he said, 'were never complete till now'—not because of the vinegar, but through their malicious envy, which was signified by the vinegar which they made him drink. And it is as though a man had laboured for a long time, and finally, after long labour, was not given his pay. Just so our Lord cultivated their love for more than thirty-two years, and wanted nothing but love as payment for all his hard labour. But at the end of his life, which was (as it were) in the evening, when workmen are paid their wages for the day, see how they paid him, not with the spiced drink of honey-sweet love, but with the vinegar of sour envy and the gall of bitter malice. 'Oh!' said our Lord then, '*it is finished*. All my labour on earth, all my sufferings on the cross do not grieve or distress me at all compared with this, that I should throw away like this all that I have done. This vinegar that you offer me, this bitter payment, completes my sufferings.' This vinegar of a sour heart, and of bitter thoughts, more than anything else quenches Greek fire, that is, the love of our Lord; and whoever carries it in her heart towards woman or man is no better than a Jew. She offers God this vinegar, and takes her part in completing Jesus' suffering on the cross. People throw Greek fire on to their enemies, and defeat them in that way. You must do the same when God stirs up hostility towards you in any of your enemies. Solomon gives instructions on how you must throw it: *If your enemy is hungry, feed him; if he is thirsty, give him drink. In this way you will heap burning coals on his head*—that is, 'if your

hungreð, fed him; to his þurst ȝef him drunch.' Þet is to
understonden, ȝef he efter þin hearm haueð hunger oðer þurst, ȝef
him fode of þine beoden þet Godd do him are; ȝef him drunch of
teares, wep for his sunnen. 'Þus þu schalt', seið Salomon, 'rukelin on
5   his heaued bearninde gleden'; þet is to seggen, þus þu schalt ontenden
his heorte for te luuie þe—for 'heorte' is in Hali Writ bi 'heaued'
understonden. O þulli wise wule Godd seggen ed te dome, 'Hwi
luuedest tu þe mon oðer þe wummon?' 'Sire, ha luueden me.' 'ȝe,' he
wule seggen, 'þu ȝulde þet tu ahtest. Her nabbe Ich þe nawt muches
10 to ȝelden.' ȝef þu maht ondswerien, 'Alle wa ha duden me, ne na
luue ne ahte Ich ham, ah, Sire, Ich luuede ham for þi luue,' þet luue he
ah þe, for hit wes iȝeuen him, ant he hit wule þe ȝelden.

    Migge, as Ich seide, þet acwencheð Grickisch fur is stinkinde
flesches luue, þe acwencheð gastelich luue þet Grickisch fur bitacneð.
15 Hweat flesch wes on eorðe se swete ant se hali as wes Iesu Cristes
flesch? Ant þah he seide himseolf | to his deore deciples, *Nisi ego abiero,*
Paraclitus non veniet ad uos: þet is, 'Bute Ich parti from ow, þe Hali
Gast—þet is, min ant mines Feaderes luue—ne mei nawt cumen to
ow. Ah hwen Ich beo from ow, Ich chulle senden him ow.' Hwen Iesu
20 Cristes ahne deciples, hwil þet ha fleschliche luueden him neh ham,
foreoden þe swetnesse of þe Hali Gast, ne ne mahte nawt habben baðe
togederes, demeð ow seoluen: nis he wod oðer heo þe luueð to swiðe
hire ahne flesch, oðer eani mon fleschliche, swa þet ha ȝirne to swiðe
his sihðe oðer his speche? Ne þunche hire neauer wunder ȝef hire
25 wonti þe Hali Gastes froure. Cheose nu euchan of þes twa, eorðlich
elne ant heouenlich, to hweðer ha wule halden, for þet oðer ha mot
leten; for i þe tweire monglunge ne mei ha habben neauer mare
schirnesse of heorte, þet is, as we seiden ear, þet god ant te strengðe of
alle religiuns, ant in euch ordre. Luue makeð hire schir, griðful, and
30 cleane. Luue haueð a meistrie biuoren alle oþre, for al þet ha rineð, al
ha turneð to hire ant makeð al hire ahne. *Quemcumque locum calcauerit*
pes uester—pes uidelicet amoris—uester erit. Deore walde moni mon
buggen a swuch þing þet al þet he rine þerwið al were his ahne; ant ne
seide hit þruppe feor, ane þurh þet tu luuest þet god þet is in anoðer,
35 wið þe rinunge of þi luue þu makest wiðuten oþer swinc his god þin
ahne god, as Sein Gregoire witneð? Lokið nu hu muchel god þe
ontfule leoseð. Streche þi luue to Iesu Crist, þu hauest him iwunnen.
Rin him wið ase muche luue as þu hauest sum mon sumchearre, he is

33 þerwið] CT, þeremide N, to A

enemy is hungry, feed him; if he is thirsty, give him drink.' That means, if he hungers or thirsts after your harm, give him the food of your prayers so that God may have mercy on him; give him a drink of tears, weep for his sins. 'In this way', says Solomon, 'you will heap burning coals on his head'; that is to say, in this way you will kindle his heart to love you—since 'head' in Holy Scripture is taken to mean 'heart'. This is what God will say on the day of Judgement: 'Why did you love that man or that woman?' 'Lord, they loved me.' 'Yes,' he will say, 'you paid back what you owed. I have nothing much here to repay you for.' If you could answer, 'They did every kind of harm to me, and I did not owe them any love at all, but, Lord, I loved them for love of you,' he owes you that love, because it was given to him, and he will repay it to you.

The urine, as I said, which extinguishes Greek fire is stinking carnal love, which extinguishes the spiritual love which is signified by Greek fire. What flesh on earth was as sweet and as holy as Jesus Christ's flesh was? And yet he said himself to his dear disciples, *If I do not go away, the Paraclete will not come to you*: that is, 'Unless I leave you, the Holy Spirit—that is, my love and my Father's—cannot come to you. But when I have left you, I will send him to you.' When Jesus Christ's own disciples, while they loved him near to them in the flesh, had to forgo the comfort of the Holy Spirit, and could not have both together, judge for yourselves: surely that man is mad, or that woman, who has too much love for her own flesh, or for any man in the flesh, so that she longs too much to see him or talk to him? She should never be surprised if she lacks the comfort of the Holy Spirit. Everyone should choose now which of these two things, earthly and heavenly comfort, she wants to settle for, as she must give up the other; because if she mixes the two she can never again have purity of heart, which is, as we said before, the virtue and the strength of all religious ways of life, and of every order. Love makes her pure, calm, and chaste. Love has a power greater than all others, for whatever she touches she takes over completely and makes all her own. *Whatever place your foot treads on— that is, the foot of love—shall be yours.* Many people would pay a great deal for something which would make everything they touched with it entirely their own; and was it not mentioned a long way back that simply by loving the good in someone else, with the touch of your love, without any other effort, you make his good your own, as St Gregory testifies? See now how much good the envious lose. Reach out with your love to Jesus Christ, and you have won him. Touch him with as much love as you have once felt for some special person, and he is

þin to don wið al þet tu wilnest. Ah hwa luueð þing þet leaueð hit for
leasse þen hit is wurð? Nis Godd betere uneuenlich þen al þet is i þe
world? 'Chearite' is cherte of leof þing ant of deore. Vndeore he makeð
Godd ant to un|wurð mid alle þet for ei worltlich þing of his luue
5 leaskeð; for na þing ne con luuien riht bute he ane. Swa ouer-swiðe he
luueð luue þet he makeð hire his euening. 3et Ich dear segge mare:
he makeð hire his meistre, ant deð al þet ha hat as þah he moste nede.
Mei Ich pruuien þis? 3e, witerliche, Ich, bi his ahne wordes; for
þus he spekeð to Moyses, þe monne meast him luuede, in
10 Numeri: *Dimisi iuxta uerbum tuum. Non dicit 'preces'.* 'Ich hefde', quoð
he, 'imunt to wreoke mine wreaððe i þis folc. Ah þu seist I ne schal
nawt; þi word beo iforðet.' Me seið þet luue bindeð. Witerliche luue
bint swa ure Lauerd þet he ne mei na þing don bute þurh luues leaue.
Nu preoue herof, for hit þuncheð wunder. *Ysaias: Domine, non est qui*
15 *consurgat et teneat te.* 'Lauerd, þu wult smiten,' seið Ysaie. 'Weilawei,
þu maht wel; nis nan þet te halde.' As þah he seide, '3ef ei luuede þe
riht, he mahte halden þe ant wearnen þe to smiten.' *In Genesy, ad Loth:*
Festina, et cetera. Non potero ibi quicquam facere donec egressus fueris illinc.
Þet is, þa ure Lauerd walde bisenchen Sodome, þer Lot, his freond,
20 wes inne, 'Hihe þe', quoð he, 'utward, for hwil þu art bimong ham, ne
mei Ich nawt don ham.' Nes þis wið luue ibunden? Hwet wult tu mare?
Luue is his chamberleng, his conseiler, his spuse, þet he ne mei nawt
heole wið, ah teleð al þet he þencheð. *In Genesy: Num celare potero*
Abraham que gesturus sum? 'Mei Ich', quoð ure Lauerd, 'heolen
25 Abraham þing þet Ich þenche to donne? Nai, o nane wise.' Nu con þes
luuien þe þus spekeð ant þus deð to alle þe him inwardliche leueð ant
luuieð. Þe blisse þet he 3arkeð ham, as ha is uneuenlich to alle
worldes blissen, alswa ha is untalelich to worldliche | tungen. *Ysaias:*
Oculus non uidit, Deus, absque te que preparasti diligentibus te. Apostolus:
30 *Oculus non uidit, nec auris audiuit, et cetera.* 3e habbeð of þeos blissen
iwriten elleshwer, mine leoue sustren.

Þis luue is þe riwle þe riwleð þe heorte. *Confitebor tibi in directione (id*
est, in regulatione) cordis. Exprobratio malorum: Generatio que non direxit
cor suum. Þis is þe leafdi Riwle. Alle þe oþre seruið hire, ant ane for
35 hire sake me hat ham to luuien. Lutel strengðe Ich do of ham, for
hwon þet þeos beo deorewurðliche ihalden. Habbeð ham þah
scheortliche i þe eahtuðe dale.

28 alswa] CFNTSL, alswa as A

yours to do anything you like with. But who loves something and gives it up for less than it is worth? Surely God is incomparably better than everything in the world? 'Charity' means the holding dear of loved and precious things. Those who slacken in their love because of any worldly thing make God cheap, and value him far too little, since he is the only creature that can truly love. He loves love so much to excess that he makes her his equal. I am bold enough to say even more: he makes her his master, and does everything she commands as if he were forced to. Can I prove this? Yes, certainly I can, by his own words; because this is how he speaks to Moses, who loved him more than any man did, in the Book of Numbers: *I have forgiven according to your word.* He does not say *'prayers'*. 'I had intended', he says, 'to wreak my anger on this people. But you say I must not; let your word stand.' It is said that love binds. Certainly love binds our Lord in such a way that he can do nothing except with love's permission. Now for a proof of this, since it seems astonishing. *Isaiah says, Lord, there is no one to rise and hold you.* 'Lord, you wish to strike,' says Isaiah. 'Alas, you may well; there is no one to hold you.' As if he were saying, 'If anyone truly loved you, he would be able to hold you and prevent you from striking.' *In Genesis, God says to Lot: Make haste, etc. I cannot do anything there until you have left the place.* That is, when our Lord wanted to destroy Sodom, where Lot, his friend, was, he said, 'Leave here quickly; because while you are among them, I can do nothing to them.' Surely here he was bound by love. What more do you want? Love is his chamberlain, his counsellor, his wife, from whom he can keep no secrets, but to whom he confides everything that he thinks. *He says in Genesis: Can I conceal from Abraham what I intend to do?* 'Can I conceal from Abraham', said our Lord, 'what I intend to do? No, not at all.' Now someone who speaks and acts in this way towards all who trust him and love him in their hearts knows how to love. Just as the joy that he is preparing for them cannot be compared with any earthly joy, so it cannot be described by any earthly tongue. *Isaiah: Lord, no eye but yours has seen what you have prepared for those who love you. The Apostle says: No eye has seen, nor ear heard, etc.* You have something written about these joys elsewhere, my dear sisters.

This love is the rule that rules the heart. *I will praise you with uprightness of heart (that is, by its regulation). The reproach of the wicked: A generation which did not guide its heart rightly.* This is the lady Rule. All the others serve her, and you are told to love them for her sake alone. I do not attach much importance to them, as long as this one is devotedly kept. You have them briefly set out, however, in the eighth part.

Biuoren on earst Ich seide þet ʒe ne schulden nawiht as i vu bihaten
for te halden nan of þe uttre riwlen; þet ilke Ich segge ʒetten. Ne
nane ne write Ich ham buten ow ane. Ich segge þis forþi þet oþre
ancren ne seggen nawt þet Ich þurh mi meistrie makie ham neowe
5 Riwle. Ne bidde Ich nawt þet ha halden ham; ah ʒe ʒet moten
changin, hwen se ʒe eauer wulleð, þeose for betere. Aʒein þinges þe
beoð biuoren, of ham is lutel strengðe.

Of sihðe ant of speche, ant of þe oþre wittes, is inoh iseid. Nu is þis
leaste dale, as Ich bihet on earst, todealet ant isundret o lutle seoue
10 stucchen.

Me let leasse of þe þing þet me haueð ofte. Forþi ne schule ʒe beon
bute as ure breðren beoð ihuslet inwið tweolf moneð fiftene siðen: (i)
Midwinter Dei (ii) Tweofte Dei (iii) Condelmeasse Dei (iiii) a
Sunnedei midwei bitweonen þet ant Easter, oðer Ure Leafdi Dei ʒef
15 he is neh þe Sunnedei, for þe hehnesse (v) Easter Dei (vi) þe þridde
Sunnedei þrefter | (vii) Hali Þursdei (viii) Witsunnedei (ix) Midsumer [1▸
Dei (x) Seinte Marie Dei Magdaleine (xi) þe Assumptiun (xii) þe
Natiuite (xiii) Seinte Mihales Dei (xiiii) Alle Halhene Dei (xv) Seint
Andrews Dei. Aʒein alle þeose beoð cleanliche ischriuene ant
20 neomeð disceplines—neauer þah of na mon bute of ow seoluen—ant
forgað an dei ower pitance. ʒef ewt ilimpeð misliche þet ʒe ne beon
nawt ihuslet i þeose isette tearmes, beoð hit þe neste Sunnedei; oðer
ʒef þe oþer terme is neh, abideð aþet tenne.

ʒe schulen eoten from Easter aþet te Hali Rode Dei þe leatere, þe
25 is in heruest, euche dei twien bute þe Fridahes ant Umbridahes,
ʒongdahes ant uigilies. I þeos dahes ne i þe Aduent ne schule ʒe
nawt eoten hwit bute neode hit makie. Þe oþer half-ʒer feasten al,
bute Sunnedahes ane, hwen ʒe beoð in heale ant i ful strengðe; ah
riwle ne tweast nawt seke ne blodletene.

30 ʒe ne schulen nawt eoten flesch ne seim bute for muche secnesse,
oðer hwa se is ouer-feble. Potage eoteð bliðeliche, ant wunieð ow to
lutel drunch. Noðeles, leoue sustren, ower mete ant ower drunch

26–7 ant . . . dahes] CFNT, *similar wording in* LP, *om.* A

Guide for Anchoresses, Part 8

I said earlier, at the beginning, that you should not commit yourselves to keeping any of the outer rules by a vow; I say the same now. And I am not writing them for anyone apart from you. I mention this so that other recluses may not claim that I am presuming to lay down a new Rule for them. I do not ask that they should observe them, and even you may change them for better ones whenever you wish. Compared with the matters dealt with earlier, they are of little importance.

Enough has been said about sight, speech, and the other senses. Now this last part is subdivided, as I promised at the beginning, into seven smaller sections.

People care less about what they have often. For this reason you should take Communion, as our brothers do, only fifteen times a year: (i) Christmas Day (ii) the feast of the Epiphany (iii) Candlemas Day (iv) a Sunday midway between that and Easter, or Lady Day if it is near the Sunday, because of its importance (v) Easter Day (vi) the third Sunday after Easter (vii) the feast of the Ascension (viii) Whit Sunday (ix) the feast of the Nativity of John the Baptist (x) the feast of St Mary Magdalen (xi) the Assumption (xii) the Nativity of the Blessed Virgin (xiii) the feast of St Michael (xiv) the feast of All Saints (xv) the feast of St Andrew. In preparation for all these, make a full confession and receive the discipline—but never from anyone apart from yourselves—and go without your pittance for one day. If anything goes wrong, so that you cannot take Communion at these set times, let it be the next Sunday; or if the next time is near, wait until then.

From Easter until the second feast of the Holy Cross, which falls in the autumn, you should eat twice every day except for the Fridays and Ember Days, Rogation Days and vigils. On these days and in Advent you should not eat dairy produce unless you have to. For the remaining half of the year you should fast all the time, Sundays only excepted, when you are healthy and have all your strength; but the rule does not apply to those who are ill or have been let blood.

You should not eat meat or fat except in the case of serious illness, or when someone is very weak. Be willing to eat vegetable dishes, and accustom yourselves to little drink. Nevertheless, dear sisters, your

haueð iþuht me ofte leasse þen Ich walde. Ne feaste ȝe na dei to
bread ne to weattre bute ȝe habben leaue.

Sum ancre makeð hire bord wið hire gest utewið. Þet is to muche
freondschipe; for of alle ordres, þenne is hit uncundelukest ant meast
5 aȝein ancre ordre þe is al dead to þe world. Me haueð iherd ofte þet
deade speken wið cwike, ah þet ha eten wið cwike ne fond Ich ȝet
neauer.

Ne makie ȝe nane gestnunges, ne ne tulle ȝe to þe ȝete nane
uncuðe hearloz. Þah þer nere nan oðer uuel bute hare meadlese nurð,
10 hit walde letten oðerhwile heouenliche þohtes. Ne limpeð nawt to
ancre of oþer | monnes ealmesse to makien hire large. Nalde me [1
lahhen a beggere lude to bismere þe leaðede men to feaste? Marie ant
Marthe ba weren sustren, ah hare lif sundrede. Ȝe ancren beoð
inumen ow to Marie dale, þe ure Lauerd seolf herede: '*Maria optimam
15 partem elegit.*' 'Marthe, Marthe,' quoð he, 'þu art in muche baret.
Marie haueð icore bet, ant ne schal hire na þing reauin hire dale.'
Husewifschipe is Marthe dale. Marie dale is stilnesse ant reste of alle
worldes noise, þet na þing ne lette hire to heren Godes steuene. Ant
lokið hwet Godd seið, þet na þing ne schal ow reauin þis dale. Marthe
20 haueð hire meoster; leoteð hire iwurðen. Ȝe sitten wið Marie stan-
stille ed Godes fet, ant hercnið him ane. Marthe meoster is to feden
poure ant schruden as hus-leafdi; Marie ne ah nawt to entremeatin
þrof. Ȝef ei blameð hire, Godd seolf ihwer wereð hire, as Hali Writ
witneð (*Contra Symonem: duo debitores, et cetera. Contra Martham:*
25 '*Maria optimam partem*', *et cetera. Contra apostolos, murmurantes, 'Vt quid*
perditio hec?': '*Bonum*', *inquit, 'opus', et cetera*). On oðer half, nan ancre
ne ah to neomen bute meaðfulliche þet hire to neodeð. Hwerof,
þenne, mei ha makien hire large? Ha schal libben bi ealmesse ase
meaðfulliche as ha eauer mei, ant nawt gederin for te ȝeouen. Ha nis
30 nawt husewif, ah is a chirch-ancre. Ȝef ha mei spearien eani poure
schraden, sende ham al dearnliche ut of hire wanes. Vnder semblant of
god is ofte ihulet sunne. Ant hu schulen þeose riche ancres þe tilieð
oðer habbeð rentes isette don to poure nehburs dearnliche hare
ealmesse? Ne wilni ha nawt to habbe word of a large ancre, ne for te
35 ȝeouen | muchel ne beo nan þe grediure for te habben mare. For [11
hwon þet gredinesse beo rote of þet gederunge, of hire bitternesse al
beoð þe bohes bittre þe of hire spruteð. Bidden hit for te ȝeouen hit

food and drink have often seemed to me less than I would like. Do not fast on bread and water on any day unless you have permission.

Sometimes a recluse has a meal with her guest outside her quarters. That is showing too much friendliness, for it goes against the nature of any form of religious life, and most of all that of a recluse, who is utterly dead to the world. One has often heard of the dead speaking with the living, but I have never found yet that they ate with the living.

Do not give lavish entertainments, or encourage strange beggars to come to the gate. Even if there were no harm in it apart from the disturbance they make, it would sometimes be a hindrance to heavenly thoughts. It is not proper for a recluse to be generous with someone else's donations. Would not a beggar who invited people to a feast be loudly laughed to shame? Mary and Martha were two sisters, but their way of life diverged. You recluses have followed Mary's way, which Our Lord himself praised: '*Mary has chosen the best part.*' 'Martha, Martha,' he said, 'you are in a great bustle. Mary has chosen better, and nothing will take her part away from her.' Being a housewife is Martha's part. Mary's part is silence and peace from all the noise of the world, so that nothing may prevent her from hearing God's voice. And look what God says, that nothing will take this part away from you. Martha has her role; let her be. You should sit with Mary, absolutely still at God's feet, and listen to him alone. Martha's role is to feed and clothe the poor, as the lady of the house does; Mary should have nothing to do with this. If anybody criticizes her, God himself defends her on every occasion, as Holy Scripture shows (*Against Simon: 'Two debtors', etc. Against Martha: 'Mary [has chosen] the best part', etc. Against the apostles, complaining, 'What is the point of this waste?' '[She has done] a good work', he said, etc.*). On the other hand, no recluse should accept more than will supply her needs without excess. So what has she to be generous with? She must live on charity as moderately as she can, and not gather together things to give away. She is not a housewife, but a church-recluse. If she can spare any poor scraps, she should send them secretly out of her house. Under an apparent good, sin is often concealed. And how are these rich recluses who cultivate lands, or have a fixed income, to offer charity secretly to their poor neighbours? She should not wish to have the reputation of a generous recluse, or be any greedier to have more in order to give much away. Whenever greed is the root of that gathering, all the branches that spring from it share in its bitterness. A recluse has no right to ask for something in

nis nawt ancre rihte. Of ancre curteisie, of ancre largesce is icumen
ofte sunne ant scheome on ende.

Wummen ant children, ant nomeliche ancre meidnes, þe cumeð
iswenchet for ow, þah ȝe spearien hit on ow, oðer borhin oðer bidden
5 hit, makieð ham to eotene wið chearitable chere ant leaðieð to
herbarhin.

Na mon ne eote biuoren ow bute bi ower meistres leaue, general
oðer spetial: general as of Freres Preachurs ant Meonurs, spetial of
alle oþre. Ne leaðie ȝe nane oþre to eoten ne to drinken bute alswa
10 þurh his leaue. 'Liht is', me seið, 'leaue.' Nawiht ne ȝirne Ich þet me
for swucche boden telle ow hende ancren; ihwear þah ant eauer
ȝemeð ow þet nan from ow þurh ower untuhtle ne parti wið scandle.

Ed gode men neomeð al þet ow to nedeð; ah þet lokið ow wel, þet ȝe
ne kecchen þe nome of gederinde ancren. Of mon þet ȝe misleueð
15 þurh his fol semblant oðer bi his wake wordes, nowðer ne neome ȝe
ne leasse ne mare. Neode schal driuen ow for te bidden ei þing; þah
eadmodliche schawið to gode men ant wummen ower meoseise.

Ȝe, mine leoue sustren, bute ȝef neod ow driue ant ower meistre
hit reade, ne schulen habbe na beast bute cat ane. Ancre þe haueð ahte
20 þuncheð bet husewif ase Marthe wes, ne lihtliche ne mei ha nawt beo
Marie, Marthe suster, wið griðfullnesse | of heorte; for þenne mot ha [11ᵃ]
þenchen of þe kues foddre, of heordemonne hure, olhnin þe heiward,
wearien hwen he punt hire, ant ȝelden þah þe hearmes. Ladlich þing
is hit, wat Crist, hwen me makeð i tune man of ancre ahte. Nu þenne,
25 ȝef eani mot nedlunge habben hit, loki þet hit na mon ne eili ne ne
hearmi, ne þet hire þoht ne beo nawiht þron ifestnet. Ancre ne ah to
habben na þing þet utward drahe hire heorte.

Na chaffere ne driue ȝe. Ancre þet is chepilt—þet is, buð for te
sullen efter biȝete—ha chepeð hire sawle þe chapmon of helle. Þing
30 þah þet ha wurcheð ha mei þurh hire meistres read for hire neode
sullen. Hali men sumhwile liueden bi hare honden.

Nawt, deore dehtren, ne wite ȝe in ower hus of oðer monne
þinges—ne ahte ne claðes, ne boistes ne chartres, scoren ne cyrograffes, ne þe chirch-uestemenz ne þe calices—bute neode oðer

8 general] *om.* A; *Salu, p. 184*

order to give it away. From a recluse's courtesy, from a recluse's generosity, sin and shame have often come in the end.

As for women and children—and especially the recluses' maid-servants—who have taken trouble on your account, even if you have to do without something yourself or borrow or beg it, encourage them hospitably to eat and invite them to stay.

No man should eat in your presence without your director's permission, general or special: general in the case of Dominican and Franciscan friars, special in all other cases. Do not invite anyone else to eat or drink without asking his permission in the same way. 'Asking costs nothing,' they say. I have no desire at all that you should be seen as courtly recluses because of such invitations; but in all circumstances take care that you do not let anyone go away scandalized at your bad manners.

Take all that you need from good people; but see that you do not get the reputation of being acquisitive recluses. From anyone you distrust because of his impudent manner or his idle chatter, accept nothing whatever. You should be forced by necessity to ask for anything; nevertheless, humbly reveal your difficulties to good men and women.

You, my dear sisters, unless you are forced by necessity and your director advises you to, must not keep any animal except a cat. A recluse who keeps livestock is more like a housewife, as Martha was, and cannot easily be Mary, Martha's sister, in serenity of heart; because then she has to think about the cow's fodder and the herdsman's wages, cajole the hayward, curse him when he impounds the cow, and pay damages all the same. It is a dreadful thing, God knows, when people complain in the village about the recluse's cattle. For this reason, if anyone is forced by need to keep livestock, she should see that it does not cause annoyance or damage to anybody else, and that she is not preoccupied with it. A recluse ought not to own anything that attracts her heart outwards.

Do not carry on any business. A recluse who is a tradeswoman—that is, who buys to sell at a profit—is selling her soul to the tradesman of hell. However, she may, on her director's advice, sell things she has made to supply her needs. Holy men have supported themselves in the past by the work of their hands.

Do not keep anything in your house, dear daughters, that belongs to other people—livestock or clothes, caskets or deeds, tallies or indentures, or the church vestments or the chalices—unless you are

strengðe hit makie oðer muchel eie. Of swuch witunge is muchel vuel ilumpen ofte siðen.

Inwið ower wanes ne leote ȝe na mon slepen. Ȝef muchel neod mid alle makeð breoken ower hus, hwil hit eauer is ibroken habbeð
5 þrinne wið ow a wummon of cleane lif deies ant nihtes.

Forþi þet wepmen ne seoð ow ne ȝe ham, wel mei don of ower clað beo hit hwit, beo hit blac, bute hit beo unorne, warm, ant wel iwraht, felles wel itawet; ant habbeð ase monie as ow to neodeð to bedde ant to rugge.
10 Nest flesch ne schal nan werien linnene clað bute hit beo of hearde ant of greate heorden. Stamin habbe hwa se wule; hwa se wule beo buten. Ȝe schulen in an hetter ant igurd liggen, swa leoðeliche þah þet ȝe mahen honden put|ten þerunder. Nest lich nan ne [113 gurde hire wið na cunne gurdles bute þurh schriftes leaue, ne beore
15 nan irn ne here ne ilespiles felles, ne ne beate hire þerwið, ne wið scurge ileadet, wið holin ne wið breres, ne biblodgi hireseolf, wiðute schriftes leaue. Nohwer ne binetli hire, ne ne beate biuoren, ne na keoruunge ne keorue, ne ne neome ed eanes to luðere disceplines, temptatiuns for te acwenchen. Ne for na bote aȝein cundeliche
20 secnesses nan uncundelich lechecreft ne leue ȝe ne ne fondin wiðuten ower meistres read, leste ow stonde wurse.

Ower schon i winter beon meoke, greate, ant warme. I sumer ȝe habbeð leaue bearuot gan ant sitten, ant lihte scheos werien.

Hosen wiðute vampez ligge in hwa se likeð. Ischeoed ne slepe ȝe
25 nawt, ne nohwer bute i bedde. Sum wummon inohreaðe wereð þe brech of here ful wel icnottet, þe streapeles dun to þe vet ilacet ful feaste; ah eauer is best þe swete ant te swote heorte. Me is leouere þet ȝe þolien wel an heard word þen an heard here.

Ȝef ȝe muhen beo wimpelles, ant ȝe wel wullen, beoð bi warme
30 cappen, ant þeruppon hwite oðer blake veiles. Ancren summe sungið in hare wimplunge na leasse þen leafdis. Ah þah seið sum þet hit limpeð to euch wummon cundeliche for te werien wimpel. Nai, wimpel ne heaued-clað nowðer ne nempneð Hali Writ, ah wriheles ane. *Ad Corinthios: Mulier uelet caput suum.* 'Wummon', seið þe apostle,
35 'schal wreon hire heaued.' 'Wrihen', he seið, nawt 'wimplin': wrihen

forced to by necessity or violence or because of great danger. Much harm has often arisen from such custody.

Do not let any man sleep on the premises. Furthermore, if some great emergency results in damage to your house, while it is insecure have a woman of respectable character to stay with you day and night.

Because men do not see you, or you them, it does not matter at all whether your clothing is white or black, as long as it is plain, warm, and well-made, the skins properly cured; and have as many bedclothes and garments as you need.

Nobody should wear linen next to the skin unless it is made of stiff and coarse fibres. Anyone who wishes may wear an undergarment of rough wool; anyone who wishes may do without one. You should sleep in a robe, and wearing a belt, but so loosely fastened that you can put your hands under it. Nobody should wear a belt of any kind next to the skin except with her confessor's permission, or wear anything made of iron or hair or hedgehog skins, or beat herself with them, or with a scourge weighted with lead, with holly, or with thorns, or draw blood, without her confessor's permission. She should not sting herself anywhere with nettles, or scourge the front of her body, or mutilate herself with cuts, or take excessively severe disciplines at any one time, in order to subdue temptations. Nor should you put your trust in any unnatural remedy for natural sicknesses, or try it without your director's advice, lest you should be the worse for it.

Your shoes in winter should be supple, roomy, and warm. In summer you have permission to go around barefoot and wear light shoes.

Anyone who wants to may sleep in stockings without feet. Do not sleep wearing shoes, or anywhere except in bed. Sometimes a woman may wear drawers of haircloth tightly fastened, with the legs firmly cross-gartered down to the feet; but a mild and gentle heart is always best. I would rather have you bear a harsh word well than a harsh hair shirt.

If you can do without wimples, and you are quite willing to, have warm caps, and white or black veils over them. Some recluses sin no less than ladies in wearing wimples. But nevertheless, someone may say that it is natural for every woman to wear a wimple. No, Holy Scripture makes no mention of wimple or head-cloth, only of 'covering'. *To the Corinthians: Let the woman cover her head.* 'A woman', says the apostle, 'must cover her head.' 'Cover', he says, not 'wimple':

ha schal hire scheome as sunfule Eue dohter, i mungunge of þe sunne
þet schende us on earst alle, ant nawt drahe þe wriheles to tiffunge ant
to prude. Eft wule | þe apostle þet wummon wreo i chirche hire neb [11.
ӡetten, leste uuel þoht arise þurh hire onsihðe: *et hoc est propter*
5 *angelos.* Hwi þenne, þu chirch-ancre, iwimplet openest þi neb to
wepmonnes ehe? Toӡeines þe þe sist men spekeð þe apostle, ӡef þu
þe ne hudest. Ah ӡef þet ei þing wriheð þi neb from monnes ehe, beo
hit wah, beo hit clað i wel-itund windowe, wel mei duhen ancre of oðer
wimplunge. Toӡeines þe þe þus ne dest spekeð þe apostle, nawt
10 toӡeines oþre þet hare ahne wah wriheð wið euch monnes sihðe. Þer
awakenið ofte wake þohtes of, ant werkes oðerhwiles. Hwa se wule
beon isehen, þah ha atiffi hire nis nawt muche wunder; ah to Godes
ehnen ha is lufsumre þe is for þe luue of him untiffet wiðuten.

Ring ne broche ne habbe ӡe, ne gurdel imembret, ne glouen ne
15 nan swuch þing þet ow ne deh to habben. A meoke surpliz ӡe mahen
in hat sumer werien.

Eauer me is leouere se ӡe doð greattre werkes.

Ne makie ӡe nane purses for te freondin ow wið, bute to þeo þet
ower meistre ӡeueð ow his leaue, ne huue ne blodbinde of seolc ne
20 laz buten leaue; ah schapieð ant seowið ant mendið chirche claðes ant
poure monne hettren. Na swuch þing ne schule ӡe ӡeouen wiðuten
schriftes leaue, na mare þen neomen þet ӡe ne seggen him fore—as of
oðre þinges, kun oðer cuððe, hu ofte ӡe underuengen, hu longe ӡe
edheolden. Tendre of cun ne limpeð nawt ancre beonne. A mon wes
25 of religiun, ant com to him efter help his fleschliche broðer, ant he
tahte him to his þridde breðer, þe wes dead biburiet. Þe ondswerede
wundrinde, 'Nai,' (quoð he) 'nis he dead?' 'Ant Ich', quoð þe hali
mon, | 'am dead gasteliche. Na fleschlich freond ne easki me [114
fleschlich froure.' Amites ant parures worldliche leafdis mahen inoh
30 wurchen; ant ӡef ӡe ham makieð, ne makie ӡe þrof na mustreisun.
Veine gloire attreð alle gode þeawes ant alle gode werkes. Criblin ne
schal nan of ow for luue ne for hure. Taueles ne forbeode Ich nawt,
ӡef sum riueð surpliz oðer measse-kemese; oþre riuunges ne riue ha
nawt, nomeliche ouer-egede, bute for muche neode.

---

1 sunfule Eue] C²V, Eue sunfule A　　　6 þe²] C², *om.* A

she must cover her shame as a daughter of sinful Eve, in memory of
the sin which brought us all to destruction in the beginning, and not
turn the covering into adornment and finery. What is more, the apostle
would like women in church to cover their faces as well, in case looking
at them should give rise to sinful thoughts: *and this is on account of the
angels*. Why, then, do you, as a church-recluse, wear a wimple and
leave your face open to a man's gaze? The apostle is talking about
those of you who see men, if you do not conceal yourselves. But if
anything hides your face from men's eyes, whether it is a wall or cloth
in a well-secured window, there is no need for the recluse to have any
other wimpling. The apostle is referring to those of you who do not do
this, not the others who are concealed by their own wall from any
man's sight. Often unhealthy thoughts arise from this, and sometimes
acts as well. If anyone wants to be looked at, it is hardly surprising that
she adorns herself; but the woman who remains outwardly unadorned
for love of God is more beautiful in his eyes.

Do not own rings or brooches or ornamental girdles or gloves or
anything of that kind that you are not supposed to have. When it is hot
in summer you may wear a light garment of white linen.

The plainer the things you make, the better I am pleased.

Do not make any purses to win friends, except for those people your
director allows, or caps, or silk bandages, or girdles, without permission;
but cut and sew and mend church vestments and poor men's clothes.
You must not give away anything of this kind without your confessor's
permission, any more than you should accept it without telling him
beforehand—and the same applies to other matters, such as how often
you should receive relations or friends, and how long you should have
them to stay. A recluse ought not to be too attached to her family.
There was once a religious whose own brother came to him for help,
and he referred him to a third brother, who was dead and buried. He
answered in amazement, 'Surely not! Isn't he dead?' 'And I', said the
holy man, 'am dead in a spiritual sense. No earthly friend should ask me for
earthly help.' Amices and decorative panels for vestments can very well
be made by ladies in the world; if you do make them, avoid any
ostentation. Vainglory poisons all virtues and all good works. None of
you should do sieve-work for love or money. I do not forbid you to
make narrow lace borders, if one of you is trimming a surplice or an
alb; but she should not make other kinds of trimming, especially over-
elaborate ones, unless it is absolutely necessary.

Helpeð ow wið ower ahne swinc se forð se ȝe eauer mahen, to schruden ow seoluen ant feden ȝef neod is, ant þeo þe ow seruið.

As Sein Ierome leareð, ne beo ȝe neauer longe ne lihtliche of sum þing allunges idel, for ananrihtes þe feond beot hire his werc þe i
5   Godes werc ne swinkeð, ant tuteleð anan toward hire. For hwil he sið hire bisi, he þencheð þus: 'For nawt Ich schulde nu cume neh hire; ne mei ha nawt iȝemen to lustni mi lare.' Of idelnesse awakeneð muchel flesches fondunge. *Iniquitas Sodome: saturitas panis et ocium*—þet is, Sodomes cwedschipe com of idelnesse ant of ful wombe. Irn þet lið
10 stille gedereð sone rust; weater þe ne stureð nawt readliche stinkeð.

Ancre ne schal nawt forwurðe scolmeistre, ne turnen ancre-hus to childrene scole. Hire meiden mei learen sum oðer meiden þet were pliht of to leornin among wepmen oðer bimong gromes, ah ancre ne ah to ȝemen bute Godd ane (þah bi hire meistres read ha mei sum rihten
15 ant helpen to learen).

ȝe ne schulen senden leattres ne underuon leattres ne writen bute leaue.

ȝe schulen beon idoddet, oðer ȝef ȝe wulleð ischauen, fowr siðen i þe ȝer to lihtin ower heaued (beo bi þe her ieueset | hwa se swa is [11
20 leouere), ant as ofte ileten blod, ant ȝef neod is oftre. Þe mei beo þer buten, Ich hit mei wel þolien. Hwen ȝe beoð al greiðe ilete blod, ȝe ne schule don na þing þe þreo dahes þet ow greueð, ah talkið to ower meidnes, ant wið þeawfule talen schurteð ow togederes. ȝe mahen swa don ofte hwen ow þuncheð heuie, oðer beoð for sum worltlich
25 þing sare oðer seke—þah euch worltlich froure is unwurðe to ancre.

Swa wisliche witeð ow in ower blodletunge ant haldeð ow i swuch reste þet ȝe longe þrefter mahen i Godes seruise þe monluker swinken, ant alswa hwen ȝe feleð eani secnesse. Muchel sotschipe hit is leosen for an dei tene oðer tweolue.
30 Wesscheð ow hwer se neod is as ofte as ȝe wulleð, ant ower oþre þinges. Nes neauer fulðe Godd leof, þah pouerte ant unorneschipe beon him licwurðe.

Vnderstondeð eauer of alle þeose þinges þet nan nis heast ne forbod þet beoð of þe Uttre Riwle, þet is lute strengðe of, for hwon þet te inre

Help yourselves with your own labour as far as you possibly can, to clothe and, if necessary, support both yourselves and those who work for you.

As St Jerome advises, never be completely unoccupied for any length of time or without good reason, since the Devil offers his own employment straight away to the woman who is not employed in God's business, and whispers to her at once. For while he sees her busy, he thinks, 'It would be useless for me to approach her now; she cannot find the time to listen to my teaching.' Much temptation of the flesh arises from idleness. *The iniquity of Sodom: a surfeit of bread and idleness*—that is, the wickedness of Sodom came from idleness and a full belly. Iron which lies still soon gathers rust; standing water soon begins to stink.

A recluse should not degenerate into a schoolmistress, or turn her cell into a children's school. Her maid may give instruction to some other girl if it would be undesirable to have her taught with men or boys, but a recluse ought not to devote her attention to anyone other than God (although on her director's advice she may offer guidance and help with learning).

You must not send letters or receive letters or write anything without permission.

You should have your hair cropped, or shaved if you wish, four times a year to lighten your head (anyone who prefers may have her hair trimmed); and be let blood as often, and if necessary more often. If anyone can do without this, I have no objection. When you have just been bled, you should not do anything for the three days you are recovering, but talk to your maidservants and entertain each other with edifying stories. You may do this often when you are feeling depressed, or are upset or ill for some earthly reason—though every earthly comfort is of little value to a recluse.

Look after yourselves so carefully during your blood-letting, and take things so easily, that you may labour more vigorously in God's service for a long time afterwards; and the same applies when you feel at all ill. It is very foolish to lose ten or twelve days for the sake of one.

Wash yourselves wherever necessary as often as you wish, and your things as well. Filth was never dear to God, although poverty and plainness of dress are pleasing to him.

Where all these matters are concerned, you should always understand that nothing which comes under the Outer Rule is a command or a

beo wel iwist, as Ich seide i þe frumðe. Þeos mei beon ichanget hwer
se eani neod oðer eani skile hit easkeð, efter þet ha best mei þe leafdi
Riwle seruin as hire eadmode þuften—ah sikerliche wiðuten hire þe
leafdi feareð to wundre.

5　Ancre þe naueð nawt neh honde hire fode, beoð bisie twa wummen,
an eauer þe leaue ed hame, anoþer þe wende ut hwenne driueð neod;
ant þeo beo ful unorne wiðuten euch tiffunge, oðer a lutel þuftene
oðer of feier ealde. Bi þe wei as ha geað, ga singinde hire beoden, ne
ne halde na tale wið mon ne wið wummon, ne sitte ne ne stonde, bute
10　þet leaste þet ha eauer mei ear þen ha ham cume. Nohwider elles ne
ga | heo bute þider as me send hire wiðute leaue, ne ne eote ha ne ne [1
drinke ute. Þe oþer beo eauer inne, ne wiðute þe ȝeten ne ga wiðute
leaue. Ba beon obedient to hare dame in alle þing bute i sunne ane. Na
þing nabben þet heo hit nute, ne underuo na þing ne ne ȝeoue
15　nowðer wiðuten hire leaue. Na mon ne leoten in, ne þe ȝungre ne
speoke wið na mon bute leaue. Ne ga ha nawt ut of tune wiðuten siker
fere, ȝef hit swa mei beon, ne ne ligge ute. Ȝef heo ne con o boke,
segge bi Pater Nostres ant bi Auez hire ures, ant wurche þet me hat
hire wiðute gruchunge. Habbe eauer hire earen opene toward hire
20　dame. Nowðer of þe wummen ne beore from hare dame, ne ne bringe
to hire, nane idele talen ne neowe tidinges, ne bitweonen hamseolf ne
singen ne ne speoken nane worldliche spechen, ne lahhen swa ne
pleien þet ei mon þet hit sehe mahte hit to uuel turnen. Ouer alle
þinges, leasunges ant luðere wordes heatien. Hare her beo icoruen,
25　hare heaued-clað sitte lahe. Eiðer ligge ane. Hare cop beo hehe
isticchet ant bute broche. Na mon ne seo ham unleppet ne open-
heaued. Lah locunge habben. Heo ne schulen cussen na mon, ne cuð
mon ne cunnesmon, ne for na cuððe cluppen, ne weschen hare
heaued, ne lokin feaste o na mon, ne toggin wið ne pleien. Hare weden
30　beon of swuch schape, ant al hare aturn swuch, þet hit beo edscene
hwerto ha beoð iturnde. Hare lates lokin warliche, þet nan ne mahe
edwiten ham in hus ne ut of hus. On alle wise forbeoren to wreaðen

15　leoten in] CT, leote ȝe in A, lessent entrer F, introducat L, leten heo in N

prohibition, since this rule matters little as long as the Inner Rule is observed, as I said at the beginning. The former may be changed wherever any need or any reason requires it, depending on how it may best serve the lady Rule as its humble maidservant—but certainly without it the lady comes to grief.

For a recluse who does not have her food near at hand, two women are needed, one always to remain at home, another to go out when the need arises; and the latter should be very plainly dressed, without any kind of personal adornment, either a little maidservant or else advanced in years. As she goes on her way she should recite her prayers, and should not stop to chat with anyone, man or woman, or sit down or stand about more than she can possibly help before she comes home. She should not go anywhere else than where she is sent, or eat and drink while out, without permission. The other one should always remain inside, and not go outside the gates without permission. Both should be obedient to their mistress in everything except what is sinful. They should not own anything without her knowledge, or accept or give anything without leave from her. They should not let any man in, and the younger should not speak to any man without permission. If at all possible, she should not leave the village without a trustworthy companion, or spend the night elsewhere. If she is illiterate, she should say her hours with *Our Father*s and *Hail Mary*s, and do whatever work she is told to do without any grumbling. She should always keep her ears open for her mistress's call. Neither of the women should carry from their mistress, or bring to her, any trivial stories or items of news, or sing or talk in a worldly manner between themselves, or laugh and romp in such a way that anyone who saw it might misconstrue it. Above all, they should hate lies and malicious talk. Their hair should be cut short, and their head-cloths sit low on the forehead. Each of them should sleep on her own. The necklines of their dresses should be sewn high at the front, and without a brooch. Nobody should see them without a cloak, or bareheaded. They should keep their eyes lowered. They must not kiss any man, either friend or relation, or embrace him, however close the acquaintance, or wash men's hair, or stare at any man, or indulge in horseplay with him. The cut of their clothes, and their dress in general, should be of a kind that makes it obvious what way of life they have chosen. They should watch their behaviour carefully, so that they give no occasion for criticism indoors or out. They should make every effort not to incur their

hare dame, ant as ofte as heo hit doð, ear ha drinken oþer eoten
makien | hare *Venie* o cneon dun biuoren hire, ant seggen, '*Mea culpa*', [1
ant underuon þe penitence þet ha leið upon hire, lutinde hire lahe. Þe
ancre þrefter neauer mare þet ilke gult ne upbreide for na wreaððe,
5 bute ʒef ha eftsone falle i þet ilke, ah do hit allunge ut of hire heorte.
Ʒef ei strif ariseð bitweone þe wummen, þe ancre makie eiðer to
makien oþer *Venie* o cneon to þer eorðe, ant eiðer rihte up oþer, ant
cussen on ende, ant te ancre legge on eiðer sum penitence, mare upo
þe ilke þe greatluker gulte. Þis is a þing, witen ha wel, þet is Gode
10 leouest, sahtnesse ant some, ant te feond laðest; forþi he is eauer
umben to arearen sum leaððe. Nu sið þe sweoke wel þet hwen fur is
wel o brune ant me wule þet hit aga, me sundreð þe brondes; ant he
deð hond þet ilke. Luue is Iesu Cristes fur, þet he wule þet bleasie aa i
þin heorte; ant te deouel blaweð for te puffen hit ut. Hwen his
15 blawunge ne geineð nawt, he bringeð up sum uuel word oðer sum
oþer nohtunge hwerþurh ha tohurten eiðer frommard oþer; ant te Hali
Gastes fur cwencheð hwen þe brondes þurh wreaððe beoð isundret.
Forþi halden ham i luue feaste togederes, ant ne beo ham nawt of
hwen þe feond blawe, nomeliche ʒef monie beon iueiet somet ant wel
20 wið luue ontende. Þah þe ancre on hire meidnes for openliche gultes
legge penitence, to þe preost noðeleater schriuen ham hwen neod is—
ah eauer þah wið leaue.
Ʒef ha ne cunnen nawt þe mete graces, seggen in hare stude *Pater
Noster* biuoren ant *Aue Maria*, ant efter mete alswa ant a *Credo* mare,
25 ant segge þus on ende: 'Feader, Sune, Hali Gast, an almihti Godd,
ʒeoue ure dame his grace | se lengre se mare, ant leue hire ant us ba [1
neomen god ende. Forʒelde alle þe us god doð, ant milci hare sawle
þe us god idon habbeð, hare sawle ant alle Cristene sawles.'
Bitweone mel ne gruseli nawt, nowðer frut ne oðerhwet, ne drinken
30 bute leaue; ant te leaue beo liht in al þet nis sunne. Ed te mete na
word, oðer lut ant teo stille. Alswa, efter þe ancre Complie aþet Prime
ne don na þing ne seggen hwerþurh hire silence mahe beon isturbet.
Nan ancre seruant ne ahte bi rihte to easkin iset hure, bute mete ant

25 an] CFNT, *om.* A   29 gruseli] gruchesi ʒe A (ch *written in another hand over*
an erasure, with a horizontal line through the ascender of h), gruuesi C, manguent F, gruselie
ʒe N, gruse ʒe T; *Tolkien, Corpus MS, p. 220*

mistress's anger, and as often as they do, before they eat or drink they should make their *Venia* on their knees before her, and say, '*My fault*', and accept the individual penance that she gives them, bowing low to her. The recluse should never rebuke them again for that offence afterwards, however angry she is, unless they commit it again, but put it completely out of her mind. If any quarrel arises between the women, the recluse should see that each of them makes her *Venia* to the other, kneeling on the ground, and each of them should raise the other up, and finally they should kiss each other, and the recluse should impose some penance on each of them, heavier for the one who was more at fault. Concord and unity, as they should realize, is something very dear to God, and most hateful to the Devil; so the Devil is always plotting to stir up some discord. Now the treacherous fiend knows well that when a fire is burning strongly and you want to put it out, you separate the brands; and he does just the same. Love is the fire of Jesus Christ, who wishes it to blaze at all times in your heart; and the Devil blows in order to put it out. When his blowing does no good, he brings up some malicious remark or some other trivial thing which makes them recoil from each other; and the fire of the Holy Ghost goes out when the brands are separated by anger. So they should hold fast together in love, and it should be nothing to them when the Devil blows, especially if there are many joined together and well-kindled with love. Although the recluse may impose penance on her maids for manifest faults, they should nevertheless make their confession to the priest when necessary—but always with permission, even so.

If they do not know the graces for meals, they should say in their place *Our Father* and *Hail Mary* beforehand, and also after the meal with a *Creed* as well, and finally say as follows: 'May Father, Son, Holy Ghost, one almighty God, grant our mistress his grace in ever-increasing measure, and allow both her and us to make a good end. May he recompense all our present benefactors, and have mercy on the souls of our past benefactors, both on theirs and on all Christian souls.'

They should not nibble between meals, either fruit or anything else, or drink without permission; and permission should be easily gained for everything that is not sinful. There should be no talking at meals, or very little and in a low voice. Also, between the recluse's Compline and Prime they should not do or say anything by which her silence might be disturbed.

It is not proper that any recluse's servant should ask for a fixed wage,

clað þet ha mei flutte bi, ant Godes milce. Ne misleue nan Godd, hwet se tide of þe ancre, þet he hire trukie. Þe meidnes wiðuten, ʒef ha seruið þe ancre alswa as ha ahen, hare hure schal beon þe hehe blisse of heouene. Hwa se haueð ehe of hope toward se heh hure, gleadliche wule ha seruin ant lihtliche alle wa ant alle teone þolien. Wið eise ant wið este ne buð me nawt blisse.

5

ʒe ancres ahen þis leaste lutle stucche reden to ower wummen euche wike eanes aþet ha hit cunnen. Ant muche neod is þet ʒe neomen to ham muche ʒeme, for ʒe mahen muchel beon þurh ham igodet, ant iwurset. On oðer half, ʒef þet ha sungið þurh ower ʒemeles, ʒe schule beo bicleopet þrof biuore þe hehe Deme. Ant forþi as ow is muche neod, ant ham ʒet mare, ʒeornliche leareð ham to halden hare Riwle, ba for ow ant for hamseolf, liðeliche ant luueliche; for swuch ah wummone lare to beonne, luuelich ant liðe ant selthwenne sturne. Ba is riht þet ha ow dreden ant luuien, ant þah þet ter beo eauer mare of luue þen of drede; þenne schal hit wel fearen. Me schal healden eoli ant win ba i wunden efter Godes lare, ah mare of softe eoli þen of | bitinde win—þet is, mare of liðe wordes þen of suhinde. For [1 þerof kimeð þinge best, þet is, luue eie. Lihtliche ant sweteliche forʒeoueð ham hare gultes hwen ha ham icnaweð ant bihateð bote.

10

15

20

Ase forð as ʒe mahen, of mete ant of claðes, ant of oþre þinges þet neode of flesch easkeð, beoð large toward ham, þah ʒe nearowe beon ant hearde to ow seoluen. Swa deð þe wel blaweð: went te nearewe of þe horn to his ahne muð ant utward þet wide. Ant ʒe don alswa as ʒe wulleð þet ower beoden bemin wel ant dremen i Drihtines earen, nawt ane to ower ahnes ah to alle folkes heale—as ure Lauerd leue þurh þe grace of himseolf þet hit swa mote. Amen.

25

Hwen ower sustres meidnes cumeð to ow to froure, cumeð to ham to þe þurl earunder ant ouerunder eanes oðer twien ant gað aʒein sone to ower note gastelich, ne biuore Complie ne sitte ʒe nawt for ham ouer riht time, swa þet hare cume beo na lure of ower religiun ah gastelich biʒete. ʒef þer is eani word iseid þet mahte hurten heorte, ne beo hit nawt iboren ut ne ibroht to oþer ancre þet is eð hurte. To him hit schal beon iseid þe lokeð ham alle. Twa niht is inoh þet ei beo

30

apart from food and clothing enough for her to manage on, and the mercy of God. She should never fear that God will fail her, whatever may happen to the recluse. If her lay servants serve the recluse as they are supposed to, their reward will be the exalted bliss of heaven. Whoever looks with the eye of hope towards such a high reward will be happy to serve, and easily tolerate all miseries and troubles. Bliss is not bought by comfort and pleasure.

You recluses should read this last short section to your women once a week until they know it well. And it is most important that you take much care with them, as you can be greatly helped by them, and greatly harmed. On the other hand, if they should sin through your lack of care, you will be called to account for it before the high Judge. And as this is very important for you, and still more for them, do your best to teach them, gently and lovingly, to keep their Rule, both for your sake and their own—for that is what women's teaching should be like, loving and kindly and seldom stern. It is proper that they should both fear and love you, but nevertheless there should always be a greater degree of love than fear; then all will go well. According to God's teaching, both oil and wine must be poured into wounds, but more soothing oil than stinging wine—that is, more kind words than sharp ones. For out of this comes the best of things, that is, fear caused by love. Forgive them their faults readily and kindly when they acknowledge them and promise to make amends.

As far as you can, be liberal towards them with food and clothes and other things which their bodily needs require, even if you are sparing and hard on yourselves. This is what the good trumpeter does: he puts the narrow end of the horn to his own mouth, and the wide end outwards. And you should do the same if you want your prayers to ring loudly and musically in the Lord's ears, not only for your salvation but for everyone else's—and may Our Lord grant through his special grace that it may be so. Amen.

When your sisters' maids pay you a visit, come to them at the window in the morning and afternoon once or twice, and go straight back to your spiritual duties, and do not linger at table too long before Compline on their account, so that their visit may not mean the loss of any of your spiritual observances, but spiritual gain. If anything is said which might cause hurt feelings, it should not be taken further or told to another recluse who is easily hurt. It should be told to the man who has charge of them all. Two nights are enough for anyone to be asked to stay, and

edhalden, ant þet beo ful seldene; ne for heom ne breoke silence ed te
mete, ne for blodletunge, bute ȝef sum muche god oðer neod hit
makie.

Þe ancre ne hire meiden ne plohien worldliche gomenes ed te þurle,
5 ne ne ticki togederes; for ase seið Seint Beornard, vnwurðe þing is to
euch gastelich mon, ant nomeliche to ancre, euch swuch fleschlich
froure, ant hit binimeð gastelich, þet is, wiðute met utnume murhðe—
ant þet is uuel change, as is iseid þruppe.

Of þis boc redeð hwen ȝe beoð eise euche dei leasse oðer mare. Ich
10 hopie þet hit | schal beon ow, ȝef ȝe hit redeð ofte, swiðe biheue, [1
þurh Godes muchele grace; elles Ich hefde uuele bitohe mi muchele
hwile. Me were leouere, Godd hit wite, do me toward Rome þen for te
biginnen hit eft for te donne. Ȝef ȝe findeð þet ȝe doð alswa as ȝe
redeð, þonckið Godd ȝeorne. Ȝef ȝe ne doð nawt, biddeð Godes
15 are, ant beoð umben þeronuuen þet ȝe hit bet halden efter ower
mihte.

Feader, Sune, Hali Gast, an almihti Godd, wite ow in his warde. He
gleadie ow ant frouri ow, mine leoue sustren, ant for al þet ȝe for him
dreheð ant dreaieð ne ȝeoue ow neauer leasse hure þen altogedere
20 himseoluen. Beo he aa iheiet from world into worlde aa on ecnesse.
Amen.

Ase ofte as ȝe habbeð ired eawiht heron, greteð þe Leafdi wið an
Aue for him þet swonc herabuten. Inoh meaðful Ich am þe bidde se
lutel.

25 *Explicit.*

Iþench o þi writere i þine beoden sumchearre, ne beo hit ne se lutel.
Hit turneð þe to gode þet tu bidest for oþre.

19 hure] CFNTSP, *om.* A

that should be very rarely; do not break silence at meals on their account, or because of blood-letting, unless some great benefit or need requires it.

The recluse and her maid should not play worldly games at the window, or romp together; for as St Bernard says, every such pleasure of the flesh is unworthy of someone in the spiritual life, and especially a recluse, and it deprives them of spiritual joy, which surpasses it immeasurably—and that is a poor exchange, as was said above.

Read some of this book in your free time every day, whether more or less. I hope that if you read it often it will be of much use to you, through God's great grace; otherwise I would have wasted the long time I spent on it. As God is my witness, I would rather set out to Rome than start writing it again. If you find that you are practising what you read, thank God sincerely. If you are not, pray for God's mercy, and try to observe it better in the future as far as you can.

May Father, Son, Holy Ghost, one almighty God, have you in his keeping. May he give you joy and comfort, my dear sisters, and, in return for all that you suffer and endure for him, give you no less reward than his whole self. May he be glorified world without end, for ever and ever. Amen.

Whenever you have read anything in this book, greet Our Lady with a *Hail Mary* for the man who laboured on it. I am moderate enough in asking for so little.

The End.

Remember your scribe sometimes in your prayers, no matter how little. It will benefit you if you pray for others.

TEXTUAL COMMENTARY

FULL notes on sources and textual points are available in the editions mentioned in Further Reading, and only a selection is offered here. Sources have been cited regularly for direct quotations in the texts but only occasionally for other borrowings. Biblical references are to the Vulgate Bible.

Hali Meiðhad

Title. *Epistel . . . froure*: only in MS Bodley 34. *meidene*: may be genitive singular or plural. The word is used of both male and female virgins in ME. From the early Christian centuries, girls could be professed as virgins from the age of fourteen in a ceremony involving a ring (for betrothal to Christ) and, from the thirteenth century, a nuptial veil. It was not necessary to enter a religious community to be consecrated as a virgin (the ceremonial profession of virginity has been exclusively reserved to nuns only since 1950). See further R. Metz, *La Femme et l'enfant dans le droit canonique mediéval*, Variorum Repr. (London, 1985), 'La femme', §2, 'La Vierge consacrée', esp. art. VII, 'La Couronne et l'anneau dans la consécration des vierges . . .', originally published in *Revue des sciences religieuses*, 28, Strasburg, 1954). The description of *HM*'s purpose as the *froure* ('comfort, support, encouragement') of virgins can be compared to the author's comment in *AW* (see Corpus MS 41^b/23–4; Salu, p. 68, 'I write about the solitary life to encourage (*frourin*) recluses').

2/1–2. *Avdi . . . tui*: Ps. 44: 11, a text widely quoted in virginity literature. *HM*'s interpretation is derived from Alan of Lille (see Millett, *Hali Meiðhad*, pp. xxvii–xxviii, and 1/11–12n., 1/12–13n., 1/16–21n.).

2/26–7. *'Syon'. . . 'heh sihðe'*: see Introduction, pp. xviii–xix.

6/4. *alle . . . gode*: Rom. 8: 28.

8/3. *buggen ham brudgume*: twelfth-century canon law affirmed that, in a marriage contract, the wife's gift to the husband (*maritagium* or *dos*, 'dowry') must equal the husband's to the wife (*donatio*, 'dower'), though in the early Middle Ages, when female labour and skills were more highly valued, it could be smaller. In the thirteenth century, contributions to the dowries of poor girls became a form of Christian charity for the first time, and rank was sometimes weighed against insufficient money in negotiations. See further David Herlihy, *Medieval Households* (Cambridge, Mass., 1985), 98–103 and M. M. Sheehan, 'The Influence of Canon Law on the Property Rights of Married Women in England', *Medieval Studies*, 25 (1963), 109–24.

8/11–21. *þet unþeaw . . . þerwiðinnen*: *HM*'s denunciation of sexual intercourse, though vehement, is confined to the concupiscence attending it and does not condemn God's institution of it as such (see Millett, *Hali Meiðhad*, pp. xxx–xxxii, and 4/24–5n., 4/30–2n.).

8/28. *Et concupiscet . . . tuum*: Ps. 44: 12.

10/26–7. *þet eadi lond . . . brudgume brude*: Matt. 22: 30, Mark 12: 25, Luke 20: 34–6.

10/28. *'lond of unlicnesse'*: a Neoplatonic idea (cf. Plotinus, *Enneads*, i.8.13, 'we are become dwellers in the place of unlikeness, where, fallen from our resemblance to the divine, we lie in gloom and mud') which reaches *HM* through St Bernard of Clairvaux, *Sermo 27 in Cantica*, *PL* 183. 916, §6; see further Millett, *Hali Meiðhad*, 6/15–16n.

10/29. *utlahe*: for the idea of life on earth as exile, see Heb. 11: 13–16, 13: 14, and Millett, *Hali Meiðhad*, pp. xxvi–xxviii.

10/32–5. *as Seinte Pawel leareð . . . wiðute wemmunge*: 1 Thess. 4: 3–5. Incorruption in a saint's body was frequently taken as a proof of virginity, as in the cult of St Audrey (D. H. Farmer (ed.), *The Oxford Dictionary of Saints* (Oxford, 1978), s.v. Etheldreda).

12/5–10. *þe prophete . . . þet he wule*: based on Joel 1: 17. The idea that subjection to passion makes one the Devil's beast of burden has a wide medieval currency (see Millett, *Hali Meiðhad*, 6/29n., 6/32–7/2n.).

12/15. *þe ontfule deouel*: the Devil's pride and envy of God was the reason for his fall and, in a doctrinal consensus following Gregory the Great's sixth-century *Moralia in Job*, this extended to man when God created humanity to take the place of the fallen angels (see further J. Burton Russell, *Lucifer: The Devil in the Middle Ages* (Ithaca, 1984), 94–104, esp. p. 97).

12/17. *ure Leafdi . . . earst*: according to Augustine (*De sancta virginitate*, ch. 4, *PL* 40. 398), Mary was supposed to have taken a vow of virginity before the Annunciation.

14/5–27. *Forþi . . . teares*: the battle of Lechery and Virginity is based on Alan of Lille's *Summa de arte praedicatoria* (*PL* 210. 122, but see also Millett, *Hali Meiðhad*, 8/7–31n.), tr. Gillian R. Evans, *The Art of Preaching* (Kalamazoo, Mich., 1981), 36–7). See further Millett, *Hali Meiðhad*, 8/8–20n.

16/8. *Eunuchus . . . et cetera*: Isa. 56: 4–5.

16/14. *þet swete song*: based on Rev. 14: 3–4, and a heavenly reward frequently discussed in virginity literature. See further *HM* 16/20–20/4, *SM* 44/28–9.

16/28–9. *Non omnes . . . capiat*: Matt. 19: 11–12.

18/4. *crune upo crune*: virgins do not only receive the heavenly reward of eternal life (the traditional interpretation of the golden crown of Exod. 25: 25) but an extra, smaller crown (the *aureola* of 20/12). This is given to those who aspire to perfection, usually virgins, martyrs, and doctors, since these respectively conquer the flesh, the world, and error. See further Millett, *Hali Meiðhad*, 10/5–9n., 11/17–20n.

18/4–6. *Alswa Seinte Pawel . . . halden*: cf. 1 Cor. 7: 8, 25–6.

20/12. *aureola*: see note to 18/4 above.

20/17–21. *3et of þes þreo . . . baþe*: a patristic interpretation of Matt. 13: 23 (the parable of the sower), much used in virginity literature. See Millett, *Hali Meiðhad*, pp. xxxviii–xxxix.

20/29. *liues writ*: see Rev. 3: 4–5, 20: 12–15.

22/18. *þeos doð hare cunde*: unfavourable comparison of human with animal sexual habits goes back as far as Pliny and is found in the works of patristic and later medieval theologians; see further Millett, *Hali Meiðhad*, 12/27–13/3 n.

24/20–1. *Wa . . . iteiet*: probably a reference to Augustine, *Confessions*, Bk. 4, ch. 6, §11 (*PL* 32. 697).

26/15. *þis worldes hweol*: the image is of Fortune's wheel. See H. R. Patch, *The Goddess Fortuna in Medieval Literature* (Cambridge, Mass., 1927), ch. 5.

28/25–31. *3ef . . . bileaue*: based on Hildebert of Lavardin's Letter to Athalisa (*Ep.* 1. 21, *PL* 171. 194). The thirteenth-century English poem *Dame Sirith* tells of such a consultation for adulterous purposes (no. VI in Bennett and Smithers).

30/22–3. *For ase Seinte Pawel seið . . . ane*: 1 Cor. 6: 18.

32/18–25. *Efter al þis . . . limpeð to donne*: a common topic in the literature on the *molestiae nuptiarum* 'tribulations of marriage' (see Introduction, p. xix); cf. Abelard's report of Heloise's use of the topic in her arguments against marriage: 'Will he [the philosopher] put up with the constant muddle and squalor which small children bring into the home?' (*The Letters of Abelard and Heloise*, tr. Betty Radice (Harmondsworth, 1974), 71).

32/26–8. *Seinte Pawel bilukeð . . . derf drehen*: 1 Cor. 7: 28.

34/28–9. *Eadi is his spuse . . . ne pineð*: on the tradition of spiritual pregnancy, see Millett, *Hali Meiðhad*, p. xli.

34/32. *marheʒeue*: the 'morning gift' presented by the husband to the wife on the morning after the consummation of their marriage (distinct from the dowry and dower of the marriage contract; see note to 8/3 above). Frequently used of Christ's rewards to his chosen in heaven (see note to *SW* 102/21–3).

36/1–2. *of hwas wlite . . . fulle to bihalden*: on Christ's beauty cf. *SW* 100/9–10 and note to *AW7* 120/1–32. Christ as the best of all suitors is a topic much used in virginity literature from the fourth century onwards; see Millett, *Hali Meiðhad*, pp. xliii–xliv, and 20/9–10 n., 20/10–11 n.

36/7–19. *3ef þe were leof . . . hire in heouene*: see note to *HM* 34/28–9 above.

38/14–15. *under hwit . . . under grene ant gra*: 'white', 'black', and 'grey' probably refer to the colours of the religious orders' habits; Alan Fletcher argues for the possibility that 'grei' refers to the Franciscans, which would date *HM* after 1224 ('Black, White and Grey in *Hali Meiðhad* and *Ancrene Wisse*', forthcoming in *Medium Ævum*).

38/26–7. *þe eadi sunegilt Marie Magdaleine*: Gregory the Great's generally accepted identification (*Homiliarum in Evangelia*, Bk. 2, Hom. 25, *PL* 76. 1189) of the Magdalene (Luke 8: 2) with the female sinner of Luke 7: 37 made her one of the 'great penitents'—exemplary reformed sinners who demonstrated God's capacity for mercy (see further Marie Collins, 'Will and the Penitents . . .', *Leeds Studies in English*, 16 (1985), 290–3).

40/4–5. *'Efter þi word . . . mi Lauerdes þrel'*: Luke 1: 38.

40/7–8 *'For mi Lauerd . . . eadi alle leoden'*: Luke 1: 48.

40/13. *eolie in a lampe*: the image is from the parable of the wise and foolish virgins (Matt. 25: 1–13).

40/16–24. *Haue eauer . . . cwenes of heouene*: in his *Summa de arte praedicatoria* (see note to *HM* 14/5–27), Alan of Lille advises the preacher to make use of examples at the end of his sermon to prove what he has said (ch. 1, *PL* 210. 114).

40/18–20. *Seinte Katerine . . . Seinte Cecille*: Catherine, Margaret, and Juliana are semi-legendary virgin martyrs of the fourth century (and the subjects of Katherine Group Lives; see Introduction, pp. xx–xxi), Lucy and Agnes are virgin martyrs of the fourth century, and Cecilia (who may never have been martyred) according to fifth-century legend remained virgin and converted her spouse. For details of their Lives, cults, martyrdoms, feasts, and attributes see their entries in D. H. Farmer, *The Oxford Dictionary of Saints* (Oxford, 1978).

40/30. *ear ha agulten . . . heamen*: Adam and Eve fell through pride and disobedience, not lust; but it was generally assumed by patristic writers that they remained virgin until after the Fall, and that the element of uncontrolled desire always present in sexual intercourse was the result of the Fall (cf. 8/10–27). See Millett, *Hali Meiðhad*, pp. xxix–xxx.

42/9–11. *For as Seinte Pawel seið . . . ouercume hire seolf*: 1 Cor. 9: 24–7.

42/12. *his ahne turn*: the image is from wrestling; a *turn* is 'a movement, device, or trick, by which a wrestler attempts to throw his antagonist' (*NED*).

42/12–13. *as þe apostle seið . . . asailet*: probably a reference to Jas. 1: 12.

42/16–17. *under . . . mengen*: a common image in the Psalms; see Pss. 16: 8, 35: 8, 56: 2, 60: 5, etc., and cf. *SW* 106/11.

Seinte Margarete

44/10–22. *Ich, an Godes þeowe, Teochimus . . . biȝet hit iwriten of þe writers þa*: the claim of Teochimus to have acquired the contemporary records (*cartae*, see Mack, 4/4 n.) seems at odds with his later claim to direct witness of the dragon and transcription of Margaret's prayers (82/28–31). *SM* follows its Latin source at both points (text printed by Mack, pp. 127–42, hereafter referred to by page and line number): see Mack, 128/11–15, 141/35–142/8. The two claims may not have been perceived as self-contradictory, but in *SM* they are certainly unharmonized (cf. note to 58/7–8 below) and opportunist 'authentication' is characteristic of saints' legends (cf. H. Delehaye, *Les Légendes hagiographiques*, 4th edn. (Brussels, 1955), 67–8) and of the tradition of Margaret's *vita*. Teochimus' claim to be an eye-witness is thought to be a later addition in the Greek legend (Mack, 4/4 n.); in the Latin tradition his role fluctuates and not all versions include him.

44/27–8. *þet eadie meiden þe we munneð todei*: 20 July (see 82/33–84/1). J. A. W. Bennett (*The Oxford History of English Literature*, i/2, *Middle English Literature*, ed. and completed by D. Gray (Oxford, 1986), 281) suggests that *SM* was written after the establishment of St Margaret's Day as a major feast in the English Church by the Council of Oxford in 1222.

44/28. *þet seli meidnes song*: see note to *HM* 16/14 above.

46/12. *wes ant wiste*: for the origin and meaning of *wes* in this alliterative collocation, which also occurs at 46/22 below, see Patrick Stiles, 'eME (AB) *wes*: a reflex of IE *wes*- 'to pasture, tend (livestock)?', *Zeitschrift für vergleichende Sprachforschung*, 98 (1985), 295–301.

48/1–3. *Ich habbe a deore ʒimstan . . . biwit wel*: images of treasure and flowers are typical of virginity literature (cf. *HM* 8/34–10/2 and Millett, *Hali Meiðhad*, 5/12–27 n.), though Margaret's specific association with the pearl (Latin *margarita*) dates from the later thirteenth-century *Golden Legend* version of her life by James of Voragine.

48/16–17. *heþene godes . . . heðene*: i.e. Roman gods and Romans. Olibrius' men unhistorically use Christian religious distinctions.

52/12–15. '*Lauerd, in þe . . . hoker of me . . .*': based on Pss. 30: 2 and 24: 3.

54/15–20. '*Helle-hundes . . . hornes . . .*': Ps. 21: 17, 21, 22.

54/20. *þe an-ihurnde hornes*: a surprising use of the unicorn (traditionally subdued by virgins), but *SM* here follows the Latin (Mack, 132/11–12) and the unicorn's reputation for general ferocity was in any case undiminished in contemporary bestiary lore: he is, for instance, 'la plus egre beste . . . del mont' in Guillaume le Clerc's twelfth-century Anglo-Norman *Bestiaire* (ed. R. Reinsch (Leipzig, 1892), l. 1381). *AW* uses the unicorn as a figure of wrath (Corpus MS 54ᵃ/14–15; Salu, p. 89).

56/16. *þe seoueðe time of þe dei*: in the synoptic Gospels darkness accompanies Christ's crucifixion from the sixth to the ninth hour (see e.g. Matt. 27: 45).

56/19–26. '*Deorewurðe Drihtin . . . þi meiden*': expansion of common psalm-motifs from the Latin source; cf. e.g. Pss. 26: 9, 36: 33, 37: 22.

56/23. *Widewene warant, ant meidenes mede*: cf. Ps. 67: 6.

56/26. *Min ahne flesliche feader . . . draf me awei*: not mentioned in the earlier account of Margaret's fostering (46/2–4), where the Latin has 'she was hated by her father' (Mack, 128/28), as Mack, 18/33 ff. n., points out. Juliana is also rejected by her father; see *Iuliene*, p. 17, ll. 192–5 (MS B).

58/7–8. *Heo þa ant monie ma*: *SM*'s Teochimus retrospectively claims to have been one of these (82/29–31) in spite of *SM*'s omission of the Latin's 'Theotimus was also in the dungeon' (Mack, 133/18) at this point (see Mack, 20/16 ff. n. and note to 44/10–22 above).

58/32–60/9. *þu wrahtest . . . to fordo me*: Expansion of common psalm-motifs from the Latin source; cf. e.g. Pss. 68:35, 103:9, 19, 26, 145:6, 148:3–8.

60/26. *biheold . . . riht half*: it is difficult to see why MSS B and R agree, against the Latin MS tradition (Mack, 134/18 n. 1), that the devil was on Margaret's right hand rather than her left. It is possible that the original reading was *luft* 'left' rather than *riht*; the apparently tautologous use of *lokin* would then be at least partly explained by its alliterative function (cf. *SW* 100/3 *ne mahte Ich nawt aʒein þe leome of his wlite lokin ne bihalden*).

62/7–8. *Ich me seolf smelle of þe*: a sweet smell is a traditional attribute of Christ and of virgins; cf. e.g. Ambrose, *De virginibus* Bk. 1, ch. 7 (*PL* 16. 210, §39), commenting on S. of S. 4: 11.

62/15. *castel of strengðe*: cf. Ps. 60: 4.

62/18. *swotest ant swetest*: the two ME forms probably correspond to the different senses distinguished by Latin *suavissimus* (ME *swotest* = 'most gentle, most fragrant') and *dulcissimus* (ME *swetest* = 'most pleasant, most dear'): see John H. Fisher, 'Chaucer's Use of *swete* and *swote*', *JEGP* 50 (1951), 326–31, and cf. *AW7* 120/6, *AW8* 136/27. The odour vs. taste basis of the distinction is generally observed (cf. *HM* 6/32, 24/21 vs. *HM* 10/33, *SM* 62/8, *SW* 102/14).

64/33. *Rufines*: mentioned in *AW* as 'Ruffin þe deouel, Beliales broðer, in ower [i.e. 'your'] Englische boc of Seinte Margarete' (Corpus MS 66ᵃ/18–19; Salu, p. 108). On the possible origin of his name, see d'Ardenne, *Iuliene*, p. xxv.

66/35–68/30. *Eoten meaðeliche . . . hwet ha seggen*: much expanded from the Latin source, using 'remedies against temptation' material: cf. e.g. *De modo bene vivendi ad sororem* (*PL* 184. 1286–88, 1298–1300).

68/13–16 translates a Latin verse also quoted and paraphrased in *AW* (Corpus MS 65ᵃ/17–23; Salu, p. 106) where it is a mnemonic for 'the objects of holy meditation' (see further Mack, 34/18 ff. n.). For 68/27–30 cf. *AW*'s recommendations not to speak to any man (even one's confessor) often or long without a witness (Corpus MS 17ᵃ/2–6; Salu, p. 30).

68/10–12. *makieð þe engles . . . in helle*: cf. *HM* 14/25–7.

72/3–31. *Sathanas þe unseli . . . of þe worlde*: the demon's account has parallels in the *Testament of Solomon* (a Christian compilation of Jewish demonology, possibly of the fifth century): see Mack, pp. xxvi–xxviii.

72/6–7. *i Iames ant i Manbres bokes*: a lost apocryphal work, of which a fragment is preserved in an eleventh-century English manuscript; see Mack, p. xxix, and Price, 'The Virgin and the Dragon: The Demonology of Seinte Margarete', *Leeds Studies in English*, 16 (1985), 345 n. 27.

72/9. *we liuieð bi þe lufte*: demons were believed to inhabit both hell and the 'dark atmosphere' below the moon; the first, as Aquinas explains, for their punishment, and the second because of their function of proving human virtue (*Summa Theologiae* 1a, 64, 4).

72/11–24. *ant mest rihtwise men . . . meiden*: cf. note to *HM* 12/15.

72/28. *ne warp þu me . . . into helle*: according to Aquinas, devils deem it a punishment 'to be expelled from a place (i.e. earth) where they could do harm to men' (*Summa Theologiae*, 1a, 64, 4).

72/29–31. *For Salomon . . . of þe worlde*: see Mack, p. xxviii (*c*), for the tradition of Solomon and the demons.

74/22. *Daviðes bone*: Ps. 25: 2.

76/18. *a loft-song*: Ps. 92: 1.

76/31. *stihen alle martyrs . . . to heouene*: according to Augustine, martyrdom could constitute a form of baptism (the 'baptism of blood'). Like baptism, it gave remission of sins and Augustine (*Sermones de sanctis*, 285, *PL* 38. 1295, §5) argues that martyrs leave the world perfect and hence are prayed to, but not for.

78/3. *Malcus*: the naming here of an executioner who has not been previously mentioned is puzzling, but it is paralleled in the Latin source (although the MS used by Mack substitutes 'one of them', perhaps because the scribe also found it puzzling). See Mack, 139/23 n. 4.

78/13–19. *þu folkes Feader . . . weole ant wunne*: cf. Isa. 40: 12.

78/19. *boc writ*: see note on *AW8* 140/16 below.

80/15. *leaf þet leode se lah*: perhaps a reference to Ps. 44: 11–12 (the text of *HM*; see *HM* 2/1–5).

80/32. *an Godd unagin*: the word *unagin* is recorded only here (MS B only; MS R has *inmagin*) and in *SJ* (p. 3, l. 4, MS B; omitted in MS R); its origin and meaning are uncertain. The B scribe (and perhaps the author as well) probably understood it as meaning 'without beginning', but it may have originated in the OE description of the Trinity (used more than once by Ælfric) as *an angin*, 'a common origin [of all created things]'. The noun *angin* was already obsolescent by the end of the twelfth century, and the phrase *an angin* could have seemed odd to those who took it as meaning that the Trinity had, rather than was, a single beginning; both factors may have contributed to confusion in sense and form with another epithet used in OE for the Divinity, *unagunnen* 'without beginning'.

82/19–20. *Sanctus . . .*: cf. the angelic song of praise heard by Isaiah in the temple (Isa. 6: 3), used in the offering of the Mass.

82/26–32. *Com Ich, Teochimus . . . te worlde*: see note on *SM* 44/10–22 above.

82/33–84/1. *i þe moneð . . . twentuðe dei*: see note on 44/27–8 above.

82/34. *Efterliðe*: 'the second mild month, July' only here in ME: *MED* s.v. **after-** *prefix* 2(g).

Sawles Warde

86/1–2. *Si sciret paterfamilias . . . domum suam*: Matt. 24: 43, Luke 12: 39.

92/21–3. *Ich habbe . . . alle forwerede*: as Bennett and Smithers (423/129) point out, the 'thousand tongues of steel' are based ultimately on a passage in Virgil (*Aeneid*, Bk. 6, ll. 625–7), quoted by Jerome (*Ep.* 66, *PL* 22. 641), describing the punishment of offenders in the classical underworld:

> non, mihi si linguae centum sint oraque centum,
> ferrea vox, omnis scelerum comprendere formas,
> omnia poenarum percurrere nomina possim

('Even if I had a hundred tongues and a hundred mouths, a voice of iron, I could not include all the types of crime or list all the punishments by name'). The idea became a commonplace of OE vernacular homily and of ME homiletic and visionary literature.

94/5. *rueð up*: (MS R *ruueð*, MS T *runeð*) 'stands up, stands on end'. See G. V. Smithers, 'Four Cruces in Middle English Texts', *English and Germanic Studies*, 2 (1948–9), 62–4.

94/24–5. *hu þe unwiht . . . ure hus*: 1 Pet. 5: 8.

94/32–3. *Pe apostle . . . flið ananriht*: Jas. 4: 7.

100/23. *Nihe wordes*: SW explains *De custodia*'s 'degrees and positions' (Southern and Schmitt, 358/26) with the usual number of angelic hosts, enumerated in Dionysus' *Celestial Hierarchies* (*c.*AD 500) and adopted by the later Middle Ages (following Gregory the Great) as Seraphim, Cherubim, Thrones, Dominations, Virtues, Powers, Principalities, Angels, and Arch-angels.

100/27–30. *þe makieð . . . gastelich sihðe*: cf. Heb. 11: 13.

102/5. *cunfessurs*: originally those who confessed their faith in time of persecution without being martyred. Later generalized to male saints (Wilson, 71/286n., cites Edward the Confessor) not already included in some special class.

102/8–17. *Ich iseh . . . sittende ihereð*: *De custodia*'s monks (Southern and Schmitt, 359/4–5) are omitted, and expanded treatment given to the reward of virgins in heaven.

102/21–3. *Þe imeane blisse . . . þe seoueðe*: on the traditional seven joys of the soul see G. Shepherd, '"All the wealth of Croesus . . ."', *MLR* 51 (1956), 161–7, and for a table of Anselm's differing arrangements of the joys see Southern and Schmitt, p. 10. In *AW* (Corpus MS 24^b/16–22; Salu, p. 41), two of the joys in particular are promised as morning-gifts (see note to *HM* 34/32) to the recluses: agility of movement and clarity of sight in exchange for enclosure and obscurity on earth.

102/32–4. *as ure Lauerd seide . . . ure alesnesse*: John 17: 3.

102/36–7. *alle Godes reades . . . sea-dingle*: based on Ps. 35: 7. On the rare *sea-dingle* see Wilson, 74/320n.

104/15–21. *Neomeð nu . . . neomen in*: cf. Anselm's explanation in *De beatitudine*, ch. 14, '*De gaudio*' (Southern and Schmitt, 285/30–/286/11): though the joy of heaven is too great for an individual to contain, that individual's joy can nonetheless be multiplied by participation in the joys of other heavenly inhabitants, and when to this is added the joy of seeing God, the blessed will be immersed in joy 'inside and outside' (286/9–10).

106/7–10. *hwet mei tweamen us . . . haueð iʒarket*: Rom. 8: 35–9.

106/11. *under his wengen*: not in *De custodia*, but a frequent phrase in the Psalms (as Hall, 2.523/340, points out); cf. note to *HM* 42/16–17.

106/12–14. *Varpeð ut . . . is fleme*: based on 1 John 4: 18.

108/13. *wrat*: here 'copied'. (The scribe's verses appear only in MS R).

Ancrene Wisse, *Part 7*

110/3. *schireð ant brihteð* here and *schir ant of briht sihðe* (110/19) express a similar complex of ideas, although the similarity cannot be fully brought out in translation. On the abstract level, love purifies (*scireð*) and enlightens (*brihteð*) the heart; on the metaphorical level, it makes the troubled waters of the heart clear (see *NED* s.v. **Shire** *adj.* 2), and unclouds its sight so that it can see God (see *MED* s.v. **bright** *adj.* 4. (a)).

110/3–4. *Exercitio corporis . . . ad omnia*: 1 Tim. 4: 8.

110/5–8. *Si linguis . . . michi prodest*: 1 Cor. 13: 1, 3 (with altered order of phrases).

110/12. *þe hali abbat Moyses*: a desert father of the fourth century; see Shepherd, 19/15 ff. n.

110/21. *þis mong . . . þe heorte*: the underlying image is of troubled waters: the verb *woreð* is used transitively in ME to mean 'trouble' (literally of water, figuratively of the heart; see Millett, *Hali Meiðhad*, 24/10 n. and cf. the adjective *wori*, 110/26).

110/21. *þe ehnen of þe heorte*: cf. Eph. 1: 18.

110/27–8. *Omnia munda . . . est mundum*: Titus 1: 15.

110/28–9. *Habe caritatem . . . uidelicet rationis*: based on Augustine, *In epistolam Joannis*, Tr. 7, §8 (*PL* 35. 2033), with *uoluntate rationis* added by the author (as Shepherd, 19/35 n., explains) to restrict the application of this widely current but potentially dangerous phrase.

112/2–3. *Minus te amat . . . propter te amat*: Augustine, *Confessions*, Bk. 10, ch. 29 (*PL* 32. 796).

112/6. *Plenitudo legis est dilectio*: Rom. 13: 10.

112/7. *Quicquid precipitur . . . caritate solidatur*: *Homiliarum in Evangelia*, Bk. 2, Hom. 27 (*PL* 76. 1205, §1).

112/9. *Seinte Mihales weie*: the archangel's scales in which the soul's good and bad deeds are weighed after death.

112/18–19. *Omnia subiecisti . . . semitas maris*: Ps. 8: 8–9.

112/23–4. *Christus dilexit . . . semetipsum pro ea*: Eph. 5: 25.

112/29–30. *leattres isealet . . . leattres iopenet*: the terminology is borrowed from royal administration ('letters closed' were sent by the king under seal to individual subjects, 'letters patent' were open letters to his subjects in general), probably because it provided an apt metaphorical expression of the idea that the Old Testament allegorically foreshadowed the New (see Shepherd, 21/4 n., 21/5 n., and, for more detail, Beryl Smalley, *The Study of the Bible in the Middle Ages*, 3rd edn. (Oxford, 1983), 6–14).

112/34. *eorðene castel*: it is not clear how transparent the allegory is meant to be here. Salu (p. 172 n. 2) explains *eorðene castel* as a 'castle with earthworks', but the phrase does not seem to occur elsewhere in Middle English, and the point may be precisely that thirteenth-century castles were built of stone, not earth, and it is only the human body which is a 'castle of clay' (for the image of the body as a castle, see Introduction, pp. xxv–xxvi, and cf. *SW* 98/5–9).

114/24–6. *schawde þurh cnihtschipe . . . to donne*: see Shepherd, 22/8 f. n. Shepherd is likely to be right in assuming that the author is referring to an 'ideal' rather than historical past (see Juliet R. Barker, *The Tournament in England 1100–1400* (Cambridge, 1986), p. 101), and his citation of Geoffrey of Monmouth's legendary *History of the Kings of Britain* is apposite; but this does not mean that the author is necessarily referring to Geoffrey. It is more probable, given the romance affinities of his *tale*, that he is thinking of the love-tournaments of late twelfth-century romance (see Maurice Keen, *Chivalry* (New Haven, 1984), 91–4).

114/30. *efter monies wene*: the three-nail crucifix became fashionable in devotional imagery around 1200, though the older style with four nails and separate fastening of each foot persisted (see Shepherd, 22/13 n.).

114/33. *Relicto . . . fugerunt*: Matt. 26: 56.

114/34–5. *Dabis . . . tuum*: Lam. 3: 65.

114/36. *Scuto . . . uoluntatis*: Ps. 5: 13.

116/3. *Oblatus . . . uoluit*: Isa. 53: 7.

116/12. *þe þridde reisun*: it is not at all clear what the other two are. Shepherd's suggestion that it refers to the three functions of the shield as a protection against evil, a means of crowning us in heaven, and a memorial, is perhaps the most probable; but see also Shepherd, 22/36 f. n. and R. A. Waldron, 'Enumeration in "Ancrene Wisse"', *Notes and Queries*, 214 (1969), 86–7, for alternative theories.

116/19. *Fowr heaued-luuen*: this classification is also found in two early thirteenth-century Latin works, Richard Wetheringsette's *Summa Brevis* (*c.*1215–22) and the rather later *Moralia super Evangelia*; see R. H. Rouse and S. Wenzel, review of Dobson, *Moralities on the Gospels*, *Speculum*, 52 (1977), 651.

116/23. *Giwerie*: though the Jews were not expelled from England until 1290, anti-semitism intensified in the late twelfth century. Mob violence and intellectual polemic were among its manifestations and some of the clerics on whose works the author of *AW* drew wrote against the Jews (see B. Blumenkranz, 'Anti-Jewish Polemic and Legislation in the Middle Ages: Literary Fiction or Reality?', no. XXII in his *Juifs et Chrétiens: Patristique et Moyen Age*, Variorum Repr. (London, 1977), esp. pp. 130–1, 134).

116/33–5. *Si dimiserit . . . dicit Dominus*: Jer. 3: 1.

116/37. *Immo . . . uenienti*: see Luke 15: 20.

118/4. *Seint Austin seið*: the reference has not been identified, but Augustine discusses the restoration of spiritual virginity (the loss of physical virginity being irreparable, as *HM* 8/31 – 10/5 stresses) more than once (see *De symbolo*, *PL* 40. 1191–2, and *Sermo* 188, *PL* 38. 1005, cited by Cooper, p. 297).

118/7. *Restituit . . . in integrum*: Job 12: 23.

118/10. *beað of blod*: for the healing bath of blood as a medieval narrative *motif*, see Shepherd, 24/5 ff. n.

118/14. *Preo beaðes*: the basis of this classification is probably 1 John 5: 8, with spirit, water, and blood corresponding to baptism, penitence, and redemption.

118/19–20. *Qui dilexit . . . sanguine suo*: Rev. 1: 5.

118/21–2. *Nunquid potest . . . obliuiscar tui*: Isa. 49: 15.

118/24. *In manibus . . . te*: Isa. 49: 16.

120/1–32. *3ef hit is . . . wurð a nelde*: lists of the qualities of Christ which attract love are a feature of contemporary devotional writing (see Shepherd, 25/4 ff. n. for examples).

120/6. *swotest ant swetest*: see note to *SM* 62/18.

120/25–30. *Al Creasuse weole* . . . *Moysese heale*: a standard list of types: see Shepherd, ' "All the wealth" ', cited in note to *SW* 102/21–3 above.

120/26. *Absalones schene wlite*: 2 Sam. 14: 25–6.

120/28. *Asaeles swiftschipe* . . . *urn*: 2 Sam. 2: 18.

120/29. *Samsones strengðe*: Judg. 15: 14–17.

120/30. *Cesares freolac; Alixandres hereword*: Caesar Augustus and Alexander the Great were standard types of generosity and power or fame, regularly linked with the Biblical figures of 120/26–30 (see Shepherd, ' "All the wealth" ', cited in note to *SW* 102/21–3 above).

120/30. *Moysese heale*: Moses is said to have died at the age of one hundred and twenty, with his teeth and eyesight intact (Deut. 34: 7).

122/7–8. *Non est qui* . . . *a calore eius*: Ps. 18: 7.

122/12. *Ignem ueni mittere* . . . *ut ardeat*: Luke 12: 49.

122/16–17. *Vtinam frigidus* . . . *de ore meo*: Rev. 3: 15–16.

122/23–4. *En* . . . *duo ligna*: 3 Kgs. 17: 12. In medieval etymologies of Biblical names, Sarepta (Zarephath) was usually derived from *incendium*, 'burning'. The allegory of the widow as the Church, Elijah as Christ, and the pieces of wood as the cross, based on Augustine (*Sermo* 11, *PL* 38. 97–9), was used by several contemporary writers (see Shepherd, 26/32 n.).

122/35. *Grickisch fur*: a liquid incendiary whose basic ingredients were naphtha, pitch, and sulphur, used mainly for defence in siege warfare; see J. R. Partington, *A History of Greek Fire and Gunpowder* (Cambridge, 1960). Shepherd (27/11 ff. n.) takes 'the blood of a red man' literally, but it is probably an alchemical 'secret name' for a more mundane ingredient (as in Jonson's *Alchemist*, where the 'red man' is sulphur); see M. P. Crosland, *Historical Studies in the Language of Chemistry* (London, 1962), ch. 1, on alchemical terminology. For other uses of the image of 'Greek fire', see Ian Bishop, ' "Greek Fire" in "Ancrene Wisse" and Contemporary Texts', *Notes and Queries*, 224 (1979), 198–9, and, for a (parodic) recipe, see the (late twelfth-century?) romance *The Rise of Gawain (De ortu Waluuanii)* ed. and tr. Mildred Leake Day (New York, 1984), pp. xx–xxi and xxv–xxvii, and pp. 68–77.

124/6–8. *as Salomon seið* . . . *luue acwenchen*: S. of S. 8: 7.

124/16. *þe niðfule Giws*: on medieval anti-semitism, see note to 116/23.

124/18. *Consumatum est*: John 19: 30.

124/26. ibid.

124/36–7. *Si esurierit* . . . *caput eius*: Prov. 25: 21–2; see also Rom. 12: 20.

126/6. *'heorte'* . . . *'heaued'*: glosses on Rom. 12: 20 (see previous note) usually explain 'head' in this way.

126/7–12. *O þulli wise* . . . *wule þe ȝelden*: based on Matt. 5: 46 and Luke 6: 32–5.

126/16–17. *Nisi ego* . . . *veniet ad uos*: John 16: 7.

126/31–2. *Quemcumque* . . . *uester erit*: Deut. 11: 24.

126/33–4. *ne seide hit þruppe feor*: Corpus MS 77ᵃ/12–17; Salu, pp. 125–6.

126/36. *Sein Gregoire witneð*: from *Cura Pastoralis*, Part 3, ch. 10 (*PL* 77. 63), quoted at Corpus MS 77ᵃ/16–17; Salu, p. 126.

128/10. *Dimisi . . . uerbum tuum*: Num. 14: 20. *Non dicit 'preces'* is the author's addition.

128/12–13. *Me seið þet luue . . . luues leaue*: a commonplace, used by Augustine (*Manuale*, 20, *PL* 40. 960) and others; see Shepherd, 30/5 ff. n.

128/14–15. *Domine, non est . . . teneat te*: Isa. 64: 7.

128/18. *Festina . . . fueris illinc*: Gen. 19: 22.

128/23–4. *Num celare . . . gesturus sum*: Gen. 18: 17.

128/29. *Oculus non uidit . . . diligentibus te*: Isa. 64: 4.

128/30. *Oculus non uidit . . . et cetera*: I Cor. 2: 9, paraphrasing Isa. 64: 4.

128/30–1. *3e habbeð . . . leoue sustren*: possibly a reference to the descriptions of heaven and its rewards in *Hali Meiðhad* and *Sawles Warde*.

128/32–3. *Confitebor tibi . . . cordis*: Ps. 118: 7 (with gloss, *id est, in regulatione*, by author).

128/33. *Exprobratio malorum*: an addition by the author: 'the reproach of the wicked [on the other hand is that it is] a generation . . .'.

128/33–4. *Generatio que . . . cor suum*: Ps. 77: 8.

128/34. *þe leafdi Riwle*: cf. *AW8* 140/33–142/4.

Ancrene Wisse *Part 8*

130/1. *Biuoren on earst*: see Corpus MS 2ᵃ/20–2ᵇ/27: Salu, pp. 3–4.

130/9. *as Ich bihet on earst*: Corpus MS 4ᵇ/9–15; Salu, p. 6. See Introduction, p. xxxiii.

130/12. *ure breðren*: probably the brothers (other than priests) belonging to the author's order.

130/12–19. See List of Proper Names for these feasts.

130/20. *disceplines*: probably penitential scourging as Dobson, *Origins*, p. 73, suggests (the Latin *disciplina* is translated at another point in *AW* (Corpus MS 99ᵃ/16–17) as *beatunge* 'beating').

130/21. *pitance*: customary or occasional extra dish, usually of fish or eggs (D. Knowles, *The Monastic Order in England*, 2nd edn. (Cambridge, 1963), 463).

130/24–6. See List of Proper Names for further details.

130/26. *uigilies*: the day and night preceding church feasts (with, from the eleventh century, an obligation of fasting).

130/27. *hwit*: 'dairy produce', more luxurious than the standard fare of vegetable stews (*potage*; see 130/31), and possibly including eggs (*NED* s.v. *white meat*).

132/14–15. *Maria optimam . . . elegit*: Luke 10: 42, much quoted and commented on in anchoritic rules; see Alexandra Barratt, 'Anchoritic Aspects of *Ancrene Wisse*', *Medium Ævum*, 49 (1980), 38–40.

132/24–6. *Contra Symonem . . . 'opus', et cetera*: see Luke 7: 36–50; Luke 10: 38–42; Matt. 26: 8–10; Mark 14: 4–6.

134/8. *Freres Preachurs ant Meonurs*: the mention of Dominican and Franciscan friars is an addition to the original text, and is important for the dating of the revised version of *Ancrene Wisse* (the Dominicans arrived in England in 1221, the Franciscans in 1224). The author's openly expressed admiration for their piety and sexual restraint (see Corpus MS 16^b/13–15; Salu, p. 29) contrasts markedly with the stereotype of the cynical and dissolute friar found in later Middle English writers such as Chaucer and Langland.

134/31. *Hali men*: probably, as Hall (2.390/14) suggests, the desert fathers, whose Lives (*PL* 73, 74) are important models in eremitic and reclusive literature.

134/32–136/1. *Nawt, deore dehtren, . . . muchel eie*: for the practice of entrusting church plate and other valuables to recluses see H. Mayr-Harting, 'Functions of a Twelfth-Century Recluse', *History*, 60 (1975), 337–52.

136/34. *Mulier . . . caput suum*: 1 Cor. 11: 6.

138/4–5. *et hoc . . . angelos*: see 1 Cor. 11: 10. Hall (2.394/51–5) cites Honorius of Autun's explanation of *angelos* as priests.

138/24–9. *A mon wes . . . fleschlich froure*: added in revision, this story is given a reference in the Latin translation of *Ancrene Wisse* to the *Lives of the Fathers* (see note to 134/31). As Hall (2.396/73) points out, it is also found in Odo of Cheriton's fables and Jacques de Vitry's *exempla* (both early thirteenth century).

138/31. *criblin*: this verb normally means 'to sieve'; here it probably refers to drawn-thread work, the precursor of modern lace.

140/3–4. *ne beo ʒe . . . allunges idel*: Cooper compares Jerome, *Ep.* 125, *PL* 22. 1078, §11.

140/8. *Iniquitas Sodome . . . et ocium*: Ezek. 16: 49.

140/11–12. *Ancre ne schal . . . childrene scole*: a common prohibition in anchoritic rules (see Warren, pp. 112–13, for examples).

140/16. *writen*: Hall (2.398/99), comparing a similar prohibition in the Gilbertine Rule, suggests that *writen* means here 'compose or copy books'; the verb *writen* could mean either (cf. *SM* 78/19–20, and notes on *SW* 108/13, *AW8* 148/26–7).

140/21–3. *Hwen ʒe beoð . . . schurteð ow togederes*: on monastic blood-letting (*minutio*) which was regarded as a vacation by the thirteenth century, see Knowles, *Monastic Order*, pp. 455–6, and on the recreational function of talk after blood-letting, see G. Olson, *Literature as Recreation in the Later Middle Ages* (Ithaca, 1982), 'Monastic *recreatio*', 109–15. *Talen* here may mean either 'stories' or, more broadly, 'talk' of any kind.

142/20–1. *Nowðer of þe wummen . . . neowe tidinges*: gossip is frequently warned against in anchoritic rules (see Warren, pp. 108–9). *AW* cites a proverb, 'from mill and from market, from smithy and from anchorhouse, one hears the news' (Corpus MS 23ᵃ/18–19; Salu, p. 39).

144/2. *Venie . . . Mea culpa*: Hall (2.400/150) explains as 'acknowledgement of fault and petition for pardon, usually in the form of a genuflection or of a profound bow (curvatio)'.

146/17–18. *of softe eoli . . . bitinde win*: cf. Luke 10: 34. Cooper notes a similar use of this image in Gregory, *Moralia*, Bk. 20, §14, *PL* 76. 143–4, and *Regula Pastoralis*, Bk. 2, ch. 6, *PL* 77. 38.

146/30. *biuore Complie*: Compline is recited in the early evening, after the second meal of the day (for a full timetable of the recluse's day see Ackerman and Dahood, pp. 37–8).

148/5. *ticki*: Hall (2.405/219) suggests 'pat, caress each other, or possibly, romp, play the child's game of "ticky"'. The basic sense of 'tick' is 'touch or tap lightly' (see *NED* s.v. *Tick* v.); 'Tick' or 'Ticky' is still the normal name, in the area where *Ancrene Wisse* was written, for the children's chasing game based on touch (see Iona and Peter Opie, *Children's Games in Street and Playground* (Oxford, 1969), 66–7). Since the author has just mentioned games, and seems to see the indulgences he describes as unworthy of those in the spiritual life rather than immoral in themselves, the second and more innocent of Hall's suggestions is more likely here.

ase seið Seint Beornard: possibly the letter ascribed to Bernard (*Ep.* 462, *PL* 182. 665) suggested by Hall (2.405/220), but the verbal correspondence is not close.

148/9–16. *Of þis boc . . . efter ower mihte*: the author is probably drawing here on the very similar conclusion to Augustine's *Ep.* 211, the basis of the Augustinian Rule (*PL* 33.965, §16).

148/12–13. *Me were leouere . . . eft for te donne*: see *Patience*, ed. J. J. Anderson (Manchester, 1969), 52/52 n. for further examples of this stock phrase for an arduous task (many English clerics did have to go to Rome in the course of their duties).

148/23–4. *Inoh meaðful . . . bidde se lutel*: for the suggestion that these lines make a covert identification of the author of *AW* see Dobson, *Origins*, pp. 327–68.

148/26–7. *Iþench on þi writere . . . for oþre*: found only in the Corpus MS, and probably the scribe's farewell to the reader (*writere* can mean both 'writer' and 'scribe' in this group of texts; see note on 140/16 above).

A NOTE ON THE LANGUAGE

In 1929[1] J. R. R. Tolkien pointed out that the language of the Corpus manuscript of *Ancrene Wisse* (A) was practically identical with that of the main Katherine Group manuscript, MS Bodley 34 (B). This 'language AB' showed not only a consistent phonology and morphology, but also a distinctive and regular spelling-system. Tolkien placed it in the West Midlands, about 1225, and argued that it must also have been the language in which the works themselves were originally composed. The reasoning behind this conclusion has been questioned, on the ground that works can be 'translated' by scribes from one written form of Middle English to another;[2] but there is no supporting evidence in this case for 'translation' from a different dialect, and Tolkien's case has been strengthened by Dobson's convincing identification of 'Scribe B' of the Cleopatra manuscript of *Ancrene Wisse*—who uses a closely similar, though not identical, form of 'language AB'—with the author himself.[3]

'Language AB' belongs to a part of England remote enough to have escaped the main impact of both the Viking invasions of the later Anglo-Saxon period and the Norman Conquest. Although in certain respects—notably a much-simplified system of noun and adjective declension—it has moved some distance from Old English, in others—particularly the conjugation of verbs—it has remained close to it. The general regularity of its phonology and morphology indicates a relatively undisturbed development from Old English, and its preservation of some Old English spelling-conventions suggests that this continuity extended to the written as well as the spoken language. Its geographical closeness to Wales is reflected in a handful of Welsh words, the earlier Scandinavian settlements in the area in a more substantial element of Norse vocabulary, and the effects of the Conquest in a large number of Romance borrowings; but these alien elements have for the most part been integrated into existing inflexional patterns.

Tolkien's arguments for the uniformity of 'language AB' were based on its spelling, phonology, and morphology; later scholars have noted that there is rather more internal variation in its syntax and vocabulary. R. M. Wilson has pointed out that the word-order of *Ancrene Wisse* seems to be considerably closer to modern usage than that of *Seinte Margarete* and *Hali Meiðhad*,[4] and Cecily

---

[1] '*Ancrene Wisse* and *Hali Meiðhad*', *Essays and Studies*, 14 (1929), 104–26.

[2] See Michael Benskin and Margaret Laing, 'Translations and *Mischsprachen* in Middle English Manuscripts', in *So Meny People Longages and Tonges: Philological Essays in Scots and Mediaeval English Presented to Angus McIntosh*, ed. Michael Benskin and M. L. Samuels (Edinburgh, 1981), 55–106, for full references and discussion.

[3] See Dobson, *Cotton Cleopatra*, pp. xciii–cxl.

[4] 'On the Continuity of English Prose', in *Mélanges de linguistique et de philologie: Fernand Mossé in memoriam* (Paris, 1959), 486–94. Wilson, however, is working from the Nero text of *Ancrene Wisse*, which tends to modernize the word-order of the original.

Clark has analysed the different proportions of Romance borrowings in *Ancrene Wisse* and the works of the Katherine Group (highest in *Ancrene Wisse*, lowest in the saints' lives).[5] The significance of these internal variations is not entirely clear. They may indicate that *Ancrene Wisse* was written later than the other works, or by another—perhaps younger—author, but they are probably also influenced by the content and style of the individual works. Cecily Clark relates the higher proportion of Romance borrowings in *Ancrene Wisse* to its relatively abstract content; and there is a wide stylistic gap between the saints' lives of the Katherine Group, with their elevated, half-poetic language and extensive use of traditional alliterative collocations, and *Ancrene Wisse*, whose broader stylistic range embraces not only Latinate theological terminology and a courtly diction influenced by French, but an English which can be highly colloquial and idiomatic.[6]

'Language AB' is a complex phenomenon. It cannot be taken simply as a record of the spoken English of its time and place. Its orthography is conservative, the product of a local scribal tradition which was probably developed during the later twelfth century and retains some links with Old English; its morphology may also have been standardized to some extent; and the syntax and vocabulary of the works preserved in it reflect not only current usage but the stylistic traditions (in Latin and French as well as English) on which they draw. The most convenient short summary of its main features can be found in the introduction to Geoffrey Shepherd's edition of *Ancrene Wisse Parts 6 and 7*, pp. xiv–xxi, but the standard works by d'Ardenne and Zettersten mentioned in Further Reading are essential for more advanced study and reference.

---

[5] '*Ancrene Wisse* and Katherine Group: A Lexical Divergence', *Neophilologus*, 50 (1966), 117–24.

[6] See Cecily Clark, ' "Wið Scharpe Sneateres": Some Aspects of Colloquialism in *Ancrene Wisse*', *Neuphilologische Mitteilungen*, 79 (1978), 341–53; and Janet Bately, 'On Some Aspects of the Vocabulary of the West Midlands in the Early Middle Ages: The Language of the Katherine Group', in *Medieval English Studies Presented to George Kane*, ed. Edward Donald Kennedy, Ronald Waldron, and Joseph S. Wittig (Woodbridge, 1988), 55–77.

GLOSSARY

FOR reasons of space the glossary is selective; a little over four-fifths of the forms in the texts are included. Fuller glossaries, and more detailed information on grammar and etymology, can be found in the individual editions listed in 'Further Reading'.

ʒ (modern *gh*, *y* consonant) is placed after *g*, *i* consonant (modern *j*) after *i* vowel, þ/ð (modern *th*) after *t*, and *u/v* consonant (modern *f* or *v*) after *u/v* vowel (modern *u*). Past participles formed with an *i-* prefix are normally placed with the verb they belong to rather than under *i* (so, for example, **idemet** will be found in the entry for **demen**, but a reference is given under *i* where no other form of the verb occurs, or where the relationship between the participle and other parts of the verb is not immediately obvious. Cross-references for variant spellings are given except where they would fall in the immediate neighbourhood of the main entry.

Up to three citations for each text are given for the words included; but if they occur more than three times in any one text, only the first instance (followed by '*etc.*') is given. Where a word is easily recognizable, glossing has sometimes been reserved for its more obscure forms (so that, for instance, the adjective **strong** is glossed only in its comparative form **strengre**). Emended forms are not separately indicated here, but all divergences from the base manuscripts are recorded in the list of variants at the foot of each page of the text.

The abbreviations for *Ancrene Wisse* Parts 7 and 8 are shortened in the Glossary to *A7* and *A8*. The grammatical abbreviations used are given below.

1, 2, 3	first, second, third person	*neut.*	neuter
acc.	accusative	*nom.*	nominative
adj.	adjective	*num.*	numeral
adv.	adverb	*obj.*	object
art.	article	*ord.*	ordinal
auxil.	auxiliary	*orig.*	originally
comp.	comparative	*pa.*	past tense
conj(s).	conjunction(s)	*pers.*	person
cons.	consonant	*personif.*	personified
dat.	dative	*pl.*	plural
def.	definite	*poss.*	possessive
demons.	demonstrative	*p.p.*	past participle
fem.	feminine	*ppl.*	participial
fut.	future	*pr.*	present tense
gen.	genitive	*prep.*	preposition
imp.	imperative	*pron.*	pronoun
impers.	impersonal	*pr.p.*	present participle
indecl.	indeclinable	*recipr.*	reciprocal
indef.	indefinite	*refl.*	reflexive
infin.	infinitive	*rel.*	relative
infl.	inflected	*sg.*	singular
interj.	interjection	*subj.*	subjunctive
interrog.	interrogative	*superl.*	superlative
masc.	masculine	*v.*	verb (infinitive)
n.	noun	*wk.*	weak declension
neg.	negative		

a *adv. see* **aa.**
a *interj.* oh, ah *HM* 2/20, *SW* 98/33.
a *pron. 3 pl. see* **ha** *pron. 3 pl.*
a, an *indef. art.* a, an; a (*before cons.*) *HM*
4/21 *etc.*, *SM* 46/3 *etc.*, *SW* 86/3 *etc.*,
A7 112/26 *etc.*, *A8* 130/13 *etc.* an
(*usually before vowel or h*) *HM* 6/21 *etc.*,
SM 44/10 *etc.*, *SW* 90/11 *etc.*, *A7*
112/34 *etc.*, *A8* 136/12 *etc.*
a, an *adj.* one; a *HM* 22/19[1, 2] *etc.*, *A7*
122/25, — **dei** one day *SM* 46/21, **ed**
— **time** at one time *A7* 120/29. **an**
(*before cons.*) *HM* 6/20 *etc.*, *SM* 58/1,
72/26, 80/32, *SW* 104/30, 106/12, *A7*
114/29, 124/13, *A8* 130/21 *etc.* **en; ed**
— **cherre** at one time *HM* 20/25. **ane**
infl. alone *SM* 68/28, *A7* 112/8,
120/29, 128/5, *acc. masc. HM* 6/1, *SM*
50/15, 70/20, *acc. fem. SW* 98/12, —
hwile for a time *HM* 16/1, *SW* 98/21,
dat. HM 40/33 *etc.*, *SM* 54/19, 58/9
etc., *SW* 98/4, *A7* 110/23, 32, 118/13,
A8 132/21 *etc.* —**dale** partly *HM* 22/2,
him— by himself *HM* 34/35, þe— on
your own *SM* 70/19. **anes** *gen. sg.* (*after
poss. pron.*) alone *HM* 16/20[1, 2], 26/5,
own *HM* 24/27, 26/2, *pl.* 26/22. **ane**
pl. HM 20/7, *dat. pl. A8* 130/3, 28, in
— **lut wordes** in a few words *HM*
32/27. *See also* **ane** *adv.*
aa *adv.* always, for ever *HM* 14/5 *etc.*, *SM*
58/4 *etc.*, *SW* 88/25 *etc.*, *A7* 124/12,
A8 144/13 *etc.*, — **on echnesse** to all
eternity *SW* 92/16, — **on ecnesse**
HM 24/25, *SM* 54/27 *etc.*, *A8* 148/20,
— **mare** for ever *SM* 60/2, 68/18. **a**
SM 66/6, *SW* 92/13 *etc.*, — **mare** for
ever, evermore *HM* 18/20, *SM* 50/22.
See also **abuten** *prep.*
abeoren *v.* endure, put up with *HM*
14/35, *SW* 92/33.
abideð *pr. 3 sg.* awaits *HM* 14/34, **abit**
SM 80/14. **abid** *imp. sg.* wait for *SM*
78/7. **abideð** *imp. pl.* wait *A8* 130/23.
abuggen *v.* pay for *HM* 26/3, 40/35.
aboht *p.p. HM* 24/21.
abufen *adv.* above *SM* 72/10.
abute(n) *prep.* about, around; **abute** *HM*
32/19, *SW* 88/3, **abuten** *SM* 58/17
etc., *SW* 94/25, *A7* 118/1.
abuten *adv.* about, around *HM* 16/10,
26/15, *SM* 78/6, *SW* 86/29, *A7*
112/33.

abuten *prep.* forever without; **world**
—**ende** for all eternity *A7* 122/1.
acaste *see* **akeasten.**
acouerin *v.* recover; **up** — rise again
HM 28/19, **acourin** *HM* 10/5.
acoueret *p.p. HM* 8/34.
acouerunge *n.* recovery *HM* 24/9, *SW*
92/15.
acwaldest *pa. 2 sg.* destroyed *SM* 62/31.
acwenchen *v.* extinguish *A7* 124/1, 8,
A8 136/19. **acwencheð** *pr. 3 sg. A7*
124/9 *etc.*
acwikeð *pr. 3 sg.* revives *HM* 14/24.
acwikieð *pr. 3 pl. SW* 92/12. **acwiket**
p.p. HM 18/22.
acwitin *v.* buy off, ransom *A7* 116/23, 25.
adamantines *n. gen. sg.* of adamant *HM*
32/30.
afeallen *v.* cast down *SM* 60/13.
auealleð *pr. 3 sg. SM* 70/23. **aueallet**
p.p. HM 14/26, **auellet** *SM* 62/4.
aga *pr. sg. subj.* go out, be extinguished
A8 144/12.
ageasteð *pr. 3 sg.* frightens, terrifies *HM*
28/2.
agrette *pa. 3 sg.* addressed *SW* 98/23.
agrisen *v.* frighten, be afraid; **makeð þe
to** — frightens you *HM* 28/3. **agras**
pa. 3 sg. hire — frightened her *SM*
62/35. **agrisen** *p.p. SM* 58/23.
agulteð *pr. 3. pl.* offend, transgress *SW*
88/20. **agulten** *pa. 3 pl.* sinned *HM*
40/30.
aȝein *adv.* back *HM* 14/3, *SM* 48/14,
82/27, *A7* 116/29, 36, 118/4, *A8*
146/29.
aȝein *prep.* against *HM* 12/27, 14/31,
36/12, *SM* 54/24 *etc.*, *SW* 86/20,
88/1, 18, *A7* 114/34, 116/6, 124/13,
A8 132/5, 136/19, in comparison with
HM 4/33, *SW* 100/1, *A7* 120/32,
124/27, *A8* 130/6, towards, upon *SW*
100/3, on account of, in anticipation of
HM 28/1, 32/7, *A8* 130/19, in response to *SW* 102/16, *A7* 118/1.
aȝeines *prep.* against *HM* 36/12, *SW*
88/5 *etc.*, in return for *HM* 6/20, in
comparison with *SW* 102/3, *A7* 110/2.
aȝeinwart *adv.* back, back again *HM*
38/8.
ah *conj.* but *HM* 4/2 *etc.*, *SM* 44/10 *etc.*,
SW 86/26 *etc.*, *A7* 110/4 *etc.*, *A8* 130/5
etc.

ah *pr. 1 sg.* ought, owe, own *SM* 82/28; **hah** own *SM* 50/9, 27. **ahest** *pr. 2 sg.* ought *HM* 10/7, 34/15. **ah** *pr. 3 sg. HM* 2/8, 34/10, *SW* 106/33, *A7* 112/26, 120/6, *A8* 132/22 *etc.*, owes *A7* 126/12. **ahen** *pr. 1 pl. SW* 86/4, *pr. 2 pl. A7* 122/28, *A8* 146/7, *pr. 3 pl. SW* 104/4, *A8* 146/3. **ahte** *pa. 1 sg.* owed *A7* 126/11. **ahtest** *pa. 2 sg.* ought *HM* 30/20, owed *A7* 126/9. **ahte** *pa. 3 sg.* owned *A7* 114/8, 120/31, ought *A8* 144/33, **hahte** *SM* 46/11. **ahten** *pa. 1 pl.* owned *SM* 72/14, *pa. 3 pl.* ought *SM* 70/1.

ahef *pa. 3 sg.* lifted up; — hire heorte summoned up her courage *SM* 52/11.

ahne *adj. wk.* own *HM* 30/31, 32/31, 42/12, *SM* 56/26, 68/15, *SW* 104/10 *etc.*, *A7* 112/30 *etc.*, *A8* 138/10, 140/1, 146/24. **ahnes** *gen. pl. A8* 146/26. **ahne** *pl. SM* 66/16, 68/1, *SW* 96/23, *A7* 126/20, 128/8.

ahon *p.p.* hung, suspended *SM* 48/11.

ahte *n.* livestock *HM* 26/17, *A8* 134/19, 24, 33, **hahte** sheep *SM* 46/13.

ahte *v. see* **ah** *pr. 1 sg.*

akeasten *v.* cast down *SM* 66/30. **akeasteð** *pr. 3 sg. HM* 8/27. **acaste** *pa. 3 sg. SM* 44/22. **akeasten** *pa. 3 pl. SM* 44/4. **akeast** *p.p. HM* 4/11, 20, 32, **akest** *SM* 62/12.

akeldeð *pr. 3 sg.* cools *A7* 124/11.

aken *v.* ache *HM* 30/33. **akeð** *pr. 3 pl.* (*with pers. obj.*) *HM* 28/6.

akennesse *n.* conception *HM* 40/3.

al *adj.* all, every *HM* 2/21[2] *etc.*, *SM* 44/22 *etc.*, *SW* 86/12 *etc.*, *A7* 110/12[1,2] *etc.*, *A8* 142/30, **alle** *HM* 26/6 *etc.*, *A7* 110/9, 126/10, *dat. HM* 34/25, *A8* 132/17. **alles** *gen.* — **weis** in every way *HM* 24/11, — **cunnes** of every kind *SM* 48/6, *SW* 90/34 *etc.*, *A7* 120/34. **alle** *pl. HM* 2/28 *etc.*, *SM* 44/17 *etc.*, *SW* 88/1 *etc.*, *A7* 110/1[1,2] *etc.*, *A8* 146/26. **on** — **cunne** in all kinds of *A7* 112/14. **alre** *gen. pl. HM* 24/28 *etc.*, *SM* 46/12 *etc.*, *A7* 120/5. **al** *as n.* all, everything *HM* 2/21[1] *etc.*, *SM* 46/11 *etc.*, *SW* 94/8 *etc.*, *A7* 110/2 *etc.*, *A8* 134/13, 144/30, 148/18. **alle** *dat.* **mid** — whole, altogether *SM* 58/23 *etc.*, *A7* 122/18, indeed *SW* 98/16, *A7* 118/29, 128/4, furthermore *A8* 136/4, **wið** —

altogether *HM* 16/25. **alle** *pl. HM* 4/6 *etc.*, *SM* 44/24 *etc.*, *SW* 86/13 *etc.*, *A7* 118/34, 120/31, 128/26, *A8* 144/27, **al** (*with elision before* as) *HM* 20/5. **alre** *gen. pl. HM* 14/30 *etc.*, *SM* 66/20, *SW* 92/24, 96/20.

al *adv.* all, entirely, quite *HM* 8/19 *etc.*, *SM* 46/23 *etc.*, *SW* 86/10 *etc.*, *A7* 112/22 *etc.*, *A8* 130/27 *etc.*

al *conj.* although *HM* 38/9, 19.

aleid *p.p.* sated *HM* 22/7.

alesen *v.* save, deliver *HM* 12/22, *SW* 100/13. **ales** *imp. sg. SM* 78/29.

alesendnesse *n.* redemption, salvation *HM* 10/6, **alesnesse** *SW* 102/34.

aliggen *v.* cease, fail *SM* 50/21. **alið** *pr. 3 sg. SM* 50/21, 68/17, 70/6. **alei** *pa. 3 sg.* subsided *SM* 64/19.

alle, alles *see* **al** *adj.*

allunge *adv.* entirely, completely *HM* 40/30, *SM* 60/23, 70/15, *A7* 118/37, 122/18, *A8* 144/5, **allunges** *A8* 140/4.

alre *see* **al** *adj.*

alswa *adv.* so, as, also, just (as) *HM* 10/34 *etc.*, *SM* 56/10, *SW* 88/24 *etc.*, *A7* 110/16 *etc.*, *A8* 134/9 *etc.*, **alse** likewise *HM* 10/35.

alwealdent *adj.* almighty *HM* 36/23, *SW* 100/9, *as n. HM* 30/26, *SW* 98/32.

am *pr. 1 sg.* am *HM* 40/33, *SM* 48/24 *etc.*, *SW* 88/35 *etc.*, *A8* 138/28, 148/23. *neg. form:* **nam** am not *A7* 120/2[1,2,3] *etc.* See **aren, art, beon, is, wes.**

amead *adj.* mad, out of one's mind *HM* 32/31.

amites *n. pl.* amices, ecclesiastical linen scarves *A8* 138/29.

amurðrin *v.* murder *SW* 88/3.

an *def. art., adj. see* **a, an.**

an *pron.* one *HM* 10/25[1], 20/19, *SM* 46/16 *etc.*, *SW* 100/24 *etc.*, *A7* 110/24, 120/31, *A8* 142/6, — **efter** — one after another *HM* 22/22, — **efter** oðer *A7* 112/36, **moni** — many people *HM* 34/17, **þreo** — three in one *SW* 100/6. **anes** *gen.*; — **heorte** the heart of one of them *SW* 104/16.

anan *adv.* at once, immediately *HM* 30/5 *etc.*, *SM* 68/18, *SW* 92/12, *A7* 118/1, *A8* 140/5.

ananriht *adv.* immediately *HM* 14/13, *SM* 76/28, 82/8, *SW* 94/33, 104/28,

ananrihtes *A8* 140/4.

ancre *n.* anchoress, recluse *A8* 132/3
etc., *gen. sg. A8* 134/1¹,²,³ *etc.*
chirch- — church-recluse *A8* 132/30,
138/5. **ancres** *pl. A8* 132/32, 146/7.
ancren *pl. A8* 130/4 *etc.* **ancrene** *gen.*
pl. AW (heading).

ancre-hus *n.* anchoritic cell *A8* 140/11.

ane *adv.* alone, only *HM* 4/17, *A7*
128/34, *A8* 142/25, simply *A7* 126/34,
nawt — not only *HM* 22/23 *etc.*, *SM*
68/9, *A7* 112/22, 114/35, *A8* 146/26.
See also **a, an** *adj.*

anewil *adj.* stubborn *A7* 120/33.

angoise *n.* suffering *HM* 32/8.

an-hwet *pron.* one thing, something *SM*
50/23.

an-ihurnde *adj. as n. gen. pl.* unicorns
SM 54/20.

anlepi *adj.* only *SM* 56/27, individual
SW 104/17.

anuald *adj.* one, single *SM* 62/19.

are *n.* glory *SM* 50/21, mercy *A8*
148/15. **do** — have mercy *A7* 126/3.

areachen *v.* describe, interpret *SM*
60/28. **araht** *pa. 3 sg. SM* 44/11.

arearen *v.* raise *A7* 114/5, stir up *A8*
144/11. **areareð** *pr. 3 sg. A7* 124/35.
areare *pr. sg. subj. HM* 18/21. **arerde**
pa. 3. sg. SM 44/15.

aren *pr. 3 pl.* are *SM* 56/27, 64/17,
70/15, *SW* 92/15, 100/28. *See* **am,
art, beon, is, wes.**

ariste *n.* resurrection *SM* 44/2.

art *pr. 2 sg.* are *HM* 8/30 *etc.*, *SM* 48/21
etc., *A7* 114/10 *etc.*, *A8* 132/15. *neg.*
form: **nart** are not *SM* 64/35, 70/32.
See **am, aren, beon, is, wes.**

arudden *v.* rescue, deliver *SW* 92/28,
arudde *SM* 54/7, *A7* 114/14. **arude**
imp. sg. SM 54/17. **arudde** *pa. 3 sg.*
SM 60/21, 62/5, *A7* 114/18. **arud** *p.p.*
A7 116/5.

astenche *v.* assail with a stench *SM*
64/9.

astoruen *p.p.* destroyed *SM* 62/3.

aswinden *v.* vanish *SM* 64/29.

atiffi *pr. sg. subj.* dress elegantly *A8*
138/12.

atter *n.* venom *SM* 56/33.

attreð *pr. 3 sg.* poisons *A8* 138/31.

attri *adj.* poisonous *HM* 12/25, *SM*
66/19.

aturn *n.* attire, dress *HM* 20/8, *A8*
142/30.

aturnet *p.p.* dressed *SW* 98/13.

atwa *see* **otwa.**

aþet *prep.* until *HM* 12/11 *etc.*, *SM*
48/35, 70/10, *SW* 86/22, *A7* 122/11,
A8 130/23 *etc.*, **aðet** *SW* 92/12, 22.

aþrusmeð *pr. 3 sg.* smothers *SW* 92/16.

aueallet, auealleð, auellet *see* **afeallen.**

aureola *n.* heavenly crown *HM* 20/12.

awariede *adj.* accursed *SM* 54/24,
70/33, **aweariede** *HM* 38/9. **awariede** *pl. SM* 52/8, **aweariede** *pl. as*
n. wicked women *HM* 28/28.

awarpen *v.* overthrow *SM* 52/16. *p.p.*
HM 42/12, *SM* 62/3, 66/11,
70/16.

awed *p.p.* maddened, enraged *SM*
76/33.

aweiwart *adv.* away *SM* 62/2.

awundret *p.p.* astonished; **beoð** — of
marvel at *HM* 36/1.

ba *adj.* both *SM* 56/13, *SW* 92/24,
104/30, *A7* 118/18, 120/36, *A8*
132/13, 144/26, — **twa his honden**
both his hands *A7* 118/27.

ba *adv.* both; — **ant** both and *HM* 18/19
etc., *SM* 50/17 *etc.*, *SW* 86/22, 29, *A8*
146/13, 15.

ba *pron.* both *HM* 4/26, 14/5, 24/34, *SW*
96/4, 106/22, *A7* 110/25, *A8* 142/13.

bald *adj.* brave *SW* 96/22, 26.

baldeliche *adv.* bravely, boldly *SM* 74/2,
freely, openly *SM* 78/9.

bale *n.* suffering, torment *HM* 2/21 *etc.*,
SW 92/1 *etc.*

bale *adj.* cruel *SM* 66/2.

balefule *adj. wk.* dreadful *SM* 60/14,
fierce *SM* 62/6.

balesið *n.* suffering *SM* 84/2.

banles *adj.* boneless; **blodles ant** —
without real life or vitality *SM* 74/13.

baret *n.* turmoil *A8* 132/15.

baðe *adv.* both, too, as well *HM* 2/29
etc., *SM* 74/10, 13, 78/8, *A7* 112/36,
baþe *SM* 56/21, 76/1.

baþe *pron. pl.* both *HM* 20/21, **baðe** *SM*
80/31, *A7* 118/32, 126/21.

bead *see* **beoden** *v.*

beah *see* **buhest.**

bearmes *n. gen. sg.* lap *HM* 32/20.

bearmes (*cont.*):
  bearmes *pl.* in hare — in their arms *SM* 82/18.
bearn *n.* child *HM* 30/15 *etc.*
bearn-team *n.* offspring *HM* 26/31.
beawbelez *n. pl.* ornaments, costly presents *A7* 112/36.
bed *see* **bidden.**
beddin *v.* cohabit *HM* 38/5.
beieð *pr. 3 sg.* bows, pays homage *SM* 50/18. **beieð** *pr. 3 pl. SM* 56/21, 68/4, **beið** *SM* 60/5. **beie** *pr. sg. subj.* bend *HM* 14/2. **bei** *imp. sg.* incline *HM* 2/4, 11, *SM* 78/18, do homage *SM* 54/37. **beide** *pa. 3 sg.* gave way *SM* 82/7, *pa. sg. subj. SM* 74/5.
bemin *pr. pl. subj.* resound (like a trumpet) *A8* 146/25.
bene *n.* prayer *SM* 78/26. **benen** *pl. SM* 68/2, 78/18, 80/2.
beo *see* **beon.**
beodefule *adj. pl.* prayerful, suppliant *SM* 68/1.
beoden *n. pl.* prayers *SM* 58/8 *etc.*, *A7* 126/3, *A8* 142/8, 146/25, 148/26.
beoden *v.* offer *A7* 122/30. **beot** *pr. 3 sg. A8* 140/4. **beodeð** *pr. 2 pl. A7* 124/28. **bead** *pa. 3 sg. A7* 114/7.
beon *v.* be *HM* 4/28 *etc.*, *SM* 44/13 *etc.*, *SW* 86/9 *etc.*, *A7* 112/8 *etc.*, *A8* 138/12 *etc.*, **beo** *HM* 4/12 *etc.*, *A7* 112/9 *etc.*, **beonne** *infl. infin. HM* 8/16, *A8* 138/24, 146/14. **bið** *pr. 3 sg.* is, will be *HM* 8/34 *etc.*, *SM* 56/5 *etc.*, *SW* 86/23, 94/20. **beoð** *pr. 3 pl. HM* 2/29 *etc.*, *SM* 44/17 *etc.*, *SW* 86/13 *etc.*, *A7* 110/14 *etc.*, *A8* 130/7 *etc.* **beo** *pr. sg. subj. HM* 2/6 *etc.*, *SM* 46/35 *etc.*, *SW* 86/26 *etc.*, *A7* 118/2 *etc.*, *A8* 132/36 *etc.*, **ibeo** *SM* 60/32. **beon** *pr. pl. subj. HM* 6/9 *etc.*, *SM* 44/8 *etc.*, *SW* 94/16 *etc.*, *A8* 130/21 *etc.* **beo** *imp. sg. HM* 2/12 *etc.*, *SM* 46/32 *etc.* **ibeo** *p.p. SW* 106/2, **ibeon** *SM* 64/28, *A7* 114/32.
  See **am, aren, art, is, wes.**
beore *v.* carry *SM* 60/14. **berest** *pr. 2 sg. HM* 6/5. **bereð** *pr. 3 sg. SM* 48/3, *SW* 90/10, *A7* 124/31, — to incites *HM* 22/15, — forð distends *HM* 30/34. **beoreð** *imp. pl.* — me genge accompany me *SM* 80/25. **beore** *pr. sg. subj.* wear *A8* 136/14, carry *A8* 142/20. **beorinde** *pr.p. SM* 76/15. **ber** *pa. 3 sg.* lifted *SM* 78/11, carried *SM* 82/26.

beren *pa. 3 pl. SM* 82/18. **iboren** *p.p.* carried *HM* 8/6, taken *A8* 146/33, born *HM* 30/12 *etc.*, *SM* 60/31, 72/13, 78/27, **ibore** *HM* 32/18, 36/32, *SM* 74/8, *SW* 94/10, **iborene** *pl. SM* 60/31.
beoð *see* **beon.**
bere *n.* uproar, clamour *HM* 28/3, *SW* 86/22.
beren, berest, bereð *see* **beore.**
besmen *n. pl.* rods *SM* 52/8.
bet *adv.* better *A8* 132/16, 148/15, **þuncheð** — seems more like *A8* 134/20.
beten *v.* atone for *HM* 18/27. **beten** *pr. pl. subj. HM* 22/11. **ibet** *p.p.* atoned *SW* 90/14.
bi *prep.* by; **beoð** — be in possession of, have *A8* 136/29, **don** — do to *HM* 36/34, 38/1, serve *SW* 104/4.
biblodgi *pr. sg. subj.* make bloody *A8* 136/16. **biblodeget** *p.p.* bloodied, stained *SM* 46/31.
bicleopest *pr. 2 sg.* speak to *HM* 28/22. **bicleopet** *p.p.* called (to account) *A8* 146/11.
bicluppeð *pr. 3 sg.* embraces *HM* 36/7, — abuten comprehends *HM* 16/10.
bicoruen *p.p.* cut off; **hefdes** — beheaded *SM* 76/29.
bidden *v.* pray *SM* 56/19 *etc.*, ask, beg *A8* 132/37, 134/16, tell, command *SM* 80/18. **bidde** *pr. 1 sg. SM* 62/33 *etc.*, *SW* 108/16, *A8* 130/5, 148/23. **biddest** *pr. 2 sg. SM* 62/25, **bidest** *A8* 148/27. **bit** *pr. 3 sg. HM* 8/7, *SW* 100/17. **biddeð** *pr. 3 pl. SM* 80/10. **bidden** *pr. pl. subj. SW* 108/17, *A8* 134/4. **bidde** *imp. sg. HM* 8/25. **biddeð** *imp. pl. SW* 108/13, *A8* 148/14. **bed** *pa. 3 sg.* commanded *SM* 56/14, 74/34, prayed *SM* 58/8, 82/31, 84/4. **ibeden** *p.p. SM* 58/26, 80/4.
bifunden *p.p.* contrived *HM* 28/14.
bigan *v.* bespatter *HM* 34/2.
bigoten *p.p.* suffused *SW* 100/31, **bigotten** immersed *SW* 104/21.
biȝeotene *infl. infin.* gain *HM* 6/24, 26/14. **biȝet** *pr. 3 sg.* obtains *SM* 78/20. **biȝeoteð** *pr. 3 pl. HM* 26/14. **biȝet** *pa. 3 sg. SM* 44/22.
biȝete *n.* gain *HM* 24/7, 34/21, *A7* 120/34, *A8* 146/32.

bihaten *v.* promise *A8* 130/1. **bihate** *pr. 1 sg. HM* 16/6. **bihat** *pr. 3 sg. HM* 38/8. **bihateð** *pr. 3 pl. A8* 146/20. **bihet** *pa. 1 sg. A8* 130/9. **biheten** *pa. 1 pl. HM* 20/30, *pa. 3 pl. HM* 6/26. **bihaten** *p.p. HM* 16/12, *SM* 80/21, *A7* 112/15.

biheaste *n.* promise *HM* 16/11, 34/16, *SM* 50/29.

biheue *n.* advantage *HM* 22/30, *A7* 110/24 *etc.*

biheue *adj.* beneficial *A8* 148/10.

bihoueð *pr. 3 sg. impers.* is necessary (to) *HM* 4/19 *etc.*, is fitting *SW* 86/26, me — I need *HM* 22/34. **bihofde** *pa. 3 sg.*; him — it needed *A7* 118/9.

bileaue *n.* faith *HM* 4/19, 16/35, 28/31, *SM* 46/14 *etc.*, *SW* 94/32, 96/3, *A7* 118/8.

bilehwit *adj.* innocent *SM* 82/13.

biliue *adv.* quickly, immediately *SM* 48/20.

bilukeð *pr. 3 sg.* summarizes, encompasses *HM* 32/27. **biloke** *p.p.* locked up *SW* 98/9.

biluueð *pr. 3 sg. impers.* is pleasing (to) *SW* 98/20, 22.

bineomen *v.* deprive of *A7* 116/6. **binimeð** *pr. 3 sg. A8* 148/7. **bineomeð** *pr. 3 pl. HM* 32/7. **bineome** *pr. sg. subj. SW* 86/11. **binumen** *p.p.* taken away *SM* 72/14.

binetli *pr. sg. subj.* sting with nettles *A8* 136/17.

biremen *v.* lament *HM* 40/35.

bireowe *v.* cause to regret *HM* 6/23.

bireowsið *pr. 3 pl.* repent *HM* 38/27. **birewsinde** *pr.p. SM* 68/23.

bireowsunge *n.* repentance *HM* 12/11, 18/21.

biseon *v.* look (at), regard *HM* 16/19, *SW* 92/30, 108/1, **biseonne** *infl. infin. SM* 68/35. **bisið** *pr. 3 sg.*; — him *refl.* considers *SW* 106/3. **bisih** *imp. sg.*; — þe *refl.* consider *HM* 28/20. **biseoð** *imp. pl. A7* 122/28. **biseh** *pa. 1, 3 sg. HM* 40/7, *SM* 54/15, *SW* 100/20.

bismere *n.* shame *HM* 14/20, **to** — shamefully *HM* 28/4, to shame *A8* 132/12.

bisocnen *n. pl.* entreaties *SW* 102/16.

bisteaðed *p.p.* beset *SM* 48/10.

bisteken *p.p.* locked out *SW* 88/13.

bit *see* **bidden.**

bitacneð *pr. 3 sg.* signifies *HM* 2/27, *A7* 124/11, 126/14. **bitacnið** *pr. 3 pl. A7* 122/25. **bitacnede** *pa. 3 sg. A7* 124/19. **bitacnet** *p.p. HM* 4/3.

bitacnunge *n.* sign, token *A7* 114/31.

bitechen *v.* surrender *SM* 50/32. **biteache** *pr. 1 sg.* commend *SM* 78/8. **bitahte** *pa. 3 sg. SM* 46/10. **bitaht** *p.p. SM* 46/34, *SW* 94/18 *etc.*

bitel *adj.* biting, keen *SM* 76/35.

bitellunge *n.* excuse *A7* 116/6.

biteon *v.* bestow *A7* 120/1. **biteo** *pr. 1 sg. A7* 124/28. **bitohe** *p.p.*; uuele — misspent, used badly *A8* 148/11.

bitimde *pa. 3 sg.* (it) happened *SM* 46/18.

bitrumme *v.* surround *SM* 78/5. **bitrummet** *p.p. SM* 54/16.

bitterlukest *adv. superl.* most bitterly *HM* 30/15.

bituhe *prep.* between, among *HM* 28/33, *SM* 84/10, — **Godes earmes** in God's arms *HM* 40/24, **bituhen** *HM* 28/8, *SM* 56/35, *A7* 114/15, **bituhhe** *HM* 22/14, *SW* 94/6 *etc.*, **bituhhen** *SW* 96/7, *A7* 118/15.

bitunde *pa. 3 sg.* confined *SM* 72/29, enclosed *SM* 72/35.

biturn *imp. sg.*; — þe *refl.* turn *A7* 116/36. **biturde** *pa. 3 sg.*; — hire *refl.* (she) turned about *SM* 64/19. **biturnd** *p.p.* directed towards *A7* 112/25.

biþenchen *v.* think (of); — on contrive *SM* 52/1. **biþencheð** *pr. 3 pl.*; — ham *refl.* reflect *HM* 6/31. **biþoht** *p.p.*; — him *refl.* considered *SM* 48/35.

biwiten *v.* keep, defend *SW* 86/4, **biwite** *SM* 64/5, **biwitene** *infl. infin. HM* 18/7. **biwit** *pr. 3 sg. SM* 48/3, **biwiteð** *SW* 88/1. **biwiteð** *pr. 3 pl. HM* 26/13, 20. **biwite** *imp. sg. SM* 46/34.

blac *adj.* pale *SW* 88/30.

blakien *v.* grow pale *SM* 58/24.

blamon *n.* black man *SM* 60/27.

bleasie *pr. sg. subj.* blaze *A7* 122/14, *A8* 144/13.

bleinin *n. pl.* blisters *SM* 74/20.

bleo *n.* countenance *SM* 54/27, 58/24, 60/30.

blikinde *pr.p.* shining *SM* 64/37, 76/35. **blikeden** *pa. 3 pl.* shone *SM* 58/12.

bliðeliche *adv.* gladly *HM* 14/35, 36/6, *SM* 80/23, *SW* 100/19, 106/24, *A8* 130/31, bluðeliche *SW* 90/23.

bliþeluker *adv. comp.* more gladly *HM* 2/9.

blodbinde *n.* bandage *A8* 138/19.

blostme *n.* flower *HM* 8/35, *SM* 48/3, 60/31.

blowinde *pr.p.* flowering *SM* 60/38. iblowen *p.p.* in full flower *SM* 60/31.

bluðeliche *see* bliðeliche.

boc-felle *n.* parchment *SM* 82/31.

boden *n. pl.* offers, invitations *A8* 134/11.

bohes *n. pl.* branches *A8* 132/37.

bohte *see* buggen.

boistes *n. pl.* caskets *A8* 134/33.

bold *n.* abode *SW* 94/3.

bone *n.* (1) destroyer *SM* 60/22 *etc.*

bone *n.* (2) prayer *SM* 52/12 *etc.* bonen *pl. SM* 82/31.

bord *n.* table; makeð hire — takes her meal *A8* 132/3.

bote *n.* remedy *SM* 68/28, *SW* 92/1, *A8* 136/19, remission *SM* 80/11, amends *A8* 146/20, *gen. sg.* remedy *HM* 28/28.

bottnede *pa. 3 sg.* cured *SM* 44/15. botneden *pa. 3 pl.* were healed *SM* 82/17.

brech *n.* drawers *A8* 136/26.

breres *n. pl.* thorns (on a branch used as a scourge) *A8* 136/16.

broke-rugget *adj. pl.* hunchbacked *HM* 22/24.

brond *n.* sword, blade *SM* 76/35. brondes *pl.* brands *A8* 144/12.

bruche *n.* breach (of chastity) *HM* 10/11 *etc.* bruchen *pl.* sins *SM* 80/11.

bruchele *adj. wk.* frail *HM* 10/21, fragile *HM* 10/31.

brudlac *n.* marriage *HM* 2/17, 42/25. brudlakes *gen. sg.*; — dei wedding-day *HM* 8/6.

bruken *v.* have, get *HM* 26/2, enjoy *HM* 28/31, *SM* 76/25.

brune *n.* burning, fire *HM* 8/12, 38/31, 40/35, *SM* 68/34, *SW* 90/26, 92/7, *A7* 124/13, 14^{1,2}, o — alight, burning *A8* 144/12.

buggen *v.* buy *HM* 8/3, *A7* 120/11, pay for *A7* 126/33. buð *pr. 3 sg. A7* 116/7, *A8* 134/28, 146/6. buggeð *pr. 3 pl. HM* 6/32. bugge *pr. sg. subj. A7*

120/10. bohte *pa. 3 sg. SW* 86/28, 100/8, *A7* 116/7^{1,2}, 16. iboht *p.p. HM* 30/15, *A7* 120/13. ibohte *ppl. adj. wk. HM* 28/5.

buhest *pr. 2 sg.* submit *SM* 54/35.

buheð *pr. 3 sg.* obeys *SM* 50/18, bends *A7* 122/29. buheð *pr. 3 pl.* pay homage (to) *HM* 4/14, *SM* 56/21, 60/4, 68/4. buh *imp. sg. SM* 54/36, 78/17. beah *pa. 3 sg.* bowed *SM* 80/34, fell *SM* 82/7. buhe *pa. sg. subj. SM* 74/4. ibuhe *p.p.* bowed down *HM* 22/24.

buhsum *adj.* obedient *HM* 2/12, *SW* 100/12.

buhsumnesse *n.* obedience *HM* 36/13.

bur *n.* chamber, mansion *SM* 76/11, 80/14, 82/8.

burde *n.* (1) lady *SM* 72/28. *gen. pl. SM* 80/17.

burde *n.* (2) nature *HM* 10/29.

burh *n.* town *SM* 46/3 *etc.*, *A7* 122/23, buri dwelling, habitation *SW* 94/2.

burnes *n. gen. sg.* spring; — drunch water from a spring *SM* 58/7.

burðerne *n.* carrying (of a child), pregnancy *HM* 30/6, burþerne *HM* 30/28, 32/34, weight *HM* 32/2.

busteð *pr. 3 sg.* beats *HM* 28/5.

bute *conj.* unless *HM* 12/32 *etc.*, *SM* 66/5 *etc.*, *SW* 86/10 *etc.*, *A7* 112/4^2 *etc.*, *A8* 130/27 *etc.*, — 3ef unless *HM* 6/28 *etc.*, *A8* 134/18, 144/5, 148/2, — 3if *SM* 50/24.

bute *prep.* but, except, without *HM* 4/17 *etc.*, *SM* 44/13 *etc.*, *SW* 92/1 *etc.*, *A7* 110/14 *etc.*, *A8* 130/12 *etc.*, buten *HM* 10/11 *etc.*, *SM* 54/11 *etc.*, *SW* 102/14 *etc.*, *A7* 118/32, *A8* 130/3 *etc.*

butte *n.* uterus *HM* 30/34.

buue *prep.* above *SW* 100/24, buuen *SW* 100/21.

cader *n.* cradle *HM* 32/20. cader-clutes baby-clothes *HM* 34/2.

cake *n.* loaf *HM* 34/8.

cangun *n.* fool *HM* 28/21.

carien *v.* grieve *HM* 24/15, be troubled, concerned *SW* 96/1, 5, look after, worry about *HM* 4/30 *etc.*, carie care *HM* 4/18.

chaffere *n.* bargain *HM* 8/5, trade *A8*

134/28, **cheaffeare** *HM* 24/7, **cheaf-fere** *HM* 22/32.

chap *n.* bargain, price; **liht** — easy terms, cheaply *A7* 120/16.

chapmon *n.* trader *A8* 134/29.

charbucle *n.* ruby *HM* 38/20, 22.

charden *pa. 3 pl.* turned; **— aȝein** turned back *SM* 48/14.

chastieð *pr. 3 sg.* controls *HM* 12/34. **chasti** *pr. sg. subj.* disciplines *SW* 86/11.

chearite *n.* charity *A7* 128/3.

cheosen *v.* select, choose *SW* 96/16. **cheose** *pr. 1 sg. SM* 46/25. **cheoseð** *pr. 3 sg. HM* 34/35. **cheose** *pr. sg. subj. A7* 126/25. **chure** *pa. 2 sg. SM* 76/24. **cheas** *pa. 3 sg. HM* 12/20, 40/32, **ches** *SM* 46/9. **icoren** *p.p. SM* 70/21, **icore** *SM* 80/25, *A8* 132/16, **icorene** *ppl. adj. as n. pl.* elect, chosen *HM* 6/9, 38/31, 42/18, *SM* 44/16, 46/14, 64/8.

cheowest *pr. 2 sg.* eat *HM* 32/4. **cheoweð** *pr. 3 sg.* nags, scolds *HM* 28/4.

chepeð *pr. 3 sg.* sells, trades *A8* 134/29.

chepilt *n.* tradeswoman *A8* 134/28.

chere *n.* countenance, demeanour *HM* 28/22, *SM* 48/19, *SW* 98/18, *A8* 134/5.

cherre *n.* occasion; **ed en** — at one time *HM* 20/25.

cherte *n.* love, holding dear *A7* 128/3.

cheuese *n.* mistress *SM* 46/26.

chideð *pr. 3 sg.* scolds *HM* 34/9, **chit** *HM* 28/4.

chirch-ancre *see* **ancre**.

chirch-uestemenz *n. pl.* church vestments *A8* 134/34.

chulle *see* **wulle**.

chure *see* **cheosen**.

cleanliche *adv.* completely, fully *A8* 130/19.

cleannesse *n.* purity *HM* 10/12, *A7* 120/7.

cleanschipe *n.* purity *HM* 18/26.

cleopien *v.* call *HM* 40/8, **clepien** call on *SM* 46/28. **cleopeð** *pr. 3 sg. HM* 2/7 *etc.*, *SW* 88/10. **cleopieð** *pr. 3 pl. HM* 28/17, *SM* 54/1. **cleopede** *pa. 3 sg. SM* 48/20 *etc.* **icleopet** *p.p. HM* 2/26 *etc.*, *SM* 44/17 *etc.*, *SW* 88/8.

cluppen *v.* embrace *A8* 142/28.

cluppunge *n.* embrace *HM* 2/18. **cluppunges** *pl. A7* 118/16.

cnawen *v.* know *SW* 102/33. **cnaweð** *pr. 3 pl. SW* 88/27.

cnawlechunge *n.* knowledge *SW* 102/32.

cneolin *v.* kneel; **on cneon** — fall to the knees *SM* 78/10.

cniht *n.* knight *A7* 114/27. **cnihtes** *gen. sg. A7* 116/12. **cnihtes** *pl. A7* 114/25, **knihtes** *SM* 46/28, 48/14.

cnihtschipe *n.* (knightly) prowess *A7* 114/25, 116/15.

cnurnede *adj. pl.* gnarled *SM* 60/29.

cokkunge *n.* struggle *HM* 42/11.

colen *n. pl.* ashes *SW* 92/11.

com, com(e) *see* **cumen**.

con, const *see* **cunnen**.

cop *n.* top (of a dress), neckline *A8* 142/25.

copni *pr. 1 sg.* long for, await eagerly *SM* 80/14.

cost *see* **cunnen**.

coste *n.* cost; **bi liues** — on pain of death *SM* 56/15.

crahien *v.* stretch out the neck *SM* 58/22.

creft *n.* skill *HM* 32/11.

crenge *v.* (?)bend haughtily; **— wið swire** arch the neck *SM* 58/22.

criblin *v.* do 'sieve-work' *A8* 138/31 n.

crohe *n.* pot *HM* 34/9.

culure *n.* dove *SM* 64/16 *etc.* **culures** *gen. sg. SM* 76/8, **culurene** *gen. pl. SM* 54/22.

cume *n.* coming *SM* 80/14, 82/23, *SW* 90/2, visit *A8* 146/31.

cumeliche *adv.* becomingly *SM* 76/21.

cumen *v. SW* 88/24, 90/7, 98/13, *A7* 116/29, 32, 126/18, **cume** *HM* 6/14, *SW* 86/6, *A8* 140/6, **cumene** *infl. infin. SW* 102/4. **cume** *pr. 1 sg. SW* 90/18, 98/26. **cumest** *pr. 2 sg. SW* 90/16. **kimeð** *pr. 3 sg. HM* 14/18 *etc.*, *SM* 70/28, *SW* 90/9, 94/12, *A7* 118/3, *A8* 146/19. **cumeð** *pr. 3 pl. A8* 134/3, 146/28[1]. **cume** *pr. sg. subj. HM* 24/4, *SM* 54/22, 76/7, 80/7, *SW* 86/22, 90/4, 94/18, *A8* 142/10. **cum** *imp. sg. SM* 80/13[1,2], 80/14, **— aȝein** come back *A7* 116/36, **cvm** *SM* 76/23. **cumeð** *imp. pl. A8* 146/28[2].

cuminde *ppl. adj.*; *as n. pl.* those

cumen (*cont*.):
  approaching *SW* 88/12. com *pa. 1 sg.*
  SM 82/26, *SW* 94/13, *A7* 122/13, *pa.*
  3 sg. SM 46/18 *etc.*, *A7* 112/29, 114/3,
  24, *A8* 138/25, 140/9. comen *pa. 3 pl.*
  SM 72/30, 82/12, 17. come *pa. sg.*
  subj. HM 38/7, *SW* 88/32. icumen
  p.p. SM 70/17, *SW* 90/1, *A8* 134/1, *as*
  adj. SW 88/27, icume *SM* 48/20,
  ikumen *SM* 70/25.
cun *n.* family *HM* 30/11, *SM* 70/17, 25,
  SW 92/25, *A8* 138/24, kun *A8*
  138/23. cunnes *gen. sg. A7* 114/20,
  alles — of every kind *SM* 48/6 *etc.*,
  SW 90/34, *A7* 120/34. cunne *gen. pl.*
  SM 44/5, *A7* 112/14, *A8* 136/14.
cunde *n.* kind, nature *HM* 8/18 *etc.*, *SM*
  56/33 *etc.*, *SW* 102/10, *A7* 114/20,
  source *SM* 70/28, doð hare — mate
  naturally *HM* 22/18.
cundeliche *adj. pl.* natural *A8* 136/19.
cundeliche *adv.* naturally *A7* 124/4, *A8*
  136/32.
cunne(s) *see* cun.
cunnen *v.* can, know, be able; con *pr. 1*
  sg. SW 90/24, 94/27, 104/35. const
  pr. 2 sg. SM 52/1, *A7* 122/2, cost *SM*
  72/6. con *pr. 3 sg. HM* 38/7, *SW*
  90/3, *A7* 120/4 *etc.* cunnen *pr. 3 pl.*
  HM 32/11, *SW* 96/26, *A8* 144/23,
  146/8. cunne *pr. sg. subj. SM* 84/7.
  cuðe *pa. sg. subj. A7* 110/8. cuðest *pa.*
  2 sg. subj. SM 56/7.
cunnesmon *n.* kinsman *A8* 142/28.
cunnið *pr. 3 pl.* try *SM* 66/8.
cunreadnes *n. pl.* tribes *SW* 100/34.
cuð *adj.* known, familiar; — mon friend
  A8 142/27.
cuðen *v.* make known *SW* 100/11, *SM*
  84/7. cuðe *pr. 1 sg. SM* 66/31, show
  A7 114/17. cuðeð *pr. 3 sg. SM* 76/20.
  cuðe *pr. sg. subj. SM* 48/8. cuð *imp. sg.*
  SM 48/21 *etc.* icud *p.p. A7* 120/14,
  icudde *ppl. adj. pl.* known, tried *SM*
  44/4.
cuð(ð)e *n.* acquaintanceship *A8* 142/28,
  kun oðer — relations or friends *A8*
  138/23.
cwakien *v.* quake *SM* 76/14, tremble
  SW 104/30. cwakieð *pr. 3 pl. SM*
  58/31.
cwalhus *n.* prison *SM* 48/35, cwalmhus
  SM 56/15 *etc.*

cwalm *n.* plague *HM* 26/17.
cwarterne *n.* prison, dungeon *SM*
  48/35.
cwauien *v.* tremble *SM* 76/15.
cwedschipe *n.* wickedness *A8* 140/9.
cwellere *n.* executioner *SM* 80/34.
  cwelleres *pl. SM* 52/7, 21.
cwemen *v.* please *HM* 4/18, *SW* 86/20.
cwemest *adj. superl.* most pleasing *HM*
  10/7.
cwencheð *pr. 3 sg.* goes out, is extinguished *A8* 144/17. cwenctest *pa. 2*
  sg. destroyed *SM* 62/31.
cweðeð *pr. 3 sg.* declares; — þe al cwite
  surrenders you completely *HM* 36/26.
  cweð *pa. 3 sg.* spoke, said *SM* 64/19
  etc., quoð *HM* 16/29 *etc.*, *SM* 48/21
  etc., *SW* 94/13 *etc.*, *A7* 122/24 *etc.*, *A8*
  132/15 *etc.* cweþen *pa. 3 pl. SM*
  48/14.
cwicliche *adv.* vigorously, actively *A7*
  124/12.
cwikede *pa. 3 sg.* came to life; — of took
  life from *HM* 38/10.
cwite *adj.* free *HM* 36/26; *see* cweðeð.
cyrograffes *n. pl.* written agreements,
  indentures *A8* 134/33.

dahes *see* dei.
dale *n.* part, share *HM* 26/2 *etc.*, *SM*
  82/4, *A7* 128/37, *A8* 130/9 *etc.*, *pl.*
  HM 6/32, 24/22.
deadbote *n.* penance *HM* 12/12, 18/22,
  SW 90/15.
deadlich *adj.* mortal *HM* 18/8. deadliche *wk. HM* 10/25. deadliche *pl. A7*
  118/3.
deadliche *adv.* dreadfully, severely *SM*
  82/13.
deaf *adj.* deaf *SM* 78/28. deaue *pl. SM*
  54/2, 74/13, *as n. pl. SM* 44/15, 82/17.
dealen *v.* separate *A7* 120/35.
dear *pr. 1 sg.* dare *SM* 72/8, *A7* 128/6.
  der *pr. 3 sg. HM* 38/12.
dearie *pr. 1 sg.* cower, quake *SM* 72/8.
dearne *adj.* secret, hidden *SM* 70/34.
  dearne *pl. SM* 56/20, 78/12. derne
  SW 102/37.
dearnliche *adv.* secretly *SM* 66/19, *A8*
  132/31, 33.
deaðlich *adj.* deathlike *SW* 88/30.
deaue *see* deaf.

deboneirte *n.* gentleness, graciousness *A7* 114/9.

defde *pa. 3 sg.* sank (in) *SM* 82/6. **def** *imp. sg.* dive *SM* 72/34.

deh *see* **duhen.**

dehtren *see* **dohter.**

dei *n.* day *SM* 46/21 *etc.*, *SW* 86/29, *A8* 130/13 *etc.*, **al** — constantly *A7* 116/35, **þe** — **of dome** Doomsday, Judgement Day *SW* 100/33. **deies** *gen. sg. A7* 124/24, — **ant nihtes** by day and night *A8* 136/5. **dahes** *pl. A8* 130/26, 140/22, **feole 3eres ant** — many years, many a 'year and a day' *A7* 116/31.

dele *interj.* the devil!; **hu** — what the devil, what! *SM* 48/29.

deme *n.* judge *SW* 88/20, *A8* 146/11.

demen *v.* judge *SW* 96/28, 100/33, **deme** argue *SM* 56/31. **deme** *pr. 1 sg. SW* 96/28, 98/1, **demi** *SW* 96/24. **demeð** *pr. 3 sg. SW* 88/21 *etc.* **demen** *pr. pl. subj. SW* 96/30, 32. **dem** *imp. sg. SM* 56/35. **demde** *pa. 3 sg.* condemned *SM* 76/33. **idemet** *p.p.* ordained *SM* 78/13.

deopliche *adv.* seriously *HM* 2/13.

deor *n. pl.* animals *SM* 60/6.

deore *adj.* dear; **deorre** *comp.* dearer *HM* 18/6, *A7* 116/8.

deorewurðe *adj.* dear, beloved, precious *HM* 2/23 *etc.*, *SM* 56/19 *etc.*, *A7* 116/25, 122/32, **deorrewurðe** *HM* 4/15, **deorwurðe** *SM* 46/3 *etc.*

deorewurðliche *adv.* devotedly *A7* 128/36.

deorliche *adv.* closely *HM* 10/8.

depeint *p.p.* depicted, painted *A7* 118/24.

der *see* **dear.**

derf *n.* mortification, hardship, pain *HM* 14/35 *etc.*, *SM* 52/19, 66/36, *A7* 110/17.

derf *adj.* painful *HM* 40/23, *SM* 52/2, 54/37, difficult, hidden *SM* 70/34. **derue** *pl. HM* 16/34, mysterious *SM* 78/12. **derure** *comp.* more difficult *HM* 18/7.

derne *see* **dearne.**

derue, derure *adj. see* **derf** *adj.*

derueð *pr. 3 sg.* troubles, afflicts *HM* 6/11, *SW* 92/11. **derueð** *pr. 3 pl. SW* 90/34, *A7* 124/27. **derue** *pr. sg. subj. SM* 64/2, 72/34. **ideruet** *p.p. HM*

6/19, 24/33, *SM* 70/10, 78/28.

dest, deð *see* **don.**

destruet *p.p.* laid waste *A7* 112/33.

dihelnesse *n.* secrecy, mystery *SM* 70/34.

dihten *v.* manage *HM* 4/29. **diht** *pr. 3 sg. SW* 86/10, **dihteð** ordains *SW* 108/6. **dihte** *pa. 3 sg. SM* 46/3. **diueri** *pr. 1 sg.* quake, tremble *SM* 72/8.

dohter *n.* daughter *HM* 2/4 *etc.*, *SM* 56/27, *A8* 138/1. **dehtren** *pl. HM* 16/7 *etc.*, *SW* 88/6, 96/34, 98/7, *A8* 134/32.

dom *n.* judgement *SW* 88/21, 98/3, 106/24, **te leaste** — the Last Judgement *SM* 78/29. **dome** *dat. sg. SM* 56/31, **te** — Judgement Day *SM* 68/16, *A7* 126/7, **þe dei of** — Doomsday *SW* 100/33. **domes** *pl. SM* 56/20, 78/12, *SW* 102/37.

domesmon *n.* judge *SM* 56/35.

don *v.* do, carry out, act, put *HM* 4/26 *etc.*, *SM* 64/11 *etc.*, *SW* 102/28, 104/29, 106/28, *A7* 124/34 *etc.*, *A8* 132/33 *etc.*, — **o leaue** put in writing *SM* 82/32, **do** *SM* 66/36, *SW* 96/28, *A7* 120/19, — **me** set off *A8* 148/12. **donne** *infl. infin. HM* 14/31 *etc.*, *SM* 44/13, *SW* 94/16, 96/24, 108/6, *A7* 114/26, 128/25, *A8* 148/13. **do** *pr. 1 sg. SM* 66/31, *SW* 96/29, 98/1, *A7* 128/35. **dest** *pr. 2 sg. HM* 30/27, *SM* 56/1, 82/3, *A7* 110/23, 24, *A8* 138/9. **deð** *pr. 3 sg. HM* 4/28 *etc.*, *SM* 52/22, 58/18, *SW* 96/21, 23, 27, *A7* 110/16 *etc.*, *A8* 144/13, 146/23. **doð** *pr. 1 pl. A7* 110/13, *pr. 2 pl. A8* 138/17, 148/13, 14, *pr. 3 pl. HM* 22/18, 24/31, 28/28, *SW* 88/21, 102/6, *A8* 144/1, 27. **do** *pr. sg. subj. HM* 10/4, *SM* 52/13 *etc.*, *A7* 118/23, 126/3, — **ut** put out *A8* 144/5. *pr. pl. subj. A7* 114/12. **do** *imp. sg. HM* 8/7, *SM* 80/34, 82/9, *SW* 94/29, *A7* 110/23, 26. **dudest** *pa. 2 sg. HM* 6/23. **dude** *pa. 3 sg. HM* 12/19, 22/21, 38/28, *SM* 56/15 *etc.*, *A7* 112/21 *etc.*, gave *A7* 112/22, 116/24, put *A7* 114/26, 118/27, — **awei** sent away *SM* 56/26. **duden** *pa. 3 pl. SM* 74/19, *A7* 126/10, made *A7* 124/20. **dude** *pa. sg. subj. A7* 110/9. **idon** *p.p. SW* 104/4, *A7* 112/15, 116/36, 124/28, *A8* 144/28, put *HM* 34/12,

don (*cont.*):
SM 44/3, ido SM 62/24, SW 88/25, 92/25.
dosc *adj.* dark, dull SW 100/2.
draf *pa. 3 sg.* drove SM 56/26.
drahen *v.* draw, drag HM 4/9, SW 90/12, attract HM 28/30, dreaien SW 98/10, drahe A8 138/2. draheð *pr. 3 sg.* HM 8/26. dreaieð *pr. 3 pl.* HM 2/16. drahe *pr. sg. subj.* SW 108/5, A8 134/27. droh *pa. 3 sg.* took SM 56/16, traced SM 60/16, — to deaðe put to death SM 46/14. drohen *pa. 3 pl.* SM 48/17. idrahen *p.p.* HM 4/11, 20, idrahe engraved HM 20/12.
drake *n.* dragon SM 60/17, 62/11. drakes *gen. sg.* SM 58/10, drake SM 62/28. draken *pl.* SW 90/34.
dreaien *see* drahen.
dreaieð *see* drahen, dreien?
dream *n.* melody HM 18/29, drem HM 16/14. dreames *pl.* HM 18/29.
drecchunge *n.* trouble, disturbance HM 4/29.
dreccheð *pr. 3 pl.* afflict SW 90/34. idrechet *p.p.* HM 26/1.
dreden *v.* fear SW 96/10, 98/31, be concerned about SW 96/5. drede *pr. 1 sg.* SM 52/4, SW 96/11, *pr. 1 pl.* SW 94/30. dreden *pr. pl. subj.* A8 146/15.
drehen *v.* suffer, endure HM 4/27 *etc.*, SM 52/2, 4, SW 92/13, 108/19, drehe HM 34/13. drehe *pr. 1 sg.* SM 52/20. drehest *pr. 2 sg.* HM 14/35. dreheð *pr. 3 sg.* SW 96/6, *pr. 2 pl.* A8 148/19, *pr. 3 pl.* SM 44/16. drehen *pr. pl. subj.* HM 6/11, 20/30. drehdest *pa. 2 sg. subj.* HM 24/30. dreh *pa. 3 sg.* SM 44/23. drehden *pa. 3 pl.* HM 32/15, drehheden SM 46/17. idrohe *p.p.* SM 80/28.
dreien *v.* suffer, endure SM 52/2. dreaieð *pr. 2 pl.* A8 148/19. drohen *pa. 3 pl.* SM 46/16. drohe *pa. sg. subj.* SM 76/2.
drem *see* dream.
dremen *pr. pl. subj.* resound A8 146/25.
dreori *adj.* lamentable HM 14/23, SM 54/37, sad, unhappy SM 70/10.
dreorinesses *n. pl.* miseries SW 94/4.
dreorliche *adv.* wretchedly SM 48/30.
driuel *n.* drudge HM 26/2. driueles *pl.* menials SM 74/19.

droh *see* drahen.
drohe *see* dreien.
drohen *see* drahen, dreien.
druncnið *pr. 3 pl.* drown SM 68/33. druncnede *pa. sg. subj.* SM 76/2.
drupest *adj. superl.* saddest; — alre þinge most wretched of beings SM 72/8.
drupnin *v.* be sad, downcast SW 98/28.
dude(n), dudest *see* don.
duhen *v.* manage, be effective; — of do without A8 138/8. deh *pr. 3 sg.* is proper, fitting SM 44/22, A8 138/15.
duhtie *adj. pl.* excellent SM 56/20, 78/12.
dulue *pa. sg. subj.* dig A7 110/15.
dun *adv.* down HM 18/19, 20/24, SM 78/33, A8 136/26, 144/2.
dunede *pa. 3 sg.* resounded SM 78/31.
dunriht *adv.* straight down SM 62/36.
dunt *n.* blow SM 82/6, 9, deaðes — death-blow HM 14/23, stroke of death HM 24/17. duntes *pl.* SW 92/34.
durewart *n.* doorkeeper SW 88/11.
dusten *v.* throw, fling, cast down SM 76/1. duste *pa. 3 sg.* HM 36/34, SM 62/36. idust *p.p.* SM 62/11.
dustlunges *n. pl.* flingings, tossings SW 92/35.
duuelunge *adv.* headlong SM 78/33.

e *see* þe *def. art.*
eadi *adj.* blessed, fortunate HM 4/15 *etc.*, SM 48/23 *etc.*, SW 100/14, 102/8, 104/23. eadie *wk.* SM 44/20, 27, 52/11. eadie *pl.* SM 62/25, 78/5, 80/2. eadiure *comp.* HM 10/23.
eadiest *superl.* SM 64/23, eadieste *wk.* HM 40/16.
eadinesse *n.* the state of blessedness HM 10/22.
eadmode *adj. wk.* humble A8 142/3.
eadmodliche *adv.* humbly A8 134/17.
eahtuðe *adv.* eighth A7 128/37.
ealdren *n. pl.* parents HM 24/1, 30/16.
ealmesdeden *n. pl.* charitable works HM 18/14.
ealmesse *n.* alms A8 132/11, 28, 34.
eanes *adv.* once HM 8/34 *etc.*, A8 146/8, 29, ed — at once HM 34/1, at any one time A8 136/18.
eani *adj.* any HM 16/2, 24/30, SM 60/37, 62/8, 84/7, A7 118/20,

124/35, 126/23, *A8* 132/30 *etc.* **eni**
SM 44/16, *SW* 102/37. **eanies** *gen. sg.*;
— **weis** by some means *SM* 66/9.
eani *pron.* anyone *A8* 134/25.
ear *adv.* before, previously *HM* 4/7 *etc.*,
SM 54/13, *SW* 88/16 *etc.*, *A7* 110/31
etc., **er** *SW* 106/26. **earest** *superl.*
first; **on alre** — first of all *SM* 66/20, **on** —
at first *SM* 66/23, **earst** *HM* 12/17
etc., *SM* 66/18, *A7* 112/26, **on alre** —
first of all *HM* 14/30, **on** — first, at
first *A8* 130/1, 9, 138/2.
ear *conj.* before *HM* 40/22, 30, *SM*
66/19, 30, *A7* 112/17, 118/10, *A8*
144/1, — **þen** before *SM* 54/37,
74/26, *A8* 142/10.
eardin *v.* live, dwell *HM* 38/6. **eardið**
pr. 3 pl. SM 58/34. **eardinde** *pr.p. HM*
38/8. **ieardet** *p.p. SM* 70/20.
earest *see* **ear** *adv.*
eareste *see* **earre.**
earheliche *adv.* shamefully *SM* 62/4.
earm *adj.* poor, wretched *HM* 6/21.
earme *wk. SM* 64/1. **earmest** *superl.*
SM 72/32.
earm-hwile *n.*; **moni** — many an
unhappy time, weary hour *HM* 30/8,
32/21.
earmðe *n.* misery, trouble *HM* 24/19,
26/13. **earmðen** *pl. HM* 4/29, 30/29,
32/26.
earnesse *n.* pledge; **as on** — as a pledge
HM 6/13.
earre *adj. comp.* former *HM* 4/25, *A7*
124/5, *as n. SW* 92/11, *A7* 110/26.
earste *superl.* first *A7* 118/16, *as n. SW*
88/7. **eareste** *pl. HM* 40/30.
earst *see* **ear** *adv.*
earþon *adv.* before then, before that time
SW 90/14.
earunder *n.* morning; — **ant ouerunder**
morning and afternoon *A8* 146/29.
easkunge *n.* questioning *SM* 70/32.
eateliche *adj. wk.* hideous, loathsome
SM 62/35. **eateluker** *comp. HM*
22/28. **eatelukest** *superl. HM* 36/33.
eaðe *adv.* easily, readily *A7* 122/28, **eð**
A8 146/33.
eauer *adv.* always, constantly, ever *HM*
4/9 *etc.*, *SM* 46/11 *etc.*, *SW* 88/3 *etc.*,
A7 110/13, 26, 116/32, *A8* 132/29 *etc.*,
eaure *A7* 118/14, **euer** *SM* 48/5, 6,
SW 108/5. — **umbe hwile** *HM*

24/14, — **umbe stunde** *HM* 30/6, —
ant aa for ever and ever *SM* 62/21, **aa
ant** — constantly *SM* 72/17, — **mare**
always *SW* 102/29, **as ofte as** —
whenever *SW* 106/25, **hwa se** —
whoever *SM* 78/19, 21, 28, **hwen se**
— whenever *A8* 130/6, **hwer se** —
wherever *SM* 80/6, *SW* 104/27,
hwider se — wherever *HM* 16/16, 21,
hwuch se — whatever *HM* 28/21.
eaueres *n. pl.* draught-horses *HM* 12/5, 9.
eauereuch *adj.* any *HM* 10/11, *SM*
60/24, every *HM* 12/6, *SM* 74/3,
76/10, *SW* 94/3, **eauereuich** *SM*
52/1, **in** — **time** at all times *HM*
22/21, — **an** every one, each *SW*
104/12, 106/29.
eauerȝete *adv.* ever (up to this time) *SM*
56/32, — **þickest** as thick as could be
SW 92/7.
eauroskes *n. pl.* water-frogs *SW* 92/4.
eawbruche *n.* adultery *HM* 38/2.
eawiht *n.* anything *HM* 36/27, *A8*
148/22, **eawt** *HM* 38/17, *A7* 112/4,
ewt *SM* 56/32, *A8* 130/21.
eawiht *adv.* in any way *SM* 68/18.
eawles *n. pl.* flesh-hooks *SW* 92/34,
ewles *SM* 54/14.
ec *adv.* also *HM* 8/10 *etc.*, *SW* 90/3, *A7*
112/12, 120/22.
eche *n.* aching *HM* 32/1.
eche *adj.* eternal *HM* 6/13 *etc.*, *SM* 44/6,
56/13, 74/28, *SW* 98/25 *etc.*
echelich *adj.* eternal *SM* 76/7.
echeliche *adv.* eternally *SM* 44/18 *etc.*
echen *v.* increase *SW* 92/2.
echnesse *n.* eternity *SW* 92/16, **ecnesse**
HM 24/25, *SM* 54/27, 58/5, 80/33,
A8 148/20.
ed *prep.* at *HM* 4/32 *etc.*, *SW* 92/5, 6[1,2],
A7 120/29, 126/7, *A8* 132/21 *etc.*,
from *HM* 40/10, *SM* 70/12, *A8*
134/13, — **eanes** at once, at any one
time *HM* 34/1, *A8* 136/18, **et** *HM*
28/1, 34/8, *SM* 68/16 *etc.*, *SW* 92/5[1,2]
etc.
edfleon *v.* escape, flee from *A7* 114/12.
edhalden *v.* keep back *A7* 120/4. **edhalt**
pr. 3 sg. A7 112/11, preserves *HM*
10/28. **edheolden** *pa. 2 pl. subj.* retain
(as guests) *A8* 138/24. **edhalden** *p.p.*
A8 148/1, **ethalden** kept back *HM*
36/4.

edlutien *v.* hide *A7* 122/8.
edscene *adj.* obvious, apparent *A8*
142/30, **etscene** *A7* 118/30.
edstonden *v.* resist *SM* 66/28,
etstonden *SM* 68/27, *SW* 96/21,
104/29. **edstont** *pr. 3 sg. HM* 12/34.
etstonde *pr. sg. subj. HM* 42/8.
edstode *pa. sg. subj.* stop *HM* 20/27.
etstont *imp. sg. SW* 94/33.
edwiten *v.* blame, reproach *A8* 142/32.
edwited *pr. 1 pl. HM* 32/14, *pr. 3 pl.*
abuse *SW* 92/32.
edwrenchen *v.* escape *SM* 68/32,
etwrenchen *SM* 66/12.
efne *adj.* steady *SW* 106/23.
efne *adv.* quite, completely *SM* 62/1.
eft *adv.* again *HM* 10/1 *etc.*, *SW* 90/35
etc., *A8* 148/13, moreover *A7* 116/12,
A8 138/3.
efter *adv.* later *HM* 8/15, *A7* 118/24.
efter *conj.*; — þet after *HM* 18/26.
efter *prep.* according to *SW* 86/10 *etc.*, in
search of *SW* 86/28, after *SW* 100/14
etc., — þet Ich mei as far as I can *SW*
90/24, **don** — follow the lead of *SW*
106/28.
efterwart *prep.* after; **beon** — pursue
HM 32/16.
eftsone *adv.* again *A8* 144/5.
egede *adj.* ridiculous, foolish *HM* 34/6,
10, 11, *SM* 62/4.
egge *n.* blade, (sword)-edge *SM* 54/18.
eggi *v.* incite, encourage *HM* 34/10.
eggið *pr. 3 pl. HM* 2/17, 8/8.
eggunge *n.* urging, incitement *HM* 4/8,
42/21.
ehe *n.* eye *A8* 138/6, 146/4. **ehnen** *pl.*
HM 2/11, 30/32, *SW* 88/23 *etc.*, *A7*
110/21, *A8* 138/13.
ei *adj.* any *HM* 6/12 *etc.*, *SW* 94/9,
96/31, 104/14, *A7* 124/35, 128/4, *A8*
134/16 *etc.*
ei *pron.* any, anyone *HM* 30/10, 38/17,
SM 80/6, *SW* 88/13, *A7* 128/16, *A8*
132/23, 146/34.
eie *n.* anger *HM* 38/26, *SM* 50/32, 60/5,
fear *HM* 28/1, *SW* 86/22, *A8* 146/19,
danger *A8* 136/1.
eilin *v.* afflict *SW* 102/30, **eili** *HM* 42/8.
eili *pr. sg. subj. SM* 58/32, *A8* 134/25.
eilþurl *n.* window *SM* 58/8.
eise *n.* ease, comfort *HM* 2/19, 26/4, 10,
A8 146/5, opportunity *HM* 14/28.

eise *adj.* at leisure; **hwen ʒe beoð** — in
your free time *A8* 148/9.
eisfule *adj. wk.* dreadful *SM* 58/32.
eisil *n.* vinegar *A7* 124/1 *etc.*
eiðer *adj.* either *SM* 58/14.
eiðer *pron.* each (one) *HM* 24/11 *etc.*,
SM 66/16, 21, *SW* 92/10, 19, 106/20,
A8 142/25 *etc.*
elde *n.* old age *SW* 108/21, **helde** age
SM 46/5.
elheowet *adj.* of an unearthly colour,
livid *SW* 88/30.
elles *adv.* else, otherwise *A7* 120/11, 13,
122/14, *A8* 142/10, 148/11.
elleshwer *adv.* elsewhere *A7* 128/31, in
the next world *HM* 26/6.
elleshwider *adv.* elsewhere *SW* 100/26.
elne *n.* strength *HM* 22/33, *SM* 60/10,
comfort *HM* 24/18, *A7* 126/26.
en *see* a, an *adj.*
enbreuet *p.p.* recorded, inscribed *SW*
90/13.
ende *n.* region, district *SM* 70/20, *SW*
106/16.
endelong *prep.* down *SM* 60/16.
endin *v.* carry out *HM* 8/25, end *HM*
24/18.
engel *n.* angel *HM* 10/15 *etc.* **engles** *gen.*
sg. HM 38/11, *pl. HM* 4/16 *etc.*, *SM*
60/5 *etc.*, *SW* 100/10, 21, 102/9.
englene *gen. pl. HM* 10/19, *SM*
60/35, 68/7, 84/8, *A7* 110/9, *as adj.*
angelic *HM* 4/4.
eni *see* eani *adj.*
entremeatin *v.* be concerned with *A8*
132/22.
eode *see* gan.
eoli *n.* oil *SM* 62/7, 80/1, *A8* 146/17[1,2],
eolie *HM* 40/13.
eorles *n. gen. pl.* noblemen *HM* 40/21.
eornen *v.* run; run over *HM* 34/9.
eorneð *pr. 3 sg. A7* 116/37. **eorne** *pr.*
sg. subj. SM 68/21.
er *see* ear *adv.*
erede *pa. sg. subj.* tilled, cultivated *A7*
110/15.
erndunge *n.* intercession *SM* 84/10.
este *n.* joy, pleasure *HM* 26/4, 10, *SW*
94/36, 96/12, *A8* 146/6. **estes** *pl. SW*
98/1.
et *see* ed.
ethalden *see* edhalden.
etlunge *n.* estimate; **wiðuten ei** —

inestimably *HM* 36/4, *SW* 104/15.
etscene *adj. see* **edscene.**
etscene *adv.* plainly, clearly *SW* 100/10.
etstonde(n), etstont *see* **edstonden.**
etstutten *v.* counter *SM* 68/26, *pa. 3 pl.*
stop *HM* 18/16.
etwrenchen *see* **edwrenchen.**
eð *see* **eaðe.**
eðele *adj.* 'native', born on the estate *HM*
28/5.
eðelich *adj.* worthless *HM* 8/33, 38/19,
40/12, **eðlich** *HM* 6/21. **eðeliche** *pl.*
SW 96/32, *as n. SW* 94/31, **eðliche**
HM 38/25. **eðeluker** *comp.* of lower
rank *HM* 8/4.
eðie *v.* breathe *SM* 64/23.
euch *adj.* each, every *HM* 2/3 *etc., SM*
52/36 *etc., SW* 86/16 *etc., A7* 126/29,
A8 136 /32 *etc.,* any *HM* 34/15, 38/30,
SM 58/37, 84/2, *SW* 102/28, 30, *A7*
116/6, *A8* 138/10, 142/7, — **a** every
SW 102/19, **euche** *A8* 130/25, 146/7,
148/9, **on — half** on every side *A7*
114/27, **euich** *SM* 46/14.
euchan *pron.* each one, every one *SM*
48/14, 64/6, *SW* 88/21 etc., *A7*
126/25. **euchanes** *gen. sg. SM* 56/2,
SW 100/24.
euenald *adj.* of the same age *HM* 36/31.
euene *n.* nature, quality *HM* 20/13,
38/11, 21.
euenin *v.* compare with, equal *HM*
16/18, *SW* 90/27. **eueneð** *pr. 3 sg.*; —
to puts on a level with *HM* 22/23.
euening *n.* equal *HM* 10/19, 21, 22/27,
A7 128/6.
euenunge *n.* comparison *HM* 4/35.
euer *see* **eauer.**
euesede *pa. 3 sg.* trimmed *A7* 120/26.
ieueset *p.p. A8* 140/19.
euesunge *n.* clippings, trimmings *A7*
120/27.
euich *see* **euch.**
ewles *see* **eawles.**
ewt *see* **eawiht** *n.*

fa *n.* enemy *HM* 10/16 *etc., SW* 106/12,
A7 124/37, va *A7* 124/35. **fan** *pl. SM*
52/14, *A7* 112/33, 120/29, — **fulle**
declared enemies *HM* 26/21, **uan** *SM*
44/5, **van** *A7* 114/11, 18.
fahe *adj.* specious *SW* 94/21.
falewi *pr. sg. subj.* wither *HM* 10/1.

fallinde *ppl. adj.* transitory *SW* 96/17.
famon *n.* enemy *HM* 36/27. **famen** *pl.*
SM 56/27, *A7* 124/34.
famplin *v.* feed in by hand *HM* 34/1.
fare *n.* array *HM* 16/21.
Farlac *see* **fearlac.**
feahe *imp. sg.* adorn *HM* 40/15.
feahunge *n.* adornment *HM* 38/13.
fearen *v.* go, turn out, happen *A8*
146/16, **feare**; — **wið to** be treated
HM 24/5. **fearest** *pr. 2 sg.*; — **wið** are
treating *SM* 56/9. **feareð** *pr. 3 sg. HM*
6/1, 34/18, 19, behaves *SW* 86/18, —
to wundre comes to grief *A8* 142/4.
fearen *pr. pl. subj.* appear *SM* 76/22.
ferde *pa. 3 sg.* went; — **him** *refl.*
proceeded *SM* 50/1.
fearlac *n.* fear *HM* 26/13 *etc.,* terror *SM*
58/25 *etc.,* **Fearlac** Fear (personified)
SW 88/35 *etc.,* **Farlac** *SW* 106/12
etc.
feaste *adv.* fast *A8* 144/18, tightly *A8*
136/27, **lokin** — look intently, stare
A8 142/29, **feste** hard *SM* 64/6.
feat *n.* vessel *SM* 72/31, **ueat** *HM*
10/32.
feden *v.* feed, support *A8* 132/21, 140/2,
ueden be raised *SM* 46/4. **fed** *imp. sg.*
A7 126/1. **fedde** *pa. 1 sg. SM* 82/30.
feh *n.* property *SW* 94/23, 98/8.
feier *adj.* pleasing, attractive, beautiful;
feherest *superl. HM* 36/5, *A7* 114/4,
120/2.
feierlec *n.* beauty *SM* 76/20, *SW*
102/12, **feirlec** *HM* 36/3.
felles *n. pl.* skins *A8* 136/8, 15.
feng *pa. 3 sg.* began *SM* 60/30, — **on**
began *SM* 52/12, 64/1. **fengen** *pa. 3
pl. SM* 82/14. **iuon** *p.p.* caught *SM*
48/11.
fenniliche *adv.* vilely *HM* 8/27, *SM*
70/5.
feolahes *n. pl.* fellows, equals *HM*
16/12.
feolahlukest *adv. superl.* (most suited) as
companions *SW* 102/9.
feole *adj.* many *HM* 4/30 *etc., SW*
104/11, *A7* 112/37 *etc.*
feond *n.* devil, adversary *HM* 12/22,
36/12, *SM* 44/21 *etc., A7* 116/31, *A8*
140/4, 144/10, 19, **feont** *HM* 32/32,
40/25, *SW* 88/4, 94/33, **ueont** *SM*
44/5. **feondes** *gen. sg. HM* 4/8 *etc.,*

feond (*cont.*):
SM 54/5, **ueondes** SM 46/19.
feondes *pl.* SM 52/14 *etc.*
feor *n.* value, price; **setten** — set a price
(on) *A7* 120/17.
feor *adv.* far; — þerbiuoren long before
SM 76/19, **of** — from afar SW 88/12,
100/29, **se** — ant se forð, so far SM
68/25, þruppe — a long way back *A7*
126/34. **fir** *comp.* further SM 60/3.
feorren *adv.* afar; **of** — from afar SW
88/27.
feorrene *adj.* distant, far-off *A7* 112/27.
ferd *n.* army SW 94/25.
ferde *see* **fearen.**
fere *n.* companion *A7* 116/23 *etc.*, *A8*
142/17.
ferkin *v.* feed, support HM 32/21.
ferliche *adj. wk.* dreadful SM 82/30, SW
92/10.
ferliche *adv.* suddenly SM 70/5, SW
90/8, 92/8, rapidly HM 18/18.
ferreden *n.* company SW 102/8.
feste *adv. see* **feaste.**
fet *n. pl.* feet SM 76/1, *A7* 112/17, *A8*
132/21, **uet** SM 62/23, SW 100/32,
vet *A8* 136/26.
fikelinde *ppl. adj.* deceitful SW 94/21.
fikest *pr. 2 sg.* speak flatteringly SM
66/4.
fir *see* **feor** *adv.*
firstin *pr. pl. subj.* delay, postpone SM
68/19.
fla *n.* arrow HM 12/32. **flan** *pl.* HM
14/3.
flede *v.* flow SM 60/3.
fleme *n.* outcast SW 106/14.
fleon *v.* flee SW 94/33, 108/9, **fleo** HM
42/7, SM 68/28. **fleo** *pr. 1 sg.* SM
68/24. **flið** *pr. 3 sg.* SW 94/33. **fleoð**
pr. 3 pl. SM 66/8, fly HM 14/3, SM
58/35. **flih** *imp. sg.* HM 14/28, SM
72/33. **fluhen** *pa. 3 pl. A7* 114/32.
fleoteð *pr. 3 pl.* move through the water
SM 58/35.
flesch-fulet *adj.* defiled in the flesh SM
84/9.
flih *see* **fleon.**
flihinde *ppl. adj.* flying SM 58/35.
flið *see* **fleon.**
fluhen *see* **fleon.**
flutte *v.* make shift (with) *A8* 146/1.
flutteð *pr. 3 pl.* move SW 92/8. **flute**

imp. sg. go away SW 106/22.
fluttunge *n.* support HM 22/34,
flutunge HM 24/26, provisions SM
82/29.
fode *n.* food HM 22/34, 24/26, SM
58/7, 82/30, *A7* 126/3, *A8* 142/5, *gen.*
sg. child HM 32/35.
fol *adj.* foolish, indecorous SW 86/18, *A8*
134/15.
folliche *adv.* improperly HM 14/15.
fond *pa. 1 sg.* found *A8* 132/6, **font**
supplied with SM 82/29.
fondin *v.* test, try, experience, find out
SW 98/30, 106/6, **fondi** HM 24/32.
fondeð *pr. 3 sg.* HM 34/11, SW
106/29. **fondið** *pr. 3 pl.* HM 28/16.
fondin *pr. pl. subj. A8* 136/20. **ifondet**
p.p. HM 18/26.
fondunge *n.* temptation HM 42/7, 16,
22, *A8* 140/8.
font *see* **fond.**
for *conj.* for; *in compound conjs.* — **hwon**
þet for which reason HM 12/20,
whenever SW 86/24, *A8* 132/35, as
long as *A7* 128/35, *A8* 140/34.
forbearneð *pr. 3 sg.* burns up, consumes
SW 92/11. **forberneð** *pr. 3 pl.* SM
68/34. **forbernde** *p.p.* SM 50/25.
forbeode *pr. 1 sg.* forbid *A8* 138/32.
forbeode *pr. sg. subj.* HM 12/26,
forbude *pa. sg. subj.* SW 86/12.
forbisne *n.* example HM 40/1, parable
SW 86/3, allegory *A7* 112/32.
forbod *n.* prohibition *A8* 140/33.
forbuh *imp. sg.* avoid HM 14/29.
forcoruen *p.p.* cut off HM 10/1, 16/4.
forcuðest *adj. superl.* most loathsome
HM 28/17, SM 58/16, 64/20, SW
90/32.
fordede *n.* favour *A7* 116/26.
fordemen *v.* condemn SW 98/2.
fordemest *pr. 2 sg.* SM 70/22.
fordemde *pa. 3 sg.* HM 36/36, SM
46/21. **fordemden** *pa. 3 pl.* SM
48/17. **fordemde** *ppl. adj. as n.* the
damned SW 94/6.
fordon *v.* destroy SM 48/31, **fordo** SM
52/31, 60/9, 62/1. **fordude** *pa. 3 sg.*
SM 46/21.
foreoden *see* **forgan.**
forewart *n.* agreement; **halden** — keep
one's promise HM 14/18, 16/6.
forfeare *pr. sg. subj.* die, perish SM

56/11. **forfaren** *p.p. SM* 48/32.

forgan *v.* forgo *HM* 42/2. **forgað** *imp. pl. A8* 130/21. **foreoden** *pa. 3 pl. A7* 126/21.

forgulten *v.* commit sin *HM* 42/1. **forgulte** *ppl. adj. pl.* guilty of sin *A7* 112/17.

forʒelt *pr. 3 sg.* pays *HM* 4/31. **forʒelde** *pr. sg. subj.* recompense *A8* 144/27. **forʒolden** *p.p.* repaid *HM* 10/24. **forʒeme** *pr. sg. subj.* neglect *SW* 88/26. **forʒemeð** *pr. 3 pl.*; — **ham** *refl.* are negligent *SW* 96/7. **forʒolden** *see* **forʒelt.**

forheccheð *pr. 3 sg.* turns out of doors *HM* 36/25.

forhohien *v.* scorn, despise *HM* 22/27. **forhohe** *imp. sg. HM* 22/11.

forhwi *conj.* why, for what reason *A7* 112/26, 116/5, 122/21, for which reason *HM* 20/2.

forleosen *v.* perish, be lost *SM* 46/30. **forleoseð** *pr. 3 pl.* lose *HM* 26/13. **forleas** *pa. 3 sg. HM* 12/18. **forloren** *p.p. HM* 8/34, destroyed *SM* 48/32. **forlorene** *ppl. adj. as n. pl.* the damned *SM* 46/30.

forletest *pr. 2 sg.* forsake *SM* 52/30. **forlet** *imp. sg. SM* 56/29. **forleteð** *pr. 3 pl. SM* 68/5.

forlið *pr. 3 sg.* commits adultery with *HM* 36/24.

forme *adj.* first *HM* 14/12, *SW* 96/34, *A7* 118/17.

formealte *ppl. adj. pl.* melted away *SW* 92/12.

forneh *adv.* almost, nearly *HM* 36/31, *SM* 54/12, 56/14.

forschuptest *pa. 2 sg.* degrade *HM* 22/29. **forschuppet** *p.p.* deformed *HM* 30/17.

forseoð *pr. 3 pl.* disregard *SM* 70/3.

forswelten *v.* torture, make perish *SM* 50/24.

forswolhen *v.* swallow up, devour, destroy *SM* 50/25 *etc.*, **forswolhe** *SM* 58/23, 62/29. **forswolheð** *pr. 3 pl. SW* 90/35. **forswolhe** *pr. sg. subj. SW* 94/26. **forswelh** *pa. 3 sg. SM* 60/20. **forswolhen** *p.p. SM* 64/28.

fortruste *pr. sg. subj.*; — **him** *refl.* grow over-confident *SW* 88/26.

forþi *adv.* therefore, for this reason *HM* 4/10 *etc., SM* 56/11, 64/34, 76/25, *SW* 96/27 *etc., A7* 110/18 *etc., A8* 130/11, 144/10, 18.

forþi *conj.*; — **þet** so that *HM* 2/7, 22/25, *A8* 130/3, because *SW* 104/8, *A7* 122/18, *A8* 136/6, — as *A8* 146/11.

forðlich *adj.* thriving *HM* 30/13, *as n. HM* 30/18.

forðre *adv.* further *HM* 30/28, later on *HM* 6/33.

forwalleð *pr. 3 sg.* boils *SW* 92/12.

forwerede *ppl. adj. pl.* worn out *SW* 92/23.

forwurðen *v.* be destroyed *HM* 26/18, **forwurðe** become, degenerate into *A8* 140/11. **forwurðest** *pr. 2 sg. HM* 32/6. **forwurðeð** *pr. 3 sg.* degenerates *SM* 68/36. **forwurðe** *pr. sg. subj. SM* 52/13, go astray *HM* 32/23.

foster *n.* offspring *HM* 14/4, *SM* 46/19, 48/21, foster-parent *SM* 56/22.

frakele *adj. wk.* worthless *HM* 6/19.

freamien *v.* help, strengthen *HM* 26/8. **freameð** *pr. 3 sg. HM* 26/25.

freinin *v.* ask *HM* 28/15. **freineð** *pr. 3 sg. SW* 90/4.

fremede *adj. as n. pl.* strangers *A7* 114/33.

freo *adj.* free, noble *HM* 4/6 *etc., SM* 46/24, 48/24. **freoest** *superl. A7* 120/4.

freolec *n.* freedom *HM* 4/33, generosity *A7* 112/11, 120/30.

freolich *adj.* fine, beautiful, noble *SW* 98/13. **freoliche** *wk. SM* 54/14, *pl. SM* 64/37.

fret *pr. 3 sg.* devours *HM* 26/17, gnaws *SW* 92/19. **freoteð** *pr. 3 pl. SW* 92/3.

frommard *prep.* away from *A8* 144/16.

froure *n.* comfort, support *HM* (*heading*), *SM* 74/24, *SW* 88/6, *A7* 126/25, *A8* 138/29, 140/25, 148/7, **to** — for solace *A8* 146/28.

frouri *pr. sg. subj.* support, comfort *A8* 148/18. **frourede** *pa. 3 sg. SM* 58/6.

frumscheft *n.* creation *SM* 78/14.

frumðe *n.* beginning *HM* 34/23, *A8* 142/1.

fuhel *n.* bird *SM* 48/10. **fuheles** *pl. SM* 58/35, *A7* 112/17.

ful *adj.* foul *HM* 22/31, *A7* 124/14; — **wiht** devil, demon *HM* 42/1, *SM*

ful (*cont.*):
66/4, 70/33. fule *wk. HM* 12/9, 22/6, *SM* 62/1.

fulden *see* fullen.

fule *adv.* foully *SM* 70/5.

fulen *v.* defile *SM* 66/10. fuleð *pr. 3 sg. HM* 10/17, 30/25.

fulhet *p.p.* baptized *SM* 44/18.

fulieð *pr. 3 pl.* follow, pursue *HM* 38/25.

fulitohe *adj.* badly behaved, ill-disciplined *SW* 86/9, fulitohen *SW* 106/28.

fulitoheschipes *n. pl.* indecencies, wanton behaviour *HM* 28/13.

fullen *v.* fulfil, carry out *HM* 16/34. fulden *pa. 1 pl.* filled *SM* 72/31.

fulliche *adv.* completely *HM* 8/35.

fulluht *n.* baptism *SM* 76/6, 9, 11, *A7* 118/16.

fulst *n.* help *HM* 14/12, 18, 20, *SW* 98/31.

fundeð *pr. 3 sg.* tries *SM* 60/9, 13.

fure *imp. sg.* inflame *SM* 74/24.

gan *v.* go, walk, proceed *HM* 12/19, *SM* 62/33, *SW* 86/21, 104/20, *A8* 136/23. ganne *infl. infin. SM* 50/14. ga *pr. 1 sg. SM* 66/7. geast *pr. 2 sg. SM* 74/10. geað *pr. 3 sg. SW* 94/25, *A8* 142/8. ga *pr. 1 pl. SW* 96/9. gað *pr. 3 pl. HM* 20/9, *SM* 70/3. ga *pr. sg. subj. SM* 74/10, *SW* 86/10, 88/19, 108/5, *A8* 142/8 *etc., pr. pl. subj. HM* 30/27, gan *SM* 68/18. ga *imp. sg. HM* 8/22, *SW* 104/20. gað *imp. pl. A8* 146/29. eode *pa. 3 sg. A7* 122/26. igan *p.p. HM* 10/3, i3ongen *HM* 42/23.

gast *n.* spirit *SM* 60/9 *etc., SW* 104/28. gastes *pl. SM* 82/24, *SW* 86/29, 92/30, 100/22.

gastelich *adj.* spiritual *HM* 36/12, *SW* 100/30, *A7* 126/14, *A8* 146/30 *etc.* gasteliche *dat. SM* 80/10. gasteliche *pl. HM* 36/8, *SM* 60/37.

gasteliche *adv.* spiritually *HM* 4/5, *A8* 138/28.

geað, geast *see* gan.

gederunge *n.* gathering *HM* 2/15, (sexual) intercourse *HM* 8/13, (marital) union *HM* 22/35, accumulation *A8* 132/36.

genge *n.* company; beoreð me — accompany me *SM* 80/25.

genow *n.* mouth, jaws *SM* 58/22.

gentil *adj.* noble, well-born *A7* 112/27. gentile *pl. HM* 8/2.

gerlondesche *n.* (golden) circlet *HM* 20/11.

gersum *n.* treasure *SM* 46/26.

gestnunges *n. pl.* entertainments, hospitality *A8* 132/8.

gif *see* 3ef *conj.*

gleadfulre *adj. comp.* more joyful *A7* 118/2.

glead-icheret *adj.* happy-looking *SW* 98/13.

gleadschipe *n.* joy *HM* 36/14. gleadschipes *pl. SW* 104/11, 12.

gleadunge *n.* pleasure, delight *SW* 102/22 *etc.,* gledunge *SM* 46/32.

gleam *n.* lightning *SM* 58/18, glem brightness *SM* 64/15.

gleden *n. pl.* coals *SM* 50/26, *A7* 126/5.

gledread *adj.* red-hot *SW* 90/11. gledreade *pl. SW* 92/34.

gleo *n.* joy *SM* 46/32, 54/21.

glit *pr. 3 sg.* proceeds *SM* 80/30.

god *n.* good *HM* 2/19, 22/16, *SM* 56/34, *SW* 96/15 *etc., A7* 110/13 *etc., A8* 132/32 *etc.,* benefit *SM* 74/10, virtue *A7* 126/28, — unnen wish well *SM* 80/20. godes *gen. sg.*; euch — ful full of every virtue *HM* 16/16, *SM* 52/36, 58/30, 62/20, na þing — no good thing *HM* 8/25. gode *dat.*; turne to — turn out well, benefit *HM* 6/2, 4², *A8* 148/27.

god *adj.* good *HM* 2/21 *etc., SM* 66/24, 78/9, 80/29, *SW* 88/1, 34, 102/5, *A7* 110/5 *etc., A8* 144/27¹. gode *dat. masc. as n.* good (man) *HM* 6/4¹. goder *dat. fem.*; to — heale þin for your own good *HM* 24/31. gode *pl. HM* 40/6, 15, *SW* 96/33, *A7* 116/19, 118/7, 124/12, *A8* 134/13 *etc., as n. SM* 66/7, 72/21, *A7* 112/20.

godlec *n.* goodness *SM* 60/33, 66/15, 76/13, *SW* 104/4.

gomeful *adj.* joyful *SM* 60/32.

gomenin *v.* rejoice *SM* 72/22, talk pleasantly *SM* 66/18. gomeni *pr. 1 sg. SM* 54/10. gomeneð *pr. 3 sg.*; me — *impers.* I rejoice *SM* 60/36.

gra *n.* (1) fiend, monster *SM* 54/8, 58², 62/22.

gra *n.* (2) grey fur; grene ant — green

(cloth) and grey fur, rich clothes *HM* 38/15.

gras *pa. 3 sg.* felt horror; **ham** — *impers.* (they) were aghast *SM* 58/10.

greate, greattre *see* **gret.**

greatluker *adv.* more seriously *A8* 144/9.

greden *v.* cry out *HM* 42/4. **gredde** *pa. 3 sg. SM* 74/16.

gref *n.* suffering *A7* 116/4.

grei *n.* grey (clothing) *HM* 38/15.

greiðe *adj. pl.* ready; **al** — just *A8* 140/21.

greiðeð *pr. 3 sg.* prepares *HM* 14/13, 24/32. **greiðede** *pa. 3 sg. HM* 18/12, *A7* 118/14.

gremien *v.* anger *HM* 24/15, *SM* 74/16, **gremie** disturb *SM* 64/7.

grene *n.* green (cloth); — **ant gra** rich clothes *HM* 38/15.

grenin *v.* grow green *HM* 10/2, 30/32, grow pale, pine *HM* 26/30.

gret *adj.* great *SW* 90/10. **greate** *pl.* coarse *A8* 136/11, roomy *A8* 136/22, **greattre** *comp.* plainer *A8* 138/17.

greueð *pr. 3 sg.* afflicts, troubles *HM* 28/27, 42/15, (*impers.*) *A8* 140/22.

grimfule *adj. pl.* fierce, terrible *SW* 92/31.

grimliche *adv.* terribly *SM* 62/27.

grisle *n.* horror *SM* 68/16, *SW* 94/4, **ham to** — to their horror *SW* 92/2.

grislich *adj.* grisly, dreadful, horrible *SM* 58/10, 60/28, *SW* 92/28. **grisliche** *wk. SM* 54/8 *etc.*, *SW* 92/30, *pl. SW* 90/35. **grisluker** *comp. SW* 92/5.

grið *n.* peace *SM* 80/10.

griðful *adj.* calm *A7* 126/29.

griðfullnesse *n.* serenity *A8* 134/21.

grome *n.* anger *HM* 12/24, 27, 28/7, *SM* 72/20, 74/16, 76/32. **gromen** *pl.* annoyances *HM* 4/30.

gromes *n. pl.* boys *A8* 140/13.

gromeð *pr. 3 sg.* angers *SM* 72/20. **gromede** *pa. 3 sg. SM* 76/32.

gromful *adj.* terrible *SM* 58/30.

gruchunge *n.* grumbling *A8* 142/19.

grunde *n.* bottom *SM* 76/2, *SW* 90/26, **helle** — the depths of hell *HM* 36/32, **ibroht to** — overthrown *SM* 62/28.

grune *n.* snare, trap *SM* 48/11.

grure *n.* horror, terror *HM* 42/5, *SM*

54/31, 58/25, 68/16, *SW* 92/2 *etc.*

grurefule *adj. pl.* terrible *SW* 92/31.

gruseli *pr. pl. subj.* nibble *A8* 144/29.

gult *n.* offence, fault *A8* 144/4. **gultes** *pl. A8* 144/20, sins *HM* 38/27.

gultest *pr. 2 sg.* offend, sin *HM* 30/26. **gulteð** *pr. 3 sg. SW* 86/18, *SM* 72/22, *pr. 3 pl. SM* 68/18. **gulte** *pa. 3 sg. A8* 144/9.

gume *n.* bridegroom *HM* 10/26.

gurde *pr. sg. subj.* belt *A8* 136/14. **igurd** *p.p.* girded *SM* 76/21, *as adj.* wearing a belt *A8* 136/12.

ʒarkin *v.* prepare *SM* 80/11. **ʒarkeð** *pr. 3 sg. HM* 42/17, *A7* 128/27. **iʒarket** *p.p. SM* 64/30, 74/32, *SW* 106/10.

ʒarow *adj.* ready *A7* 116/32. **ʒarowe** *pl. SM* 64/17, *SW* 100/33.

ʒe *adv.* yes *HM* 24/11, *SM* 48/25 *etc.*, *SW* 90/20 *etc.*, *A7* 126/8, 128/8, **ʒeoi** *A7* 116/5.

ʒe *pron. 2 pl.* you *HM* 14/15, *SM* 52/33 *etc.*, *SW* 94/11 *etc.*, *A7* 110/31 *etc.*, *A8* 130/1 *etc.* **ow** *acc. recipr.* each other *HM* 14/21, *A8* 140/23. **ow** *acc., dat. HM* 28/8, *SM* 52/35 *etc.*, *SW* 90/1 *etc.*, *A7* 110/32 *etc.*, *A8* 130/3 *etc.* **ow** *refl.* yourselves *A7* 122/22, 124/9, 12¹, *A8* 130/31 *etc.* — **seolf** *SM* 80/22, — **seoluen** *SM* 74/30, *A7* 126/22, *A8* 130/20, 146/23. **ower** *poss. adj.* your *SM* 54/2, 80/19, 84/3, *A7* 122/27, *A8* 130/21 *etc.*

ʒef *conj.* if *HM* 6/30 *etc.*, *SM* 46/15 *etc.*, *SW* 86/5 *etc.*, *A7* 110/10 *etc.*, *A8* 130/14 *etc.*, — þet *A8* 138/7, 146/10, **bute** — unless *HM* 6/28 *etc.*, *A8* 134/18, 144/5, 148/2, **swa** — if *SM* 44/17, **ʒif** *SM* 48/21, 50/26, **bute** — unless *SM* 50/24, **gif** *SM* 50/11.

ʒef *v. see* **ʒeouen.**

ʒeien *v.* cry out *SM* 70/14, 82/14. **ʒeiʒeð** *pr. 3 sg. A7* 116/35. **ʒeieð** *pr. 3 pl. SW* 94/7. **ʒeide** *pa. 3 sg. SM* 52/23, 82/9.

ʒeincume *n.* return *A7* 118/1.

ʒelden *v.* give in return *SW* 104/5, yield *SW* 108/22, pay *A8* 134/23, repay *A7* 126/10, 12. **ʒelt** *pr. 3 sg. A7* 124/24. **ʒeldeð** *pr. 3 pl. SW* 98/18. **ʒulde** *pa. 2 sg. A7* 126/9. **ʒulden** *pa. 3 pl. A7* 124/25.

ʒelpeð *pr. 3 sg.* boasts *SW* 96/27.
ʒeme *n.* heed; **nim** — take heed *HM* 2/6 *etc.*, *SM* 50/6, *SW* 94/21, 104/16, *A7* 112/25, *A8* 146/9.
ʒemeles *adj.* negligent *SW* 86/17. ʒemelese *pl. SW* 88/28.
ʒemen *v.* heed, pay attention *A8* 140/14, ʒeme *SW* 96/16. ʒemeð *imp. pl. refl.* take care *A8* 134/12.
ʒeohðe *n.* itch *HM* 8/12.
ʒeoi *see* ʒe *adv.*
ʒeomerliche *adv.* brutally *SM* 52/23.
ʒeomerunge *n.* groaning, outcry *HM* 32/10.
ʒeorne *adv.* carefully, earnestly, eagerly *HM* 2/10 *etc.*, *SM* 46/15, 64/18, *SW* 98/6, *A8* 148/14.
ʒeornliche *adv.* earnestly, eagerly *SM* 44/25, *SW* 94/25 *etc.*, *A8* 146/12.
ʒeoue *n.* gift *HM* 10/4, *A7* 112/15, 22.
ʒeouen *v.* give, grant *HM* 16/6, 10, 28/28, *A7* 120/24, 31, *A8* 132/35 *etc.*, ʒeoue *HM* 8/23, *A7* 120/6, 18, ʒeouen (*passive*) be given *A7* 118/37, 120/1. ʒeouene *infl. infin. A7* 120/10. ʒeuest *pr. 2 sg. HM* 24/4. ʒeueð *pr. 3 sg. HM* 6/13 *etc.*, *SW* 90/31, 96/3, *A7* 112/12, *A8* 138/19. ʒeoueð *pr. 3 pl. HM* 8/4. ʒeoue *pr. sg. subj. HM* 40/17, *A8* 144/26, 148/19, ʒeue *SW* 108/11. ʒeoue *pr. pl. subj. A8* 142/14. ʒef *imp. sg. SM* 54/21, 78/24, *A7* 126/1, 2², 3. ʒef *pa. 3 sg. HM* 18/33, *SM* 46/8, 82/9, *A7* 112/16, 21, 25. ʒeue *pa. sg. subj. A7* 110/10. iʒeuen *p.p. SM* 80/5, *A7* 112/22, 114/34, 126/12, provided for *HM* 8/2, iʒeue *SM* 48/2, 74/32.
ʒer *n.* year *HM* 22/19, *SM* 64/29, *A8* 140/19, *pl. A7* 124/22. ʒeres *pl. SM* 46/5, *A7* 116/31 (*see also* dei).
ʒerde *n.* rod *SM* 62/17.
ʒerdede *pa. 3 sg.* beat *SM* 52/23.
ʒet *adv.* yet, still, further *HM* 10/31 *etc.*, *SW* 100/10, 104/13, *A7* 112/19 *etc.*, *A8* 130/5, 132/6, 146/12, even *HM* 22/18, *SM* 76/27, *SW* 104/35, *A7* 112/20, 120/23.
ʒete *n.* gate *A8* 132/8. ʒeten *pl. SM* 64/17, *A8* 142/12.
ʒette *adv.* still, yet *A7* 120/16. ʒetten *HM* 10/22, 38/12, 18, *A7* 118/35, *A8* 130/2, moreover *A8* 138/4.

ʒetti *pr. 1 sg.* grant, give *SM* 80/11. ʒetteð *pr. 3 sg. SW* 100/19. ʒette *imp. sg. SM* 78/24, *A7* 122/2. ʒettede *pa. 1 sg. SM* 74/32, *pa. 3 sg. HM* 18/27. iʒettet *p.p. HM* 10/4, *SM* 48/28 *etc.*
ʒeuest, ʒeue(ð) *see* ʒeouen.
ʒif *see* ʒef *conj.*
ʒimmes *n. pl.* precious stones *HM* 20/13, *SW* 100/16.
ʒimstan *n.* jewel *SM* 48/2, 62/17, 74/32. ʒimstanes *pl. SM* 58/13.
ʒirne *pr. 1 sg.* long for, want *A7* 122/3, 14, *A8* 134/10. ʒirne *pr. sg. subj. A7* 126/23. ʒirnde *pa. 3 sg. SM* 46/15.
ʒisceunge *n.* avarice *HM* 36/15, 21.
ʒiscið *pr. 3 pl.* covet *HM* 26/12.
ʒong *n.* progress *HM* 16/20.
ʒont *prep.* throughout *SM* 82/32.
ʒuheðe *n.* youth *SW* 108/21, ʒuheþe *SM* 50/6.
ʒulde(n) *see* ʒelden.
ʒung *adj.* young *SM* 56/8. ʒungre *comp.* as *n. A8* 142/15.
ʒuren *v.* yell, howl *SM* 70/14.

ha *pron. 3 sg. fem.* she *HM* 2/7 *etc.*, *SM* 44/23 *etc.*, *SW* 86/10 *etc.*, *A7* 114/21 *etc.*, *A8* 132/28[1, 2] *etc.*, it *HM* 8/35 *etc.*, *A7* 110/21. heo *HM* 2/8 *etc.*, *SM* 46/3 *etc.*, *SW* 88/14, *A7* 112/11 *etc.*, *A8* 142/11, 14, 17. hire *acc., dat.* her *HM* 2/7 *etc.*, *SM* 46/7[1, 2, 3] *etc.*, *SW* 86/10 *etc.*, *A7* 112/25 *etc.*, *A8* 132/16[1] *etc.*, it *HM* 42/19, *SM* 54/7, *SW* 86/7 *etc.*, *A7* 116/12 *etc.*, *A8* 132/37. hire *refl.* herself *HM* 4/28 *etc.*, *SM* 64/19, 74/2, *SW* 96/19, 20, 98/9, *A7* 116/31 *etc.*, *A8* 132/28 *etc.* hire *poss. adj.* her *HM* 2/9 *etc.*, *SM* 44/22 *etc.*, *SW* 88/3 *etc.*, *A7* 112/11 *etc.*, *A8* 132/3[1,2], its *SM* 58/37, *A8* 132/36. hiren *disjunctive* hers *A7* 112/13.
ha *pron. 3 pl.* they *HM* 6/10 *etc.*, *SM* 44/17 *etc.*, *SW* 88/27 *etc.*, *A7* 112/3 *etc.*, *A8* 130/5 *etc.*, a *SM* 76/21, heo *HM* 18/32 *etc.*, *SM* 54/32 *etc.*, *SW* 92/1, 102/14, 15, *A7* 124/19, *A8* 142/27, 144/1. ham *acc., dat.* them *HM* 6/11 *etc.*, *SM* 50/24 *etc.*, *SW* 86/12 *etc.*, *A7* 110/15 *etc.*, *A8* 130/3 *etc.*, — twa the two of them *HM* 30/14, heom *A8* 148/1. ham *refl.*

themselves *HM* 6/31[1] *etc.*, *SM* 70/8,
SW 88/29, *A8* 144/18[1], 21. **ham**
recipr. each other *HM* 28/9, 10, *SM*
66/15, *SW* 92/18, 19. **hare** *gen.*
(*partitive*) of them *SW* 86/17. **hare**
poss. adj. their *HM* 2/16 *etc.*, *SM*
44/5[1,2] *etc.*, *SW* 86/22[1,2] *etc.*, *A7*
114/12 *etc.*, *A8* 132/9 *etc.*, — o**þres**
each other's *HM* 24/16, **heore** *HM*
18/29. **hare** *pron.* theirs *HM* 16/19,
SW 88/23[1, 2, 3]

habben *v.* have, possess, own *HM* 6/20,
26/21, 28/33, *SM* 46/25 *etc.*, *SW*
88/12, 108/2, *A7* 110/19 *etc.*, *A8*
132/35 *etc.*, **habbe** *HM* 6/6, 22/3, 20,
SM 54/35, 82/4, *A8* 132/34, 134/19.
habbe *pr. 1 sg. HM* 6/31, 34/15, *SM*
44/11 *etc.*, *SW* 92/21 *etc.*, *A7* 110/31
etc. **hauest** *pr. 2 sg. HM* 6/18 *etc.*, *SM*
60/2, *SW* 90/19, 22, *A7* 116/1. **haueð**
pr. 3 sg. HM 2/3 *etc.*, *SM* 50/11 *etc.*,
SW 88/6 *etc.*, *A7* 112/12 *etc.*, *A8*
130/11 *etc.*, **hafeð** *SM* 44/18. **habbeð**
pr. 1 pl. SW 96/30, *pr. 2 pl. SM*
44/24, 80/20, *A7* 122/21, 128/30, 36,
A8 136/23, 148/22, *pr. 3 pl. HM* 2/19
etc., *SM* 60/5 *etc.*, *SW* 94/7, 106/30,
A8 132/33, 144/28, **habbet** *SM*
54/16. **habbe** *pr. sg. subj. HM* 6/12
etc., *SW* 88/34. **habben** *pr. pl. subj.*
SM 80/22, *A8* 132/2. **haue** *imp. sg.*
HM 8/24, 40/13, 16, *SM* 46/29 *etc.*,
A7 110/24, 26[1, 2]. **habbeð** *imp. pl. A8*
136/4. **hefde** *pa. 1 sg. SW* 100/25, *A7*
110/10, 128/10, *pa. 3 sg. HM* 4/25,
33, *SM* 46/5 *etc.*, *SW* 100/30, *A7*
114/10 *etc.* **hefden** *pa. 3 pl. HM*
18/26, *SM* 64/29, 82/25, *SW* 100/28,
29, 104/19, *A7* 114/23. **hefde** *pa. 1 sg.*
subj. SW 92/22, *A8* 148/11. **hefdest**
pa 2 sg. subj. HM 24/30, 26/32. **hefde**
pa. 3 sg. subj. SM 56/33, *SW* 92/24,
A7 118/9. **hefden** *pa. 3 pl. subj. HM*
26/22. *neg. forms*: **nabbe** *pr. 1 sg. SM*
54/19, 60/10, *A7* 126/9. **naueð** *pr. 3*
sg. HM 4/22, *SW* 92/14, *A7* 114/30,
A8 142/5. **nabbeð** *pr. 3 pl. HM* 8/3,
SM 68/35. **nabbe** *pr. sg. subj. HM*
26/30. **nabben** *pr. pl. subj. HM* 26/11,
A8 142/14. **nefde** *pa. 3 sg. SM* 76/14,
pa. sg. subj. A7 110/10. **nefden** *pa. pl.*
subj. HM 22/15.

hades *n. pl.* persons (of the Trinity) *SM*

62/20, 80/31, **hat** states *HM* 20/17.
hah , hahte *v. see* **ah** *v.*
hahte *n. see* **ahte.**
halewende *adj.* healing *SM* 74/23,
halewinde wholesome *SM* 56/34,
halwende *SM* 62/7, 80/1.
half *n.* side, flank; **upon hire riht** — to
her right *SM* 60/26, **on his Feader**
riht — on the right hand of his Father
SW 100/8. **halue** *dat.*; **on hire riht** —
at her right side *SM* 82/11.
halhe *n.* saint *HM* 16/15. **halhen** *pl. HM*
4/16, *SW* 102/17. **halhene** *gen. pl. A8*
130/18.
halheð *pr. 3 sg.* sanctifies *A7* 118/18.
halhunge *n.* sanctification *SM* 76/7.
haliliche *adv.* in holiness *SW* 102/6.
halschipe *n.* integrity *HM* 4/14, 30/21.
halsi *pr. 1 sg.* entreat *SM* 72/25.
halwende *see* **halewende.**
ham *see* **ha** *pron. 3 pl.*
hamseolf *pron. pl.* themselves *SM* 66/26,
68/8, *A7* 110/16, *A8* 142/21, 146/13,
bi — in private *HM* 28/11,
hamseolue *SM* 68/35, **hamseolfen**
HM 6/34, **hamseoluen** *SM* 66/10 *etc.*,
A7 110/33.
hantið *pr. 3 pl.* practise *HM* 22/9, 28/18.
hare *see* **ha** *pron. 3 pl.*
hat *n. pl. see* **hades.**
hate *pr. 1 sg.* command, call *SM* 54/36.
hat *pr. 3 sg. HM* 16/31[1, 2] *etc.*, *SW*
88/17, 31, *A7* 128/7, 35, *A8* 142/18,
hateð *SW* 88/18. **het** *pa. 3 sg. SM*
46/23 *etc.* **ihaten** *p.p. HM* 18/7,
20/12, *SM* 46/1, 78/1, 80/35, *SW*
86/9, 88/8, 98/25. **hatte** *passive* be
called, named; *pr. 1 sg. SM* 64/27, *SW*
88/35, *pr. 3 sg. SM* 48/27.
haue, hauest, haueð *see* **habben.**
he *pron. sg. masc.* he, it *HM* 2/7[1, 2] *etc.*,
SM 44/2 *etc.*, *SW* 86/5 *etc.*, *A7* 110/8
etc., *A8* 130/15 *etc.* **him** *acc., dat.* him
HM 2/9 *etc.*, *SM* 44/16 *etc.*, *SW* 88/5
etc., *A7* 110/11[1, 2] *etc.*, *A8* 132/21 *etc.*
him *refl.* himself *HM* 18/1 *etc.*, *SM*
48/35 *etc.*, *SW* 106/3 *etc.*, *A7* 114/26.
his *poss. adj.* his *HM* 2/8 *etc.*, *SM*
44/1[1, 2, 3] *etc.*, *SW* 86/5 *etc.*, *A7* 110/18
etc., *A8* 134/10 *etc.* **hise** *pl. HM* 16/17,
SM 46/19 *etc.*
heafden *see* **heaued.**
heale *n.* health *HM* 30/21, *A7* 120/30,

heale (*cont.*):
salvation *SM* 52/35 *etc.*, *SW* 100/13, 106/34. in — healthy *A8* 130/28, to goder — þin for your own good *HM* 24/31, him to wraðer — to his destruction *SM* 60/21.
healewi *n.* drug *HM* 12/25, *SM* 66/20.
heamen *n. pl.* inhabitants *HM* 40/30.
heane *n.* oppressor, tyrant *HM* 10/15. **heaneð** *pr. 3 sg.* afflicts, oppresses *HM* 10/16, *SM* 54/16, 56/31. **heaneð** *pr. 1 pl. SM* 72/15. **heane** *pr. 2 pl. SM* 70/26.
hearloz *n. pl.* beggars *A8* 132/9.
heasci *pr. sg. subj.*; — wið be angry with *HM* 26/36.
heast *n.* command *A8* 140/33. **heaste** *dat. SM* 70/25. **heastes** *pl.* commandments *SM* 58/36, *A7* 112/8.
heatel *adj.* cruel *SW* 94/2, *A7* 120/35. **heatele** *wk. SM* 54/7. **hetelest** *superl. SM* 82/5.
heateliche *adj. wk.* vicious, cruel *SM* 56/4.
heateð *pr. 3 sg.* hates *SW* 92/17. **heatieð** *pr. 1 pl. SM* 72/16, *pr. 3 pl. HM* 28/18, *SW* 92/19. **heatien** *pr. pl. subj. A8* 142/24.
heaued *n.* head; —-cla ð head-cloth *A8* 136/33, 142/25, —-sunne mortal sin *A7* 116/31, —-luuen *pl.* chief kinds of love *A7* 116/19. **heued**; —-þeawes cardinal virtues *SW* 108/7. **heafden** *pl.* heads *SM* 54/31.
hechelunge *n.* gnashing *SW* 92/8.
hefde(n), hefdest *see* habben.
heh *adj.* high, lofty, exalted, blessed *HM* 2/27 *etc.*, *SM* 48/12 *etc.*, *A7* 112/22, *A8* 146/4, *as n. SM* 68/9, *A7* 122/6, of — from above *HM* 2/28, on — upwards *HM* 14/33, above, aloft *SM* 52/7 *etc.*, *SW* 100/14, *A7* 122/9, aloud *SM* 60/24. **hehe** *wk. HM* 2/26 *etc.*, *SM* 44/13 *etc.*, *A7* 112/37, 122/9, *A8* 146/3, 11. **hehe** *as n.* height, exalted position *HM* 4/2, 16/27. **herre** *comp. HM* 12/14[1,2], *SM* 54/13. **hest** *superl. A7* 120/2, on — in the highest place *SW* 88/20. **heste** *wk. HM* 36/32, *as n. sg. A7* 120/9. **heste** *pl. HM* 4/16, *as n. pl. SM* 50/8, 68/11.
hehen *v.* extol, honour, worship *SM* 46/33, **heien** *SM* 54/2. **heie** *pr. 1 sg.*

SM 80/27. **hehest** *pr. 2 sg. SM* 48/25, **heiest** *SM* 74/15. **heheð** *pr. 3 sg. SM* 48/16. **heieð** *pr. 3 pl. SM* 58/33. **heie** *pr. sg. subj. SM* 74/11. **heien** *pr. pl. subj. SM* 76/5. **hehede** *pa. 3 sg. SM* 50/2. **heheden** *pa. 3 pl. SM* 44/9. **ihehet** *p.p.* raised *HM* 20/22, **iheiet** *SM* 62/21, 84/13, *A8* 148/20.
hehnesse *n.* eminence, importance *HM* 2/28, *A8* 130/15. in — in heaven *SM* 82/22, 23.
hehschipe *n.* eminence, exalted state *HM* 4/21, 16/9, 18/13, *SM* 62/20, 80/31.
heie(n), heiest, heieð *see* hehen.
helde *see* elde.
helest, heleð *see* heolen.
hellene *adj.* infernal *HM* 36/36.
hende *adj.* gracious, courtly *HM* 6/8, *A8* 134/11. **hendest** *superl. A7* 120/3.
henlunges *n. pl.* objects of contempt *SM* 68/7.
heo *pron. 3 sg. see* ha *pron. 3 sg.*
heo, heom *pron. 3 pl. see* ha *pron. 3 pl.*
heolen *v.* conceal (from) *A7* 128/24, **heole** *A7* 128/23. **helest** *pr. 2 sg. HM* 2/21. **heleð** *pr. 3 sg. SM* 68/22. **ihulet** *p.p. A8* 132/32.
heonne *adv.* hence, out of here *SM* 72/27.
heonneuorð *adv.* henceforth *SM* 64/8, 72/27.
heordemonne *n. gen. sg.* herdsman *A8* 134/22.
heorden *n. pl.* fibres *A8* 136/11.
heore *see* ha *pron. 3 pl.*
heoueriche *n.* the kingdom of heaven *SM* 82/4, *A7* 120/20. *gen. sg. SM* 68/14.
her *adv.* here; —abuten on this, in this matter *A8* 148/23, —bi by this *HM* 20/21, 40/9, —towart in comparison with this *HM* 24/9, —þurh by, through this *HM* 32/16, *SW* 92/23.
herbarhin *v.* stay, be lodged *A8* 134/6.
here *n.* army *HM* 2/24, 4/7.
herede(n), herestu *see* herien.
hereword *n.* renown *A7* 120/30.
herien *v.* praise, honour *HM* 10/13 *etc.*, *SM* 46/19 *etc.*, *SW* 104/24. **herie** *pr. 1 sg. SM* 80/27. **herestu** *interrog. pr. 2 sg. SM* 48/25. **herieð** *pr. 3 pl. SM* 56/22, 58/33, *SW* 104/22. **herien** *pr. pl. subj.*

SM 76/5. **herede** *pa. 3 sg. A8* 132/14.
hereden *pa. 3 pl. SM* 44/9. **heriende**
pr.p. SM 60/24, 76/30.
herre, hest(e) *see* **heh.**
het *see* **hate.**
hetelest *see* **heatel.**
heteueste *adv.* firmly *SM* 60/29, 62/35.
hetter *n.* robe *A8* 136/12. **hettren** *pl.*
clothes *A8* 138/21.
hetterliche *adv.* rapidly, urgently *SM*
46/24.
heued-þeawes *see* **heaued.**
heuel *adj.* woven; — **bedd** mattress *HM*
18/18.
hihendliche *adv.* suddenly, quickly *SM*
58/9, 78/26, 80/35.
hihin *v.* hasten *HM* 42/24. **hihe** *imp. sg.*
(*refl.*) *SM* 80/14, *A7* 128/20.
him *see* **he, hit.**
hine *n.* servant *HM* 10/15, 18, 26/2.
hinen *pl. HM* 4/29, *SW* 86/13 *etc.*
hird *n.* host, troop, retinue, household,
court *SM* 44/29 *etc.*, *SW* 86/12 *etc.*, *A7*
112/37, **hirt** *SM* 50/8.
hirde *n.* shepherd *SM* 64/10.
hirdmen *n. pl.* servants *HM* 26/34.
hire, hiren *see* **ha** *pron. 3 sg.*
his *pron. see* **he, hit.**
his *v. see* **is.**
hise *see* **he.**
hit *pron. 3 sg. neut., nom., acc.* it *HM* 4/9
etc., *SM* 44/22 *etc.*, *SW* 86/10 *etc.*, *A7*
110/23 *etc.*, *A8* 130/22 *etc.* **his** *poss.*
adj. HM 30/7 *etc.* **him** *dat. HM* 30/9.
him *refl. SW* 106/27.
hofles *adj.* unreasonable *HM* 38/17, *SM*
72/19.
hoker *n.* contempt *SM* 52/15, *A7* 114/8,
(something) contemptible *HM* 38/17.
hokeres *pl.* insults *SM* 74/18, *SW*
92/32.
hokerlich *adj.* shameful *SM* 72/19.
hokerluker *comp. HM* 12/28.
hokerliche *adv.* disdainfully *HM* 32/5.
holin *n.* holly *A8* 136/16.
holke *n.* (chest) cavity *SW* 92/6.
hond *adv.* just, exactly *A8* 144/13.
hondhwile *n.* moment *HM* 8/33, *SM*
70/6. **honthwile** *HM* 38/32.
hondlið *pr. 2 pl.* touch; — **ow** touch
each other *HM* 14/21.
horedom *n.* adultery *HM* 36/35.
horlinges *n. pl.* fornicators *HM* 22/9.

houeret *adj.* hunchbacked *SM* 78/27.
hu *adv.* how, what, in what way *HM* 2/19
etc., *SM* 44/25 *etc.*, *SW* 86/3 *etc.*, *A7*
116/16 *etc.*, *A8* 132/32, 138/23[1,2], —
dele! *interj.* what! *SM* 48/29.
hude *n.* hide *HM* 34/8, skin *SM* 74/19.
hudest *pr. 2 sg.* hide *A8* 138/7. **hut** *pr. 3
sg. SM* 68/22. **hudden** *pa. 3 pl. SM*
54/31.
huler *n.* lecher *HM* 28/5.
hure *n.* reward, wages *HM* 4/31, *A7*
124/21 *etc.*, *A8* 134/22 *etc.*
hure *adv.* especially; **ant** — let alone *HM*
36/27, *SM* 70/33, *SW* 92/33.
hurne *n.* corner *SM* 58/9.
hut *see* **hudest.**
huue *n.* cap *A8* 138/19.
hwa *pron.* who, which; *interrog. HM* 16/7,
8, *A7* 110/15, 128/1. *rel.* (one) who
SW 96/18. **hwam** *acc., dat.* whom *HM*
6/26 *etc.*, *SW* 88/11. **hwas** *gen.* whose
HM 16/12 *etc.*, *SM* 58/30, 68/5,
70/25. — **se** *indef.* who, whoever *HM*
16/29 *etc.*, *SM* 78/19 *etc.*, *SW* 108/14,
A7 124/31, *A8* 130/31 *etc.*, **hwam se**
dat. SW 102/15.
hweat *see* **hwet** *adj.* and *pron. interrog.*
hwen *conj.* when, since, if *HM* 6/18 *etc.*,
SM 54/10 *etc.*, *SW* 86/25, 90/8,
94/19, *A7* 116/32 *etc.*, *A8* 130/28 *etc.*,
hwenne *A8* 142/6. **hwen se eauer**
indef. whenever *A8* 130/6.
hwenne *adv. interrog.* when *HM* 28/33,
32/23, *SW* 86/5, 90/4.
hweonene *adv. interrog.* where from,
whence *SW* 88/32, 90/4, 16,
hweonne *SM* 70/27.
hwer *conj.* where *SM* 60/26 *etc.*
hwer *adv.* where; *interrog. A7* 120/1,
— **in** in what *HM* 24/12, — **of** where
from *SW* 104/2, from what *A8* 132/27,
— **to** to what end *SM* 72/5, *SW* 104/2,
A7 116/4, *rel. A8* 142/31, — **uore** why
HM 14/4, — **uore se eauer** for
whatever reason *HM* 38/16. — **þurh**
rel. through which *A8* 144/16, 32, —
wið (anything) with which *HM* 8/3.
— **se (eauer)** *indef.* wherever *SM* 80/6,
SW 86/17 *etc.*, *A8* 140/30, 142/1.
hwet *adj. interrog.* what *SM* 48/25, 70/25,
28, **hweat** *SM* 64/20, *A7* 126/15.
hwet *pron. interrog.* what *HM* 2/13 *etc.*, *SM*
52/33, 54/34, *SW* 106/7, *A7* 110/30

hwet (*cont.*):
  etc., **hweat** *A7* 118/2. — ꝫef what if
  HM 26/29, 34/6. **hwet** *rel. HM* 2/6 *etc.*,
  SM 56/6, 68/30, 80/21, *SW* 88/32[1,2]
  etc., *A7* 122/6[1,2], *A8* 132/19, **hweat** *SM*
  68/30, *A7* 120/17. **hwet** *indef.* — **se**
  HM 18/14, 36/28, *SM* 64/27, 70/35,
  SW 96/10, *A8* 146/1. **hwet** *interj.*
  indeed *HM* 32/20.
hweðer *conj. interrog.* whether *HM* 24/
  32.
hweðer *pron. interrog.* which of two *SW*
  92/9, *A7* 126/26.
hwi *adv. interrog.* why *HM* 8/16, 26/19,
  SM 70/29, 72/15, 16, *SW* 104/2, *A7*
  126/7, *A8* 138/5, *rel. A7* 120/6.
hwider *adv.* where to; — **se (eauer)** *indef.*
  wherever *HM* 16/16, 21, 20/9, *SW* 102/
  14.
hwil *conj.* while *HM* 4/19 *etc.*, *SM* 44/14
  etc., *SW* 98/23, 106/23, *A8* 136/4, 140/
  5, — þet while *SM* 64/13, 68/27, 78/
  7, *A7* 126/20, **hwile** *SM* 72/29.
hwile *n.* time *SM* 48/1, 50/31, 56/8, *SW*
  100/6, 26, *A8* 148/12, **ane** — for a
  while *HM* 16/1, *SW* 98/21, **eauer**
  umbe — constantly *HM* 24/14, **of ane**
  lutle — momentary *HM* 40/34, **þe** —
  in the meantime *SM* 66/32.
hwilinde *adj.* transitory *HM* 22/10, 24/7,
  SW 94/9.
hwit *adj. as n.* dairy produce *A8* 130/27.
hwon *pron. interrog.*; **to** — what *SM* 70/15.
hwon *rel. adv.* see **for**.
hwuch *adj. interrog.* what, of what nature
  HM 2/18 *etc.*, *SM* 52/30, *SW* 86/6 *etc.*
  hwucche *dat. sg.*; **o** — **wise** in what way
  SM 48/35. **hwucche** *pl. HM* 28/16, *SW*
  86/14.
hwuch *pron. interrog.* which *HM* 20/18,
  SW 88/12 *etc.* — **se** *indef.* whoever *HM*
  18/2, *SW* 90/12, whatever *HM* 28/21,
  SM 70/35. **hwucche** *pl. HM* 20/14.

I *pron. 1 sg.* see **Ich**.
ibeden see **bidden**.
ibeo, ibeon see **beon**.
ibet see **beten**.
ibidde *pr. 1 sg.*; — **me** *refl.* pray *SM* 78/7;
  ibide *imp. sg. SM* 78/9.
iblend *p.p.* blinded, deceived *SM* 64/32,
  iblent *SM* 70/3.
iblowen see **blowinde**.

iboht(e) see **buggen**.
ibore(n), iborene see **beore**.
iborenesse *n.* birth *HM* 30/7, 32/35.
iborhen *p.p.* saved *HM* 10/6, 16/32, *SM*
  72/13, *SW* 102/16.
ibreuet *p.p.* written down *SM* 72/7.
ibrowden *p.p.*; — **on** modelled on *HM* 10/
  14.
iburst *p.p.* enraged *SW* 94/25.
Ich *pron. 1 sg.* **I** *HM* 4/7 *etc.*; *SM* 44/10 *etc.*,
  SW 88/34[1,2] *etc.*, *A7* 110/8 *etc.*, *A8* 130/1
  etc., **I** *HM* 6/26, *SM* 48/2 *etc.* **me** *acc.*,
  dat. me, myself *HM* 2/4 *etc.*, *SM* 48/1
  etc., *SW* 88/35 *etc.*, *A7* 114/13 *etc.*, *A8*
  132/1 *etc.* **me** *refl.* myself *HM* 40/28,
  SM 60/15, 78/7[2], *A8* 148/12[2]. **mi** *poss.*
  adj. my *HM* 2/12 *etc.*, *SM* 46/30 *etc.*, *SW*
  90/23 *etc.*, *A7* 110/9 *etc.*, *A8* 130/4, 140/
  7, 148/11, **min** *HM* 34/15, *SM* 46/33
  etc., *SW* 96/2, 35, 108/21, *A7* 122/3
  126/18. **mines** *gen. A7* 126/18. **mine** *pl.*
  HM 16/4, *SM* 50/7 *etc.*, *SW* 96/3, 100/
  4, *A7* 110/29 *etc.*, *A8* 134/18, 148/18.
icluhte *ppl. adj.* closed *SM* 78/16.
icnawen *v.* recognize, understand *HM* 20/
  18. **icnaweð** *pr. 3 pl.* acknowledge,
  confess *A8* 146/20. **icnawe** *pr. sg. subj.*
  HM 20/31. **icnawen** *p.p.*; we beoð —
  we recognize *SM* 82/15.
icnawlecheð *pr. 3 pl.* admit *HM* 6/31.
icnottet *p.p.* fastened *A8* 136/26.
icnut *p.p.* tied *HM* 28/20.
icore(n), icorene see **cheosen**.
icoruen *p.p.* cut *A8* 142/24.
icud(de) see **cuðen**.
icumen see **cumen**.
icunnet *p.p.* connected by kinship *A7* 120/
  3.
icweme *adj.* pleasing *HM* 34/36, *SW* 106/
  19.
icwemen *v.* please *SW* 108/20. **icwemet**
  p.p. SW 104/19.
icwiddet *p.p.* prophesied *SW* 100/30.
idoddet *p.p.* cropped *A8* 140/18.
idoruen *p.p.* distressed *SM* 82/14.
idrechet see **dreccheð**.
idrencte *p.p.*; — **of** dipped in *HM* 12/25.
idrohe see **drehen**.
iferen *n. pl.* companions *A7* 116/19.
ifont *pa. 3 sg.* — **ed** obtained from *HM* 40/
  10.
iforðet *p.p.* accomplished *A7* 128/12.
igederet *p.p.* united (as consorts) *HM* 28/

34, **wel** — well matched *HM* 24/11.

ignahene *ppl. adj. pl.* consumed with anxiety *HM* 26/10.

igodet *p.p.* benefited, helped *A7* 112/1, *A8* 146/9.

igret *p.p.* magnified *SM* 84/12.

iȝemen *v.* pay attention *A8* 140/7.

iȝeue(n) *see* ȝeouen.

iȝongen *see* gan.

iȝotten *p.p.* dissolved *HM* 38/32.

ihal *adj.* intact *HM* 14/1, whole *SW* 90/35.

ihehet, iheiet *see* hehen.

ihente *v.* catch *HM* 18/9. **ihente** *pr. sg. subj. HM* 18/18.

iheuen *p.p.* raised *SM* 78/11.

ihulet *see* heolen.

ihuret *p.p.* hired *HM* 26/2.

ihuslet *p.p.*; **beon** — receive Communion *A8* 130/12, 22.

ihwear *adv.* everywhere; — **ant eauer** in all circumstances *A8* 134/11, **ihwer** *HM* 34/20, *SM* 64/4, on every occasion *A8* 132/23.

ikennet *p.p.* begotten *SM* 56/24, born *SM* 70/17.

ikepte *pa. 3 sg.* saved *HM* 16/25.

ikepunge *n.* restraint *HM* 20/28.

ikumen *see* cumen.

ilahet *p.p.* (1) made lawful *HM* 18/8, 20/26.

ilahet *p.p.* (2) brought low *HM* 18/14.

ilatet *p.p.*; **wraðeliche** — bad-tempered *HM* 28/24.

ile *n.* hard skin (of heel) *SM* 60/19.

ilefde *pa. sg. subj.* believed *SM* 74/27.

ilened *p.p.* granted *SM* 44/18, **ilenet** *SM* 70/27, 78/13.

ilered *see* learen.

ilespiles *n. gen. sg.* hedgehog *A8* 136/15.

ilich *adj.* like *HM* 4/14 *etc.*, *SM* 64/35, *SW* 92/5, 102/34, — **as þah** as though *A7* 124/20. **ilikest** *superl. SW* 102/9.

iliche *n. dat.* form, likeness *SM* 76/8. *pl.* equals, fellows *HM* 12/4.

iliche *adv.* alike *HM* 16/33, 20/11, *SW* 102/20, 104/22.

ilicnesse *n.* likeness *HM* 20/34, **to Godes** — in God's image *HM* 22/25.

iliht *p.p.* descended, alighted *HM* 20/34.

ilihtet *p.p.* lightened, cheered *SW* 98/19.

ilikest *see* ilich.

ilimpeð *pr. 3 sg.* happens *HM* 30/10, *A8* 130/21. **ilumpen** *p.p. A8* 136/2.

ilke *adj.* same *HM* 4/33 *etc.*, *SM* 44/20 *etc.*, *SW* 90/32 *etc.*, *A7* 110/32, 114/17, 20, *A8* 144/4. *as n. SW* 92/13¹, *A8* 130/2 *etc.*, **mit tet** — at that moment *SM* 60/18, 82/9, **wið þet** — *SM* 72/34, 76/16, **wið þis** — *SM* 70/14.

iloket *p.p.* ordained *SM* 60/7.

ilome *adv.* often *HM* 30/10, *SM* 68/15, *SW* 86/18, **ofte ant** — often *SW* 90/20, 106/33.

iloten *p.p.* assigned *HM* 8/30.

iluuet *p.p.* loved *HM* 22/14.

imeane *adj.* common, shared *HM* 16/33 *etc.*, *SW* 102/21.

imembret *p.p.* with links or plates of precious metal *A8* 138/14.

imerred *see* merren.

imotet *p.p.* spoken *SM* 82/2.

imuneget *see* munegin.

imunt *p.p.* intended *A7* 128/11.

inc *pron. 2 dual acc., dat.*, (both of) you *HM* 8/31, — **baðe** *SM* 80/30. **incker** *gen.*; — **noðres tale** neither of your accounts *SW* 106/21, **inker** of you *HM* 26/35, *poss. adj.* your *HM* 2/20.

inȝong *n.* entry *SW* 88/3.

inoh *adv.* enough *HM* 4/32 *etc.*, *SM* 62/24, *A8* 130/8 *etc.*

inohreaðe *adv.* perhaps *HM* 28/27, 42/8, *A8* 136/25.

inre *adj.* inward, inner *A7* 118/17, 124/8, *A8* 140/34.

inread *adj.* ruddy, red-complexioned *A7* 124/4.

in-seil *n.* seal *SM* 52/5.

inwarde *adj. wk.* innermost, inmost *SM* 64/18, — **helle** the depths of hell *HM* 22/9, 38/10, *SW* 90/12.

inwart *adv.* within *SM* 56/18.

inwið *adv.* inside *SM* 68/34, *SW* 86/8, 19, — **i** in, within *HM* 6/5 *etc.*

inwið *prep.* in, within, inside *HM* 2/15 *etc.*, *SM* 74/15, *A7* 112/34, 122/27, *A8* 130/12, 136/3, in the midst of *HM* 32/6.

ipaiet *p.p.* pleased; — **of** contented with *HM* 24/11.

is *pr. 3 sg.* is *HM* 2/3 *etc.*, *SM* 44/13 *etc.*, *SW* 86/8 *etc.*, *A7* 110/2 *etc.*, *A8* 130/7 *etc.*, **his** *SM* 44/26, 84/9. *neg. form*: **nis** is not *HM* 4/11 *etc.*, *SM* 68/27, 80/6, 82/15, *SW* 86/17 *etc.*, *A7* 110/17 *etc.*, *A8* 132/29 *etc. See* **am, aren, art, beon, wes.**

ischepen *see* **schuptest.**

ischriuene *ppl. adj. pl.* confessed *A8* 130/19.

iscrippet *p.p.*; — **ut** scratched out *HM* 20/29.

iseid *see* **seggen.**

iseinet *p.p.* blessed *SM* 84/12.

iseon *v.* see, perceive *SM* 54/23 *etc.* **iseo** *pr. 1 sg. SM* 48/9 *etc., SW* 94/24, 98/12. **isið** sees (to) *pr. 3 sg. HM* 26/8. **iseoð** *pr. 3 pl. SW* 90/33, 92/2. **iseh** *pa. 1 sg. SM* 82/30, *SW* 92/27 *etc.* **isehen** *pa. 3 pl. SM* 54/33. **isehe** *pa. sg. subj. SW* 92/26. **isehe** *p.p. SM* 62/5, **isehen** *SM* 60/38 *etc., SW* 90/19 *etc., A8* 138/12.

ismeðet *p.p.* glossed over *HM* 24/3, 34/16.

ismiret *p.p.* anointed *HM* 10/34.

isoht *see* **sechen.**

isoðet *p.p.* verified, proved *SW* 100/29.

isped *p.p.* given success *SW* 108/15.

ispillet *p.p.* wasted *A7* 110/11.

istald *p.p.* established *HM* 16/26.

istelet *adj.* bound with steel *SW* 92/34.

isticchet *p.p.* sewn *A8* 142/26.

istopen *p.p.* advanced *SM* 68/25.

istrahte *ppl. adj. pl.* extended *A7* 114/29.

isturbet *p.p.* disturbed *A8* 144/32.

iswenchet *ppl. adj.* having taken trouble *A8* 134/4.

iswunken *see* **swinken.**

itake *see* **tac.**

itald *see* **tellen.**

itawet *p.p.* cured *A8* 136/8.

iteiet *p.p.* attached *HM* 24/21, **iteit** bound *SM* 80/32.

itiden *v.* happen *HM* 26/29.

itimeð *pr. 3 sg.* happens *HM* 30/15, 32/13.

itricchet *p.p.* betrayed *HM* 6/27.

ituht *see* **tuhten.**

ituinet *p.p.* enclosed *SM* 76/13, **itunet** *SM* 80/32.

ituket *see* **tukin.**

iturnde *see* **turnen.**

ituðet *p.p.* granted *SM* 58/27, 80/4.

iþeinet *p.p.* served *SM* 84/13.

iþench *imp. sg.*; — **o** bear in mind *A8* 148/26.

iþuht *see* **þuncheð.**

iunnen *v.* wish *HM* 8/25. **ivnnen** *p.p.* granted *HM* 12/4.

iueiet *see* **veien.**

iuon *see* **feng.**

iwenet *p.p.* weaned *SM* 46/7.

iwis *adv.* indeed, certainly *SM* 52/31, **iwiss** *HM* 28/17, *A7* 116/5.

iwist *p.p.* (1) brought up *SM* 46/6.

iwist *p.p.* (2) *see* **witen** *v.* (2).

iwraht(e) *see* **wurchen.**

iwunet *p.p.* accustomed *SW* 98/10, 106/28, *A7* 114/26.

iwurget *p.p.* worshipped *SM* 44/13.

iwurset *p.p.* harmed *A8* 146/10.

iwurðen *v.* become *HM* 22/32, 28/25, *SM* 56/14, 70/15, *A7* 116/28, be *HM* 34/34, *SM* 66/14, *SW* 86/25, 104/1, *A8* 132/20, happen *HM* 40/5, *SM* 46/27, 50/8, 52/25, **iwurðe** *SM* 76/5. **iwurðest** *pr. 2 sg. HM* 28/25. **iwurðeð** *pr. 1 pl. SM* 72/20, *pr. 3 pl. SW* 92/1. **iwurðe** *pr. sg. subj. HM* 26/35, 30/3, 4, *SM* 60/11, 84/12. **iwurðe** *p.p.*; — **to** turned into *HM* 6/25.

iacinct *n.* jacinth *HM* 38/21, 22.

kearf *see* **keorue.**

kecchen *pr. pl. subj.* get, acquire *A8* 134/14.

keis *n.* servants, henchmen *SW* 88/5.

keli *v.* cool *HM* 22/3.

kempe *n.* champion, victor *HM* 38/12, *SM* 60/9, 62/12. **kempen** *pl. SM* 44/4. **kempene** *gen. pl. HM* 20/10, 42/14, *SM* 74/32.

kenchinde *adv.* laughing *HM* 14/26.

kene *adj.* brave *A7* 114/27, 116/12.

kennen *v.* make known *SM* 72/21. **kenne** *pr. sg. subj. SM* 48/8. **ken** *imp. sg. SM* 70/29, 72/2.

kenschipe *n.* courage *SM* 62/11.

keorue *pr. sg. subj.* cut *A8* 136/18. **kearf** *pa. 3 sg. A7* 120/27. **kurue** *pa. sg. subj. A7* 110/15.

keoruunge *n. pl.* wounds made by cutting *A8* 136/18.

kepe *pr. 1 sg.* care, like *SM* 74/9, await *SM* 80/13. **kepeð** *pr. 3 sg.*; — **half dale** go halves *HM* 36/26. **kepte** *pa. sg. subj.* restrained *HM* 20/27, would want *A7* 110/15, would care for *A7* 112/12, would accept *A7* 116/30.

kimeð *see* **cumen.**

kine-bern *n.* royal offspring *SM* 48/32, 56/24.

kineriche *n.* kingdom *HM* 16/6.
kinewurðe *adj.* royal *SM* 76/29.
knihtes *see* **cniht.**
kumelich *adj.* decent *HM* 22/16.
kun *see* **cun.**
kurue *see* **keorue.**

ladli *adj.* loathsome, hateful, bad *HM* 22/32, **ladlich** *SM* 60/28, *A8* 134/23. **ladliche** *wk. HM* 22/7, 28/3, *SM* 66/27, dreadful *SM* 80/19. **ladluker** *comp. HM* 22/13. **ladlukeste** *superl. as n. HM* 36/6.
ladliche *adv.* cruelly *SM* 52/29.
lah *adj.* low, base, humble *HM* 40/4, *SM* 80/15, *A8* 142/27. **lahe** *pl. HM* 38/25, *SW* 96/32, *A7* 112/23. **lahre** *comp.* more debased *HM* 22/32. **lah** *as n. sg. HM* 4/2, *A7* 122/7, *pl. SM* 68/9, *SW* 100/31. **laheste** *superl. as n. SM* 68/12.
lah *adv.* low, humbly *SM* 68/11, **lahe** *HM* 4/1, 21, 20/34, *SM* 64/17, 70/29, 72/4, *A8* 142/25, 144/3.
lahe *n.* law *HM* 16/25, 18/17, *SM* 60/6, *SW* 102/10, *A7* 112/6, **i—of wedlac** legally married *HM* 18/11.
lahe *adv. see* **lah** adv.
laheliche *adv.* lawfully *HM* 12/8.
lahte *pa. 3 sg.* thrust, darted *SM* 58/16.
lam *n.* clay *HM* 10/30, 38/1, **mon of—** earthly man *HM* 4/23, 20/1.
lami *adj.* earthly *HM* 42/20.
lane *n.* loan *SW* 98/6.
lanhure *adv.* at least *HM* 16/24, 18/12, 20/27, *SM* 64/2, 22, 82/14, *A7* 114/17.
lare *n.* teaching *HM* 2/12, 13, *SW* 106/29, *A8* 140/7, 146/14, 17.
large *adj.* generous *A7* 120/4, *A8* 132/11 *etc.*
largeliche *adv.* generously *HM* 24/29.
largesce *n.* generosity *A8* 134/1.
lates *n. pl.* looks, behaviour *SM* 66/21, *A8* 142/31.
lað *n.* hatred *SW* 94/27, **laððe** *HM* 28/32, **leaððe** *A8* 144/11.
lað *adj.* hateful *HM* 24/17, 26/35, *SM* 54/9, 56/34, 66/30, *A7* 122/15. **laðe** *wk. HM* 36/35, *pl. SW* 92/3. *pl. as n.* those one hates *HM* 26/1, those who hate each other *HM* 34/19. **laðest** *superl. HM* 12/16, 26/32, 36/25, *SM* 68/20, *SW* 94/3, *A8* 144/10, **loþest** *SM* 48/4.

laði *v.* be hateful (to) *HM* 6/22.
lauerdom *n.* lordship *HM* 8/19, **—on** lordship over *HM* 12/18.
laz *n.* girdle *A8* 138/20.
leaf *n.* leaf (of book) *SM* 44/11. **leaue** *dat.*; **o —** in writing *SM* 82/32.
leafdi *n.* lady *HM* 4/14 *etc.*, *SM* 62/33 *etc.*, *A7* 112/27 *etc.*, *A8* 142/2, 4, **þe —** Our Lady *A8* 148/22, **lefdi** *SM* 50/27, *SW* 106/28, 108/4. **leafdis** *pl. HM* 2/19, 6/30, *A8* 136/31, 138/29.
leafdischipe *n.* rank as lady *HM* 4/24.
léafeð *see* **leuen** *v.* (3).
leanin *v.* grow thin *HM* 30/32.
learen *v.* teach, learn *A8* 140/12, 15. **leare** *pr. 1 sg. SM* 80/22. **learst** *pr. 2 sg. HM* 2/13. **leareð** *pr. 3 sg. HM* 2/8, 10/32, *SW* 86/3, 96/16, *A8* 140/3, *pr. 3 pl. SW* 108/4. **leare** *pr. sg. subj. SW* 88/16. **leareð** *imp. pl. HM* 2/16, 8/8, 34/25. **leaðie** *pr. sg. subj. HM* 40/26. **leaðie** *imp. pl.* invite *A8* 134/9, **leaðieð** *A8* 134/5. **leaðede** *pa. sg. subj.* invited *A8* 132/12.
leaððe *see* **lað** *n.*
leaue *n.* (1) permission *A8* 132/2 *etc.*
leaue *n.* (2) *see* **leaf.**
lechecreft *n.* medical treatment *A8* 136/20.
ledene *n.* language *SM* 82/34, *A7* 110/8, **on Englische —** in English *HM* 2/27, **o Latines —** in Latin *HM* 20/12. **ledenes** *pl.* nations *SW* 100/34.
lefden *see* **leue** *v.* (2).
lefdi *see* **leafdi.**
lefmon *see* **leofmon.**
leggen *v.* lay; inflict *SM* 74/4, **legge** lay *SM* 56/30. **leið** *pr. 3 sg. SM* 70/29, *A7* 116/23, *A8* 144/3. **leide** *pa. 3 sg. A7*

leggen (*cont.*):
116/24. **leiden** *pa. 3 pl.*; — **on** laid on
SM 52/9, 21, 76/35. **legge** *pr. sg. subj.*
SM 80/7, *A8* 144/8, 21.
lei *n.* (1) law *SM* 44/11.
lei *n.* (2) fire, flame *SM* 74/24. **leie** *dat. SM*
58/19, 74/21.
lei *v. see* **liggen**
leide(n) *see* **leggen**.
leifen *n.* mire *HM* 28/18, **leiuen** *SM* 66/
26.
leirwite *n.* punishment for fornication *HM*
42/3.
leiti *v.* burn, blaze *SM* 74/24. **leiteð** *pr. 3*
sg. SM 66/3. **leitið** *pr. 3 pl. SM* 64/36.
leitede *pa. 3 sg. SM* 58/18. **leitinde**
pr.p. SM 78/32.
leið *see* **leggen**.
leiuen *see* **leifen**.
lenden *n. pl.* loins *SM* 74/24. **lendene** *pl.*
back *HM* 32/1.
lengere *adv. comp.* longer *SW* 106/15.
lengre *SM* 46/7, *SW* 100/20, *A8* 144/
26.
leode *n.* people *SM* 80/15. **leoden** *pl. HM*
40/8. **leodes** *gen. pl.* of nations *SM* 78/
11.
leof *adj.* dear, pleasing, attractive *HM* 10/9
etc., *SM* 48/4, *A7* 128/3, *A8* 140/31. *as*
n. beloved *SM* 80/13, 14, *A7* 118/2.
leoue *wk. SM* 64/18, *A7* 114/28. **leoues**
gen. sg. as n. A7 114/26, 122/11. **leoue**
pl. A7 110/29 *etc.*, *A8* 130/32, 134/18,
148/18, *as n. pl.* those one loves *HM* 26/
1. **leouere** *comp.* more pleasing; **me is**
— I would rather *A8* 136/27, 138/17,
me were — *A8* 148/12, **hwa se is** —
whoever prefers *A8* 140/20, **leuere** *SM*
46/7. **leouest** *superl. SM* 44/27, *A8*
144/10. **leoueste** *superl. wk.* best-loved
HM 30/15, *pl.* dearest *HM* 16/33, 18/3.
leofliche *adj. wk.* lovely, fair, beautiful *SM*
52/9 *etc.* **leoflukest** *superl. HM* 10/11,
SM 50/19.
leofliche *adv.* lovingly *SM* 80/22, finely
SW 98/13.
leofmon *n.* beloved, lover *HM* 4/13 *etc.*,
SM 48/28 *etc.*, *A7* 112/24 *etc.*, **lefmon**
SM 46/10.
leome *n.* radiance, light *SM* 56/25 *etc.*, *SW*
98/20, 100/3, 6, **to** — **ant to liue** to life
SM 44/15.
leomeð *pr. 3 sg.* blazes *SM* 66/3.

leor *n.* face, countenance *SM* 46/27, *SW*
88/30, 100/2.
leote *v.* allow *HM* 8/24, 42/14, value *HM*
14/34, *A7* 120/16, *pr. 1 sg. SM* 66/12,
14^{1,2}. **let** *pr. 3 sg. SW* 86/25, 98/17,
— **leasse** of cares less about *A8* 130/11,
— **lutel to** cares little for *HM* 28/27.
leoteð *pr. 3 pl. SM* 66/25, — **ham** *refl.*
consider themselves *HM* 38/25. **leote**
pr. sg. subj. SW 88/11. **leoten** *pr. pl. subj.*
A8 142/15. **let** *imp. sg. SM* 46/30 *etc.*,
SW 98/14. **leote** *imp. pl. A8* 136/3,
leoteð *A8* 132/20. **lette** *pa. 1 sg.*;
— **don** caused to be put *SM* 82/32,
pa. 3 sg. considered *HM* 40/4, 10,
allowed *A7* 116/16.
leoð *n.* song *HM* 18/20.
leoðe *imp. sg.* release, loose *SM* 66/32,
72/24, 82/14, **leoþe** *SM* 64/23.
leoðede *pa. 3 sg. SM* 64/25.
leoðebeie *adj. pl.* supple *SM* 70/27.
leoðeliche *adv.* loosely *A8* 136/12.
leoue, leouere *see* **leof**.
lerden *see* **learen**.
lessere *adj. comp.* of less worth *SW* 106/
18.
let *adj.* late *HM* 32/22.
let *v. see* **leote, leten**.
leten *v.* let go, give up *A7* 126/27, leave *A7*
116/32. **lete** *pr. sg. subj.*; **lif** — suffer
death *SM* 74/26. **let** *imp.* stop *SM* 50/
23. **leoteð** *imp. pl. SM* 80/19. **lette** *pa.*
3 sg. SW 86/28.
lette *see* **leote, leten, letten**.
letten *v.* hinder *A8* 132/10. **letteð** *pr. 3*
pl. SM 66/25, 68/31. **lette** *pr. sg. subj.*
A8 132/18.
lettunge *n.* hindrance, delay *SW* 104/28.
leue *v.* (1) grant, allow; *pr. sg. subj. HM* 42/
19, 20, *A8* 144/26, 146/26.
leue *v.* (2) trust, believe in, accept *SM* 50/
26. **leue** *pr. 1 sg. SM* 48/28. **leuest** *pr. 2*
sg. SM 82/16, **leuestu** *interrog. pr. 2 sg.*
SM 48/29. **leueð** *pr. 3 sg. SM* 48/16,
pr. 3 pl. A7 128/26. **leue** *imp. pl. SM* 52/
35, *A8* 136/20. **lefden** *pa. 3 pl. SM* 46/
20.
leuen *v.* (3) remain, stay *SW* 106/15.
leafeð *pr. 3. sg. HM* 22/7.
leuere *see* **leof**.
lich *n.* body *SM* 52/9 *etc.*, *A8* 136/13.
liche *dat sg.* form *SM* 58/10, 62/29.
licome *n.* body *HM* 10/30, 34, 22/3, *SM*

54/6,*A7* 114/28 *etc.* **licomes** *gen. sg.* of the body, physical *HM* 12/3 *etc.*, *SM* 44/5, 48/1, 52/35.

licomlich *adj.* bodily, physical, carnal *SW* 96/12,*A7* 110/4. **licomliche** *wk. HM* 8/12, 14/9,*pl. HM* 2/17, 8/8,*A7* 110/2.

licomliche *adv.* in the body *HM* 4/4.

licunge *n.* pleasure, delight *HM* 6/7, 12, 20, *SM* 68/17, *SW* 96/7, 12.

licwurðe *adj.* pleasing, acceptable *HM* 10/9, *SW* 106/19,*A8* 140/32.

liflade *n.* life, way of life, biography *HM* 4/4 *etc.*, *SM* (*heading*), 78/20, 82/31.

lifsiðe *n.* life, life-time *SW* 90/14. **lifsiðen** *pl. HM* 38/33.

liggen *v.* lie down, sleep *A8* 136/12. — **under** be subject to *HM* 26/32. **list** *pr. 2 sg. HM* 6/22. **lið** *pr. 3 sg.* lies; — **in** belongs to *SM* 50/22. **ligge** *pr. sg. subj. A8* 136/24, 142/17, 25. **lei** *pa. 3 sg. SM* 82/17, **lomp ant** — fell in accord with *SM* 50/2.

liheð *pr. 3 pl.* deceive *HM* 34/24. **lihe** *pr. sg. subj. HM* 24/23.

lihtinde *pr.p.* descending *SM* 64/13, 82/12.

lihtschipe *n.* lightness, ease of movement *SW* 102/23.

likeð *pr. 3 sg.* pleases *HM* 4/27, *SM* 48/1, *SW* 102/18,*A8* 136/24, **hwil þe god** — for as long as it pleases you *SM* 78/9.

limmel *adv.* limb from limb *SM* 56/1.

limpeð *pr. 3 sg.* falls to *HM* 32/25, *SW* 106/30, **limpet** *SW* 94/29, belongs *HM* 36/17, befits *A8* 132/10, 136/32, 138/24. **lomp** *pa. 3 sg. SM* 50/2. **ilumpen** *p.p. A8* 136/2.

linnunge *n.* ceasing *SM* 62/21, *SW* 100/9.

lire *n.* flesh; **lið ba ant** — limb from limb *HM* 18/19.

list *see* **liggen**.

litunge *n.* painted design, painting *A7* 116/10, 11.

lið *n.* limb, joint *HM* 18/19.

lið *v. see* **liggen**.

liðe *adj.* gentle, kindly *A8* 146/14, *pl. A8* 146/18.

liðeliche *adv.* courteously *SW* 98/23, gently *A8* 146/13, with good will *SM* 78/21.

liðerede *pa. 3 sg.* streamed, was lathered *SM* 52/10.

liueneð *n.* support *HM* 24/27, provisions *A7* 112/37, 122/33.

locunge *n.* looking; **lah — habben** keep the eyes lowered *A8* 142/27, **lokunge;** — **on** attention *HM* 28/2.

loft-song *n.* song of praise *SM* 76/18, *SW* 102/23. **loft-songes** *pl. SW* 104/23.

lomen *n. pl.* tools *A7* 110/14, 16.

lomp *see* **limpeð**.

lonke *n.* side *HM* 32/1.

loþest *see* **lað**.

lufsum *adj.* lovely, desirable *SM* 68/5. **lufsume** *wk. SM* 46/27 *etc.* **lufsumre** *comp. HM* 10/13,*A8* 138/13.

lufsumlec *n.* beauty *SM* 50/20.

lufte *n. dat.* air *SM* 58/35, 72/9.

lupe *n.* leap *HM* 20/25.

lure *n.* loss *HM* 2/22 *etc.*,*A8* 146/31. **luren** *pl. HM* 4/34.

lusteð *pr. 3 sg.* pleases *HM* 22/15. **luste** *pa. sg. subj. HM* 14/3.

lusti *adj.* rejoicing *SW* 104/22.

lut *pron.* few *HM* 16/34, 18/3, *SW* 96/25.

lut *adj.* short *HM* 16/9, 32/27, few *A8* 144/31. **lute** *wk.*; **is — strengðe of** matters little *A8* 140/34.

luteð *pr. 3 sg.* lurks, lies hidden *HM* 38/15.

lutinde *see* **leat**.

lutle *adj.* little; **of ane — hwile** momentary *HM* 40/34, — **hwile** *adv. phrase* for a short time *SM* 48/1, *SW* 100/6.

lutlen *adv.* a little *SM* 64/19, — **ant** — gradually, little by little *SM* 68/32.

lutlin *v.* lessen, diminish *HM* 4/23, *SW* 104/32, **lutli** *SM* 50/21.

luðere *adj.* cruel *SM* 48/19 *etc.*, terrible *HM* 38/26, **luðre** wicked *SM* 56/30. **luðere** *pl.* evil *SM* 48/12, malicious *A8* 142/24, severe *A8* 136/18, *as n. pl.* evil men *SM* 46/31. **luðerest** *superl. SM* 74/25.

luðerliche *adv.* cruelly, violently *SM* 52/9, 21, shamefully *SM* 70/4, 74/26, 27, wretchedly *SM* 48/32.

luuefule *adj. pl.* amorous *SM* 66/23.

luuelich *adj.* loving *A8* 146/14. **luueliche** *wk.* gracious *SM* 68/6, *pl.* loving *SM* 66/20.

luueliche *adv.* lovingly *HM* 2/8, *A8* 146/13.

luuewende *adv.* beloved *SM* 60/7.

ma *adv.* more *HM* 20/25.
ma *adj. comp.* more *SM* 44/8, *as pron.* more
(people) *HM* 26/19, *SM* 58/8, *SW* 96/
6.
mahe *n.* stomach *HM* 32/5.
mahe(n), maht, mahte(n), mahtu *see*
mei.
mahte *n.* power *SM* 54/25.
make *n.* mate *HM* 22/19, equal *A7* 124/
32.
makeles *adj.* matchless *SM* 60/37,
makelese *wk. SM* 50/20, 72/23.
makunge *n.* cause *HM* 38/14.
man *n.* complaint *A8* 134/24.
mare *adj. comp.* more, greater *HM* 6/12
etc., *SM* 84/7, *A8* 144/8, 146/12, *as n.*
HM 6/17 *etc.*, *SM* 66/22, 80/5, *A7* 112/
15 *etc.*, *A8* 132/35, 146/16 *etc.*
mare *adv.* more *HM* 10/13 *etc.*, *SM* 64/2
etc., *SW* 92/18 *etc.*, *A7* 116/30 *etc.*, *A8*
144/26, as well *A8* 144/24, þe — the
more *HM* 34/3, *SM* 54/26, *SW* 92/11.
See also aa, eauer, na, ne *conj.*, neauer.
marheȝeue *n.* morning gift *HM* 34/32.
marhen *n.* morning *HM* 28/10, *SM* 74/1.
maumez *n. pl.* idols *SM* 44/9, 50/7, 74/7.
me *pron. 1 sg. see* Ich.
me *pron. indef.* one, you *HM* 8/15 *etc.*, *SM*
56/18 *etc.*, *SW* 88/17 *etc.*, *A7* 110/17
etc., *A8* 130/11 *etc.*, — seið it is said
HM 14/28, 38/18, *A7* 120/4, 124/1,
128/12, *A8* 134/10, — dude it was
done *SM* 76/3.
me *conj.* but *HM* 28/8, *SM* 54/5, 56/4, 60/
37, *A7* 116/4.
meadlese *adj. wk.* immoderate *A8* 132/9.
meadschipe *n.* madness *HM* 32/31.
mealles *n. pl.* clubs *SW* 92/34.
meallið *pr. 3 pl.* beat *SW* 90/33.
meanden *pa. 3 pl.* pitied *SM* 52/27.
meane *adj.* common, shared *SW* 102/20.
measse-kemese *n.* alb *A8* 138/33.
meast *adj. superl.* greatest *SM* 52/32 *etc.*
measte *wk. A7* 120/14², al þet — deal
(for) the most part *SM* 72/9, þe alre —
poure the poorest of all *HM* 34/35.
measte *pl. A7* 118/35, 120/14¹.
meast *adv.* most *HM* 22/2 *etc.*, *SM* 70/24,
72/15¹, *A7* 112/9¹,², 128/9, most of all
SM 72/15², 16, *A8* 132/4, mest
especially *SM* 72/11. — alle almost all
HM 8/2.
meastling *n.* brass *HM* 6/26.

meaðeliche *adv.* moderately *SM* 66/35.
meaðeluker *comp. SM* 66/35.
meaðen *n. pl.* maggots *SW* 92/6.
meaðful *adj.* temperate *SW* 96/35,
moderate *A8* 148/23.
meaðfulliche *adv.* in moderation *A8*
132/27, moderately *A8* 132/29.
mede *n.* reward *HM* 6/9 *etc.*, *SM* 52/3, 56/
23, money *HM* 28/29, to — of in
payment for *SM* 74/17. meden *pl. SM*
64/29.
medi *v.* pay, reward *HM* 28/29.
mehes *n. pl.* kinswomen *SM* 70/19.
mei *pr. 1 sg.* can, may *SM* 66/3, 68/21, *SW*
90/24², *A7* 118/23, 128/8, 24, *A8* 140/
21. maht *pr. 2 sg. HM* 20/18, 31, 28/24,
SM 50/12, *A7* 114/11 *etc.*, mahtu *SM*
74/29. mei *pr. 3 sg. HM* 2/12 *etc.*, *SM*
48/15 *etc.*, *SW* 86/9 *etc.*, *A7* 110/19 *etc.*,
A8 132/28 *etc.* mahe *pr. 1 pl. SM* 72/11,
mahen *SW* 86/21. mahen *pr. 2 pl. SW*
94/11, 104/10, *A8* 136/13 *etc.*, muhen
A8 136/29. mahe *pr. 3 pl. HM* 16/17,
SW 102/13, mahen *HM* 16/18 *etc.*, *SM*
66/30, 68/25, *A7* 124/8, *A8* 138/29,
muhe *HM* 20/6, muhen *HM* 20/4, 38/
5. mahe *pr. sg. subj. HM* 14/29, 22/13,
24/28, *SM* 54/25 *etc.*, *SW* 102/30, 106/
3, *A7* 122/8, *A8* 142/31, 144/32.
mahen *pr. pl. subj. SM* 66/31. mahte
pa. 1 sg. SM 44/12, *SW* 100/3 *etc.*, pa. 3
sg. SM 54/30, 64/31, *A7* 114/2, 118/12.
mahten *pa. 3 pl. HM* 16/27, 38/5, *A7*
114/5, mahte *A7* 126/21. mahte *pa. sg.
subj. HM* 2/19, 4/28, 16/7, *SM* 60/28
etc., *SW* 90/28 *etc.*, *A7* 110/9 *etc.*, *A8*
142/23, 146/32. mahten *pa. pl. subj.*
HM 14/30, *SM* 52/16.
meide *n.* maiden, virgin, girl *SM* 52/28,
meiden *HM* 2/3 *etc.*, *SM* 44/20 *etc.*, *SW*
100/15, *A7* 118/4, 6, 7, *A8* 140/12²,
maid *A8* 140/12¹, 148/4. meidenes *gen.*
sg. and pl. HM 10/35 *etc.*, *SM* 56/23 *etc.*,
meidene *HM* (*heading*), *SM* 50/10, 52/
2. meidnes *pl. HM* 18/5 *etc.*, *SM* 44/25
etc., *SW* 102/8, *A8* 134/3.
meidenhad *n.* virginity *HM* (*heading*),
10/35, *A7* 120/9.
meies *n. pl.* kinsmen *SM* 70/19.
mein *n.* power *SM* 62/29, virtue *SM* 68/
35.
meinful *adj.* powerful *SM* 50/19, 52/36.
meistre *n.* master *A7* 128/7, director *SW*

88/15, *A8* 134/18, 138/19. **meistres**
gen. sg. A8 134/7 *etc.*

meistreð *pr. 3 sg.* rules, directs *SW* 88/4.

meistrie *n.* mastery, power *HM* 8/20, *A7*
126/30, **þurh mi** — out of
presumption *A8* 130/4. **meistries** *pl.*
wonders *A7* 114/6.

meið *n. gen. sg.* virginity; — **þeawes** the
virtues of virginity *HM* 2/3.

meiðhad *n.* virginity *HM* 2/28 *etc.*, *SM*
44/26 *etc.*, *A7* 118/8. **meiðhades** *gen.*
sg. HM 8/30 *etc.*, *SM* 44/28.

mel *n. pl.* meals *A8* 144/29.

mel-seotel *n.* banqueting seat *SM* 62/16.

menske *n.* honour *HM* 12/24 *etc.*, *SM* 44/
28, 46/10, 68/6. **mensken** *pl. HM* 20/
15.

menskeð *pr. 3 sg.* honours *HM* 20/2.

meokelec *n.* meekness, humility *HM* 36/
16 *etc.*

meokeschipe *n.* meekness, humility *HM*
40/1, 13.

meoseise *n.* difficulties *A8* 134/17.

meoster *n.* occupation, role *SW* 96/28,
100/24, *A8* 132/20, 21.

merren *v.* harm, ruin, corrupt *HM* 14/20,
SM 50/1, 62/29. **merrest** *pr. 2 sg. HM*
38/18. **merreð** *pr. 3 sg. SM* 70/12.
merden *pa. 3 pl. HM* 8/18. **merren** *pr.*
pl. subj. be corrupted *HM* 12/2.
imerred *p.p. HM* 8/20.

mest *see* **meast** *adv.*

met *n.* measure *HM* 18/1, **wiðute** —
beyond measure *SW* 90/26, 102/22,
104/3, *A8* 148/7.

mete *n.* (1) moderation, temperance,
measure *HM* 36/12, *SW* 88/16, 19,
96/13.

mete *n.* (2) food, meals *HM* 32/5, 38/2,
A7 110/33, *A8* 130/32 *etc.*

mete *pa. 2 sg.* measured *SM* 78/15.

mi *see* **Ich.**

mid *prep.* with *HM* 10/1, *SM* 56/6, *SW*
86/28, 98/2, *A7* 110/18 *etc.*, **mit** *SM*
60/17, 82/9, — **alle** *intensive* entirely,
indeed *SM* 58/23, 70/22, *SW* 98/16, *A7*
118/29, 122/18, 128/4, *A8* 136/4.

migge *n.* urine *A7* 124/1 *etc.*

mihte *n.* virtue *HM* 10/7 *etc.*, *SM* 62/30,
72/13, rank *SM* 48/15, power *SM* 50/
20 *etc.*, *A7* 114/7, *A8* 148/16. **mihtes** *pl.*
virtues *HM* 10/7, 38/35, *SM* 76/25.
mihte *gen. pl. HM* 12/16², *SM* 44/27.

milce *n.* kindness, mercy, pity, grace *HM*
18/15, *SM* 46/29 *etc.*, *SW* 104/5, 108/
11, *A7* 118/2, *A8* 146/1.

milci *pr.sg. subj.* have mercy *A8* 144/27.

milc-strunden *n. pl.* streams of milk *HM*
32/3.

min(e), mines *see* **Ich.**

mis *n.* wrong; **on** — **forte donne** into
wrong-doing *HM* 14/30.

misbileaue *n.* false faith *SM* 52/30.

misbileuede *p.p. as adj. pl.* infidel *SM* 44/
8.

misfeare *pr. sg. subj.* is defective *HM* 30/
11, come to harm *HM* 30/14.

misleueð *pr. 2 pl.* distrust *A8* 134/14.
misleue *pr. sg. subj. A8* 146/1.

mislich *adj.* various; **moni** — all kinds of
SM 44/11, *SW* 86/19. **misliche** *pl. SW*
92/35, improper *HM* 10/2.

misliche *adv.* cruelly *SM* 44/3, wrongly;
ilimpeð — goes wrong *A8* 130/21.

mislimet *adj.* deformed *SM* 78/27.

mit *see* **mid.**

moder-bern *n. pl.* people *SM* 46/16.

modie *adj. pl.* proud *HM* 6/30.

mon *n.* man; **monne** *gen. pl.* men, people
SM 66/36, *A7* 110/8, 120/3, 128/9, *A8*
134/32, 138/21.

mong *n.* exchange *SW* 92/10, admixture,
pollution *A7* 110/21.

monglunge *n.* mingling, adulteration *A7*
110/20, 126/27.

moni *pron.* many a one; **monies** *gen. sg.*
many; **efter** — **wene** according to the
opinion of many *A7* 114/30.

monluker *adv. comp.* more vigorously *A8*
140/27.

monne *see* **mon.**

monslahe *n.* murderer *SM* 62/3, 64/8.

mot *n.* argument, speech *SM* 56/8.

mot *pr. 1 sg.* must, may *SM* 46/32 *etc.* **most**
pr. 2 sg. HM 14/32 *etc.*, *SM* 82/3, *SW*
102/24, 104/20. **mot** *pr. 3 sg. HM* 14/5,
16/31, *SM* 60/3, *A7* 122/8, 126/26, *A8*
134/21, 25. **moten** *pr. 2 pl. A8* 130/5.
mote *pr. 3 pl. HM* 34/4, **moten** *HM*
18/32, *SM* 44/27 *etc.* **mote** *pr. sg. subj.*
HM 40/5, *SM* 52/2 *etc.*, *SW* 108/19,
22, *A8* 146/27. **moste** *pa. sg. subj.*
might *SM* 46/15, 58/26, had to *A7*
128/7.

motin *v.* argue *SM* 72/33.

muche *adj.* much, great, huge *HM* 2/19

muche (*cont.*):
etc., *SM* 54/31, 58/24, 68/10, *SW* 96/8
etc., *A7* 116/27, 126/38, *A8* 130/30 *etc.*,
— **deale** a great deal *HM* 22/12,
26/12, *SM* 60/27, *SW* 92/13, **muchel**
HM 4/21 *etc.*, *SM* 60/18, *SW* 96/5,
104/7, 17, *A7* 112/15, 122/6, 126/36,
A8 136/1 *etc.*, *as n. HM* 26/12, *SW* 86/
11 *etc.*, *A7* 112/14, 118/5, 120/18, *A8*
132/35. **muchele** *wk. HM* 2/22 *etc.*, *SM*
46/4 *etc.*, *SW* 104/4, *A7* 112/11, 122/3,
A8 148/11^{1,2}. **muchele** *pl. A7* 114/6, *as
n. SW* 104/18.
muche *adv.* much, greatly *HM* 12/28 *etc.*,
SM 52/28, 80/4, *SW* 96/20 *etc.*,
muchel *HM* 2/27 *etc.*, *SM* 46/16, 80/
23, *SW* 104/5, *A7* 118/10, *A8* 146/9,
muchele *HM* 36/3, *SM* 64/5.
muches *n. gen. sg.* much; **nawt** — nothing
much *A7* 126/9.
muchli *v.* increase *HM* 42/9, **mutlin** *SM*
68/22.
muhe(n) *see* **mei**.
munde *n.* mind, memory; **ine** — in mind
SM 80/23.
munde *adj. pl.* present, in mind *SM* 62/33.
munegin *v.* remember *SM* 68/15.
munegeð *pr. 3 sg.* calls on *SM* 78/29,
pr. 3 pl. SM 80/24. **imuneget** *p.p. SM*
62/31, 80/2, mentioned *SM* 80/6.
munegunge *n.* remembrance *SW* 90/1
etc., **mungunge** *A7* 116/13, *A8* 138/1.
munien *v.* remember, call to mind *SM* 68/
12, **munne** mention, tell of *SW* 104/8,
munnen *HM* 20/33. **munieð** *pr. 1 pl.*
commemorate *SM* 46/1, **munneð** *SM*
44/28. **munieð** *pr. 3 pl. SM* 80/5,
munneð *SM* 78/25, 80/24. **munneð**
imp. pl. SM 84/4.
mustreisun *n.* show, ostentation *A8* 138/
30.
mutlin *see* **muchli**.

na *adj.* no, (*with neg.*) any *HM* 6/4 *etc.*, *SM*
48/15 *etc.*, *SW* 90/24 *etc.*, *A7* 110/16
etc., *A8* 130/20 *etc.*, **nan** (*usually before a
vowel or h*) *HM* 6/3 *etc.*, *SM* 44/12^1 *etc.*,
SW 88/24 *etc.*, *A7* 120/21, *A8* 132/9 *etc.*
nanes *gen. sg.* — **cunnes** (*with neg.*) of
any kind *SM* 60/10, 62/27. — **weis** in
no way *HM* 24/18, 23, 38/5, *SM* 50/12,
SW 104/21, *A7* 114/11. **nane** *dat. sg.*; **o**
— **wise** in no way *HM* 28/23, *A7* 128/

25. **nane** *pl. A7* 124/7^{1,2}, *A8* 132/8^{1,2} *etc.*
na *adv.* no *SW* 100/20, 106/15, 18, *A8*
136/31, not *SM* 58/24, — **mare** no
more *HM* 22/17, *SM* 62/25, 30 (*with
neg.*), any more *A8* 138/22.
nabbe(n), **nabbeð** *see* **habben**.
nahhi *v.* approach, come near *A7* 120/21.
nahtes *adv.* at night *HM* 32/7.
nalde, **naldest** *see* **wulle**.
nam *see* **am**.
nan *pron. sg.* none, not one *HM* 16/17 *etc.*,
SM 44/12^2 *etc.*, *SW* 86/18, 88/18, *A7*
110/19 *etc.*, *A8* 130/2. **nane** *dat. sg. A8*
130/3, **nane** *pl. HM* 18/32 *etc.*, *SW* 102/
13.
nart *see* **art**.
nat *see* **witen** *v.* (1).
naueð *see* **habben**.
naut *see* **nawiht** *adv.*
nawiht *n.* nothing *HM* 34/13, *SW* 96/11,
22, (*with neg.*) anything *SM* 74/30, **nawt**
HM 4/22 *etc.*, *A7* 110/2 *etc.*, *A8* 134/32,
140/6, **noht** *SM* 50/23, 54/9, 70/22,
SW 94/22, 31. **ne beo ham** — it should
be nothing to them *A8* 144/18, **nis hit**
— it is not worthwhile *HM* 22/33.
nawiht *adv.* not, not at all *HM* 4/17, 12/
35, *SM* 56/9 *etc.*, *SW* 94/30, *A7* 124/27,
A8 130/1, 134/10, 26, **naut** not *SM* 52/
13, **nawt** *HM* 4/2 *etc.*, *SM* 56/5 *etc.*, *SW*
86/7 *etc.*, *A7* 110/33 *etc.*, *A8* 130/4 *etc.*,
— **ane** not only *HM* 24/14 *etc.*, *SM* 68/
9, *A7* 112/21, 114/35, *A8* 146/26.
nawt *adj.* worthless *HM* 6/26.
ne *adv.* not (*usually with another neg.*); *HM*
4/17 *etc.*, *SM* 44/12 *etc.*, *SW* 86/12 *etc.*,
A7 110/14 *etc.*, *A8* 130/1 *etc.*
ne *conj.* nor *HM* 10/26^2 *etc.*, *SM* 46/30^{1,3}
etc., *SW* 90/29^{2,3} *etc.*, *A7* 110/15^{1,3} *etc.*,
A8 130/2 *etc.* **ne** ... **ne** neither; —
leasse — **mare** neither less nor more,
nothing whatever *A8* 134/16.
nease *n.* nose *SM* 58/15, *SW* 92/20.
nease-gristles *n. pl.* cartilage of the nose
SW 92/4.
nease-þurles nostrils *SM* 58/15.
neauer *adv.* never; — **mare** never *HM* 14/
6, 38/7, *SM* 72/22, *A8* 144/4, (*with neg.*)
ever *HM* 24/24, *SM* 72/27, *SW* 92/14,
104/32, **neuer mare** *SM* 50/20, — **þe**
leatere nevertheless *HM* 10/2, — **se**
however *HM* 26/11, 32/12, — **se** ...
monie however many *A7* 118/2, — **so**

however *SM* 52/2, — **swa** however *HM*
28/12, however much *HM* 28/10, 14.
neb *n.* face *HM* 28/7, 30/31, *A7* 114/3, *A8*
138/3, 5, 7, **þet dumbe** — **habbeð**
which lack the power of speech *HM* 22/
17. **nebbe** *dat. sg. HM* 14/20, *in adv.*
phrase — **to** — face to face *HM* 14/14,
SW 102/35. **nebbes** *pl. SW* 92/31.
nebschaft *n.* face *SM* 50/7, **nebscheft**
HM 36/2.
nede *adv.* necessarily, of necessity *HM* 14/
6 *etc.*, *SM* 64/23, 72/3, *A7* 128/7.
nedeð *pr. 3 sg.* is necessary *A8* 134/13,
neodeð *A8* 132/27, 136/8.
nedlunge *adv.* of necessity *SM* 66/31, *A8*
134/25, **nedunge** *SM* 82/3.
nefde(n) *see* **habben.**
neh *adj.* near *A8* 130/23. **neste** *superl. wk.*
A8 130/22.
neh *adv.* near; **nower** — nowhere near
HM 6/34, *SW* 104/34. **neorre** *adv.*
comp. A7 114/2.
neh *prep.* almost as *HM* 10/30, near *HM*
18/10, *SM* 66/13, *A7* 126/20, *A8* 130/
15, 140/6, — **honde** near at hand *A8*
142/5.
nelde *n.* needle *A7* 120/32.
nemeð *see* **neomen.**
nempneð *pr. 3 sg.* mentions by name *A8*
136/33. **nempne** *imp. sg. A7* 120/17.
nempnede *pa. 1 sg. HM* 4/7.
neodelukest *adv. superl.* most diligently
SM 66/8.
neodeð *see* **nedeð.**
neoleachunge *n.* approach *A7* 118/5, 6.
neomen *v.* take, accept *HM* 22/20, 40/22,
A7 118/38, *A8* 132/27, 138/22, receive
A7 114/15, **neome** *SW* 104/33, *A7*
114/13, — **god ende** make a good end
A8 144/27, — **in** enter *SW* 104/21, —
nan ende come to any end *SW* 104/33.
neome *pr. 1 sg. SM* 80/28. **nimest** *pr. 2*
sg. — **se deopliche** take so seriously
HM 2/13. **nimeð** *pr. 3 sg. HM* 10/26,
22/22, undertakes *SW* 88/22,
accommodates *SW* 104/18. **neomen** *pr.*
pl. subj.; — **3eme** consider *A8* 146/8,
neome *SW* 94/21. **nim** *imp. sg. HM* 34/
36, *SM* 80/28, — **þe** *refl.* turn *HM* 6/
17, 36/7, take *HM* 34/33, —**3eme**
take note, consider *HM* 2/6 *etc.*, *SM* 50/
6. **neomeð** *imp. pl. SM* 52/6, *SW* 104/
15, *A7* 112/25, *A8* 134/13, receive *A8*

130/20, **nemeð** *SM* 46/24.
neorre *see* **neh** *adv.*
neoðer *adv.* lower *HM* 20/24, *SM* 72/28.
neowcin *n.* affliction, suffering, adversity
SM 44/17, **nowcin** *SM* 60/10, 80/28,
SW 96/2, 4, 35. **neowcins** *pl. SW*
102/3.
nere(n), nes *see* **wes.**
nesche *adj.* soft; *as n.* softness *SW* 96/4 *etc.*
nesches *gen. sg.* nawiht — any kind of
softness *SW* 96/11. **nesche** *pl. SW* 96/
1.
nest *prep.* next (to) *HM* 20/9, *SW* 88/13,
A8 136/10, 13.
neste *see* **neh** *adj.*
neuer *see* **neauer.**
nim, nimest, nimeð *see* **neomen.**
nis *see* **is.**
nið *n.* envy *A7* 124/15, 19, 25.
niðfule *adj. pl.* envious *A7* 124/16.
no *adv.* not *SM* 56/1, 82/1, 4.
noht *n. see* **nawiht** *n.*
nohtunge *n.* trifle *HM* 6/22, 28/10, *A8*
144/16.
nohwider *adv.* nowhere *A8* 142/10, — **of**
þe wei nowhere out of the way *SM* 60/
2.
nomeliche *adv.* especially *HM* 12/29, 28/
14, 30/9, *SM* 44/25, *A7* 120/7, *A8*
134/3 *etc.*
note *n.* occupation *A8* 146/30.
noðeleater *adv. comp.* nevertheless *A8*
144/21, **noðeletere** *SM* 74/12.
noðeles *adv.* nevertheless, all the same
SM 64/24, 66/31, *A8* 130/32.
noðres *pron. gen. sg.* neither *SW* 106/21.
nowcin *see* **neowcin.**
nule, nulle(n), nulleð *see* **wulle.**
nurrice *n.* nurse *HM* 32/24. **nurrices** *gen.*
sg. HM 32/35.
nurð *n.* clamour *HM* 28/3, *SW* 86/22,
outcry *SM* 80/19, disturbance *A8* 132/
9.
nuste, nute(n) *see* **witen** *v.* (1).
nutteð *pr. 3 pl.* profit by, deserve *SM* 44/
18.
nuðe *adv.* now *HM* 10/23, *SM* 60/15
etc., *SW* 100/28, **nuþe** *SM* 64/32.

ofdrahen *v.* attract *A7* 116/8, 18.
ofdraheð *pr. 3 sg. A7* 112/15.
ofdred *p.p.* afraid *SW* 94/19, **ofdret** *HM*
38/26.

ofearnest *pr. 2 sg.* earn *HM* 10/19.
ofearneð *pr. 3 sg. SW* 94/9.
offearen *v.* frighten *SW* 88/28 *etc.*
offearet *p.p.* afraid *HM* 12/14, 26/12.
offruht *ppl. adj.* frightened *SM* 58/25,
    offruhte *pl. SW* 98/28.
ofgan *v.* win, earn *A7* 114/16, *p.p. A7* 112/
    14.
ofþunchunge *n.* remorse *HM* 22/8.
ofþunchunges *pl.* regrets *HM* 6/21.
ohwider *adv.* anywhere *SW* 86/24.
olhnin *v.* cajole *A8* 134/22.
olhnung *n.* flattery *SM* 50/32.
omidhepes *adv.* in the middle *SM* 60/23.
onde *n.* envy, hatred, malice *HM* 36/15,
    21, *SM* 72/17, *A7* 124/16, 26.
ondfule *adj. wk.* malicious *A7* 124/19,
    ontfule envious *HM* 12/15, malignant
    SM 56/33, *as n.* the envious *A7* 126/37.
onont *prep.* of the same rank as *HM* 8/3,
    concerning *HM* 14/35, in respect of *HM*
    38/22, *SW* 96/20, through *SW* 88/24,
    — **hire** for her own part *A7* 124/33.
onsihðe *n.* sight *SW* 98/19, 100/25, *A8*
    138/4.
ontenden *v.* kindle *A7* 122/11 *etc.*,
    ontende *A7* 122/27. **ontent** *pr. 3 sg.*
    inflames *SM* 72/20. **ontendeð** *imp. pl.*
    SM 74/18. **ontende** *ppl. adj. pl. A7* 124/
    6, *A8* 144/20.
ontfule *see* **ondfule**.
open-heaued *adj.* bareheaded *A8* 142/
    26.
ord *n.* beginning *SM* 58/5.
ordfrume *n.* beginning *SM* 58/4, 80/29.
orhel *n.* pride *SM* 62/4.
otwa *adv.* in two *SM* 60/23, asunder *SM*
    52/5, **atwa** *SM* 62/1.
oþer *adj.* other *HM* 18/6, *A7* 126/35, *A8*
    144/16[1], 146/33, second *HM* 14/14,
    SW 88/8, next *A8* 130/23, **þe** — **half-**
    3er the remaining half of the year *A8*
    130/27, — **monnes** another person's,
    someone else's *A8* 132/11, **oðer** other
    HM 4/17 *etc.*, *SW* 92/29, *A8* 132/9 *etc.*,
    another *A7* 120/11[2], second *SW* 96/35,
    A7 118/17[1], next *SM* 50/4. **oþre** *pl.*
    HM 6/11 *etc.*, *SM* 64/35, *SW* 88/24, *A7*
    116/29, *A8* 130/3 *etc.*, **oðre** *SM* 46/13,
    A7 124/30, *A8* 138/23.
oþer *pron.* (an)other, the other *HM* 22/
    20, 26/36, 30/14, *A8* 142/12 *etc.*, — ...
    — one thing ... another *HM* 16/30–31,

oðer *HM* 6/12 *etc.*, *SM* 52/16 *etc.*, *SW*
    92/16 *etc.*, *A7* 112/36. **oþres** *gen. sg. A7*
    110/24, **hare** — each other's *HM* 24/
    16, **oðres** *SM* 66/16, *SW* 92/17, 19,
    104/9. **oþre** *pl. HM* 10/33 *etc.*, *A7* 118/
    18 *etc.*, *A8* 134/9[1,2] *etc.*, **oðre** *HM* 4/34
    etc., *SW* 100/21. **oþres** *gen. pl. HM* 16/
    18, **oðres** *SW* 104/15.
oðer *conj.* or *HM* 6/22 *etc.*, *SM* 44/16 *etc.*,
    SW 86/24 *etc.*, *A7* 112/1[1,2] *etc.*, *A8* 130/
    14 *etc.*, **oðer** ... **oðer** either ... or *SW*
    86/18–19, *A7* 110/23–24 *etc.*, **oþer**
    HM 28/15, 32, 38/25, *A8* 144/1.
oðerhwet *n.* anything else *A8* 144/29.
oðerhwile *adv.* sometimes *SW* 90/36, *A8*
    132/10, **oðerhwiles** *HM* 30/7, 38/14,
    SM 66/12, *A8* 138/11.
ouer-egede *adj.* over-elaborate *A8* 138/
    34.
ouereorninde *adj.* overflowing *HM* 18/1.
ouer-feble *adj.* very weak *A8* 130/31.
ouerfullet *p.p.* filled to overflowing *HM*
    18/1.
ouergart *n.* arrogance, pride *SM* 60/13,
    62/4.
ouergeað *pr. 3 sg.* surpasses *HM* 20/20,
    transcends *A7* 116/22. **ouergan** *p.p. SM*
    70/19.
ouerguld *p.p.* gilded *SM* 58/11.
ouerhardi *adj.* over-confident *SW* 88/28.
ouerherren *n. pl.* overlords *HM* 26/16.
ouerhohe *n.* arrogance *HM* 38/4, **hauest**
    — **of** despise *HM* 38/17.
ouerstihen *v.* surpass *HM* 12/30.
ouer-swiðe *adv.* excessively *A7* 128/5.
ouerunder *n.* afternoon; **earunder ant** —
    morning and afternoon *A8* 146/29.
ouerwarpen *p.p.* overthrown, destroyed
    HM 32/4.
ouerweieð *pr. 3 sg.* outweighs *A7* 112/10.
ow, ower *see* **3e** *pron.*
owðer *pron.* either *HM* 30/14.

pappes *n. pl.* breasts *HM* 32/3.
parures *n. pl* apparels, decorative panels
    (on vestments) *A8* 138/29.
pilche-clut *n.* scrap of hide *SW* 92/35.
piment *n.* spiced drink *A7* 124/25.
pine *n.* torment, suffering, torture *HM* 22/
    10, *SM* 44/1 *etc.*, *SW* 92/2 *etc.*, *A7* 110/9
    etc., — **ouer** — torment upon torment
    HM 32/9. **pinen** *pl. HM* 40/22, *SW* 90/
    34, 92/36, 102/2.

pineð *pr. 3 sg.* suffers *HM* 34/29, lies in labour *SM* 78/25. **pine** *imp. sg.* torment *SM* 62/24. **pinet** *p.p. A7* 124/18.

pinfule *adj. wk.* painful *SM* 44/23.

pinsunges *n. pl.* mortifications *A7* 110/2.

pinunge *n.* pain; — þrahen labour pains *HM* 32/7.

pitance *n.* pittance, extra dish *A8* 130/21 n.

pliht *n.* danger, trouble; þet were — of for whom it would be undesirable *A8* 140/13.

plohe-speche n. playful speech *SM* 66/21.

plohien *pr. pl. subj.* play *A8* 148/4.

preoue *n.* proof *A7* 128/14.

procunges *n. pl.* goadings *HM* 2/16.

prokie *v.* incite, spur *HM* 42/8. **prokest** *pr. 2 sg. HM* 42/1. **prokieð** *pr. 3 pl. HM* 8/7.

prude *n.* pride *HM* 36/21, 29, 38/4, *SM* 72/3, *SW* 98/3, finery *A8* 138/3.

psalmwruhte *n.* psalm-maker, psalmist *HM* 2/2, **salmwruhte** *A7* 122/7.

punt *pr. 3 sg.* impounds *A8* 134/23.

quoð *see* **cweðeð**.

ra *n.* roe-deer *SM* 48/11.

rad *see* **rit**.

rahte *see* **reache**.

rake *n.* throat, jaws *SM* 62/5.

raketehe *n.* chain *SW* 90/11.

ran *see* **rineð**.

rarinde *pr.p.* howling, roaring *SM* 72/35.

rarunge *n.* roaring *SW* 92/31.

reache *v.* reach, extend *SM* 64/15. **rahte** *pa. 3 sg. SM* 60/19.

read *n.* advice *HM* 2/20 *etc.*, *SM* 52/24 *etc.*, *A8* 134/30, 136/11, 140/14. **reades** *pl.* recommendations *HM* 16/33, designs *SW* 102/36.

reade *pr. 1 sg.* advise *HM* 16/30, *SM* 52/35. **read** *pr. 3 sg. HM* 8/10, **readeð** *SW* 96/16, **reat** *HM* 16/31, 18/2. **reade** *pr. sg. subj. SW* 94/16, *A8* 134/19. **readde** *pa. 3 sg. HM* 34/23.

readliche *adv.* soon, swiftly, readily *A8* 140/10, **redliche** *SM* 60/21, 28, 62/5.

readwisest *adj. superl.* most crafty *SM* 64/33.

reasde *pa. 3 sg.* rushed *SM* 60/17.

reat *pr. 3 sg. see* **reade**.

reat *pa. 3 sg.* dragged *SM* 56/18.

readere *adv.* sooner *A7* 110/18.

reauers *n. pl.* robbers *HM* 26/16.

reauin *v.* seize, rob *A7* 118/38, deprive of *A8* 132/16, 19. **reaueð** *pr. 3 sg. HM* 26/25. **reauede** *pa. 3 sg. SM* 66/1.

reccheð *pr. 3 sg.* travels, pursues *SM* 58/37.

reden *v.* read *A8* 146/7. **redeð** *pr. 3 sg. SM* 78/21. **redeð** *pr. 2 pl. A8* 148/10, 14, *imp. pl. A8* 148/9. **ired** *p.p. SW* 108/14, *A8* 148/22, **iredd** *SM* 44/11.

redliche *see* **readliche**.

rehest *adj. superl.* fiercest *SM* 64/33.

religiun *n.* spiritual observances *A8* 146/31, **of** — (person) in orders, a religious *A8* 138/25. **religiuns** *pl.* religious orders, ways of life *A7* 112/5, 126/29.

remden *pa. 3 pl.* wept, cried out *SM* 52/26, 74/21.

remunge *n.* wailing *SW* 92/7.

reng *n.* rank *HM* 18/23.

rentes *n. pl.* revenue (from property); — isette fixed income *A8* 132/33.

reodien *v.* strive, make an effort *SW* 90/25.

reowfule *adj. wk.* merciful *SM* 54/18.

reowfulnesse *n.* pity, compassion *HM* 36/14.

reowliche *adj. wk.* dreadful *SM* 62/5.

reowliche *adv.* dreadfully *SM* 52/31, **reuliche** miserably *SM* 48/32.

reowðe *n.* pity, pitiful sight *HM* 14/24, compassion *SM* 52/26, **rewðe** *SM* 52/23, 74/22.

reowðful *adj.* pitiable *SW* 92/29. **reowðfule** *wk. A7* 124/17.

reschte *pa. 3 sg.* crackled *SM* 74/21.

reue *n.* governor *SM* 52/23 *etc.* **reues** *gen. sg. SM* 74/4. **reuene** *gen. pl. SM* 74/25.

reufulliche *adv.* wretchedly *SM* 48/29.

reuliche *see* **reowliche**.

rewðe *see* **reowðe**.

riche *n.* kingdom *HM* 26/26.

richedom *n.* riches, wealth *HM* 2/19, 26/33.

richesce *n.* riches *HM* 26/24.

riht n. right *SW* 96/28[1], 98/1. **rihte** *dat. sg. HM* 10/20, *SW* 98/2.

riht *adj.* true *HM* 16/35, right *SM* 62/36, 82/11, *SW* 100/8, correct, just *SW* 96/30, 98/3, 106/12, *A8* 146/15, 31. **rihte** *wk. HM* 28/31, *SM* 46/14, **wel** — only right *SW* 98/22.

riht *adv.* truly, properly, well *HM* 4/19, 6/ 31, *SM* 80/21, *SW* 96/28², *A7* 128/ 5, 17, directly *SW* 98/26, — **noht** nothing at all *SM* 54/9.

rihten *v.* guide, direct *A8* 140/14. **rihte** *pr. sg. subj.* SW 86/13, 94/15, —**up** should raise up *A8* 144/7. **rihte** *pa. 3 sg.* *SM* 78/34. **iriht** *p.p.*; — **up** made erect *HM* 22/25.

rihtwise *adj. wk.* righteous *SW* 96/32, *pl.* *SM* 72/12, 17, *as n. pl.* the righteous *SM* 52/34, 66/6.

rihtwisnesse *n.* justice *HM* 36/11, (*personif.*) Justice *SW* 88/9 *etc.*

rikenin *v.* describe *SW* 90/29. **irikenet** *p.p. HM* 28/33.

rineð *pr. 3 sg.* touches *A7* 126/30. *pr. sg. subj.* **rine** *A7* 126/33. **rin** *imp. sg. A7* 126/38. **ran** *pa. 3 sg. SM* 78/34.

rinunge *n.* touch *A7* 126/35.

rit *pr. 3 sg.* rides *HM* 12/9. **rad** *pa. 3 sg.* went, fell *SM* 72/35.

riue *adj.* plentiful *HM* 6/25.

riueð *pr. 3 sg.* sews, trims *A8* 138/33. **riue** *pr. sg. subj. A8* 138/33.

riuunges *n. pl.* trimmings *A8* 138/33.

riwle *n.* rule, religious rule A7 128/32, 34, *A8* 130/5 *etc.* **riwlen** *pl. A8* 130/2.

riwleð *pr. 3 sg.* rules *A7* 128/32.

rixleð *pr. 3 sg.* rules *HM* 8/21, *SM* 76/20, *SW* 100/9, 108/12.

ro *n.* rest *SM* 78/8.

rode-taken *n.* sign of the cross *SM* 60/21.

rotunge *n.* rotting, corruption *HM* 10/34.

rueð *pr. 3 sg.* stands on end *SW* 94/5.

rug *n.* back *HM* 14/32. **rugge** *dat. sg.* **to** — (clothes) to wear *A8* 136/9.

ruglunge *adv.* backwards *SM* 72/35.

ruhe *adj. wk.* rough *SM* 62/36.

rukelin *v.* heap *A7* 126/4.

rune *n.* (1) torrent *SM* 54/30, course *SM* 58/37.

runes *n.* (2) *pl.* secrets *SW* 102/36.

sahe *n.* something said; **i** — in the telling *HM* 34/10, — **þet ich segge** what I say *SM* 58/1. **sahen** *pl.* speeches *SW* 98/5.

sahede *pa. 3 sg.* cut *SM* 82/7.

sahtnesse *n.* concord *A8* 144/10.

salde *pa. 3 sg.* sold *A7* 120/26.

salmwruhte *see* **psalmwruhte.**

saluz *n. pl.* greetings *A7* 112/31.

salui *pr. 1 sg.* heal *SM* 80/8. **salue** *imp.* *sg. SM* 52/18, 82/10.

samblant *see* **semblant.**

sar *n.* pain, injury, misery *HM* 24/14 *etc.*, *SM* 52/18 *etc.*

sar *adj.* severe, intense, painful *HM* 28/7, 32/1. **sare** *wk. A7* 124/23, **sore** *HM* 32/8. **sarre** *comp. HM* 24/20.

sare *adv.* sorely, severely *HM* 6/19 *etc.*, painfully *SM* 62/26, 72/25. **sarre** *comp.* more intensely *HM* 12/14.

sariliche *adj. wk.* dreadful *SM* 60/18.

sariliche *adv.* wretchedly *HM* 4/20, *SM* 62/24.

sarre *see* **sar** *adj., adv.*

sauurure *adj. comp.* more palatable *HM* 24/25.

sawle *n.* soul; **sawulene** *gen. pl.* souls *SM* 52/35.

sawter *n.* Psalter *HM* 2/2.

schad *n.* discrimination *SW* 96/15, **tweire** — discrimination between two things *HM* 22/16.

schal *pr. 1 sg.* shall, must *HM* 40/35, *SM* 70/15, *A7* 114/14. **schalt** *pr. 2 sg. HM* 6/6 *etc.*, *SM* 50/26 *etc.*, *A7* 116/36 *etc.*, **schaltu** *SW* 106/15. **schal** *pr. 3 sg. HM* 4/21 *etc.*, *SM* 46/27 *etc.*, *SW* 86/21 *etc.*, *A7* 112/8 *etc.*, *A8* 132/16 *etc.* **schulen** *pr. 1 pl. SW* 106/11, *pr. 2 pl. A7* 122/27, *A8* 130/24 *etc.*, **schule** *A7* 124/2, 34, 35, *A8* 130/11 *etc.*, **schulen** *pr. 3 pl. HM* 18/ 20^{1,2} *etc.*, *SM* 44/26 *etc.*, *SW* 96/17, 98/ 30, 104/24, *A7* 112/9 *etc.*, *A8* 132/32, 142/27, **schule** *HM* 6/1, 30/32. **schule** *pr. sg. subj. HM* 34/1, *SM* 48/9, *A7* 120/ 17. **schuldest** *pa. 2 sg. subj. HM* 22/26. **schulde** *pa. 1, 3 sg. subj. HM* 22/20, 28/ 33, *SM* 56/6 *etc.*, *A8* 140/6. **schulden** *pa. pl. subj. A7* 114/31, *A8* 130/1, **schulde** *SW* 94/33.

schan *pa. 3 sg.* shone *SM* 46/23.

schapieð *imp. pl.* cut (out) *A8* 138/20.

schawere *n.* mirror *SW* 100/4.

schawi *pr. pl. subj.* let (us) show *HM* 20/30.

schefte *n. gen. pl.* created things, creatures *SM* 62/18.

schendest *pr. 2 sg.* harm, destroy *SM* 56/ 5. **schent** *pr. 3 sg.* abuses *HM* 28/4. **schende** *pa. 3 sg. A8* 138/2. **ischend** *p.p.* disgraced *SM* 68/24.

schendlac *n.* dishonour, shame *HM* 14/ 19, *SW* 92/32.

schene *adj.* shining *HM* 16/19, 20/8, *SW* 100/4, radiant *SM* 76/17, *SW* 102/8, *A7* 120/26, beautiful *SM* 50/7. **schenre** *comp. HM* 36/7, *SW* 102/27.

schenre *adv. comp.* more brightly *HM* 20/11, *SM* 64/36, 84/6.

schentfulliche *adv.* shamefully *A7* 122/1.

scheome *adj.* shameful *HM* 32/11², *A7* 114/12.

scheomeliche *adv.* shamefully *HM* 24/5 *etc.*

scheop *see* **schuptest**.

scher *pa. 3 sg.* sheared *SM* 82/6.

schilinde *pr.p.* resounding, ringing *SM* 76/23.

schilt *pr. 3 sg.* protects *A7* 114/35. **schilde** *pr. sg. subj. HM* 28/15, *pa. 3 sg. SW* 100/4.

schir *adj.* pure *A7* 110/5 *etc.*

schireð *pr. 3 sg.* purifies *A7* 110/3.

schireue *n.* governor of a district or city, high official *SM* 46/20, 48/9.

schirnesse *n.* purity *A7* 112/4, 126/28.

schraden *n. pl.* scraps *A8* 132/31.

schrift *n.* confession *HM* 12/12, 18/22, *SM* 68/21, *SW* 90/15, **under** — in a state of penitence *HM* 22/11. **schrifte** *dat. sg. SM* 68/19, 23. **schriftes** *gen. sg.* confessor *A8* 136/14, 17, 138/22.

schriuen *pr. pl. subj.* make confession *A8* 144/21.

schruden *v.* clothe *A8* 132/22, 140/2.

schrudes *n. pl.* garments *SM* 76/21.

schucke *n.* demon *HM* 36/36, *SM* 56/7, 72/33. **schuckes** *gen. sg. SM* 48/9, **schucke** *SM* 58/20.

schulde(n), schuldest *see* **schal**.

schuldi *adj.* guilty; — **towart Godd** guilty before God *HM* 30/25.

schule(n) *see* **schal**.

schunien *v.* avoid *HM* 30/22, *SW* 96/16, be shunned *SW* 106/21.

schuppent *n.* creator *SM* 62/19.

schuptest *pa. 2 sg.* created *SM* 78/14. **scheop** *pa. 3 sg. HM* 8/16, 17. **ischepen** *p.p. SM* 78/14.

schurteð *imp. pl.* entertain *A8* 140/23.

scoren *n. pl.* tallies *A8* 134/33.

se *adv.* so, as such a *HM* 2/13¹⁺², *etc.*, *SM* 50/18¹⁺² *etc.*, *SW* 86/19 *etc.*, *A7* 112/22 *etc.*, *A8* 140/1¹, 148/23, 26, —...**as** as ...as *HM* 10/17, 12/29, 18/10, *SM* 62/10, —...—as...so *HM* 6/17–18 *etc.*

se *adv. rel., conj.* as *HM* 12/14¹, *A8* 138/17, 140/1², **sone** — as soon as *HM* 14/18 *etc.*, *SM* 48/20, 78/25, *A7* 118/3, —... —...the...the; — **lengre** — **mare** in ever-increasing measure *A8* 144/26.

sea-dingle *n.* abyss of the sea *SW* 102/37.

sechen *v.* seek *SW* 88/3, **seche** come, advance *SM* 72/8. **seche** *pr. 1 sg.*; — **upon** attack *SM* 66/18. **secheð** *pr. 3 sg. HM* 14/14. **secheð** *pr. 3 pl.* seek *A7* 114/14. **seche** *pr. sg. subj. SW* 88/33. **sechinde** *pr.p. SW* 94/25. **isoht** *p.p. SM* 80/1.

seggen *v.* say, speak, tell *HM* 2/12, 22/13, 33, *SM* 50/5 *etc.*, *A7* 120/18 *etc.*, **beo to** — means *HM* 2/6, **segge** *A7* 128/6. **segge** *pr. 1 sg. SM* 58/1, *A7* 110/33, 122/30, *A8* 130/2, 3. **seist** *pr. 2 sg. HM* 24/2, 10, *SW* 102/18, *A7* 116/4, 120/16, 128/11. **seið** *pr. 3 sg. HM* 2/3 *etc.*, *SW* 86/5 *etc.*, *A7* 110/8 *etc.*, *A8* 132/19 *etc.* **seggen** *pr. pl. subj. SM* 68/30, *A8* 130/4 *etc.* **sei** *imp. sg. HM* 22/1, *SM* 70/24, 27, *SW* 102/19. **seide** *pa. 1 sg. HM* 4/20, 20/5, 26, *SW* 94/13, 106/17¹⁺², *A7* 124/10, 126/13, *A8* 130/1, 142/1. **seidest** *pa. 2 sg. HM* 26/23. **seide** *pa. 3 sg. HM* 16/27, 40/6, *SM* 48/24 *etc.*, *SW* 90/6, 102/32, 104/18, *A7* 110/12 *etc.* **seiden** *pa. 1 pl. A7* 126/28, *pa. 3 pl. SM* 52/27. **iseid** *p.p. HM* 12/7, 24/1, 26/23, *SM* 76/14, *SW* 102/19, 104/34, 106/2, *A7* 110/31, 112/20, *A8* 130/8 *etc.*

seh, sehe(n) *see* **seon**.

seheliche *adj. pl.* visible *SM* 78/17, *as n. SM* 62/18.

seim *n.* animal fat *A8* 130/30.

sel *adj.* blessed *HM* 42/25.

selcuðe *adj.* wondrous *SM* 74/11.

seldene *adv.* rarely *A8* 148/1.

selhðe *n.* happiness, blessedness *HM* 34/17, 40/29, 42/26, *SM* 72/22, 84/7, *A7* 120/24, 34. **selhðen** *pl.* joys *SM* 56/12.

seli *adj.* blessed, innocent *HM* 4/21 *etc.*, *SM* 44/28 *etc.*, *as n. pl. SW* 102/19. **selie** *pl. HM* 26/3, 28/17.

selthwenne *adv.* seldom *A8* 146/14.

seltscene *adj.* rare *HM* 24/11.

semblant *n.* appearance *A8* 132/31, sign *HM* 28/9, manner *HM* 36/13, *SW* 86/18, *A8* 134/15, **samblant** *SM* 52/19.

seme *pr. sg. subj.* appear *SM* 52/19.
semde *pa. 3 sg. SM* 58/17, 64/14.
semden *pa. 3 pl.*; — of had the
appearance of *SM* 58/12.
semliche *adj. wk.* comely *SM* 50/6.
semliche *adv.* becomingly *SM* 76/22.
seon *v.* see, look at *SW* 92/30, 102/32,
104/10, seo *SM* 74/3. sist *pr. 2 sg. A8*
138/6. sið *pr. 3 sg. HM* 12/19 *etc.*, *SM*
56/3, *A8* 140/5, 144/11. seoð *pr. 1 pl.*
SM 52/29, 68/11, *pr. 3 pl. HM* 6/10,
14/25, *SW* 100/29 *etc.*, *A8* 136/6, soð
SM 76/5. seo *pr. sg. subj. A7* 116/15, *A8*
142/26. seh *pa. 1 sg. SW* 100/10, 17,
104/35, *pa. 3 sg. SM* 46/21, 60/26, 30.
sehen *pa. 3 pl. SM* 58/10, 74/22. sehe
pa. sg. subj. HM 14/25, *SM* 64/14, *SW*
98/34, *A8* 142/23.
seoðen *adv.* then, afterwards *SW* 98/18.
seoue *num.* seven *A8* 130/9. seoueðe
ord. num. seventh *SM* 56/16, *SW* 102/
23.
seouesiðe *adv.* seven times *HM* 36/6.
set, seten *see* sitten.
sete *imp. sg.* set *A7* 120/17.
setnesse *n.* order, class *SW* 102/19.
sicles *n. pl.* shekels *A7* 120/27.
siheð *pr. 3 sg.* proceeds; — of issues from
HM 42/25. sihen *pa. 3 pl.* made their
way, ascended *SM* 82/18.
sihðe *n.* sight *HM* 14/12, 40/15, *SM* 56/
2, 5, 68/35, *SW* 86/15 *etc.*, *A7* 110/19,
22, 126/24, *A8* 130/8, 138/10, vision
HM 2/27, *SW* 102/31. sihðen *pl. SM*
72/7.
siken *v.* lament, sigh for *HM* 24/16.
siker *adj.* sure, secure *SM* 66/7, *SW* 106/
8, trustworthy *A8* 142/16, — of secure
against *SW* 96/19. sikere *pl. SW* 92/15,
104/31. sikerure *comp. pl.* the more
assured *SM* 66/17.
sikere *adv.* certainly *HM* 38/29.
sikerlec *n.* security *SM* 66/18.
sikerliche *adv.* certainly *HM* 6/1, 8/23,
SW 102/16, *A8* 142/3, in safety *SW* 96/
10, with assurance *A7* 122/30.
sikernesse *n.* security *HM* 4/28, *SW* 96/
27, 102/23.
sist *see* seon.
sitten *v.* sit; last *HM* 42/26. sit *pr. 3 sg.*
suits, pleases *HM* 6/10, *A7* 110/27,
presses on *SM* 72/25. sitte *pr. sg. subj.*
HM 4/27, sitten *pr. pl. subj.* suit, fit *SM*

76/22. sittende *pr.p.* seated *SW* 102/
17. set *pa. 3 sg.* sat *SM* 60/26, perched
SM 64/15, was placed *A7* 114/30.
seten *pa. 3 pl. SM* 82/12.
sið *n.* course of action *HM* 6/23. siðe *pl.*
times *SW* 92/5, 94/12, 106/6, siðen
A8 130/12, 140/18, ofte — often *A8*
136/2.
sið *v. see* seon
skile *n.* reason *A8* 142/2.
sleað *pr. 3 sg.* kills *HM* 26/17. slea *pr. sg.*
subj. SM 64/8. sloh *pa. 3 sg. A7* 120/29.
islein *p.p. SM* 62/3, 28, *SW* 92/24, *A7*
114/19.
sleheste *adj. superl.* most cunning *SM* 62/
28.
sloh *see* sleað.
smat *pa. 3 sg.* struck *SM* 82/5, — adun
hire cneon fell on her knees *SM* 58/27.
smeallunge *n.* (sense of) smell *SW* 86/16,
smellunge *HM* 12/1.
smeatest *adj. superl.* purest, most refined
SM 62/17.
smeche *n. gen. pl.* smoke, vapour *SM* 58/
16, *SW* 90/32.
smechunge *n.* (sense of) taste *HM* 12/1,
SW 86/16.
smellunge *see* smeallunge.
smirles *n.* ointment *HM* 10/33.
snercte *pa. 3 sg.* became scorched *SM* 74/
20.
snikeð *pr. 3 pl.* creep, crawl *SW* 92/4.
some *n.* unity *A8* 144/10.
somet *adv.* together *HM* 38/5, *SM* 68/27,
A7 112/36, 120/31, *A8* 144/19.
sometreadliche *adv.* with a single voice,
unanimously *SW* 86/20.
somnunge *n.* union, intercourse *HM* 26/
24, sompnunge *HM* 8/14, 28/8.
sompnin *pr. pl. subj.* meet together *SM*
68/29.
sonde *n.* messenger *SM* 48/8, 54/22, *SW*
88/27 *etc.* sondes *gen. sg. SW* 106/18.
sonden *pl. SW* 106/30, 108/1, *A7* 112/
28, 36.
sore *see* sar *adj.*
sorhe *n.* sorrow, misery, suffering *HM* 24/
14 *etc.*, *SM* 52/34, 54/10, *SW* 90/28.
sorhen *pl.* pains *SM* 56/10.
sorhin *v.* grieve *HM* 24/16, 26/15.
sorheð *pr. 3 sg. HM* 30/15.
sotliche *adv.* foolishly *SM* 68/25.
sotschipe *n.* foolishness *A8* 140/28.

soð *n.* truth *HM* 6/31, 24/2, *SW* 96/18, 98/36, 106/2. soðe *dat. sg.*; to — for certain *A7* 114/14.

soð *adj.* true *HM* 12/12 *etc.*, *SM* 74/12, *SW* 90/15 *etc.* soðe *wk. HM* 26/5, *A7* 122/9, 31, *dat. sg. HM* 4/19.

soð *v. see* seon.

soð-cnawes *adj.* honest; beo — admit the truth *HM* 22/2.

soðes *adv.* certainly *HM* 14/33.

soðliche *adv.* truly *HM* 6/30, *SM* 82/32.

spealie *v.* describe *SW* 104/8. spealeð *pr. 3 sg.* means *A7* 122/23.   ₁

spearien *v.* spare, save *A8* 132/30, 134/4.

speatewile *adj.* disgusting, hideous *HM* 22/4, *SM* 58/15, 64/13. speatewilre *comp. HM* 22/5.

speatewilliche *adv.* horribly, in an uncouth way *SM* 64/26.

spechen *n. pl.* talk, utterances *A8* 142/22.

spedest *pr. 2 sg.* succeed *SM* 56/9, 74/29. spede *pr. sg. subj. HM* 22/32.

sperclede *pa. 3 sg.* sparkled *SM* 58/15.

spillest *pr. 2 sg.* waste; þu — þi hwile you are wasting your time *SM* 56/8.

spitelsteaf *n.* (small) spade *A7* 110/15.

spruteð *pr. 3 sg.* grows *HM* 10/1, *pr. 3 pl. A8* 132/37.

spushad *n.* marriage *A7* 120/9.

sputte *pr. 1 sg.* incite *SM* 66/22.

stal *n.* position *HM* 4/12, steal place *SW* 102/29.

stale *n.* stealth *SW* 90/7.

stamin *n.* undergarment *A8* 136/11.

steah *see* stihen.

steal *see* stal.

stealewurðe *adj.* valiant, stalwart *SM* 70/8, 28.

steape *adj. dat. sg.* bright; — bihaldunge staring intensely *SM* 66/21. steappre *comp. pl. SM* 58/13.

steareden *pa. 3 pl.* shone *SM* 58/13.

steauene *n.* voice *SM* 70/33, steuene *SM* 76/23 *etc.*, *SW* 94/6, *A8* 132/18. steauene *gen. pl. SM* 78/35.

steoresmon *n.* steersman *SM* 78/16.

steorue *n.* pestilent creature *SM* 64/1, 70/32, *gen. pl. SM* 72/32.

steoruen *v.* die *SM* 62/32.

sterclukest *adv. superl.* most strongly *SM* 66/34.

steuene *see* steauene.

stewen *v.* restrain *SM* 68/26. stew *imp. sg.*

SM 52/24, — þe *refl.* be quiet *SM* 70/24, steu *SM* 70/32.

sti *n.* way, path *SW* 96/25.

stiche *n.* pain *HM* 32/9. stiches *pl.* stitches *HM* 32/1. stiche *gen. pl. HM* 30/7.

sticheð *pr. 3 sg.* afflicts *HM* 6/35.

stihen *v.* ascend *SM* 72/18. stiheð *pr. 3 sg. HM* 4/5, rises *SM* 64/9. stih *imp. sg. SM* 76/23. steah *pa. 3 sg. SM* 44/2, 82/8. stihen *pa. 3 pl. SM* 76/31, stuhen *SM* 82/19. istihe *p.p.* risen *HM* 12/15, 42/24, istihen *A7* 122/9.

stikelunge *adv.* intently *HM* 14/12.

stikinde *pr.p.* stabbing *HM* 32/9.

stilðe *n.* silence *HM* 36/13.

stockes *n. pl.* tree-trunks, logs; of stanes ant of — of stone and wood *SM* 44/9.

strac *see* strikeð.

straf *pa. 3 sg.* competed *A8* 120/28.

strahte *pa. 3 sg.*; — him *refl.* made his way *SM* 58/21. strahte *ppl. adj. wk.* stretched; — hond opened hand, palm *SM* 78/15.

streapeles *n. pl.* strips of cloth binding lower part of leg *A8* 136/26.

strengeluker *adv. comp.* more strongly *HM* 12/27.

strengre *adj. comp.* stronger *SM* 64/5, strengest *superl. HM* 30/7.

strengðe *n.* strength; don lutel — of attach little importance to *A7* 128/35. strengðen *n. pl.* powers *SM* 96/3.

streon *n.* offspring *HM* 2/20 *etc.*

streoneð *pr. 3 sg.* begets *HM* 36/10, 22, begets (children) *HM* 34/29. streonede *pa. 3 sg. HM* 8/11, 38/1.

streonunge *n.* begetting, engendering *HM* 30/5, 36/29.

strikeð *pr. 3 pl.* run, flow *HM* 32/3. strac *pa. 3 sg.* went *SM* 62/2, flowed *SM* 52/22. striken *pa. 3 pl. SM* 74/2.

stucche *n.* piece, section *A8* 146/7. stucchen *pl. A8* 130/10.

stude *n.* place *HM* 14/22 *etc.*, *SM* 58/19, 72/18, 80/12, *SW* 94/3, *A7* 116/14, *A8* 144/23, i — instead (of) *HM* 20/1, 28/29, in euch — in every case *SW* 88/18, i nan — nowhere *SM* 44/12. studen *pl. SW* 100/11.

studegið *pr. 3 pl.* halt *SM* 60/1.

stuhen *see* stihen.

stunde *n.* time *SW* 106/20, **umbe** — sometimes *HM* 4/31, 32/21, after a time *SM* 46/18, **vmben ane** — after a while *SW* 98/12, **eauer umbe** — always *HM* 30/7.

stureð *pr. 3 sg.* moves *A8* 140/10.

sturieð *pr. 3 pl. SM* 60/1, *imp. pl. A7* 124/12. **sturede** *pa. 3 sg. SM* 58/21, 62/2.

stutteð *pr. 3 pl.* stop, cease *SM* 60/1. **stute** *imp. sg. SM* 52/24 *etc.* **stutte** *pa. 3 sg. SM* 80/17.

sucurs *n.* help *A7* 114/12, — **of liueneð** provisions *A7* 112/37.

suhinde *pr. p.* sharp, cutting *A8* 146/18.

sulen *v.* defile *SM* 70/12. **suleð** *pr. 3 sg. HM* 12/35, 30/25, *A7* 118/18. **isuled** *p. p. SM* 46/35, **isulet** *A7* 118/12.

sulh *n.* plough *A7* 110/15.

sulli *adj.* wonderful *HM* 16/11.

sulliche *adj. wk.* wondrous *SM* 72/26.

sum *adj.* some *SM* 66/36, *A7* 126/38, *A8* 132/3 *etc.* **summes** *gen.*; — **weies** to some extent *HM* 8/15, — **weis** *SW* 96/1, 100/7, in some way *SM* 70/11. **summe** *pl. A8* 136/30.

sum *pron.* some, someone, one *HM* 30/11, *SM* 64/30, *SW* 88/26, *A8* 136/31, 138/33. **summe** *pl. SM* 52/27, *SW* 86/14[1,2].

sumchearre *adv.* sometimes *A8* 148/26, at some time, once *A7* 126/38, **sumchere** *HM* 10/1.

sumdel *adv.* to some extent *SM* 70/10, *SW* 94/11, 98/28, 102/24.

sumhweat *pron.* something *A7* 120/11, **sumhwet** *SW* 98/34, something of *SW* 102/19.

sumhwile *adv.* formerly *HM* 2/26, *A7* 114/25, *A8* 134/31.

sunderlepes *adv.* separately *SW* 102/19, 104/11.

sunderliche *adv.* separately *SW* 100/24, 104/13, 17.

sunegilt *n.* (female) sinner *HM* 38/26.

sunegin *v.* sin *SW* 96/18. **sungið** *pr. 3 pl. A8* 136/30.

surpliz *n.* white linen tunic *A8* 138/15, surplice *A8* 138/33.

sut *n.* grief, sorrow *HM* 32/34.

suteli *pr. sg. subj.* show, be revealed *SM* 52/19.

sutelliche *adv.* clearly *HM* 20/14.

suti *adj.* filthy *HM* 30/26, *SM* 66/27, 68/13.

swa *adv.* so, in this way *HM* 6/1 *etc.*, *SM* 46/16 *etc.*, *SW* 92/28 *etc.*, *A7* 110/21 *etc.*, *A8* 136/12 *etc.*, — **ȝef** if *SM* 44/17, — **þet** so that *HM* 4/22, 24/18, 26/35, *SM* 44/27 *etc.*, *A7* 126/23, *A8* 146/31, — **lengre** — **leuere** the longer the dearer *SM* 46/7.

swartede *pa. 3 sg.* blackened *SM* 74/20.

sweameð *pr. 3 sg.* grieves *HM* 30/16, *pr. 3 pl. A7* 124/27. **isweamet** *p. p. HM* 14/25.

swel *n.* swelling *HM* 30/34.

swelten *v.* suffer *SM* 54/10, perish *SM* 56/1. **swelteð** *pr. 3 sg. SM* 62/12.

swenchest *pr. 2 sg.* suffer *HM* 32/10, — **þe** *refl.* take trouble *SM* 50/31, 74/29. **iswenchet** *ppl. adj.* having taken trouble *A8* 134/4.

swengde *pa. 3 sg.* tossed *SM* 60/19.

swenges *n. pl.* strokes, tricks *SM* 66/29, 68/27.

sweoke *n.* traitor *HM* 40/27, *A8* 144/11.

swerie *pr. 1 sg.* swear, make an oath *SM* 80/2. **swerieð** *pr. 3 pl. SW* 86/20.

swete *adj. as n.* sweetness *HM* 6/32, 24/21.

swetture *adj. comp.* sweeter *HM* 24/25.

swic *see* **swike**.

swiftschipe *n.* swiftness *A7* 120/28.

swike *pr. subj. sg.* cease, renounce *SM* 50/24. **swic** *imp. sg. SM* 64/1.

swikel *adj.* treacherous *HM* 2/20. **swikele** *wk. SM* 64/2, *pl. HM* 24/34, *SM* 66/29.

swikelliche *adv.* treacherously *HM* 34/25.

swinc *n.* work, labour *SM* 64/29, *SW* 102/28, *A7* 124/21 *etc.*, *A8* 140/1. **swinkes** *pl. A7* 110/2.

swinken *v.* labour *A8* 140/28. **swinkeð** *pr. 3 sg. HM* 34/29, *pr. 3 pl. HM* 26/14. **swonc** *pa. 3 sg. A8* 148/23. **iswunken** *p. p. A7* 124/21.

swire *n.* neck *SM* 58/17 *etc.*, *A7* 118/1.

swireuorð *adv.* headlong *HM* 20/28.

swiðe *adv.* very *HM* 4/11 *etc.*, *SM* 44/25 *etc.*, *SW* 96/22 *etc.*, *A7* 114/4 *etc.*, much, greatly *HM* 10/31, 28/27, 36/28, *SM* 60/13, *SW* 88/29, *A7* 112/35, quickly *SM* 46/24 *etc.* **swiþe** *SM* 50/31. **swiðere** *comp. SW* 92/19, **swiðre** *HM* 34/10.

swonc *see* **swinken**.

swote *adj.* sweet, pleasant, gentle *HM* 10/33, 26/4, *SM* 50/20, 62/8, *SW* 102/14,

31, *A7* 110/5, *A8* 136/27. **swote** *pl. HM*
18/28. **swottre** *comp. SM* 62/8. **swotest**
superl. SM 50/19, 62/18, 78/35, *A7*
120/6.
swoteliche *adv.* tenderly *HM* 36/6, *A7*
114/4.
swuch *adj.* such (a) *HM* 4/12 *etc.*, *SM* 56/
33, 72/7, *SW* 94/8, 100/28, *A7* 116/26
etc., *A8* 136/1 *etc.*, a — such a *HM* 18/
13, *SW* 92/1, *A7* 126/33, **al** — just the
same *HM* 10/5, 40/32, **allunge** — as
completely like *HM* 40/30, **i — stude** in
such a place *A7* 116/14. **swucche** *pl.*
SW 96/33, *A7* 110/13, *A8* 134/11.
swucches *pron. gen. pl.* of such things
HM 34/14.
sy *n.* prosperity *HM* 34/17, *SM* 84/7.

tac *imp. sg.* take; — **þe** *refl.* commit
yourself *HM* 6/2. **toc** *pa. 3 sg. SM* 62/
35, 82/26. **token** *pa. 3 pl. HM* 20/2.
itake *p.p. HM* 4/18.
tadden *n. pl.* toads *SW* 92/3.
tah *see* **þah** *adv.* and *conj.*
tahte *pa. 3 sg.* directed *A8* 138/26.
taken *n.* sign *SM* 56/18, 60/17.
talde(n) *see* **tellen**.
tale *n.* talk; — **bimong alle** the talk of
everyone *HM* 30/12, conversation *A8*
142/9, news *SW* 106/18, 21, story *A7*
112/32. **talen** *pl.* stories *A8* 140/23,
142/21, **wið — tealen** speak at length
SM 72/5.
taueles *n. pl.* narrow lace borders *A8* 138/
32.
te *see* **þe** *def. art.*, *adv. demons.*, *pron.*
demons. masc., **þu** *pron.*
te *prep.* (*unstressed form of* to) to *HM* 2/25
etc., *SM* 72/30, 78/10, 80/25, *SW* 86/7
etc., *A7* 112/31 *etc.*, *A8* 130/2 *etc.*
tealen *v.* tell *SM* 72/5.
team *n.* children, offspring *HM* 36/17, 23.
teames *pl. HM* 30/3, 36/9. **teame** *gen.*
pl. HM 36/25.
tearmes *see* **terme**.
teke *prep.* besides, as well as *HM* 20/32 *etc.*
tellen *v.* count, reckon, tell, speak *HM* 20/
13, *SM* 56/2, *SW* 88/31 *etc.*, **telle** *SM*
72/5. **telest** *pr. 2 sg. HM* 38/16. **teleð**
pr. 3 sg. A7 116/23, 128/23, **telleð** *SW*
106/21. **telle** *pr. sg. subj. A8* 134/11.
tele *imp. sg. HM* 38/19, *SW* 90/21, 98/
34. **talde** *pa. 3 sg. SW* 92/22, 98/28, *A7*

114/7. **talden** *pa. 3 pl.*; **lihtliche** — to
held of little account *SW* 102/2. **itald**
p.p. **wiðuten** — not counting *SM* 76/
28.
teluken *v.* pull to pieces, tear asunder *SM*
54/6. **tolec** *pa. 3 sg. SM* 54/29. **toloken**
p.p. SM 52/34, 56/1, **toluken** *SM* 52/
29, 54/36.
temen *v.* conceive, bear children *HM* 28/
34, 36/8. **temest** *pr. 2 sg. HM* 36/23 *etc.*
temeð *pr. 3 sg. HM* 34/29, 38/2.
temeð *pr. 3 pl. HM* 30/3, 36/35. **temi**
pr. sg. subj. HM 36/29.
ten *see* **þe** *def. art.*, **þen** *conj.*
tendre *adj.* loving; — of **cun** attached to
one's family *A8* 138/24.
tendreð *pr. 3 sg.* becomes inflamed *HM*
28/7.
tene *num.* ten *HM* 20/25, *A8* 140/29.
tenne *see* **þenne** *adv.* (1).
teo *see* **þeo** *pron. demons. pl.*
teone *n.* anger, chagrin, trouble *HM* 12/
27, 24/22, 28/7, *SM* 72/19, *A8* 146/5.
teonen *pl. HM* 4/30.
teonið *pr. 3 pl.* vex *HM* 28/11.
teos *see* **þis** *adj. demons.*
ter *see* **þer** *adv. demons.*
terme *n.* time *A8* 130/23. **tearmes** *pl. A8*
130/22.
terof, terteken, terwið *see* **þer** *adv.*
demons.
tes *see* **þis** *adj. demons.*
tet *see* **þe** *def. art.*, **þet** *adj. demons.*
teuelin *v.*; — of discuss *SM* 66/15.
ti *see* **þu**.
ticki *v.* play games of 'touch' *A8* 148/5 n.
tide *n.* hour *SM* 74/7.
tide *pr. sg. subj.* happen to *A8* 146/2.
tiffunge *n.* adornment *A8* 138/2, 142/7.
tilie *v.* cultivate *A7* 110/14. **tilieð** *pr. 3 pl.*
A8 132/32. **tilede** *pa. 3 sg.* — efter
cultivated *A7* 124/22.
timeð *pr. 3 sg.* happens *HM* 40/25.
tin(e), tines *see* **þu**.
tintrohe *n.* torment *SM* 84/1. **tintreohen**
pl. SW 102/3.
tis *see* **þis** *adj.*, *pron. demons.*
tobeoreð *pr. 3 pl.* differ *HM* 28/9.
toc *see* **tac**.
todealen *v.* separate *SW* 106/9. **todealet**
divided *p.p. A8* 130/9.
to-eke *prep.* in addition to *SM* 50/18.
tofeol *pa. 3 sg.* fell *SM* 62/1.

toggin *v.* engage in horseplay, struggle amorously *A8* 142/29. **toggiŏ** *pr. 3 pl. SM* 66/22.

toȝein *prep.* against *SM* 70/8, **toȝeines** *SW* 96/35, *A8* 138/6, 9, 10.

tohurten *pr. pl. subj.* recoil *A8* 144/16.

token *see* tac.

tolec *see* teluken.

tolimet *p.p.* dismembered, torn apart *HM* 18/19, *SM* 54/36.

tolliŏ *pr. 3 pl.* wrestle amorously *SM* 66/22.

toloken, toluken *see* teluken.

torenden *v.* rend to pieces *SM* 54/14. **torendeŏ** *pr. 3 pl. SW* 90/36.

toronden *v.* tear to pieces *SM* 54/14.

tospreat *pr. 3 sg.* stretches out *A7* 122/29.

toswelleŏ *pr. 3 sg.* swells *HM* 12/24.

totoren *p.p.* torn to pieces *SM* 56/2.

toturn *n.* refuge *SM* 62/14.

totweame *pr. sg. subj.* separate *HM* 10/23. **totweamde** *pa. 3 sg.* split open *SM* 72/35, *pa. sg. subj. SM* 76/35. **totweamet** *p.p. SM* 80/31.

treowe *adj.* true, faithful *HM* 4/18 *etc.*, *SM* 46/34, 60/34, *SW* 94/32, *A7* 118/8. **treowe** *pl. SW* 106/10.

troden *n. pl.* footsteps *HM* 12/19.

trof *see* þer *adv.* demons.

trowŏe *n.* faith, honour *SW* 90/21, 23.

trukien *v.* fail, desert, deceive *HM* 4/23, 6/18. **trukeŏ** *pr. 3 sg. HM* 14/6. **trukie** *pr. sg. subj. A8* 146/2.

trume *n.* company *HM* 18/31.

tu *see* þu.

tuhen *pa. 3 pl.* proceeded *SM* 82/24.

tuht *n.* correct conduct, good behaviour *SW* 88/18.

tuhte *pr. sg. subj.* instruct, guide, discipline *SW* 86/23. **tuhten** *pr. pl. subj. SW* 108/5. **ituht** *p.p. SW* 106/26.

tukin *v.* maltreat, abuse; be maltreated *HM* 24/5. **tukest** *pr. 2 sg. HM* 30/27. **tukeŏ** *pr. 3 sg. HM* 14/16, 28/4. **ituket** *p.p.* defiled *HM* 30/5, ill-treated *A7* 114/19.

tulle *imp. pl.* encourage *A8* 132/8.

tune *n. dat. sg.* village *A8* 134/24, 142/16.

tuneŏ *pr. 3 sg.* closes *SW* 104/27. **itunet** *p.p.* enclosed *SM* 80/32, **ituinet** *SM* 76/13.

tunne *n.* jar, vat *SM* 72/29.

turden *see* turnen.

turn *n.* stratagem *HM* 42/12 n. **turnes** *pl.* wiles *SW* 96/21.

turnen *v.* turn *A7* 122/5, *A8* 140/11, **to uuel** — misconstrue *A8* 142/23, **turne** *SM* 80/12, — þe rug turn (your) back *HM* 14/32, — to gode turn out well *HM* 6/2. **turnest** *pr. 2 sg.* as þu — þin hond as you turn your hand, in a moment *HM* 22/7. **turneŏ** *pr. 3 sg.* goes *HM* 16/21, 20/9, turns out *A8* 148/27, — to hire takes over *A7* 126/31, *pr. 3 pl. HM* 6/4, — ham *refl.* transfer their loyalty *SW* 98/10. **turnden** *pa. 3 pl. HM* 8/17, were converted *SM* 82/16, **turden** *SM* 76/27. **iturnde** *ppl. adj. pl. A8* 142/31.

turnunge *n.* turning; **breines** — dizziness *HM* 30/33.

tus *see* þus.

tuteleŏ *pr. 3 sg.* whispers *A8* 140/5.

twa *n.*, *adj.* two; **tweien** *SW* 106/13. **tweire** *gen.* of two things *HM* 22/16, of the two *A7* 126/27.

tweamen *v.* separate, divide *HM* 24/17, *SW* 106/7, **twemen** *SM* 52/5.

tweast *pr. 3 sg.* applies to *A8* 130/29.

tweien, tweire *see* twa.

twemen *see* tweamen.

twien *adv.* twice *A8* 130/25, 146/29.

twinnin *v.* divide, separate *HM* 24/16, be separated *A7* 118/31. **twinni** *pr. sg. subj. HM* 10/22.

twinnunge *n.* parting *HM* 24/20, *A7* 118/30.

þa *adv.* then *SM* 44/22 *etc.*, *A7* 124/17, 26.

þa *conj.* when *HM* 16/27 *etc.*, *SM* 44/20 *etc.*, *SW* 100/20, *A7* 124/16, 128/19.

þa *def. art. pl. see* þe *def. art.*

þah *adv.* nevertheless, even so, however *HM* 6/34 *etc.*, *SM* 68/31, *SW* 96/6, 106/23, *A7* 112/34 *etc.*, *A8* 130/20 *etc.*, **ant** — even so, and yet *HM* 4/34, *SM* 48/24, *A7* 126/16, *A8* 146/15, **tah** *SW* 90/23, 100/1, **ant** — *HM* 20/25 *etc.*, *SM* 80/31, *SW* 86/12 *etc.*

þah *conj.* though, although *HM* 4/4 *etc.*, *SM* 54/8 *etc.*, *SW* 86/21 *etc.*, *A7* 110/8 *etc.*, *A8* 132/9 *etc.*, **tah** *HM* 24/30, 26/17, 40/6.

þat *pron. rel. see* þet *pron. rel.*

þe *def. art.* the *HM* 2/2 *etc.*, *SM* (*heading*)

etc., *SW* (*heading*) *etc.*, *A7* 110/3 *etc.*, *A8* 130/2 *etc.*, **e** *SW* 108/11, (*after t*) **te** *HM* 12/22 *etc.*, *SM* (*heading*) *etc.*, *SW* 86/9 *etc.*, *A7* 110/32 *etc.*, *A8* 130/24 *etc.* **þen** *masc. acc. sg.* *HM* 30/26, *SM* 58/26, *SW* 94/33, 98/17, *A7* 116/33, 124/14, **þene** *SM* 78/21, 82/9. **þen** *dat. sg.* *HM* 6/4, 36/35, **ten** *HM* 4/32, 6/15, **þene** *HM* 42/25. **þes** *masc. gen. sg.* *HM* 12/31 *etc.*, *SM* (*heading*) *etc.* **þer** *fem. dat. sg.* *HM* 18/19, *SM* 58/28 *etc.*, *A8* 144/7. **þet** *orig. neut.* *HM* 6/29 *etc.*, *SM* 44/18[1] *etc.*, *SW* 86/10[2] *etc.*, *A7* 110/ 12[1,2] *etc.*, *A8* 130/2 *etc.*, **tet** *HM* 30/15, *SM* 52/21, 78/1, *A7* 124/19. **þa** *pl.* *SM* 44/24, 52/8.

þe *adv. demons.* (*with comparatives*) on that account, (so much) the *HM* 2/9 *etc.*, *SM* 54/26[1], *SW* 86/11, 23, 92/11, *A7* 114/ 2, *A8* 132/35, 140/27, **te** *A7* 110/18.

þe *pron. 2 pers. see* **þu.**

þe *particle rel. indecl.* who, which, that *HM* 2/16[1] *etc.*, *SM* 44/8 *etc.*, *SW* 86/8[1] *etc.*, *A7* 110/2 *etc.*, *A8* 130/6 *etc.*, whom *HM* 32/ 19[2], 40/32, *SM* 44/27 *etc.*, to whom *HM* 12/3, (by) whom *A7* 112/1, (*with pers. antecedent understood*) (she) who *HM* 36/ 33, (he) who *A8* 146/23. **þe** *indef.* whoever *HM* 14/25, 22/30[1], *SW* 94/8, *A8* 140/20.

þe *pron. demons. masc.* he *A8* 138/26[2], (*preceding rel.*) — **þe he** (*who*) *SM* 58/ 23[1], *A7* 114/3[1], **te** *SM* 48/29.

þear *adv. demons. see* **þer** *adv. demons.*

þearf *pr. 2 sg.* need *HM* 8/23, **þerf** *HM* 24/ 27. **þearf** *pr. 3 sg.* *HM* 4/17, 24/35, **þerf** *HM* 34/12, **ne — us** *impers.* we do not need *SW* 96/10. **þurue** *pr. 1 pl.* *SW* 94/ 19, *pr. 2 pl.* *SW* 98/31.

þearmes *n. gen. pl.* bowels *HM* 32/1.

þeaueð *pr. 3 sg.* permits, tolerates *HM* 42/ 9. **þeauieð** *pr. 3 pl.* *SM* 66/24, 68/31.

þeaw *n.* virtue *SW* 88/1, 17. **þeawes** *pl.* qualities *HM* 40/6, 15, *SW* 88/1, *A8* 138/31, virtues *HM* 2/3, 40/18.

þeawfule *adj. pl.* virtuous *HM* 38/35, edifying *A8* 140/23.

þe-ȝet *adv.* then still *SM* 44/8.

þe-ȝet *conj.* while still *HM* 36/30, — **þe** *HM* 16/13.

þe-hweðere *adv.* none the less *SM* 62/19.

þeines *n. pl.* men *SM* 72/17.

þen *conj.* than *HM* 4/25 *etc.*, *SM* 54/13 *etc.*,

SW 102/27 *etc.*, *A7* 118/20 *etc.*, *A8* 132/ 1 *etc.*, **þene** *SM* 44/8, **ten** *SM* 58/13.

þen *acc., dat. sg. see* **þe** *def. art.*

þenchen *v.* think *HM* 2/18, 4/17, *SM* 68/ 3 *etc.*, *A8* 134/22, meditate *SW* 106/33, reflect on *SM* 68/2, imagine *A7* 120/23, **þenche** *HM* 22/5. — **þerbi** be reminded (of) *A7* 116/15. **þenche** *pr. 1 sg.* intend *A7* 128/25. **þenchest** *pr. 2 sg.* *HM* 14/33. **þencheð** *pr. 3 sg.* *A7* 128/ 23, *A8* 140/6, considers *A7* 122/5, — on *HM* 32/29. **þench** *imp. sg.* *HM* 40/ 18, 23. **þencheþ** *imp. pl.* imagine *SW* 92/23. **þohte** *pa. 3 sg.* *SM* 58/27.

þene *conj. see* **þen** *conj.*

þene *def. art. see* **þe** *def. art.*

þenne *adv.* (1) then, therefore *HM* 4/20 *etc.*, *SM* 50/1 *etc.*, *SW* 88/35 *etc.*, *A7* 114/16, 124/8, *A8* 132/4 *etc.*, **tenne** *HM* 18/7, *A8* 130/23.

þenne *adv.* (2) *see* **þeonne** *adv.*

þeo *pron. demons. fem.* she, one *HM* 30/1, *SM* 46/8, *SW* 96/19, *A8* 142/7, that *HM* 20/11. **þeo** *dat. sg.* *SM* 46/6.

þeo *pron. demons. pl.* those *HM* 12/4 *etc.*, *SM* 58/33 *etc.*, *SW* 86/15 *etc.*, *A7* 112/9, 10, *A8* 138/18, 140/2, **teo** *SW* 106/30, *A8* 144/31.

þeonewart *adv.* from there *HM* 38/7.

þeonne *adv.* (from) there, thence *HM* 38/ 6, *SW* 94/12, 106/8, **þenne** *SM* 68/28.

þeos(e) *see* **þis** *adj.* and *pron. demons.*

þeoster *adj.* dark *SW* 100/17.

þeosternesse *n.* darkness *SW* 90/33, **þosternesse** *SW* 90/30.

þeostri *adj.* dark *HM* 40/14.

þeoten *v.* howl *SM* 82/24.

þeow *n.* serf *HM* 4/26.

þeowdom *n.* servitude, bondage *HM* 2/25 *etc.*

þeowe *n.* (1) servant *SM* 44/10.

þeowe *n.* (2) (female) serf, slave *HM* 28/6, *SM* 46/25, handmaid *SM* 64/10, **þewe** *SM* 48/24.

þeowe-wummon *n.* bondwoman *SM* 48/ 22.

þer *adv. demons.* there *HM* 20/14 *etc.*, *SM* 64/13, 82/13, *SW* 86/26 *etc.*, *A7* 120/ 36, *A8* 132/9, 146/32, **þear** *SM* 52/26, 68/28, 84/6, *SW* 100/17, 106/2, **ter** *HM* 2/22 *etc.*, *SM* 46/18, 54/30, *A8* 146/15. **þer** (*forming conj.*) — **as** where *SW* 106/13, — **ase** *HM* 26/18. **þer**

þer (*cont.*):

　prefixed to prep. or adv.: þerbiuoren
before *SM* 76/19, þerefter later,
afterwards *SM* 50/25, þrefter *HM* 6/14
etc., *SM* 60/16, *A8* 130/16, 140/27,
144/4, þrinne inside *SW* 88/4 *etc.*,
þeronuuen in the future, thereafter *A8*
148/15, þerunder underneath *HM* 14/
2, þruppe above, previously *HM* 6/26
etc., *SW* 106/31, *A7* 112/20, 126/34, *A8*
148/8, þrute outside *SW* 88/13;
representing neut. pron. it, that, this:
þeraȝeines in response to it *SM* 58/31,
in comparison with it *SW* 100/17, þerbi
by that *HM* 20/31, by this *A7* 116/15,
þerfrommart away from it *HM* 34/10,
þerin in it, (in) there *HM* 4/10, 26/26,
32/13, *SM* 68/33, þerinne *SM* 76/2,
þrin *HM* 2/18 *etc.*, *SW* 90/22 *etc.*,
þrinne *A8* 136/5, þerof of it, from it,
from there *HM* 26/7, 32/3, *A8* 146/19,
terof *HM* 2/22, —... of *HM* 24/3, *A8*
138/10–11, þrof *HM* 6/7 etc., *SM* 62/9
etc., *SW* 88/4, 92/28, 104/32, *A7* 118/
14, *A8* 132/23, 138/30, 146/11, trof
SW 106/2, þron about it *HM* 22/5, *SM*
58/27, on it *HM* 20/13, *SM* 64/16, *A7*
120/16, *A8* 134/26, in this *A7* 116/16,
terteken besides, as well *SW* 92/17,
þerto to it, to that point *HM* 32/8, for
the purpose *A7* 122/22, þertoward
against it *SM* 48/5, þertowart *SW* 106/
4, with it *SW* 90/27, towards it *SW* 90/
25, þerþurh through that *HM* 42/14,
þerunder under it *A8* 136/13,
þerupon on it *SM* 80/8, þeruppon
over that *A8* 136/30, þeruore for that
(reason) *HM* 22/2, 40/24, *SW* 94/24,
for it *SM* 68/18, þerwið with it, with
that *HM* 10/34, 30/30, *SM* 78/5, *A7*
110/11, 118/12, 126/33, *A8* 136/15, of
it *SM* 68/23, terwið from this *HM* 32/
10, þerwiðinnen inside it *HM* 8/21.

þer *conj.* where *HM* 18/30, *SM* 78/25, 82/
29, *A7* 116/14, 128/19.

þer *def. art. see* þe.

þeraȝeines, — bi, —biuoren, —efter *see*
þer *adv.*

þerf *see* þearf.

þerfrommart, —in(ne), —of, —
　onuuen, —to, —toward, —towart,
　—þurh, —under, —upon, — uppon,
　—uore, —wið, —wiðinnen *see* þer

adv. demons.

þes *adv.*; — þe mare by so much the more
HM 34/3.

þes *see* þe *def. art.*, þis *adj. demons.*

þet *adj. demons.* that *HM* 2/21² *etc.*, *SM* 44/
18¹ *etc.*, *SW* 86/12 *etc.*, *A7* 114/13, 126/
11, *A8* 132/36², (*after t*) tet *HM* 24/18,
mit—ilke at that very moment, then
SM 60/18, 82/9.

þet *def. art. see* þe *def. art.*

þet *pron. demons.* that *HM* 2/3¹ *etc.*, *SM* 72/
21¹ *etc.*, *SW* 86/24² *etc.*, *A7* 110/4 *etc.*, *A8*
130/14 *etc.*, efter — he/hit is according
to what his/its nature is *SW* 88/22, 90/
24. þon *dat. sg.*; wið — þet provided that
SM 52/2.

þet *pron. rel. indecl.* who, which, what, that
HM 2/3² *etc.*, *SM* 44/13 *etc.*, *SW* 86/11
etc., *A7* 120/27 *etc.*, *A8* 130/11 *etc.*, þat
SM 82/31.

þet *conj.* that *HM* 2/8 *etc.*, *SM* 46/15 *etc.*,
SW 86/21 *etc.*, *A7* 110/1 *etc.*, *A8* 130/1
etc., so that *HM* 12/2 *etc.*, *SM* 52/13 *etc.*,
SW 88/13 *etc.*, *A7* 122/8² *etc.*, *A8* 130/
21, 132/18; *forming compound conjs. see*
efter, for, forþi *conj.*, ȝef *conj.* hwil,
þurh *conj.*

þewe *see* þeowe.

þi *see* þu.

þin(e) *see* þu.

þing *n.* thing *HM* 4/17 *etc.*, *SM* 50/13 *etc.*,
SW 90/28 *etc.*, *A7* 110/31 *etc.*, *A8* 130/
11 *etc.* þinges *pl.* *HM* 4/13, 16/31, 34/3,
SM 58/31, 34, 80/26, *SW* 90/33, *A7*
110/5 *etc.*, *A8* 130/6 *etc.*, þing *pl.* *HM* 4/
30 *etc.*, *SM* 56/20 *etc.*, *SW* 92/21 *etc.*, *A7*
110/30 *etc.*, *A8* 142/13. þinge *gen. pl.*
HM 24/28, 36/5, 17, *SM* 48/4 *etc.*, *A7*
120/2, 4, 5, *A8* 146/19. þinge *dat. pl.*
HM 10/12.

þis *adj. demons.* this *HM* 2/13 *etc.*, *SM* 44/
29 *etc.*, *SW* 86/8 *etc.*, *A7* 110/21 *etc.*, *A8*
130/8 *etc.*, þes *A7* 114/18, 22, (*after t*) tis
HM 4/9, *SM* 58/21, *SW* 86/26, 92/13,
A7 124/6, tes *HM* 16/9, *A7* 122/11.
þeos *fem. sg.* *A7* 114/20. þes *masc. acc.*
sg. *HM* 6/19, *SW* 92/26, *neut. acc. sg.* *SM*
52/27. þisse *masc. dat. sg.* *HM* 16/34,
SM 66/12, *SW* 94/9, *A7* 114/22. þeos
fem. acc., dat. sg. *HM* 40/14, *SM* 52/12,
SW 94/20, 108/13, teos *SM* 44/5. þeos
pl. these *HM* 2/19, 6/30, 18/28, *SM* 44/
6 *etc.*, *SW* 86/14 *etc.*, *A7* 116/22 *etc.*, *A8*

130/26, þeose *HM* 32/26, *SM* 64/7,*A7* 122/5, 31,*A8* 130/22, 132/32, 140/33, þes *HM* 2/23 *etc.*, *SM* 50/23, 76/9, 84/ 1,*A7* 110/25, 126/25.

þis *pron. demons.* this *HM* 2/14 *etc.*, *SM* 48/ 19 *etc.*, *SW* 88/25 *etc.*,*A7* 112/5 *etc.*,*A8* 130/3, 144/9, þes this (man)*A7* 128/ 25, (*after t*) tis *HM* 36/24,*SW* 94/26. þeos *fem. nom. sg.* this (woman) *HM* 4/ 32, 28/31, this (one)*A7* 128/36. þeos *pl. HM* 2/29 *etc.*,*SW* 86/16, A8 142/1, þeose *HM* 18/28,*SW* 92/5,*A8* 130/6, 19.

þohte *see* þenchen.

þolemode *adj. wk.* long-suffering *SM* 62/ 11.

þolemodnesse *n.* patience *HM* 36/13.

þolien *v.* suffer, allow, tolerate *HM* 4/30 *etc.*,*SM* 80/19,*SW* 86/7 *etc.*,*A7* 110/ 10,*A8* 140/21, 146/5, þolie *SW* 100/6. þoleð *pr. 3 sg. HM* 24/32. þolieð *pr. 1 pl. A7* 110/13, *pr. 3 pl. SM* 68/31. þolien *pr. pl. subj.*A8 136/28. þole *imp. sg. SM* 48/7,*SW* 106/23. þolede *pa. 3 sg. A7* 116/2, 3. þoleden *pa. 3 pl. HM* 40/22, *SW* 102/1.

þon *see* þet *pron. demons.*

þonc *n.* intent *SW* 86/19, thought *A7* 124/ 30. þonkes *pl.* thoughts *HM* 2/16, 23, 10/2, þonckes *HM* 8/7.

þosternesse *see* þeosternesse.

þrahen *n. pl.* sufferings; pinunge — labour pains *HM* 32/7.

þralunge *n.* pain, discomfort *HM* 32/1.

þreal *n.* slave, servant *HM* 6/20, 12/6, þrel *HM* 4/26, 28/5, 40/5,*SM* 64/11. þrealles *pl. HM* 2/29.

þreat *pr. 3 sg.* threatens *HM* 14/17.

þrefter *see* þer *adv. demons.*

þreohad *n.* trinity *SW* 108/12.

þreouald *adj.* threefold *SM* 62/19,*A7* 120/8.

þreste *pa. 3 sg.* pressed out, issued *SM* 58/ 16.

þrifte *n.* (healthy) development *HM* 32/ 22.

þrile *adj.* three-fold, triple *SM* 62/19.

þrin, þrinne *see* þer *adv. demons.*

þrof, þron *see* þer *adv. demons.*

þrumnesse *n.* trinity *SM* 62/19, *SW* 100/ 5.

þruppe, þrute *see* þer *adv. demons.*

þu *pron. 2 sg.* you *HM* 2/21 *etc.*, *SM* 46/32

etc., *SW* 94/3[1,2] *etc.*, *A7* 114/10 *etc.*, *A8* 132/15, 138/5, 6, (*after t*) tu *HM* 2/13 *etc.*, *SM* 46/30 *etc.*, *SW* 90/8 *etc.*, *A7* 110/23[1,2] *etc.*,*A8* 148/27. þe *acc., dat. HM* 2/16 *etc.*, *SM* 46/32 *etc.*, *SW* 90/9, *A7* 110/27 *etc.*,*A8* 138/6[1], 138/9[1], 148/ 27, (*after t*) te *HM* 6/22 *etc.*, *SM* 54/6 *etc.*,*A7* 118/25, 120/14, 128/16. þe *refl.* yourself *HM* 6/2, *SM* 50/31, 58/1, 66/ 1[1],*A7* 128/20,*A8* 138/7, — seolf yourself *HM* 24/4, 35, 30/27,*SM* 72/6, — seoluen *SM* 50/5, 54/35, 76/9, (*after t*) te *HM* 6/23 *etc.*, —seolf *HM* 22/ 29,*A7* 120/20. tines *gen. sg. masc.* your *HM* 2/4, 14. þin *poss. adj.* your (*usually before vowel or h*) *HM* 2/4 *etc.*, *SM* 50/ 32[1,2] *etc.*,*SW* 104/24, 27,*A7* 114/16 *etc.*,*A8* 144/14, tin *HM* 12/25, 26/2. þi (*before cons.*) *HM* 2/15 *etc.*, *SM* 46/29 *etc.*, *SW* 90/21 *etc.*,*A7* 114/13 *etc.*,*A8* 138/5, 7, 148/26, ti *HM* 2/4 *etc.*, *SM* 50/29 *etc.* þine *pl. HM* 28/2 *etc.*, *SM* 48/ 31 *etc.*,*A7* 114/11, 126/3,*A8* 148/26, tine *HM* 26/33,*SM* 80/3. þin *pron.* yours *HM* 10/23,*SM* 60/10,*A7* 120/ 13, 128/1. þine *pl. HM* 42/4.

þudde *pr. 1 sg.* thrust (into) *SM* 66/23, 68/ 3. *pa. 3 sg.* stamped *SM* 64/6.

þuften *n.* handmaid, maidservant *A7* 114/9,*A8* 142/3, þuftene *A8* 142/7.

þuftenes *gen. sg. HM* 40/7.

þuhte *see* þuncheð.

þulli *adj.* such (a) *HM* 34/14, 42/10, *SM* 56/8,*SW* 104/31[1,2,3] *etc.*,*A7* 122/4, 0 — wise in such a way, so*A7* 126/7. þullich *HM* 8/8, 34/12, like this *HM* 22/12. þulliche *dat.*; 0 — wise in such a way *HM* 28/32. þulliche *pl. HM* 32/ 28,*SW* 96/1, 106/33.

þullich *pron.* such (things) *HM* 34/4, such *HM* 40/27.

þuncheð *pr. 3 sg.* seems, appears *HM* 2/ 21 *etc.*,*SW* 88/31, 92/9, 100/2,*A7* 128/ 14,*A8* 134/20, *impers. HM* 12/28 *etc.*, *SM* 64/35 *etc.*, *SW* 98/19,*A8* 140/24. þuncheð *pr. 3 pl. HM* 28/2. þunche *pr. sg. subj. HM* 34/6, 40/14, 34, *impers. HM* 6/10, 28/19, 32/13,*A7* 126/24. þuhte *pa. 3 sg. impers. SM* 78/31. iþuht *p.p.*; haueð — me have seemed to me *A8* 132/1.

þurh *prep.* through, by *HM* 4/1 *etc.*, *SM* 44/27 *etc.*, *SW* 86/3 *etc.*,*A7* 114/9 *etc.*,

þurh (*cont.*):
  A8 130/4 *etc.* — þet *conj.* because,
  through (the fact) that *SM* 54/36, 66/
  24.
þurhfulleð *pr. 3 sg.* completes *A7* 124/
  29, 32.
þurhleasten *v.* continue, last *SW* 92/15.
þurh-þurli *v.* pierce *SM* 54/21.
þurhut *prep.* (right) through *SM* 82/7.
þurhwuniende *pr.p.* everlasting *SM* 56/
  13.
þurl *n.* window *A8* 146/29. þurle *dat. sg.*
  A8 148/4.
þurlin *v.* pierce; be pierced *A7* 116/16.
  iþurlet *p.p. A7* 114/27, 120/5.
þurlunge *n.* piercing *A7* 118/27.
þurs *n.* demon *SM* 62/3, 64/6.
þurue *see* þearf.
þus *adv.* thus, so, in this way *HM* 6/14
  etc., *SM* 46/12 *etc.*, *SW* 88/6 *etc.*, *A7*
  110/26 *etc.*, *A8* 138/9, 140/6, 144/25,
  tus *HM* 8/20, 14/29, 24/1.
þwertouer *prep.* across *SM* 60/16, *A7*
  122/26.

uan, ueat, ueden, ueondes, ueont, uet,
  uetles *see* u/v *consonant below.*
umbe *prep.* intent on, concerned with *HM*
  2/25, *SM* 54/17, umben intent on *A8*
  144/11, — þeronuuen intent
  (concerning it) in the future *A8* 148/15.
  vmben; — ane stunde after a while *SW*
  98/12. *See also* hwile, stunde.
unagin *adj.* without beginning *SM* 80/32
  n.
unbihefre *adj. comp.* less useful *SW*
  106/19.
unbotelich *adj.* irremediable *HM* 14/29.
unbruche *n.* integrity; wið — of bodi
  physically virgin *HM* 36/20.
unc *pron. dual acc., dat.* us; — twa the two
  of us *SM* 56/35, vnc *SM* 52/5.
uncouerlich *adj.* irrecoverable *HM* 24/6.
uncumelich *adj.* unseemly, indecent *HM*
  32/12, vnkumelich *HM* 22/17.
uncumelicheð *pr. 3 sg.* disfigures *HM*
  30/24.
uncundelich *adj.* unnatural *A8* 136/20.
  uncundelukest *superl. A8* 132/4.
uncuðe *adj. pl.* unknown, strange *A8*
  132/9.
undeadlich *adj.* immortal *HM* 10/26, *SM*
  60/33, undeaðlich *HM* 34/31.

vndeore *adj.* cheap *A7* 128/3.
underfeng, underfon *see* underuon.
underneomen *v.* receive *HM* 16/30.
  underneomeð *pr. 3 pl. HM* 16/28,
  underneome *pr. sg. subj. HM* 16/30.
undertid *n.* the third hour of the day *A7*
  122/9.
underuon *v.* receive *SM* 78/4, *SW* 104/
  16, *A8* 140/16, 144/3. underuo *pr. 1 sg.*
  SM 76/11. underueð *pr. 3 sg. HM* 32/
  5. underuo *pr. sg. subj. HM* 40/29, *pr. pl.*
  subj. A8 142/14. underfeng *pa. 3 sg. A7*
  114/1. underuengen *pa. pl. subj. A8*
  138/23. underfon *p.p. SW* 106/24,
  underuon *SW* 88/29.
unduhtie *adj. pl.* wretched *SM* 74/19.
uneuenlich *adj.* incomparable *SW* 90/27,
  A7 128/27.
uneuenlich *adv.* incomparably *A7* 128/2,
  vneuenliche *A7* 120/25.
unforgult *adj.* guiltless *HM* 38/29.
ungeinliche *adv.* threateningly *SM* 58/
  22.
unhap *n.* misfortune *HM* 26/8.
unhende *adj.* indecent, improper *HM* 8/
  11, 14/21, 28/13.
unhope *n.* despair *SW* 92/14.
unilich *adj.* unlike *HM* 18/28, unlich *HM*
  26/6.
unimete *adj.* great, immeasurable *SM* 82/
  27, *SW* 92/33, 100/32, 102/1.
unimete *adv.* immeasurably, inordinately
  SW 100/9, 104/17, *A7* 112/35.
unirude *see* unrude.
vnkumelich *see* uncumelich.
vnlaheliche *adv.* unlawfully *HM* 22/9.
unleppet *adj.* cloakless *A8* 142/26.
unlich *see* unilich.
unlust *n.* distaste *HM* 32/5.
unlusti *adj.* listless *HM* 38/29.
vnmeað *n.* excess, lack of moderation *SW*
  88/19.
unmeaðliche *adv.* immoderately *SM* 68/
  22. unmeaðlich enormously *SM* 60/
  18.
unmenskið *pr. 3 pl.* dishonour *SM* 68/8.
unmerret *adj.* inviolate *SM* 58/2,
  unharmed *SM* 60/23.
unmeteliche *adv.* immeasurably *A7* 120/
  24.
unmundlunge *adv.* unforeseen *SW* 90/8.
unmutlin *v.* diminish *SM* 54/9.
unneaðe *adv.* hardly *HM* 38/30.

unnen *pr. 3 pl.* wish *SM* 80/20.
unnet *n.* frivolous matters *HM* 14/15.
unofseruet *adj.* undeserved *SM* 72/1.
unorne *adj.* plain *A8* 136/7, plainly
dressed *A8* 142/7.
unorneschipe *n.* plainness, absence of
ornamentation *A8* 140/31.
unrecheles *adj.* heedless, careless *A7*
114/1.
unroles *adj.* unresting, incessant *HM* 32/
9.
unrude *adj.* huge *SW* 90/11. **unirude** *pl.*
SW 92/34.
unseheliche *adj. wk.* invisible *SM* 58/29.
vnseheliche *pl. SW* 86/29,
unseheliche *pl. as n. SM* 62/18.
unsehen *adj.* unseen *SM* 60/27.
unsehene *wk. SM* 58/26, *pl. SM* 74/14,
78/17.
unselhðe *n.* evil creature *SM* 58/10.
unseli *adj.* miserable, wicked *SM* 72/3. *pl.*
SM 66/6, unholy *SW* 92/30, **vnseli** *HM*
22/8.
unsulet *adj.* undefiled *SM* 84/8.
untalelich *adj.* indescribable,
inexpressible *SW* 90/29, *A7* 128/28.
untiffet *adj.* unadorned *A8* 138/13.
untodealet *adj.* undivided *SM* 76/13, 80/
32, *SW* 100/6.
untohe *adj.* wanton, unruly *HM* 8/14, 28/
3, *SW* 86/22, 108/4. **untohene** *pl. SW*
86/13.
untoheliche *adv.* in an unruly way *SW* 86/
18.
untrume *adj. pl.* infirm *SM* 82/25.
untuhtle *n.* bad manners *A8* 134/12.
untuliche *adv.* improperly *HM* 14/22.
unþeaw *n.* (corresponding) vice *SW* 88/
3, vice *SW* 88/24, wantonness *HM* 8/
11, **vnþeaw** *HM* 22/14, 23, 27.
unþeawes *gen. sg. HM* 8/19, *SW* 106/
31, *pl. HM* 14/31 *etc.*, *SW* 106/4, 108/
10, *A7* 110/20.
unþolelich *adj.* intolerable *SW* 90/28,
92/10.
unþonc *n.* displeasure; — **in his teð** in
spite of himself *HM* 42/17. **unþonkes**
adv. gen. against the will (of) *SM* 66/23,
vnþonkes *SW* 88/14.
unwarnede *adj. pl.* unprotected *SW* 94/
32.
unwarre *adj. wk.* unwary *SM* 66/20.
vnwedde *adj. pl.* unmarried *HM* 12/9.

unwemmet *adj.* immaculate, undefiled
HM 40/33, *SM* 54/23, unblemished,
unhurt *HM* 34/28, *SM* 66/34,
vnwemmet *HM* 4/15.
unweoten *n. pl.* fools *SM* 52/33.
unweotenesse *n.* ignorance *SW* 96/18.
unwepnede *adj. pl.* unarmed *SW* 94/32.
unwerget *adj.* unwearied *SW* 100/23,
104/22.
unwiht *n.* evil one, demon, devil *HM* 36/
22, 35, 42/14, *SM* 48/4 *etc.*, *SW* 86/4,
94/24. **unwihtes** *gen. sg. SW* 96/19.
unwihtes *pl. SM* 74/14, **unwiht** *SM*
74/29.
unwil *n.* despite; **hire** — against her will
HM 28/12. **unwilles** *adv. gen.*; **min** —
against my will *SM* 64/24.
unwine *n.* enemy *SW* 106/4.
unwitlese *adj. pl.* senseless *SM* 58/3.
unwitti *adj. pl.* foolish *SM* 52/24.
unword *n.* malicious talk, slander *HM* 28/
23.
unwreast *adj.* bad, depraved *A7* 116/28.
unwreste *pl. SM* 66/16, 28, 68/2,
unwreaste *SW* 88/1.
unwreaste *adv.* badly, scandalously *A7*
116/36.
unwreo *v.* uncover, reveal *SW* 102/25.
unwurð *adj.* worthless *HM* 24/9, 40/12,
SM 50/15, *A7* 128/4, little esteemed
(by) *HM* 28/26[1,2], **unwurðe** *HM* 8/5,
unworthy *A8* 140/25, **vnwurðe** *A8*
148/5. **unwurðre** *comp.* less valued
HM 28/25.
unwurðgeð *pr. 3 sg.* dishonours *HM* 30/
24.
unwurðlich *adj.* plain *HM* 28/24.
vnwurðliche *pl.* trivial *HM* 34/3.
up-aheue *adj.* upraised, lifted *SM* 76/30.
upastihunge *n.* ascension *SM* 44/2.
upbreideð *pr. 3 pl.* upbraid *SW* 92/32.
upbreide *pr. sg. subj.* rebuke *A8* 144/4.
upbrud *n.* rebuke, reproach *HM* 30/11.
ure *see* **we.**
urn *n.* running; **of** — in running *A7* 120/
28.
us *see* **we.**
utewið *adv.* outward, (on the) outside
HM 28/7, 34/19, 38/13, outside *A8*
132/3.
utnume *adj.* supreme *HM* 34/14, *A8* 148/7.
utnume *adv.* surpassingly *SM* 48/34,
vtnume *HM* 16/14.

uuel *n.* misfortune, harm, evil HM 6/3 *etc.*,
SM 60/11, 72/23, SW 92/15, 96/15,
34, A7 120/21, A8 132/9, pain HM 32/
9, illness A7 118/9, **to — turnen**
misconstrue A8 142/23, **vuel** HM 22/
16, A8 136/1. **uueles** *pl.* SW 88/17, A7
114/35.
uuel *adj.* bad, malicious HM 28/23, 30/
12, sinful A8 138/4, improper SM 66/
15, shameful SM 70/9, **vuel** SW 86/19.
uuele *wk.* SM 64/7. **uueles** *gen. sg.* A7
114/20. **uuele** *pl. as n.* SW 98/30, A7
112/21.
uuele *adv.* badly, poorly HM 4/27, A7
110/27, A8 148/11, **vuele** HM 8/2.

va *see* **fa.**
vampez *n. pl.* feet (of stockings) A8 136/
24.
uan, van *see* **fa.**
varpeð *see* **warpen,**
ueat *see* **feat.**
ueden *see* **feden.**
veien *v.* join A7 118/32. **iueiet** *p.p.* A8
144/19.
ueondes, ueont *see* **feond.**
uertu *n.* virtue HM 10/22, 31. **uertuz** *pl.*
HM 36/10.
uet, vet *see* **fet.**
uetles *n.* vessel SM 74/34.
uigilies days of fasting preceding feasts A8
130/26.
uleð *pr. 3 sg.* flatters HM 2/20.
uore *prep.* for SM 80/4, on account (of)
SM 78/4.
uorðriht *adv.* at once SM 68/19.
uostrin *v.* foster; be fostered SM 46/4.
vu *n.* vow A8 130/1.

wacliche *adv.* unworthily HM 8/2.
waker *adj.* watchful SW 88/25. **wakere** *pl.*
SM 72/11, *comp.* SW 94/16.
wala *interj.* alas HM 24/26.
wald *n.* (1) power, possession SM 46/11
etc.
wald *n.* (2) wood; **o þis** — in the woods
SM 60/6.
walde(n), waldest *see* **wulle.**
waldes *adv.* voluntarily HM 22/29, 42/3.
walewið *pr. 3 pl.* wallow HM 12/9, 10.
walh *adj.* nauseating HM 32/4.
wan *n.* dwelling, abode SM 56/17, SW 94/
2. **wanes** *pl.* HM 28/2, SM 80/9, A8

132/31, 136/3.
wanunge *n.* wailing HM 32/18,
lamentation SW 94/1.
war *adj.* wary SW 96/34, prudent SW 106/
3, **makie** — inform SM 70/31. **warre**
comp. SW 94/16.
warant *n.* protector, defender SM 56/23,
64/4.
warde *n.* custody, keeping, protection HM
4/28, SW (*heading*) *etc.*, A8 148/17.
warden *v.* guard SW 106/32. **wardi** *pr. sg.
subj.* SW 94/15.
ware *n. pl.* inhabitants SM 58/30.
wari *n.* villain, accursed person SM 48/34.
warliche *adv.* carefully SW 88/11, 96/17,
A8 142/31, **wearliche** SW 86/4.
warpen *v.* throw, cast SM 48/4, A7 124/
35, **warpe** HM 40/34, 42/3, SM 72/27,
— **honden on** seize SM 46/28. **warpe**
pr. 1 sg.; — (something) **towart** make an
attack on SM 66/13. **warpest** *pr. 2 sg.*;
— **awei þine hwile** waste your time
SM 50/31. **warpeð** *pr. 3 sg.* SM 48/5,
A7 118/1, 124/33, — **abuten** whirls
about HM 26/15, — **ut** vomits up HM
32/6. **warpeð** *pr. 3 pl.*; — **towart**
attack (with missiles) HM 4/8. **warpe** *pr.
sg. subj.* SW 88/15. **warp** *imp. sg.* SM 72/
28, 76/10. **varpeð** *imp. pl.* SW 106/12.
weorp *pa. 3 sg.* HM 38/6, A7 112/17.
warschipe *n.* prudence HM 36/11,
(*personif.*) SW 88/7 *etc.* **Warschipes** *gen.
sg.* SW 88/14.
warð *see* **wurðeð.**
wa-sið *n.* painful experience HM 32/12.
wa-siðes *pl.* troubles HM 32/35.
wast *see* **witen** *v.* (1).
wastið *pr. pl.* consume HM 26/19.
wastinde *pr.p.* HM 38/31.
wat *see* **witen** *v.* (1).
waxunge *n.* growth HM 32/21.
we *pron. 1 pl.* we HM 10/6 *etc.*, SM 44/27
etc., SW 86/4 *etc.*, A7 110/12. **us** *acc.,
dat.* HM 10/16 *etc.*, SM 52/3 *etc.*, SW
86/3 *etc.*, A7 112/15 *etc.*, A8 138/2. **us**
refl. ourselves SW 94/17 *etc.*, — **seolf**
SW 96/30, 32, — **seoluen** HM 32/15,
SW 86/4. **ure** *poss. adj.* our HM 6/8 *etc.*,
SM 44/1 *etc.*, SW 86/3 *etc.*, A7 112/2
etc., A8 130/12 *etc.* **vre** HM 10/16, 14/
4[1,2], SW 88/6. **ure** *pron. gen.* of ours A7
118/32, — **alre** of us all HM 32/14, SW
96/20.

wealden *v.* rule, possess *HM* 34/27, *A7*
112/32, 120/19, **welden** *SM* 46/12,
50/27, **wealde** *SM* 80/15. **welde** *pr. 1
sg. SM* 46/27. **wealdest** *pr. 2 sg. SM* 58/
33, 60/35. **wealt** *pr. 3 sg. HM* 6/5, **weld**
SM 50/16, **wealdeð** *HM* 34/34.
weldeð *pr. 3 pl. HM* 26/20.

weane *n.* misery, affliction, suffering *HM*
6/25 *etc.*, *A7* 114/13. **weanen** *pl. HM* 4/
6 *etc.*, *SM* 44/6, 84/1.

wearien *v.* curse *A8* 134/23.

wearliche *see* **warliche**.

wearnen *v.*; — **to** prevent (from) *A7* 128/
17.

wearð *see* **wurðeð**.

weater-bulge *n.* water-skin *HM* 30/34.

wecches *n. pl.* vigils *HM* 32/35.

wed *n.* pledge, security *A7* 116/23.

wedde *adj. pl.* mad, rabid *SM* 48/10.

weden *n. pl.* clothes *A8* 142/29.

wei *n.* way *HM* 38/7 *etc.*, *SM* 46/5 *etc.*, *SW*
96/9, *A8* 142/8. **weis** *gen.*; **alles** — in
every way *HM* 24/11, **eanies** — in any
way *SM* 66/9, **nan oðer** — in no other
way *HM* 18/6, **nanes** — in no way *HM*
24/18, 23, 38/5, *SM* 50/12, 68/26, *A7*
114/11, **summes** — to some extent *SW*
96/1, 100/7, in some way *SM* 70/11,
weies; **summes** — *HM* 8/15.

wei *interj.* alas *HM* 14/25, *SM* 70/22.

weie *n.* scale *A7* 112/9.

weila *interj.* alas *HM* 14/24, *SM* 52/29,
33.

weilawei *interj.* alas *HM* 8/5, *A7* 128/15.

weimeres *n. gen. sg.* of lamentation *HM*
18/20.

weld, welde(n), weldeð *see* **wealden**.

wele *see* **weole**.

wel-itohe *adj.* well-bred *HM* 22/13.

wel-itund *adj.* well-closed, well-secured
A8 138/8.

wem *n.* stain, mark *SM* 60/24.

wemmunge *n.* defilement *HM* 10/35.

wenden *v.* go, turn *SM* 46/6, 50/14.
wendeð *pr. 3 sg. HM* 16/16, **went**
A8 146/23, — **hit to** turns it into *HM*
26/32. **wendeð** *pr. 3 pl. SW* 102/14.
wende *pr. sg. subj. A8* 142/6, *pa. 3 sg.
SM* 46/21 *etc.* **wenden** *pa. 3 pl. SM* 44/
6. **iwend** *p.p. SM* 46/5.

wenest *pr. 2 sg.* think, expect *HM* 8/1.
weneð *pr. 3 sg. HM* 34/18, *SM* 60/14,
me — it is expected *SW* 90/8, it is

thought *A7* 124/4. **wene** *pr. 2 pl. SM*
52/33. **weneð** *pr. 3 pl. SM* 68/31, 70/
4. **wendest** *pa. 2 sg. HM* 6/24, 25.
wende *pa. 3 sg. SM* 62/1, 12. **wenden**
pa. 3 pl. SM 48/31, 66/11, 72/30.

went *see* **wenden**.

weolcne *n.* sky *SM* 60/1.

weole *n.* joy, happiness, prosperity, wealth
HM 6/28 *etc.*, *SM* 44/6 *etc.*, *SW* 94/36,
A7 120/25, **wele** *SM* 52/14. **weolen** *pl.*
HM 40/21, *SM* 56/13, 82/22. **weole**
gen. pl. HM 30/2.

weoleful *adj.* radiant *SW* 100/16.

weolefule *pl.* fortunate *HM* 26/9,
prosperous, splendid *HM* 26/34.

weolewunge *n.* pallor *HM* 32/3.

weolie *adj. as n. gen. pl.* wise (men) *A7* 120/
3.

weordes *n. pl.* hosts, troops *SM* 82/21,
wordes *SW* 100/14, orders *SW* 100/
23.

weorp *see* **warpen**.

wepmen *n. pl.* men, males *SM* 44/3, 52/
26, *A8* 136/6, 140/13. **wepmonnes**
gen. sg. A8 138/6.

were *n.* husband *HM* 4/24 *etc.* **weres** *gen.
sg. HM* 2/17 *etc.* **were** *dat. sg. HM* 12/6.

were *v. see* **werien** *v.* (1), **wes** (1).

weren *see* **wes** (1).

wereð *see* **werien** *v.* (1), (2).

wergið *pr. 2 pl.*; — **ow seluen** weary
yourselves *SM* 74/30.

werien *v.* (1) defend *SW* 96/31, 98/8.
wereð *pr. 3 sg. A8* 132/23. **werieð** *pr.
1 pl. SW* 94/17. **werie** *pr. sg. subj. SW*
94/15. **werien** *pr. pl. subj. SM* 70/9.
were *imp. sg. SM* 48/6, *A7* 122/2.

werien *v.* (2) wear *A8* 136/10 *etc.* **wereð**
pr. 3 sg. A8 136/25.

wernches *see* **wrenches**.

wes *pa. 3 sg.* (1) was *HM* 2/26 *etc.*, *SM* 44/
14 *etc.*, *SW* 98/10 *etc.*, *A7* 112/33 *etc.*, *A8*
134/20, 138/24, 26. **weren** *pa. 1 pl. A7*
112/17, *pa. 3 pl. HM* 18/14, 40/29, *SM*
44/2 *etc.*, *SW* 92/1, *A7* 112/28 *etc.*, *A8*
132/13. **were** *pa. sg. subj. HM* 2/18 *etc.*,
SM 44/12 *etc.*, *SW* 92/33 *etc.*, *A7* 110/
11 *etc.*, *A8* 140/12, 148/12. **weren** *pa.
pl. subj. HM* 8/5, *SW* 92/22. *neg. forms:*
nes *pa. 1, 3 sg. SM* 58/24, 62/10, *SW*
106/18, *A7* 112/22 *etc.*, *A8* 140/31.
neren *pa. 3 pl. HM* 18/13. **nere** *pa. sg.
subj. HM* 20/27, 30/19, *SM* 62/30, *SW*

wes (cont.):
92/29, 94/10, 106/18, A7 114/20, A8
132/9. See am, aren, art, beon, is.
wes pa. 3 sg. (2) pastured SM 46/12 n., 22.
westi adj. pl. bare HM 26/31.
westume n. form SM 46/23.
wif n. wife, woman HM 12/6 etc., SM 50/
27, SW 86/9, A7 116/20, 118/6, 7. wif
gen. sg. (in phrase — ant weres) HM 22/
34, 26/23, wifes HM 32/33. wiue dat.
sg. SM 46/25. wifes pl. HM 32/14, 34/
4, gen. pl. HM 32/11.
wiheles n. pl. wiles SM 64/30, 66/11, 70/
31, SW 94/30.
wiht n. (evil) being SM 54/24 etc., ful —
devil, demon HM 42/1, SM 66/4, 70/
33, pl. SM 58/3, 74/12, (created) beings
SM 78/17. wihte gen. pl. SM 82/22.
wile see wulle.
willeliche adv. willingly, voluntarily A7
118/31.
willes n. pl. wishes, desires SM 48/5, 66/
16.
willes adv. willingly HM 22/29, 30/27,
42/3, A7 116/2.
wilnin v. desire, wish (for), will HM 8/24,
28/16, wilni HM 8/29, 16/7. wilni pr. 1
sg. SM 58/4, 74/26. wilnest pr. 2 sg. HM
34/36, SW 102/26, A7 128/1. wilneð
pr. 3 sg. HM 30/4. wilnið pr. 3 pl. HM
26/7. wilni pr. sg. subj. A8 132/34.
wilnin pr. pl. subj. A7 110/31. wilnede
pa. 3 sg. A7 124/23.
wilnunge n. wish; efter hire — according
to its wish HM 22/21, uuel — illicit
desire SM 66/15.
wimpel n. wimple (long strip of silk or fine
linen worn round head, neck, and
upper shoulders) A8 136/32, 33.
wimpelles adj. without a wimple A8 136/29.
wimplin v. cover with a wimple A8 136/35.
iwimplet ppl. adj. wearing a wimple A8
138/5.
wimplunge n. wearing of a wimple A8
136/31, 138/9.
wise n. manner, way HM 6/15 etc., SM 50/
1, 66/12, A7 114/22, 118/36. on alle —
in every way A8 142/32, on alle cunne
— in every kind of way A7 112/14, o
þulli — in such a way, so A7 126/7, o
nane — in no way, not at all HM 28/23,
A7 128/25. wisen pl. HM 6/20.
wisent n. guide SM 62/15, wissent SM

78/16.
wisseð pr. 3 sg. directs, guides SM 50/16.
wissunge n. guidance SW 88/2, 106/27.
wiste see witen v. (1).
wit pr. 3 sg. see witen v. (2).
wit n. (the power of) reason HM 12/33 etc.,
SM 48/7 etc., SW 86/9 etc., heorte —
mind, understanding HM 42/22, ut of
þi — out of your senses A7 120/33.
witte dat. sg. SM 54/12. wittes pl.
senses HM 12/1, SW 86/15, A8 130/8.
witege n. prophet HM 2/23, SM 76/19.
witen v. (1) know, be aware of etc., HM 28/
16, SM 64/27, 70/1, 72/9, SW 94/11,
104/10, wite SM 70/1, 72/15. wat pr. 1
sg. A7 114/14. wast pr. 2 sg. HM 6/27,
SM 72/14. wat pr. 3 sg. HM 32/32, SM
50/11, SW 96/15, A8 134/24. witen pr.
1 pl. SM 72/18, pr. 3 pl. HM 26/3, SW
102/36, 104/1. wite pr. sg. subj. A8 148/
12. witen pr. pl. subj. HM 32/16, SM
66/19, A8 144/9. wite imp. sg. SM 50/
11, 15, 24. wiste pa. 3 sg. HM 16/26.
wiste pa. sg. subj. SW 86/5. neg. forms:
nat pr. 1 sg. HM 26/19, SW 90/6, pr. 3
sg. HM 6/34. nuten pr. 3 pl. HM 28/17,
SW 92/9. nute pr. sg. subj. A8 142/14.
nuste pa. 1 sg. SM 56/32, nuste pa. sg.
subj. HM 38/7.
witen v. (2) keep, guard, protect, look after
HM 10/8, SM 46/11, SW 94/17, 96/17,
31, A7 124/9, wite HM 40/32, SM 54/
23, SW 98/8, — wið protect against
HM 28/23, to witene infl. infin. SW 88/
22, 94/23, 106/31, in his keeping SW
98/32. witest pr. 2 sg. SM 60/36. wit
pr. 3 sg. HM 10/17, 33. witeð pr. 1 pl.
SW 94/18, 106/10, pr. 3 pl. SM 66/33.
wite pr. sg. subj. SM 58/2, A8 148/17,
imp. sg. HM 14/21 etc., SM 48/6, 60/11.
witeð imp. pl. A8 140/26. iwist p.p. SW
86/24, A8 142/1.
witen v. (3) blame; to — be blamed HM
22/28.
witerliche adv. truly HM 4/11, 32,
certainly SM 66/11, SW 90/20, 106/1,
A7 128/8, 12. witerluker comp. more
plainly HM 20/30, more clearly SW
102/25.
witið pr. 3 pl. fine (unjustly), mulct HM
26/16.
witlese adj. pl. without reason HM 22/23,
SM 74/12.

witte(s) *see* wit *n.*
witti *adj.* wise *SM* 44/19.
witunge *n.* custody, keeping *A8* 136/1.
wiðbreide *pr. sg. subj.* withdraw *HM* 6/
29.
wiðbuhe *v.* avoid *HM* 32/29.
wiðerin *v.* struggle *SM* 66/29.
wiðerlahen *n. pl.* villains *SM* 52/8.
wiue *see* wif.
wleateful *adj.* disgusting *HM* 32/33.
wleatewile *adj.* disgusting *HM* 8/13, *SM*
64/9.
wleatien *v.* sicken, nauseate; to — be
sickened *A7* 122/19.
wlech *adj.* lukewarm *A7* 122/15, 18,
wlecche *pl. HM* 38/30.
wlecheunge *n.* (state of) lukewarmness
HM 38/33.
wlite *n.* countenance, appearance *SM* 46/
23, *SW* 100/3, 16, 102/12, beauty,
splendour *HM* 8/29 *etc.*, *SM* 52/30, *SW*
102/7, 27, 34, *A7* 120/26.
wlonke *adj. pl.* splendid *HM* 26/34.
wod *adj.* mad, furious *SM* 56/14, 74/34,
A7 126/22. wode *pl. SM* 72/20.
wodeluker *adv. comp.* more furiously *HM*
12/27, 42/16.
wodschipe *n.* fury, frenzy *SM* 76/33.
woh *n.* harm *HM* 30/27.
wohin *v.* woo *A7* 112/31. woheð *pr. 3 sg.*
A7 112/26, 118/35, 122/4. wohede *pa.*
3 sg. A7 114/22.
wohere *n.* wooer *A7* 114/23, 122/5.
wohlech *n.* courtship; for — in courtship
A7 112/35.
wolden *see* wulle.
wondrinde *adj.* wandering, (?) wailing *HM*
32/10, *as n. gen. pl.* those who wander
SM 62/14.
wone *n.* want *HM* 24/30, 26/31, *SW* 96/2.
wonie *pr. sg. subj.* diminish, impair *SM* 48/
7.
wonlese *adj. as n. gen. pl.* hopeless *SM* 62/
15.
wonnin *v.* grow dark *HM* 30/33.
wontin *v.* be lacking *SW* 94/8, wonti *HM*
6/4, *A7* 120/22, *pr. sg. subj. HM* 30/10,
A7 126/25.
wontreaðe *n.* hardship *HM* 6/25,
wontreþe *SM* 50/13. wontreaðes *pl.*
SW 94/2.
wonunge *n.* ceasing *SM* 60/36.
wopes *n. pl.* lamentations *HM* 38/27.

wordes *see* weordes.
woreð *pr. 3 sg.* becomes troubled *SM* 68/
36, clouds *A7* 110/21. wori *pr. sg. subj.*
HM 42/22, *SM* 48/7.
worldene *n. gen. pl.* worlds; in alre —
worlt world without end *SM* 54/27.
wracfulliche *adv.* vengefully *HM* 36/36.
wrahte, wrahtest *see* wurchen.
wraðeliche *adv.* angrily; — ilatet bad-
tempered *HM* 28/24.
wraðer *adj. dat. fem.* disastrous; him to
— heale to his destruction *SM* 60/21.
wreah *see* wreon.
wreaðen *v.* anger *HM* 24/15, *A8* 142/32.
wreaðest *pr. 2 sg. HM* 30/26.
wreaðeð *pr. 3 pl. HM* 36/28, harass
HM 26/17. wraðþe *imp. sg. refl.* be
angry *SM* 58/1.
wrecchedom *n.* grief, misery *SW* 90/29.
wrenchen *v.* turn aside *SM* 50/14.
wrencheð *pr. 3 pl. SM* 60/2. wrenche
pr. sg. subj.; — ut may force out *HM* 42/
23. wrencte *pa. 1 sg.*; — adun pulled
down *SM* 64/30.
wrenches *n. pl.* tricks, wiles *SM* 48/6, 66/
28, 70/9, *SW* 94/27, wernches *SW* 86/5.
wrenchwile *adj.* eager to deceive, crafty
HM 42/1.
wreon *v.* cover *A8* 136/35, wrihen *A8*
136/35[1,2]. wrist *pr. 2 sg. HM* 42/16.
wriheð *pr. 3 sg. A8* 138/7, 10. wreo *pr.*
sg. subj. A8 138/3. wreah *pa. 3 sg.* hid *A7*
114/28.
wrihe *adj.* hidden *A7* 112/32.
wriheles *n. pl.* covering *A8* 136/33, 138/2.
wrist *see* wreon.
writ *n.* letter, treatise *HM* 6/33, 34/23,
text *SW* 108/14, liues — the book of life
HM 20/29.
writere *n.* scribe *A8* 148/26, writers *pl.*
SM 44/22.
wulle *pr. 1 sg.* wish *A7* 114/15, Ich — wel
I am very willing *SM* 56/11. *auxil.*
(*forming fut., often implying wish,
intention, etc.*) chulle (*after* Ich) will *HM*
16/10 *etc.*, *SM* 70/31, 80/23, *SW* 90/
25, *A7* 114/13, 120/19, 126/19, wile
SM 66/32, wule *SM* 46/25, 26, wulle
SM 50/32, 56/2, *A7* 122/19. wult *pr. 2*
sg. HM 14/32 *etc.*, *SM* 50/26 *etc.*, *A7*
110/26 *etc.* wule *pr. 3 sg. HM* 4/18 *etc.*,
SM 52/31, 54/6, *SW* 94/19 *etc.*, *A7*
116/32 *etc.*, *A8* 136/11, — in (*with infin.*

wulle (*cont.*):
understood) wants to get in *SW* 88/13.
wulleð *pr. 2 pl. A8* 130/6 *etc.* **wulleð** *pr.*
3 pl. SM 66/28, *SW* 102/29. **wulle** *pr.*
sg. subj. — **ha, nulle ha** whether she
wants to or not, willy-nilly *HM* 28/14–
15. **wullen** *pr. pl. subj. HM* 26/20 (*as
HM* 28/14–15), **3e wel** — you are quite
willing *A8* 136/29. *neg. forms:* **nulle** *pr. 1
sg. HM* 40/33, *SM* 50/30, 54/1, 82/1,
nule *A7* 120/18, 24. **nult** *pr. 2 sg. SM*
54/35, *A7* 120/16. **nule** *pr. 3 sg. HM* 6/9
etc. **nulleð** *pr. 3 pl. SM* 70/1. **nulle** *pr. sg.
subj. HM* 28/15. **nullen** *pr. pl. subj. HM*
26/20. **waldest** *pa. 2 sg.* wished *SM* 72/
15. **walde** *pa. 3 sg. SM* 46/15, 74/3, *A7*
118/13, 128/19. **walden** *pr. 3 pl.* were
about to *HM* 16/24, — **of** were about to
leave *HM* 18/12, **wolden** *SM* 46/28.
walde *pa. 1, 3 sg. subj.* would, would like
(to do) *HM* 14/3 *etc.*, *SM* 50/1 *etc.*, *SW*
86/6 *etc.*, *A7* 116/29 *etc.*, *A8* 132/1, 10.
waldest *pa. 2 sg. subj. HM* 12/33, *SM*
52/28. **walden** *pa. pl. subj. HM* 40/22,
SM 52/15. *neg. forms:* **naldest** *pa. 2 sg.*
would not *HM* 6/18, *A7* 114/18. **nalde**
pa. 3 sg. did not wish to *A7* 116/5, 118/
26. **naldest** *pa. 2 sg. subj. HM* 6/7. **nalde**
pa. 3 sg. subj. SW 86/7, *A7* 120/31, *A8*
132/11.

wumme *interj.* alas, woe is me *SM* 66/5,
SW 94/6.

wummone *gen. pl.* women *SM* 52/32, *A8*
146/14.

wunder *n.* wonder, remarkable thing *HM*
10/10, 36/25, *SM* 58/24, 60/37, *A7*
114/8 *etc.*, **hwuch** — what a remarkable
thing *SM* 70/2, **muche** — a great
wonder *A8* 138/12. **wundre** *dat. sg.*; **to**
— outrageously *HM* 14/17,
scandalously *HM* 24/5, shamefully *A7*
114/19, **wurche to** — commit shameful
actions *SM* 68/4, **diht to** — reduces to
chaos *SW* 86/10, **feareð to** — comes to
grief *A8* 142/4. **wundre** *gen. pl.*; **alre** —
meast the greatest of all marvels *SM*
70/18.

wune *n.* (1) habit, custom *SW* 90/7.
wune *n.* (2) *see* **wunne**.

wunien *v.* live, dwell, remain *SM* 56/17,
66/13, 80/8. **wunie** *pr. 1 sg. SM* 62/10.
wunest *pr. 2 sg. SM* 70/24. **wuneð** *pr. 3*

sg. SM 60/15, 64/34, 70/30. **wunieð** *pr.*
1 pl. HM 14/6, *SM* 72/15. **wunieð** *pr. 3
pl. HM* 4/1, 16/13, *SM* 74/14. **wunie**
pr. sg. subj. HM 4/5. **wunieð** *imp. pl.*; —
ow accustom yourselves *A8* 130/31.
wunede *pa. 3 sg. SM* 44/14, 72/29.
iwunet *p.p.* accustomed *SW* 98/10.

wunne *n.* joy, happiness, delight *HM* 6/24
etc., *SM* 44/6 *etc.*, *SW* 94/36 *etc.*, *A7*
120/22, **wune** pleasure *SM* 50/13.
wunnes *gen. sg. HM* 6/28. **wunnen** *pl.
HM* 34/28, 40/22, *SM* 56/13. **wunne**
gen. pl. HM 30/2.

wunsum *adj.* pleasant *SM* 76/5.

wununge *n.* home, dwelling-place *HM*
38/9, *SW* 94/1, 8.

wurchen *v.* act, do, make *HM* 8/24, *SM*
72/11, 74/30, *A8* 138/30, **wurche** *SM*
68/3. **wurchest** *pr. 2 sg. SM* 54/4, 64/
34, 74/14. **wurcheð** *pr. 3 sg. SM* 58/36
A7 110/17, *A8* 134/30, *pr. 3 pl. HM* 30/
30, 32/33. **wurche** *pr. sg. subj. SM* 74/
7, *A8* 142/18. **wurch** *imp. sg. SM* 50/7,
74/26. **wrahtest** *pa. 2 sg. SM* 58/32.
wrahte *pa. 3 sg. SM* 76/19, *SW* 90/14,
A7 114/5, *pa. sg. subj. SM* 56/9. **iwraht**
p.p. SM 60/2, *A7* 120/22, *as adj. HM*
22/24, *SM* 58/36, *A8* 136/7. **iwrahte**
pl. SM 44/10 *etc.*

wurgest *pr. 2 sg.* worship *SM* 74/13.
wurðgeð *pr. 3 sg.* honours *HM* 30/1.
wurge *imp. sg. SM* 50/7. **wurðgi** *pr. sg.
subj. SM* 74/7.

wurhte *n.* workman, maker *SM* 78/15,
80/26.

wursin *v.* deteriorate *SW* 104/33. **wursi**
pr. sg. subj. diminish *SW* 96/3.

wurð *n.* thing of value *HM* 24/9.

wurðes *n. pl.* fate *HM* 30/2.

wurðeð *pr. 3 sg.* becomes; — **to** turns to
HM 24/13, — **to noht** comes to nothing
SW 94/22. **wurðe** *pr. sg. subj. SM* 78/
22, 80/33, *A7* 122/20. **warð** *pa. 3 sg. SM*
46/6 *etc.*, **wearð** *SM* 48/34.

wurðfule *adj. pl.* glorious *SM* 82/21.

wurðgeð, wurðgi *see* **wurgest**.

wurðinc *n.* mire *SM* 48/4, **wurðinge** *HM*
12/5 *etc.*

wurðmund *n.* honour *SM* 60/20,
wurðmunt *SM* 76/19, 80/33.

wurðschipe *n.* honour *HM* 4/12, *SM* 70/
7, 80/32.

LIST OF PROPER NAMES

Abraham *A7* 128/25.
Absalones *gen.* Absalom *A7* 120/26.
Adam *HM* 8/17, *A7* 112/16.
Aduent Advent *A8* 130/26.
Alixandres *gen.* Alexander *A7* 120/30.
Alle Halhene Dei Feast of All Saints (1 November) *A8* 130/18.
Andrews *gen.*; Seint — Dei Feast of St Andrew (30 November) *A8* 130/19.
Antioche Antioch *SM* 46/4, 18. Antioches *gen. SM* 82/27. Antioche *dat. SM* 50/2.
Apocalipse Book of Revelations *A7* 118/19, 122/15.
Armenie Armenia *SM* 76/29.
Asaeles *gen.* Asahel *A7* 120/28.
Assumptiun Feast of the Assumption of the Blessed Virgin (15 August) *A8* 130/17.
Asye Asia *SM* 46/18.
Aue Hail Mary *A8* 148/23, Aue Marie *SW* 108/18, Aue Maria *A8* 144/24. Auez *pl. A8* 142/18.
Austin, Seint St Augustine *HM* 24/20, *A7* 112/2, 118/4.

Babilones *gen.* Babylon *HM* 2/24, 4/7, *SM* 72/30.
Belzebub Beelzebub *SM* 64/28.
Bernard, Seint St Bernard *A7* 110/22, Beornard *A8* 148/5.

Caplimet (perhaps modern Limenia; see Mack 44/31 n.) *SM* 76/30.
Cecille, Seint St Cecilia *HM* 40/20.
Cesares *gen.* Caesar Augustus *A7* 120/30.
Clete *SM* 82/28.
Complie Compline *A8* 146/30.
Condelmeasse Dei Candlemas Day, Feast of the Purification (2 February) *A8* 130/13.
Creasuse *gen.* Croesus *A7* 120/25.
Credo Creed *A8* 144/24.
Crist Christ *HM* 12/26, 28/15, 30, *SM* 64/34 *etc.*, *SW* 108/15, *A7* 112/24, 116/30, *A8* 134/24. Cristes *gen. HM* 42/18, *SM* 46/14, 64/8, 76/29. Crist *dat. HM* 10/7, Criste *SM* 44/7, 46/29, — to

wurðmund to Christ's honour *SM* 60/20, — to wurðmunt *SM* 76/19. *See also* Iesu.
Cristendom Christianity *HM* 28/30.
Cristene *adj. pl.* Christian *SM* 44/17, *A8* 144/28.

Dauið David *HM* 2/2 *etc.*, *SM* 76/18, *A7* 116/1. Dauiðes *gen. SM* 74/22.
Domesdei Judgement Day *SM* 56/12.
Drihtin God, the Lord *HM* 18/25, *SM* 44/4 *etc.* Drihtenes *gen. SM* 68/15, Drihtines *SM* 72/24 *etc.*, *A8* 146/25.

Easter *A8* 130/14, 24, — Dei Easter Day *A8* 130/15.
Efterliðe July *SM* 82/34.
Elizabeth *HM* 40/7.
Englisch *n.* English *HM* 32/28, Englis *SM* 82/34. Englische *adj. dat. HM* 2/27.
Enneis, Seinte St Agnes *HM* 40/19.
Eue Eve *HM* 8/17, *gen. A8* 138/1.

Feader (God the) Father *SM* 72/26, 74/11, *A8* 144/25, 148/17, Feder *SW* 108/11. Feaderes *gen. SM* (*heading*), *SW* (*heading*), *A7* 126/18, Fedres *SM* 44/19.
Freres friars; — Meonurs Franciscans *A8* 134/8, — Preachurs Dominicans *A8* 134/8.
Fridahes *pl.* Fridays *A8* 130/25.

Gabriel *HM* 40/3.
Giwerie Jewry; i — with the Jews *A7* 116/23, 24.
Giws *pl.* Jews *A7* 124/16, Gius *SM* 48/16. Giwes *gen. sg. A7* 124/32. Giwene *gen. pl. A7* 116/25.
Godd God *HM* 6/1 *etc.*, *SM* 46/8 *etc.*, *SW* 86/27 *etc.*, *A7* 110/11 *etc.*, *A8* 132/19 *etc.* Godes *gen. HM* 2/3 *etc.*, *SM* 44/10 *etc.*, *SW* 86/20 *etc.*, *A7* 112/5 *etc.*, *A8* 132/18 *etc.* Gode *dat. A8* 144/9.
Godspel the Gospel *SW* 86/3, *A7* 112/30, 114/33, 122/12.
Gregoire, Sein St Gregory *A7* 112/8, 126/36.

Grickisch *adj.* Greek *A7* 122/35 *etc.*

3ongdahes *pl.* Rogation Days (days of fasting and prayer in the early summer) *A8* 130/26.

Halhene Dei *see* **Alle Halhene Dei.**
Hali Chirche Holy Church *A7* 118/34.
Hali Gast the Holy Ghost *HM* 36/14, 38/ 30–31, *SM* 46/9 *etc.*, *SW* 100/6, 108/ 11–12, *A7* 126/17–18, 21, *A8* 144/25, 148/17. **Hali Gastes** *gen. SM* (heading), 44/20, *SW* (heading), 76/12, *A7* 126/ 25, *A8* 144/16–17.
Hali Rode Dei þe leatere Feast of the Exaltation of the Holy Cross (14 September) *A8* 130/24.
Hali Prumnesse Holy Trinity *SW* 100/5.
Hali Þursdei Ascension Day (fifth Thursday after Easter) *A8* 130/16.
Hali Writ Holy Scripture *A7* 126/6, *A8* 132/23, 136/33.
Healent Saviour, Redeemer *SM* 44/13 *etc.*, **Helent** *SM* 48/8, 12.
Helie Elijah *A7* 122/33, **Helye** *A7* 122/ 24, 31.

Iames *gen.* Jannes *SM* 72/6.
Ieremie Jeremiah *A7* 114/34, 116/33.
Ierome, Sein St Jerome *A8* 140/3.
Ierusalem Jerusalem *HM* 2/26, 4/2.
Iesu Jesus *SM* 56/12, 62/8, *A7* 114/22, 124/2, — **Crist** *HM* 42/19, *SM* 46/31 *etc.*, *SW* 100/7, 102/33, 108/22, *A7* 116/21 *etc.*, — **Godd** *HM* 8/5, *SM* 60/ 32, — **Cristes** *gen. HM* 4/13, 20/34, *A7* 116/15 *etc.*, *A8* 144/13. **Iesues** *gen. SM* 72/26, *A7* 124/33.
Iob Job *A7* 118/7.
Iohan John (the scribe) *SW* 108/13.
Iuhan, Sein St John *A7* 118/19, 122/15.
Iuliene, Seinte St Juliana *HM* 40/19.
Iulius July *SM* 82/34.

Katerine, Seinte St Katherine *HM* 40/ 18.

Latin Latin *SM* 82/34. **Latines** *gen. HM* 20/12.
Lauerd Lord *HM* 4/23 *etc.*, *SM* 44/26 *etc.*, *SW* 86/3 *etc.*, *A7* 112/2 *etc.*, *A8* 132/14, 146/26, — **Godd** *SW* 94/15. **Lauerdes** *gen. HM* 4/13, 40/5, *SM* 44/26, 64/10, *SW* 104/20.

Leafdi Dei; Ure — Lady Day, Feast of the Annunciation (25 March) *A8* 130/14.
Lot *A7* 128/19.
Lucie, Seinte St Lucy *HM* 40/19.

Malcus Malchus *SM* 78/3.
Manbres *gen.* Mambres *SM* 72/6.
Margarete, Seinte St Margaret *HM* 40/ 19 *n.*, *SM* (*heading*). **Margarete** *SM* 44/ 21 *etc.* **Marherete** *SM* 62/24.
Marie (the Virgin) Mary *HM* 12/17, 40/2, *SW* 100/15.
Marie Mary (sister of Lazarus and Martha) *A8* 132/12 *etc.*, *gen. sg. A8* 132/ 14, 17.
Marie Magdaleine Mary Magdalene *HM* 38/26–7, **Seinte** — **Dei Magdaleine** the feast of St Mary Magdalen (22 July) *A8* 130/17.
Marthe Martha (sister of Lazarus and Mary) *A8* 132/13 *etc.*; *gen. sg A8* 132/ 17, 21.
Midsumer Dei Feast of the Nativity of John the Baptist (24 June) *A8* 130/16– 17.
Midwinter Dei Christmas Day *A8* 130/13.
Mihales, Seinte *gen.* St Michael's *A7* 112/9, **Seinte** — **Dei** Michaelmas Day (29 September) *A8* 130/18.
Moyses (1) Abbot Moses, a desert Father *A7* 110/12.
Moyses (2) Moses *A7* 128/9. **Moysese** *gen. A7* 120/30.

Natiuite Feast of the Nativity of the Blessed Virgin (8 September) *A8* 130/ 18.

Olibrius *SM* 46/20 *etc.* **Olibrium** *dat. SM* 54/4.

Parais Paradise *SM* 72/4. **Paraise** *gen. HM* 40/29, *SM* 64/17.
Pater Noster Our Father *SW* 108/13, 18, *A8* 144/23–4. **Pater Nostres** *pl. A8* 142/18.
Pawel, Seinte St Paul *HM* 6/4 *etc.*, *A7* 110/1, 112/7, 24.
Prime *A8* 144/31.

Rode Dei *see* **Hali Rode Dei.**
Rome *A8* 148/12.
Rufines *gen.* Ruffin *SM* 64/33.

Salomon Solomon *SM* 72/29, *A7* 124/6, 35, 126/4.

Samsones *gen.* Samson *A7* 120/29.

Sarepte Sarepta *A7* 122/23, 34.

Sareptiens inhabitants of Sarepta *A7* 124/6.

Sathanas Satan *SM* 72/3.

Sawter the Psalter *HM* 2/2.

Sodome Sodom A8 128/19. **Sodomes** *gen. A8* 140/9.

Sune (God the) Son *SM* 72/26, 84/12, *SW* 100/5, 8, 17, *A7* 114/22, *A8* 144/ 25, 148/17. **Sunes** *gen. SM* (*heading*), 44/19, 76/12, *SW* (*heading*).

Sunnedei Sunday *A8* 130/14 *etc.*, **Sunnedahes** *pl. A8* 130/28.

Syon Zion *HM* 2/26 *etc.* **Syones** *gen. HM* 2/25, 4/10, 33.

Teochimus *SM* 44/10, 82/26.

Testament; þe Alde — the Old Testament *A7* 112/29.

Theodosie Theodosius *SM* 46/2.

Tweofte Dei Feast of the Epiphany (6 January) *A8* 130/13.

Þrumnesse *see* **Hali Þrumnesse.**

Þursdei *see* **Hali Þursdei.**

Umbridahes *pl.* Ember Days (set days of fasting and abstinence following the feast of St Lucy (13 December), Ash Wednesday, Whit Sunday, and Holy Cross Day (14 September)) *A8* 130/25.

Venie formula of penitence *AW* 144/2, 7.

Witsunnedei Whit Sunday *A8* 130/16.

Ysaie Isaiah *A7* 118/21, 128/15.